Recording English, Researching English, Transforming English

STUDIES IN ENGLISH MEDIEVAL LANGUAGE AND LITERATURE

Edited by Jacek Fisiak

Advisory Board:
John Anderson (Methoni, Greece), Ulrich Busse (Halle),
Olga Fischer (Amsterdam), Marcin Krygier (Poznań),
Roger Lass (Cape Town), Peter Lucas (Cambridge),
Donka Minkova (Los Angeles), Akio Oizumi (Kyoto),
Katherine O'Brien O'Keeffe (UC Berkeley, USA),
Matti Rissanen (Helsinki), Hans Sauer (Munich),
Liliana Sikorska (Poznań), Jeremy Smith (Glasgow),
Jerzy Wełna (Warsaw)

Vol. 41

Hans Sauer / Gaby Waxenberger (eds.)

Recording English, Researching English, Transforming English

With the Assistance of Veronika Traidl

Bibliographic Information published by the Deutsche Nationalbibliothek
The Deutsche Nationalbibliothek lists this publication in the Deutsche Nationalbibliografie; detailed bibliographic data is available in the internet at http://dnb.d-nb.de.

Library of Congress Cataloging-in-Publication Data
Recording English, researching English, transforming English : with the assistance of Veronika Traidl / Hans Sauer, Gaby Waxenberger (eds.).
  pages cm -- (Studies in English medieval language and literature ; v. 41)
Includes bibliographical references and index.
ISBN 978-3-631-64223-8 -- ISBN 978-3-653-03662-6 (E-Book) 1. English language--History. 2. English language--Old English, ca. 450-1100–Research. 3. English language--Middle English, 1100-1500–Research. 4. Historical linguistics. I. Sauer, Hans, editor. II. Waxenberger, Gabriele, 1956- editor. III. Traidl, Veronika.
PE1075.R43 2013
420.9--dc23
                                                                                    2013034974

ISSN 1436-7521
ISBN 978-3-631-64223-8 (Print)
E-ISBN 978-3-653-03662-6 (E-Book)
DOI 10.3726/ 978-3-653-03662-6

© Peter Lang GmbH
Internationaler Verlag der Wissenschaften
Frankfurt am Main 2013
All rights reserved.

Peter Lang Edition is an Imprint of Peter Lang GmbH.

Peter Lang – Frankfurt am Main · Bern · Bruxelles · New York · Oxford · Warszawa · Wien

All parts of this publication are protected by copyright. Any utilisation outside the strict limits of the copyright law, without the permission of the publisher, is forbidden and liable to prosecution. This applies in particular to reproductions, translations, microfilming, and storage and processing in electronic retrieval systems.

This book is part of the Peter Lang Edition list and was peer reviewed prior to publication.

www.peterlang.com

Contents

Foreword and acknowledgements..vii

Abbreviations...ix

Introduction
   Hans Sauer & Gaby Waxenberger (Munich, Germany)......................xiii

Part I. Sounds and spellings

   Homo loquens, homo scribens: On the role of writing in language change, with special reference to English
      Trinidad Guzmán-González (León, Spain)...3

   The reflection of pre-Old English sound changes in pre-Old English runic inscriptions
      Gaby Waxenberger (Munich, Germany)..17

   Middle English evidence of the elimination of velar fricatives: A prose corpus study
      Jerzy Wełna (Warsaw, Poland)..65

Part II. Words and phrases

   The chain-mail coat terminology in Old English and the dating of *Beowulf*
      Carla Morini (Perugia, Italy)..81

   Old English *geweald habban/āgan* as a stylistic set phrase, compared with Old High German and Old Saxon cognates
      Kousuke Kaita (Munich, Germany & Tokyo, Japan)......................121

   An etymological analysis of shell nouns
      Annette Mantlik (Heidelberg, Germany).......................................133

   Secondary agent constructions from a diachronic perspective
      Naděžda Kudrnáčová (Brno, Czech Republic)...............................163

Part III. Conjunctions, clauses, and sentences

Connectives before Chaucer: Conjunctive *for* and its competition
in Early Middle English
   Mary Blockley (Austin, Texas, USA)..185

A history of *Because*-clauses and the coordination–subordination
dichotomy
   Yuko Higashiizumi (Tokyo, Japan)...201

The replacement of *þe* by *þat* in the history of English
   Cristina Suárez Gómez (Palma, Spain)......................................211

Impersonal and passive constructions from a view-point of functional
category emergence
   Fuyo Osawa (Tokyo, Japan)...225

Part IV. Dialects and their representation

The southern dialect in Thomas Churchyard's
The Contention bettwixte Churchyearde and Camell (1552)
   Maria F. Garcia-Bermejo Giner (Salamanca, Spain).......................245

Scoto-Cumbrian? The representation of dialect in the works of
Josiah Relph and Susanna Blamire
   Julia Fernández Cuesta & Christopher Langmuir (Sevilla, Spain).........265

Part V. Scholars, authors and their use of the past

J.R.R. Tolkien and the historical study of English
   John Insley (Heidelberg, Germany)...287

Chinese translations of *Beowulf*
   Stella Wang (Rochester, New York, USA....................................299

Notes on contributors..329

Index..335

Foreword and acknowledgements

The present volume offers fifteen studies and it has two sources, namely papers chosen from the ICEHL 15, as well as some essays that were specially commissioned for this volume. The majority of the contributions represent a selection of papers that were delivered at the ICEHL 15, i.e. the Fifteenth International Conference on English Historical Linguistics held in Munich in August 2008. These papers were, of course, revised and updated for publication: Guzmán-González, Waxenberger, Wełna, Blockley, Higashiizumi, Suárez Gómez, Kaita, Osawa, Fernández Cuesta & Langmuir, Garcia-Bermejo Giner, and Insley. The essays specifically commissioned for this volume are those by Kudrnáčová, Mantlik, Morini, and Wang. A brief characterization of the papers is given in the Introduction, pp. xvi-xxii below.

The ICEHL 15 actually resulted in quite a number of publications, seven altogether. Two volumes of selected papers have been published (Lenker, Huber & Mailhammer 2010; Sauer & Waxenberger 2012), and the present volume is in a way the third and final one. Apart from the plenary papers and section papers, some of which are printed in those three volumes, there were also a number of workshops, and four of those also led to publications. Papers presented in the workshop "Problems in English Historical Phonology" were published in *Anglia* 127 (2009): 173-306. Papers given in the workshop devoted to the achievement and impact of Joseph Wright were published in Markus et al. 2010. Papers delivered in the workshop on historical semantics were published in Allan & Robinson 2012, and papers from the workshop on information structure and syntactic change in Meurman-Solin et al. 2012.

Our thanks for helping us with the present volume are due to many people: to the authors for their contributions, their cooperation and their patience; to all the colleagues who assisted in evaluating, selecting and editing the papers, especially Alessia Bauer, Renate Bauer, Susanne Gärtner, Judith Huber, Janin Istenits, Kerstin Kazzazzi, Ulrike Krischke, Elisabeth Kubaschewski, Ursula Lenker, Wolfgang Mager, Robert Mailhammer, Stefan Mordstein, and Birgit Schwan; to Susan Bollinger and Gill Woodman, who helped with questions of English style; to Veronika Traidl, who formatted the volume and provided expert assistance in proofreading; to Jacek Fisiak, who kindly agreed to include the volume in this series, and to Karlheinz Well from the Lang Verlag. Of course all remaining mistakes and inconsistencies are due to our own shortcomings. Nevertheless we are confident that the final result is an informative book that has been worth the time and energy of all those who were involved in its preparation and production.

Hans Sauer and Gaby Waxenberger
Munich, February 2013

References

Allan, Kathryn, & Justyna Robinson, eds. 2012. *Current Methods in Historical Semantics*. Berlin: De Gruyter Mouton.
Lenker, Ursula, Judith Huber, & Robert Mailhammer, eds. 2010. *English HistoricLinguistics 2008: Selected Papers from the Fifteenth International Conference on English Historical Linguistics (ICEHL 15), Munich 24-30 August 2008*. Volume I: *The History of English Verbal and Nominal Constructions*. (= Current Issues in Linguistic Theory 314) Amsterdam: John Benjamins.
Markus, Manfred, Clive Upton, & Reinhard Heuberger, eds. 2010. *Joseph Wright's English Dialect Dictionary and Beyond: Studies in Late Modern English Dialectology*. Frankfurt am Main: Peter Lang.
Meurman-Solin, Anneli, María José López-Couso & Bettelou Los, eds. 2012. *Information Structure and Syntactic Change in the History of English*. Oxford: Oxford University Press.
Sauer, Hans, & Gaby Waxenberger, eds., with the assistance of Veronika Traidl. 2012.*English Historical Linguistics 2008: Selected Papers from the Fifteenth International Conference on English Historical Linguistics (ICEHL 15), Munich, 24-30 August 2008*. Volume II: *Words, Texts and Genres*. (= Current Issues in Linguistic Theory 324) Amsterdam: John Benjamins.

Abbreviations

a. Dictionaries and reference works

ASPR   The Anglo-Saxon Poetic Records:

ASPR 1   *The Junius Manuscript*, ed. George Philip Krapp. New York: Columbia University Press, 1931.

ASPR 2   *The Vercelli Book*, ed. George Philip Krapp. New York: Columbia University Press, 1932.

ASPR 4   *Beowulf and Judith*, ed. Elliot v. Kirk Dobbie. New York: Columbia University Press, 1953.

ASPR 6   *The Anglo-Saxon Minor Poems*, ed. Elliot v. Kirk Dobbie. New York: Columbia University Press, 1942.

BT   *An Anglo-Saxon Dictionary*, by Joseph Bosworth and T. Northcote Toller. Oxford: Oxford University Press, 1898; *Supplement*, by T. Northcote Toller, 1921; *Enlarged Addenda to the Supplement*, by Alistair Campbell, 1972. <http://beowulf.engl.uky.edu/~kiernan/BT/Bosworth-Toller.htm>

CHEL   *The Cambridge History of the English Language*:

CHEL I   *Vol. 1: The Beginnings to 1066,* ed. Richard M. Hogg. Cambridge: Cambridge University Press, 1992.

CHEL II   *Vol. 2: 1066-1476,* ed. Norman F. Blake. Cambridge: Cambridge University Press, 1992.

CHEL III   *Vol. 3: 1476-1776,* ed. Roger Lass. Cambridge: Cambridge University Press, 1999.

DOE   *Dictionary of Old English,* eds. Angus Cameron, Ashley Crandell Amos & Antonette diPaolo Healey. Toronto: University of Toronto Press, 2009. <http://www.doe.utoronto.ca/>

DOEWC   *The Dictionary of Old English Web Corpus,* eds. Antonette diPaolo Healey, John Price Wilkin & Xin Xiang. Toronto, 2009. <http://www.doe.utoronto.ca/>

EDD	*The English Dialect Dictionary,* ed. Joseph Wright. 6 vols. London: Henry Frowde, 1898-1905.
Hall, J. R. Clark	
	A concise Anglo-Saxon dictionary. 4th edition with a supplement by H. D. Meritt. Cambridge: Cambridge University Press, 1960 [many reprints].
LALME	*A linguistic atlas of Late Mediaeval English,* ed. Angus McIntosh, M.K. Samuels & M. Benskin. Aberdeen: Aberdeen University Press, 1986.
MED	*Middle English Dictionary,* ed. Hans Kurath, Sherman M. Kuhn, John Reidy, Robert E. Lewis. Ann Arbor: University of Michigan Press, 1952-2001. online: <http://ets.umdl.umich.edu/m/med> or <http://quod.lib.umich.edu/m/med/>
ODEE	*The Oxford Dictionary of English Etymology,* ed. Charles T. Onions with the assistance of G. W. S. Friedrichsen and Robert W. Burchfield. Oxford: Oxford University Press, 1966 [many reprints].
OED	*The Oxford English Dictionary*:
OED1	*A New English Dictionary on Historical Principles,* ed. Sir James A. H. Murray, Henry Bradley, Sir William A. Craigie, Charles T. Onions. Oxford: Oxford University Press, 1884-1928. Reprinted 1933 in 10 vols. with Supplement and Bibliography under the title *The Oxford English Dictionary.*
OED2	*The Oxford English Dictionary,* 2nd edition in 20 volumes, ed. John A. Simpson and Edmund S. C. Weiner. Oxford: Oxford University Press, 1989 [incorporates the *Supplement* in 4 vols. ed. Robert W. Burchfield, 1972-1986]. Also as CD-ROM Version 3.1.
OED3	*The Oxford English Dictionary,* 3rd edition, also known as the *OED online.* In progress 2000- <http://www.oed.com> or <http://dictionary.oed.com>

b. Texts and Corpora

BNC	The British National Corpus
HC	The Helsinki Corpus of English Text: Diachronic Part, ICAME Collection of English Corpora, Second Edition

Li	The Old English Gloss to the Lindisfarne Gospels, MS London, British Library Cotton Nero D.IV
LLC	The London-Lund Corpus of Spoken English, ICAME Collection of English Corpora, Second Edition
OERC	Old English Runes Corpus
Rissanen et al.	Rissanen, Matti, Ossi Ihalainen & Merja Kytö. 1991. *The Helsinki Corpus of English Texts: Diachronic and Dialectal.* Helsinki: Department of English, University of Helsinki
Ru1	Rushworth 1 = The Old English gloss to the Rushworth Gospels, MS Oxford, Bodleian Library Auct. D. 2. 19
WSCp	The West Saxon Gospels, MS Cambridge, Corpus Christi College 140

c. Other abbreviations

a	ante
A, Adj	adjective
AP	adjective phrase
BL	London, British Library
c, ca.	circa
CL	clause
CL1	first clause in the sentence
CL2	second clause in the sentence
Co	consonant
CP	complementiser phrase/ complementiser projection
ct.	century
DP	determiner phrase/ determiner projection
EC	Ewan Clark
EETS	Early English Text Society
EModE	Early Modern English
EPP	Extended Projection Principle
F	French
Gmc	Germanic
IE	Indo-European
INFL	inflection
IP	inflection phrase/ unflectional projection
It	Italian
JR	Josiah Relph
L	Latin
ME	Middle English
MHG	Middle High German
ModE	Modern English
MP	Minimalist Program
MS, MSS	manuscript, manuscripts

N, n	noun
NP	noun phrase
NRRC	nonrestrictive relative clause
O	object
Obl	oblique
OE	Old English
OERC	Old English Runes Corpus
OHG	Old High German
OIr	Old Irish
ON	Old Norse
OS	Old Saxon
PDE	Present-Day English
PP	prepositional phrase
Pr-OE	Proto Old English
Pre-OE	Pre Old English
Pref	prefixation
Prep	preposition
RRC	restrictive relative clause
S	subject
SA	secondary agent
Scand	Scandinavian
SOV	subject–object–verb
Spec	specifier
s.v.	sub voce
SVO	subject–verb–object
T	tense
TP	tense projection / tense phrase
V	verb (predicate)
VP	verb phrase
WF	word formation
WGmc	West Germanic

Introduction

We have chosen the title *Recording English, researching English, transforming English* not just because it gets increasingly difficult to find a title for a collective volume that is eye-catching and has not yet been used, but mainly because it nicely reflects the contents of the present volume.

All of the articles are, of course, examples of linguistic research, especially of research into earlier stages of English and into the ways and causes of language change. Some are, however, also concerned with the question of how specific stages or varieties of English were recorded in writing. Thus Gaby Waxenberger shows how some of the earliest English sound changes (pre-Old English sound changes in her terminology) were reflected in the earliest runic inscriptions from England, i.e. in inscriptions from the period of ca. 400 to ca. 600; Jerzy Wełna shows how the loss of [x] was rendered in some late Middle English spellings; Julia Fernández Cuesta & Christopher Langmuir as well as Maria F. Garcia-Bermejo Giner show how certain dialects (Southern, Cumbrian) were recorded in the 16th and 18th centuries.

As to the transformation of English, Stella Wang describes how the Old English poetic language of *Beowulf* has been variously translated into Modern Chinese, and John Insley points out how J.R.R. Tolkien incorporated Old English (and other early) words and names into his novels.

Some of the contributions assembled here take up long-standing debates, but approach them from a fresh angle, adducing new material, or formulating new theories, and attempting new answers, which will certainly stimulate further discussion (e.g. Wełna, Blockley, Higashiizumi, Suárez Gómez, Osawa), whereas others open up new areas of research.[1] Thus Gaby Waxenberger emphasizes the allophonic phases of the new sounds brought about by pre-Old English sound changes. It was only when these allophones became phonemes that new characters (= runes) were required. Annette Mantlik and Naděžda Kudrnáčová deal with two topics (shell nouns and secondary agent constructions) that have so far mainly or exclusively been looked at synchronically (i.e. from a purely Modern English point of view); they now analyze them for the first time systematically from a diachronic (historical) point of view. Stella Wang provides the first study of the Chinese translations of *Beowulf*.

We have arranged the articles into five parts. Part I (Sounds and spellings) deals with questions of spelling and how sounds and sound changes are recorded by means of letters (see our remarks above on the studies by Waxenberger and Wełna). The contribution by Guzmán-González emphasizes that not only the spoken language plays a role in language change and in the standardization of a

---

[1] At least as far as we know. It is, of course, getting increasingly difficult to be abreast of the wealth of studies that have been published and are constantly being published.

langue, but also the written language, at least during certain periods such as Early Modern English.

In Part II (Words and phrases) Carla Morini lists and discusses the Old English terms for 'chain-mail' and 'chain-mail coat'. Kousuke Kaita explains the uses of the frequent Old English phrase *geweald habban/geweald agan* 'to have power'. Annette Mantlik traces the history of shell nouns and shell noun constructions (i.e. abstract nouns such as *idea* used in a construction such as "the idea was to have a better life"). Since most of the shell nouns were borrowed from French (or Latin) during the Middle English period, it seems likely that shell noun constructions are also due to French loan influence (from ca. 1220 onwards). Naděžda Kudrnáčová shows that secondary agent constructions (such as "the officer marched the soldiers"; "the man walked his bicycle") began in the 13th century; they occur mainly with verbs of movement (*run, walk, dance* etc.).

Part III (Conjunctions, clauses, and sentences) is mainly concerned with questions of syntax. Three contributions deal with the history of the conjunctions used to introduce certain clauses and show how the system has changed almost entirely. Thus clauses indicating cause or reason were mainly introduced with the conjunctions *forþon/forþy* in Old English; these were replaced by *for* (and other conjunctions) in Middle English; finally *for* in its turn was largely replaced by *because* from Late Middle English onwards.[2] Mary Blockley and Yuko Higashiizumi investigate different stages in this process, Blockley mainly looking at the use of *for* in Early Middle English, and Higashiizumi at the use of *because* in Early Modern English. The system of introducing relative clauses also changed almost completely in the history of English. Whereas in Old English invariable *þe* (either alone or in combination with the definite article) was frequently used to introduce relative clauses, this function was taken over by *that* in Middle English: Cristina Suárez-Gómez looks at the process of transition. Fuyo Osawa points at some similarities between passive and impersonal sentences: In particular, both do not express, or at least do not need to express an agent. But whereas passive sentences are still used in Modern English, impersonal constructions were relatively frequent in Old English, but were then gradually replaced by personal constructions and are unusual in Modern English ("Me thinks" > "I think").

In Part IV (Dialects and their representation) Maria F. Garcia-Bermejo Giner analyzes the representation of a stereotyped southern (Kentish) dialect in the 16th century while Julia Fernández Cuesta & Christopher Langmuir discuss how a northern (Cumbrian) dialect was represented in the 18th century.

Part V (Scholars, authors, and their use of the past) deals with some aspects of the history of scholarship and the history of translations. J.R.R. Tolkien is now most famous as a novelist (*Lord of the Rings*), but John Insley's contribution reminds us of his utmost importance as a philologist, a medievalist and an historian of the English language. Stella Wang discusses the translations of *Beowulf* into Chinese and places them in their historical and intellectual context.

---

[2] On these processes of replacement and their stages, see now also Molencki 2012.

There is, of course, no strict division between the five parts. As mentioned above, questions of spelling are not only discussed in Part I, but also in Part IV, and several of the phenomena discussed in Part II (*geweald habban*; shell nouns; secondary agent constructions) also deal with syntax, i.e. Part III. We have, however, tried to group the contributions according to their main emphasis.

After this general survey of the volume we now give a brief characterization of each of the contributions.

Part I. Sounds and Spellings

(1)   *Homo loquens, homo scribens*: Modern linguists – at least in theory, though not always in practice – often postulate the primary status of speaking and the secondary status of writing, and consequently – at least by implication – also the importance of speaking for the phenomenon of language change. **Trinidad Guzmán-González**, however, attempts to redress the balance by stressing that writing is also important for language change, at least during certain periods. She begins with general considerations concerning cultural evolution and then develops the notion of scholarly networks. She also emphasizes that written modes and sources contributed to the standardization of English in the Early Modern English period: The standardization of spelling was obviously a written phenomenon, but the grammars and monolingual dictionaries of English that were published from the late 16th/early 17th century onwards also played an important role in the process of standardization. Furthermore she points out that language planning in general is often concerned with the written language.

(2)   **Pre-Old English sound changes in pre-Old English runic inscriptions**: More than a hundred English (Old English) runic inscriptions have come down to us from the period between ca. 400 and ca. 1100. But only nine of them belong to the early period, i.e. are datable to ca. 400-600. These are important, however, for the history of the English language, because the transmission of Old English in manuscripts only began around 700. The early runic inscriptions, however, show some sound changes in progress which had been completed when the manuscript evidence began. **Gaby Waxenberger** demonstrates that the Germanic *fuþark* (rune-row) was adapted and changed to the Old English *fuþorc* in order to be able to represent the new sounds/phonemes. This was done in two ways: (1) Some new runes were created, such as ᚩ *ōs* for /o:/ and *āc* ᚪ for /a:/ (and somewhat later ᚣ for /y(:)/). (2) Some runes lost their original sound value and were therefore 're-used' for new phonemes such as the old *ōþil* rune ᛟ. After phonemicization of *i*-umlaut, the rune ᛟ denoted /œ(:)/. Waxenberger also stresses the allophonic phase of sound changes which requires no new character. The new character is only required when the allophone becomes a

phoneme. Moreover, she gives a complete list of all the authentic runic inscriptions in the Old English *fuþorc*.

(3)   **The elimination of velar fricatives**: **Jerzy Wełna** investigates the fate of the word-final velar fricative [x] <gh>, which was eventually lost in most words (e.g. in *bough, bought, brought, dough*, etc.), but was changed to or replaced by /f/ in others (e.g. *cough, enough, rough*). He focuses on its development in later Middle English, using the *Innsbruck Middle English Prose Corpus*, and concentrating on the three function words *through, though*, and *enough* /θru:, ðəʊ, ɪˈnʌf/. Middle English dialect spellings with <-ow> etc. instead of <-gh> etc. (*enow* instead of *enough*) indicate the gradual loss, although the Modern English standard spelling usually retains the <gh>. Wełna shows that the change was carried through at different speeds in the various dialects, and that the final elimination of the [x] only took place in the Early Modern English period.

Part II. Words and phrases

(4)   **The chain-mail coat terminology in Old English and the dating of *Beowulf***: **Carla Morini** provides a detailed survey of the Old English terms for 'corselet, chain-mail coat', namely *byrne, serc, hlenc, hring* etc. (plus the compounds formed with them), and their use in Old English texts, especially in the poetry, in laws, wills and glossaries. She also takes manuscript illustrations and archaeological finds into consideration. Moreover, she analyzes the corresponding Old Norse terms. She points out that the chain-mail coat was introduced into Anglo-Saxon England by the Scandinavians during the Scandinavian invasions of the 9th century, and that it did not exist in the earlier Anglo-Saxon period. From this she concludes that *Beowulf* cannot be dated early; according to her findings *Beowulf* must have been composed in the 10th century.

(5)   **Old English *geweald habban/geweald agan***: The OE set phrase (phrasal unit) *geweald habban/geweald agan* is the focus of **Kousuke Kaita's** study. He does not call it an idiom, because idioms often have a specialized meaning, whereas in this case the meaning of the whole is basically the sum of the meaning of its parts. In translations and glosses it often renders Latin *potestatem habere*. According to Kaita's investigation *geweald agan* is more frequent in verse, whereas *geweald habban* is more frequent in prose; the use of *agan* is on the whole more limited than the use of *habban*. Kaita also distinguishes whether the phrase is followed by a *to* + *-anne* infinitive or not (the latter is true in the majority of cases). The phrase is used in *Genesis B*, but not in *Genesis A*, which is one of the many signs that show that *Genesis A* and *Genesis B* were originally different poems. In the *Anglo-Saxon Chronicle* the phrase *wælstowes geweald agan* 'to be victorious', literally 'to have the battlefield's power' is frequent.

Kaita also compares the phrase to corresponding phrases (especially *giwald hebbian/giwald egan*) in Old Saxon (*Heliand*) and in Old High German, where he notices similarities as well as differences. Finally he addresses the question of whether *habban* in *geweald habban* should be regarded as an auxiliary, but he comes to the conclusion that basically it is still a full verb.

(6) **An etymological analysis of shell nouns**: Shell nouns are abstract nouns such as *attempt, decision, idea, issue, problem, thing* etc. whose precise meaning (or reference) is often only indicated in a construction with a complement that follows them, e.g. "The idea is / to make everything better", or "The decision was / that the appeal must be dimissed". Some of them belong to the most frequently used nouns in Present-Day English. However, the study of shell nouns and shell noun constructions only began in the late 1990s, and it was mainly synchronically oriented. **Annette Mantlik** now presents the first comprehensive historical analysis by investigating the etymology of 670 shell nouns. As the examples given above also show, the large majority (77% according to Mantlik, i.e. more than three quarters) are loan-words from French or Latin that were borrowed from ca. 1220 onwards. The proportion of loan-words among the group of shell nouns is thus even larger than the proportion of loan-words in the English vocabulary as a whole. This makes it also likely that shell noun constructions did not exist in Old English; probably they represent a structural borrowing from Latin & French that began in Middle English and has increased greatly since.

(7) **Secondary agent constructions**: In English, some intransitive verbs of movement can also be used transitively and causatively; the subject of the intransitive sentence then becomes the object of the transitive and causative sentence, as in "The soldiers marched." – "The officer marched the soldiers.", or "The horse jumped." – "He jumped his horse." These causative constructions are also called "secondary agent constructions" (SAs), because the object (especially if it is animate) usually also performs the action, sometimes voluntarily and sometimes because it is forced. Sometimes there is not even a corresponding intransitive construction, as in "He walked his bicycle." but not *"The bicycle walked." **Naděžda Kudrnáčová** investigates the history of the fourteen verbs that can be used in SA constructions. All of them refer to bodily movement, namely *run, walk, swim, dance, march, trot, leap, waltz, jump, prance, gallop, pace, canter, fly*. According to her material, secondary agent constructions are a relatively late phenomenon in English: they were first attested in Early Middle English, and their use increased only very gradually. The earliest attestations of secondary agent construction are apparently with *run* (early 13th ct.), followed by *walk* (1485) and *gallop* (1533), the others followed still later.

Part III. Conjunctions, clauses, and sentences

(8) **Connectives before Chaucer: conjunctive *for*:** *For* can be used as a preposition ("he speaks for them"), as a conjunction indicating cause or reason ("I don't know what she looks like, for I have never met her"), or as a complementizer with an infinitival phrase ("for the multitude to be ungrateful"). Whereas its use as a preposition goes back to Old English and is still very common today, its use as a conjunction had a shorter history: it only began in Early Middle English, and it is limited and regarded as formal today - in Old English, *forþon, forþy* was mainly used in this function, whereas in Modern English causal *for* has largely been superseded by *because*. Especially in Early Middle English, there are also a number of ambiguous uses of *for*. **Mary Blockley** gives a detailed analysis of the use of *for* in Early Middle English, concentrating on the later sections of the *Peterborough Chronicle* and on three poetic texts, namely *The Owl and the Nightingale*, *Havelok*, and *King Horn*, and she also discusses the treatment of *for* in editions of these texts and in dictionaries.

(9) **A history of *because*-clauses:** As just indicated, *because* largely replaced OE *forþon, forþy* and ME *for* as a conjunction indicating cause or reason. **Yuko Higashiizumi** gives a detailed analysis of the history of constructions with *because*, starting with the Early Modern period, and applying several parameters. One of them is the function of *because*-clauses (connection to the real world, or to the epistemic domain, or to the conversational domain), another the position of *because* (between the two clauses which it connects, before the two clauses which it connects, and before just one clause, i.e. in independent use), and yet another whether its use is hypotactic (i.e. subordinating one clause to the other), or paratactic/independent. She concludes that the paratactic and independent use of *because* has been on the increase in Present-Day English, and that constructions where *because*-clauses are connected to the epistemic and to the conversational domain are also on the increase.

(10) **The replacement of *þe* by *þat*:** English has always had several ways of introducing relative clauses, but the system changed almost completely during the transition from Old English to Middle English. **Cristina Suárez-Gómez** looks especially at the history of the invariable relativizers *þe* and *þat/that*. In (late) Old English *þe* was the most frequent invariable relativizer, but it had practically died out by 1250, and it was replaced by invariable *þat/that* (originally the neuter of the demonstrative pronoun ~ definite article). One reason (perhaps even the main reason) for the loss of *þe/the* as a relativizer was that the definite article had also taken on the invariable form *þe/the*, and *the* in the function of the definite article then ousted *the* in the function of the relative pronoun. To get a closer view of the process of the replacement of *the* by *that*,

Cristina Suárez-Gómez looks at three parameters, namely (a) their syntactic function, i.e. *þe/the* and *þat/that* as subject, object and oblique, i.e. introducing a prepositional phrase, (b) whether they introduced restrictive or non-restrictive relative clauses, and (c) whether the antecedent was animate or non-animate. She notices some differences or rather different tendencies in usage mainly during the transitional period, when both *þe/the* and *þat/that* were used as relativizers; but once *þat/that* was used as the only relativizer it also took over all the functions of *þe/the*.

(11) **Impersonal and passive constructions**: **Fuyo Osawa** points out some similarities between passive clauses (constructions) and impersonal clauses (constructions): Both do not (impersonal) or do not need to (passive) express an agent. But whereas passive clauses are still common in Modern English, impersonal constructions were common in Old English, but have practically disappeared and have been replaced by personal constructions ("Me thinks." > "I think."). Osawa gives a critical survey of previous research especially on the passive, both of non-generative and generative approaches. Whereas non-generative approaches often assume that active sentences are more basic and that passive sentences are somehow derived from them ("They gave him a book." > "A book was given to him (by them).", or "He was given a book."), generative approaches often assume that both structures are independently derived from an underlying structure. Osawa, however, criticizes both approaches and proposes a new model: According to her, Old English had a lexical-thematic structure, where a subject was not necessarily required, whereas Modern English has a functional structure, where a subject is required.

Part IV. Dialects and their representation in literature

(12) **The Southern dialect**: **Maria F. García-Bermejo Giner** stresses the fact that until fairly recently dialect in literature was usually employed for comic purposes and humorous effects and assigned to characters of lower social rank. She points out that in the 16th and 17th centuries Kentish and South-Western dialects were preferred for this purpose, but often with an admixture of other dialects. In particular she analyzes Thomas Churchyard's *The Contention bettwixte Churchyeard and Camell* (1552), one of the earliest representations of the south-eastern or Kentish dialect. A typical feature of Kentish were forms such as *cham* (< *ich am*) for 'I am', but Churchyard also used other more or less typically southern features such as *h*-dropping and insertion of intrusive *h*, voicing of initial fricatives (*bevore, zay* instead of *before, say*), and voiced alveolar plosives instead of interdental fricatives (*dat* instead of *that*). Interestingly, however, when no attempt at representing a southern dialect was made, then Churchyard also employed northern features, such as *stondes,*

knowes, loues also as a plural form of the verb (northern subject rule) and *barnes* for 'children'.

(13) **Scoto-Cumbrian? Julia Fernández Cuesta & Christopher Langmuir** analyze the representation of dialect in two 18th ct. poets from the north of England, more precisely from Cumbria (Cumberland), namely Josiah Relph (1712 – 1743) and Susanna Blamire (1747 – 1794). According to their findings the dialect spellings found in Relph and Blamire can be assigned to four groups, that is, spellings typical of Cumberland, spellings characteristic of Northern English in general, spellings shared by Northern English and Scots, and spellings probably taken over from Scots. From this influence of Scots on Relph's and Blamire's Cumbrian dialect spelling they give a certain credence to the term Scoto-Cumbrian. Moreover, in a few cases Blamire has different spelling conventions than Relph.

Part V. Scholars, authors, and their use of the past

(14) **J.R.R. Tolkien and the historical study of English**: J.R.R. Tolkien (1892-1973) is now mainly famous for his novels, especially *Lord of the Rings*, but in his official occupation he was professor of English philology, first at Leeds and later at Oxford. He published a number of important articles and editions in this capacity, but his philological training also shows in his novels. **John Insley** reviews Tolkien's professional achievement as a philologist and highlights especially his interest in personal names and place-names. Insley begins with Tolkien's early review of philological research in *The Year's Work in English Studies* (1924-1927). Then he emphasizes Tolkien's discovery and description of the Middle English AB-language, the literary West Midland dialect of the *Ancrene Wisse* and the Katherine Group (1929), as well as his article on the use of (the Northern) dialect in Chaucer's "Reeve's Tale" (1934). Moreover, Tolkien published the probably most famous essay ever written on *Beowulf*, namely "Beowulf, the Monsters and the Critics" (1936), and in 1955, he attempted a comparison of "English and Welsh", a subject which is still hotly debated today. Finally, Insley discusses Tolkien's use of names in his novels.

(15) **Chinese translations of *Beowulf***: Between 1926/27 and 2006, nine Chinese translations of *Beowulf* were published, namely by Xidi (Zheng Zhenduo) [twice], Zhipan (Liang Zhipan), Chen Guohua, Yan Yuanshu, Liang Shiqiu, Feng Xiang, Chen Caiyu, and Li Funing. These are analyzed in **Stella Wang's** contribution. She points out that most of them are indirect or secondary translations, i.e. they are based on Modern English translations or retellings of *Beowulf* and not on the Old English original (with the exception of Feng Xiang). She also discusses the translation techniques employed by the various translators; moreover she sketches the cultural and political climate in which the

translations were written and published, and their repercussions on discussions about a Chinese literary language.

Our volume thus has a broad coverage: It deals with many of the basic linguistic levels, especially with phonology and orthography, vocabulary and phraseology, syntax, and also with regional varieties. It spans the entire history of the English language, from very early Old English (pre-Old English) to the twentieth century, with an emphasis on Old English and Middle English, but also with contributions on dialect representation in the 16th to 18th centuries, and the uses of Old English words and texts in the 20th century. Moreover the origin of the contributors reflects some of the countries where English historical linguistics is at present a prominent and thriving area of research, e.g., the Czech Republic, Germany, Italy, Japan, Poland, Spain, and the USA.[3] The popularity of conferences on Old English, Middle English and the history of English as well as the publication of new handbooks such as Bergs & Brinton 2012 also attest to the vigor of the field of English Historical Linguistics.

References

Bergs, Alex, & Laurel Brinton, eds. 2012. *Historical Linguistics of English*, 2 vols. (HSK 34.1-2). Berlin: de Gruyter.
Molencki, Rafał. 2012. *Causal conjunctions in mediaeval English: A corpus-based study of grammaticalization*. Katowice: Uniwersytet Śląski, Oficyna Wydawnicza.
Sauer, Hans, & Gaby Waxenberger, eds., with the assistance of Veronika Traidl.
2012. *English Historical Linguistics 2008: Selected Papers from the Fifteenth International Conference on English Historical Linguistics (ICEHL 15), Munich, 24-30 August 2008*. Volume II: *Words, Texts and Genres*. (= Current Issues in Linguistic Theory 324) Amsterdam: John Benjamins.

---

[3] The absence of contributors from Great Britain in the present volume is accidental; there are several contributions by British scholars in Sauer & Waxenberger 2012 – otherwise the origin of the contributors is almost the same in that volume (Germany, Italy, Japan, Poland, Spain, USA); additionally, Croatia, Switzerland and the Ukraine are represented there, and Austria, Finland and Sweden should, of course, also be mentioned.

Part I. Sounds and spellings

Homo Loquens, Homo Scribens:
On the role of writing in language change, with special reference to English

Trinidad Guzmán-González (León, Spain)

Abstract

Although writing has very often been overshadowed by the insistence on the oral nature of language, in this paper I argue that it must always be considered as an essential component of the changes of particular languages – and therefore not just subsidiary to speech. Departing from an extended notion of *culture*, I provide an overview of relevant macro-sociolinguistic processes, and then focus on the notion of *scholarly network* (Guzmán-González 1999). Framed within diachronic sociolinguistics, this idea expands the nodes of a social network (Milroy 1987, Tieken-Boon van Ostade 1991, 1996) with the connections established among members via comment, controversy, quotations, traceable influences in later authors, textbooks, etc. Finally, along the lines provided by recent network models (Granovetter 1983, Barabàsi 2002), I consider prospective developments of this notion, as those launched after the new technologies' world diffusion, and, especially, all those connected with the World Wide Web.

1. Introduction

No specialist, in whatever branch of knowledge one may think of, when asked about the most specific of human features, will resist the temptation to choose precisely that on which their discipline focuses – in the case of linguists, language. This has long made me think of this old story about three blind men trying to describe an elephant by feeling a part of the animal each, and consequently producing three different (and incomplete) descriptions. It may well be that the linguists' is just one out of the three blind men's tales – but, although much of the long and complex process which made us human remains unknown, the agreement about the crucial role of language in it is general.

2. How it all began

The origin of this peculiar ability of ours – a natural target for the curiosity of diachronic linguists – is still very much debated.[1] What we know so far, brought about by the joint efforts of such diverse disciplines as anthropology, neurobiology, psychology, archaeology etc. tends to reinforce the view of language as a tri-dimensional reality crucially involved in basic traits of our species: physiology, psychology and sociability. In this context, a combination of *Gestalt* theories, *emergentism* and the theories of systems and games seems to offer plausible approximations to answers which, very probably, will never be reached in full.[2]

---

[1] I use *diachronic* in the sense employed in Guzmán-González (2005: 15), i.e. as the branch of historical linguistics whose concerns are the description and explanation of change in languages.

[2] *Emergentism*: Cf. Arsuaga 2001: 299: "*Esta teoría predica que las propiedades de un sistema, definido como un conjunto de elementos interrelacionados, dependen en gran medida de cómo*

Within the frame of joint evolution of anatomy, neurobiology and neuropsychology, the incorporation of animal protein into food habits and the erect position would have had important consequences for both the development of the brain and for the morphology of the audio and vocal tract, allowing for the articulation of wider ranges of sounds. As the relevant organs and abilities (neocortex, synaptic connections, fine psychomotricity, etc) were put into new uses, our extremely peculiar plastic cognitive ability (abstract and symbolic thought, language), perhaps the result of exaptation,[3] would have developed within a most appropriate *testing field* provided by the social nature of the species: new and more efficient social organizations, which allowed to play successfully coordination games with multiple equilibria ("the basic ecological tasks facing people", Ross 2007: 725) were advantageously built – with a crucial side-effect: we thus survived a terribly hostile medium.

As part of the genetic inheritance that made us human, language evolved once into the sophisticated cognitive tool it is and has remained the same ever since, no matter whether records have reached us or not. I am using the term *evolution* in the technical sense it has in biology: "a process of systematic shifts in gene frequencies in populations, together with the resulting changes in what animals and plants look like as the generations go by" (Dawkins 1998: 192-193). In any case, stating that the ability has suffered no further evolution conveys no denial of the fact that its particular instantiations in human communities have undergone change.

3. Language and change

It is obvious that change is inherent to any cultural outcome of human activity, and historical sciences of all kinds devote their best efforts to explaining it. In the case of *our* particular historical science, it seems that historical linguists have been able to reach consensus in a few basic things, among them, at least the following two: one, that the main objectives of historical linguistics cannot be pursued without at some point considering the social dimension of language; and two, that only those innovations implying changes in consensus on norms of usage in a speech community (Milroy 1992a: 17) should be called *linguistic change* (see below).
Another truism yet: language has been a fundamental instrument of society building, as the theory of games, mentioned above, has recently parameterized:

> The range of types of games that humans can play is, just by virtue of the complexity of human institutions, greater by orders of magnitude than what other animals encounter. Furthermore, humans, but not other animals, can construct and circulate detailed records

---

interactúen los diferentes elementos entre sí' ['This theory states that the properties of a system (i.e. a set of interrelated elements) depend to a great extent upon the way the different elements interact' – my translation].
[3] *Exaptation* refers to the co-optation during evolution of structures originally developed for other purposes.

of their own games and the games of others throughout their societies, with limits set only by conspecifics' levels of interest. [...] The foremost piece of informational scaffolding in every human environment is language. It serves as far more than a device for exchanging information [...]. In particular, humans force their thoughts to conform to evolved digital categorization spaces by continuously narrating accounts of their behavior and interpreted mental processes, both ongoing and in retrospect." (Ross 2007: 725; 729).

This has been so from the very dawn of our history – or rather and more accurately, our pre-history, given the oral nature of language. Orality is an evident and undeniable trait upon which the literature on language change has become increasingly insistent. Statements like the following pervade the literature regarding linguistic change:

[*la escritura*] *no ha impedido que la actividad lingüística siga cambiando* [...] *la lengua no se ve esencialmente afectada por la escritura* [...] *las lenguas que se escriben funcionan exactamente igual*
[Writing has not prevented linguistic activity from change [...] Language is not essentially affected by writing [...] languages equipped with writing work exactly the same] (Moreno-Cabrera 2005: 9 nota 19; my translation).

In my view, perhaps such insistence is somewhat unnecessary, and, maybe, even risky, since it might be overshadowing other important aspects – namely, writing.

3.1 Writing and change

It is true that every specimen of *Homo sapiens sapiens* can be additionally labelled as *Homo loquens*, while only a small percentage of individuals in the species have been or are *Homo scribens*. Writing constitutes a technological innovation, one of the many phenotypic outcomes of human activity – and not a particularly ancient one indeed – , in the long history of speaking primates. That writing has not stopped linguistic change is also true; perhaps, it has not been able to make it slower either, not even in times of quasi-universal literacy (but see below). And still, I feel that the written dimension is an essential component of language change in two senses: one, within the macro-linguistic level, in what concerns types and directions of changes; and another, within the micro-linguistic level, in what concerns certain linguistic changes that happened in particular languages. In what follows, I intend to sketch some of the reasons which may support my belief that the accounts on the histories of languages with writing systems and the subsequent written traditions would do well in not considering writing as merely the source of evidence, of "witnesses to the past".[4]

---

[4] Lightfoot's words – an excellent good-practice *motto* – are worth recalling in full: "The texts are witnesses to the past, but, as always, the testimony of witnesses cannot be taken at face value and must be evaluated carefully" (Lightfoot 1999: 9).

In order to make my point, I need to invoke again the social dimension of language, and in particular, certain ideas stemming from diachronic sociolinguistic theory, as those evidenced by Milroy's three general principles for the social modelling of change (1992a: 5-10):

> *Principle 1:* As language use (outside literary nodes and laboratory experiments) cannot take place *except* in social and situational contexts and, when observed, is *always* observed in these contexts, our analysis – if it is to be adequate – must take into account society, situation and the speaker/listener [...]
> *Principle 2:* A full description of the structure of a variety (whether it is 'standard' English or a dialect, or a style or register) can only be successfully made if quite substantial decisions, or judgements, of a social kind are taken into account in the description [...]
> *Principle 3:* In order to account for different patterns of change at particular times and places, we need first take account of those factors that tend to maintain language states and resist change.

3.2 Cultural evolution

Writing is, in my opinion, one of the factors Milroy refers to – and certainly not a minor one. If language cannot be cut off from society, neither can writing, an essential tool of certain cultures, especially if culture is taken as

> The transmitted way a human community has to face the surrounding world, the systems of knowledge by means of which its members organise their perception of that world and their behaviour towards the demands that world makes of them and the needs they have. In sum, the way a human society has to operate upon the world (Guzmán-González 2005: 21).

Thus defined, *culture* shows evident links with crucial concepts of biology, such as ecological niche and adaptation. As a matter of fact, research did not take long to step from the study of mere cultural change into concepts parallel to genetic evolution such as *cultural evolution*. Although the idea of considering cultural change from the evolutionary framework can be traced back to William James, Herbert Spencer or Charles Darwin himself, the first formal models did not appear until the 1980s, with the works of Lumsden & Wilson, Cavalli-Sforza & Feldman, and Boyd & Richerson (cf. Lewens 2008). Recent developments, like those by Sterelny claim that

> Central and adaptive features of human life appear to have been built by an evolution-like process. In particular, the informational and technological resources essential for human life appear to have been constructed incrementally, generation by generation (Sterelny 2003: 20).

Furthermore, he also states that

> The informational resources needed for adaptive human action can be built incrementally, by evolution-like processes, through a combination of canalised and hence accurate vertical transmission and through niche construction, where the group as a whole collectively engineers the learning environment of the next generation (Sterelny 2003: 28).

In the light of Dawkins's definition (see section 2 above), *cultural evolution* would take place when systematic phase shifts happen in a given culture, and in this same line, Richard Menary speaks of *bio-cultural evolution* or co-evolution of biological and cultural niches, where neural and external processes "complement one another, even though they have different properties. [...] Cognitive processes are, in part, constituted by the bodily manipulation of structures in the environment" (Menary 2007: 627). In this approach, writing is thought to have

> involved a phase shift in the cultural evolution of those cultures, the great majority, that have experienced it [...] since [it] has allowed many people – eventually millions, and over spans of centuries – to access representations that are exact copies of one another (Ross 2007: 715-16).

Ross has also pointed at other cognitive dispositions correlating with the ability to read and write and accelerating "the pace of further cultural innovations along similar lines". I would heartily agree with Ross's further argument ("Of course I do not imagine that the invention of writing was a phase shift in human genetic evolution...") would he not have gone on by stating "...which writing is too recent to have influenced yet" (Ross 2007: 716). Certainly I would not buy into his *yet*. I have no doubts, however, about the fact that the English or the Spanish language are vehicles for such type of evolved cultures, with multiplex political and social organizations – and that, therefore, for them the contribution of writing has been simply fundamental. It is writing which has played a crucial role in important changes, even in the most dramatic change a language may undergo, namely being completely extinct, a doom, true, which has been undergone by many languages, with and without writing traditions.[5] In any case, the controversy on whether writing systems should be implemented in order to save endangered languages which are exclusively oral, and how this implementation might alter their primeval features, is particularly revealing.[6]

---

[5] I take as *extinct* those languages which are no longer acquired by children as first languages in inter-generational contact and interaction – and for which no native competence is therefore available. In any case, I do not think fates like that of Latin and Eyak (an Alaskan Na-Dené language whose last native speaker died in 2008), though both extinct, are comparable.

[6] The controversy has been tackled from many points of view; the following quotation is interesting, as it comes from the field of law, though the author has not refrained from characterizing the situation in what seem linguistic terms: "We can see clearly the importance of this feature if we only consider what happens with a preliterate society (a society whose culture is based exclusively on human memory, rather than on written documents) the moment it should

3.3 Macro-linguistic processes

It is also writing which has made possible a number of macro-sociolinguistic processes, such as language planning and the rise of standard varieties. In principle, writing need not be involved in language planning, at least within the frame of definitions like Spolsky & Lambert's (2006: 561):

> Language management, planning, engineering, cultivation, and treatment are actions taken by formal authorities such as governments or other agencies or people who believe that they have authority, such as parents, teachers, or academies, to modify the language choices made by those they claim to have under their control.

The official support by governmental bodies or other kind of organizations implies a number of decisions (dubbing in media, teaching, publication subsidizing etc.) which are difficult to carry out without writing. Since, as Trudgill (2003: 77) points out, language planning's goals are often "to improve communications and education, and/or influence nationism and/or achieve language maintenance", the process is deeply interwoven with the rise of standard varieties. Writing need not be involved, either, in every standardization process (as a matter of fact, Bernárdez [2004: 37] mentions such processes in exclusively oral languages). But no linguist conversant with the history of the English language would ever dream of denying the role of literacy in the processes of standardization undergone by a number of its varieties.

Over the past few decades, social network analysis has clearly signalled the type of societies, the linguistic innovators and the groups leading the spread of the features of overt prestige varieties, which play such a crucial role in standardization. These tend to include economic processes involving mobility of all kinds, and therefore, loose-knit networks which generally erode diversity in linguistic patterns – the type of socio-historical circumstances that can be found in England in the late 15th and the whole of the 16th centuries (cf. Conde-Silvestre & Hernández-Campoy 2004: 138). These authors (2004: 148) have shown that the linguistic innovators (i.e. individuals marginal to many loose-knit networks, geographically and socially mobile) in this particular area ("the adoption of spellings from the variety used at the Chancery in the late fifteenth century") were "the professional lawyers [...] followed by the *upper gentry* and then, [...] by the *urban non-gentry* and the *lower gentry*". They also mention (2004: 145) Matti Rissanen's observations on the strong influence of legal and statutory texts on the process of standardization. Given the nature of the codification process in English, it is perhaps no surprise that standardization in writing should have taken place the

---

receive, for whatever reason, an entire system of writing, or even part of it, from outside sources: This society will inevitably, in putting this *foreign* system to use, deform the contents of the exclusively oral language proper to it (an exclusively oral language, and hence exclusively mental or cerebral in what concerns its memorisation)" (Pattaro 2005: 276). For the field of literature, see Goytisolo 2001.

earliest and should have been (with minor variation) further reaching than any other aspect of the language. The standard language was characterized by Lass as follows (1987: 6):

> The medium in which government and public affairs are conducted, the dialect of the universities and the church, the media, etc. In short, the mark of the educated speaker, the *passport* to the non-local world of affairs. The standard is generally the most *developed* dialect, in that it is used for all possible purposes, and there are (normally) no situations in which its use is inappropriate.

In reference to Standard English, Trudgill (2003: 128) specifically mentions writing and the fact that it is the variety "taught to non-native speakers studying the language": *taught, studying,* not *learning* it in a more or less spontaneous language contact situation. He has also distinguished three sub-processes in standardization (2003: 128): *language determination, codification* and *stabilisation*. The last two were implemented, for bad or good, along paths where writing is simply crucial: the compilation of grammars, dictionaries, textbooks, pronunciation treatises and guides etc.

3.4 Micro-linguistic processes

In this context, the debate on whether literacy (and hence, writing) may affect speech production, to what degree, and the weight it may have on subsequent linguistic changes, remains highly controversial. Teachers, schools and educational institutions in general have been essential in the standardization process undergone by English – as in other Western European languages. The history of the pronunciation of initial [h-] in stressed syllables in English is highly illustrative in this respect. The traditional view that [h-] loss is a phenomenon restricted to a number of English substandard varieties and dating from not earlier than the 18th century has been challenged by evidence of loss as early as the 12th or 13th centuries – as that found by Milroy (1983: 37-54; 1992b: 197-201) and Bravo, García & Fernández-Corugedo (1991), among others. For those who accept such evidence, the present pronunciation in standard accents might have been caused by a late restoration following 18th-century prescriptivism along very specific social judgements. Joan Beal (1999: 103-104) provides evidence, mainly in orthoepistical work, including homophone lists, that [h-] dropping in words of non-Romance origin was not frowned upon until the 18th century. Social judgement has been a prevalent factor in the choice of numerous features of the standard, especially in that century, which, among other things, saw the publication of Lowth's and Murray's grammars. "Broad", "vulgar" accents are characterizations which go hand in hand with "uneducated": and certainly, since the letter <h> was never lost in writing, school practice and its insistence on pronunciations with [h-] as more correct (because they were closer to the written form) might have played a crucial role. The road to the familiar stigmatisation of "dropping aitches" in many mainland vernaculars was thus wide open.

4. Networks: social, scholarly and other labels

In the same line, one feels tempted to think that much of the insistence on the predominance of speech over writing in language change might stem from a reaction against decades of prescriptivism, when only prestigious varieties deserved consideration in grammar and style books. Scholarship and writing go hand in hand in English, as in the rest of the Western cultures, and this is the basis upon which Santiago González and myself have devised our concept of *scholarly network*. It is framed within the social network theory and it tentatively aims at expanding the nodes of a social network by considering as well the connections established among nodes, independently of the possible personal acquaintances, via comment or controversy – and even further on, quotations and, where possible, traceable influences in later authors and works, including literary ones and even *minor* data of the kind that John Horne Tooke owned a copy of Johnson's dictionary with notes, alterations or emendations (Guzmán-González & González 2005). We first tried the concept in a case study where the treatment of the grammatical category of gender (particularly gender assignment) was mapped in a number of 18th century language treatises.[7] The scholarly network we built showed, on the one hand, the connections within the various treatises and authors[8] and, perhaps most interestingly, the connections between these and actual usage, as exemplified by the following.[9] Byron writes in *Sardanapalus*, Act III, Scene 1, lines 378-382:[10]

... No; like the dam

---

[7] Michael Maittaire's *The English Grammar Or An Essay Of The Art Of Grammar Applied To And Exemplified In The English Tongue* (1712); Samuel Johnson's *A Dictionary Of The English Language* (1747, 1755); James Harris's *Hermes, Or A Philosophical Inquiry Concerning Universal Grammar* (1751); Joseph Priestley's works (*The Rudiments Of English Grammar*, 1761; *A Course Of Lectures On The Theory Of Language And Universal Grammar*, 1762); Robert Lowth's *Short Introduction To English Grammar With Critical Notes* (1762); Lord Monboddo's *Of The Origin And Progress Of Language* (1773-1792); James Beattie's *Theory Of Language And Considerations Concerning The First Formation Of Languages* (1788), and John Horne Tooke's *Diversions Of Purley* (1786-1805). To a greater or lesser degree, all of them are representative of the current trends concerning the study of language of the period, and many are sources for subsequent authors.

[8] Thus, the main ideas on assigned gender and personification contained in Harris's *Hermès* (1751) may be traced back to John Milton, while the work itself was the source of Lord Monboddo, John Horne Tooke, James Beattie and Joseph Priestley. Of these, Monboddo relies on him almost completely, while Priestley, though basically agreeing with Harris, differs in a number of points and Horne Tooke and Beattie oppose his views explicitly and thoroughly.

[9] For complete references, see Guzmán-González & González 2005: 105-106.

[10] Byron's *Poetical Works*, ed. Page 1979.

> Of the young lion, femininely raging
> (And femininely meaneth furiously,
> Because all passions in excess are female)
> Against the hunter flying with her cub..."

While in Harris's *Hermes* we read (p. 57):

> Why the Furies were made female, is not so easy to explain, unless if be that female Passions of all kinds were considered as susceptible of greater excess than male Passions: *Talibus Alecto dictis exarsit in iras...*"

Byron's ultimate source – Harris is quoting Virgil's *Aeneydos* – is not particularly relevant for my point (he surely knew both works) – i.e. revealing the intricate paths followed by the interaction between linguistic scholarship and actual usage types.

Although the directionality writing-speech in individual usages (the choice of a particular assigned gender like feminine for the native country in marked registers, for example) may be hard to prove, I have no doubt that such interaction has contributed to the shaping and fixing of norms – and that the linguistic attitudes navigating the ties of our network have had a pervasive effect on the elaboration and implementation phases – I am following here Trudgill's phase-division of standardization processes as applied to the rise of Standard English.

Scholarly networks may demand long-time gaps – but not necessarily, especially in recent times. In many ways, scholarly networks have to do with the *small-world* network models - investigated by Rappaport, Milgram, Granovetter and Watts, among others. In these models, the typical number of links between any two nodes is very small, and besides, nodes tend to group together into small clusters (cf. Barabási 2001). Within this frame, writing becomes an important element in the architecture of scholarly networks, as the medium through which direct links between nodes (i.e. authors) separated by longer-than-average life spans may be established – thus reducing the minimum number of links between any two nodes, and additionally allowing for clustering, for example around a particular line of thought.

Scholarly networks are also related to *complex evolving* network models – "where the accent is on dynamics and evolution" and which "constantly expand by the addition of new authors [...] as well as new internal links" (Barabàsi et al. 2002: 591-592).[11] It is obvious that the possibility of adding new nodes to any scholarly network we may define always exists.

Finally, recent applications of Granovetter's theory of weak ties to such different worlds as job finding, scientific communities (White 2003), industrial organization, etc., have highlighted the role of the World Wide Web as the *great*

---

[11] As a matter of fact, Barabási's article provides a most interesting study of the social network created out of scientific collaborations – which has evident resemblances to our concept.

modifiers not only of communication media but also of personal relationships themselves, including those specifically established via the Internet and the Web – a small-world network with a diameter of only 19 links in 1999 (cf. Barabàsi 1999: 130): chats, newsgroups, blogs. Further advances in technology have re-introduced the audiovisual dimension here – but in any case the importance of the written and read word in it has not diminished.

In languages like English or Spanish, where the written word has long been an important tool for personal relationship and network building, the new information technologies have brought about new and fascinating possibilities – including language outcomes like *SMSese* or *chatelese* (cf. Morala 2001). These usages have already set off all the alarms for the various self-appointed guardians of the true essences of languages – who have already marked them as potentially dangerous, since, among other *terrible* effects, they are, in their opinion, impoverishing our linguistic inheritance. The very existence of these remarks and complaints is a symptom of the popular mind's perception of the crucial role of writing in all linguistic matters – capable even of bringing about changes (especially undesirable changes) in the language in general. Maybe it is my mother-of-teenagers' expertise in deciphering both jargons, or my historical-linguist's training (all of us are used to such apocalyptic warnings periodically coming up in linguistic historiography) but I feel that all this is opening new exciting paths for research in linguistic change, apart from traditional corpus studies based upon this kind of materials. Scholarly networks are just one of many others. Mathematicians and physicists have created frames like the scale-free models which are already allowing great advances in the understanding of complex dynamic systems like the Internet, the Web and their numerous offshoots. Apart from new insights into the social network analysis itself, new fields seem to be opening before us. Just to mention one of them, we have the new social networks exclusively created via the Web. *Wikipedia* listed as many as 133 in January 2009, of which *Facebook* alone, for example, had 43 million users in October 2007. Their huge sizes exponentially increase the potential reach of innovations. Mapping and analyzing linguistic features, innovations and prospective linguistic changes via the social network analysis in the Internet for sure conveys serious theoretical and epistemological difficulties – in spite, or perhaps precisely because of them, the task seems to me extremely tempting. And I can't see a way to exclude writing from all this.

5. Conclusion

I agree with those who claim that *Homo loquens* came first, and that *Homo scribens* is a subsequent stage, which, in any case, comprises just some specimens. But I have not seen so far irrefutable evidence that the changes undergone by a good number of living languages (English, for example) have nothing to do at all with writing. Besides, we do not know, we cannot know whether these languages would have changed along exactly the same lines, had they been exclusively oral languages. Until these proofs are brought about, I am convinced that theoretical models of language change would be impoverished if the role assigned to writing remains merely to be the only 'eye witness' we have for many languages and many past stages of languages.

References

Arsuaga, Juan Luis
    2001   *El enigma de la especie: Las causas, el curso y el propósito de la evolución*. Barcelona: Círculo de Lectores.

Barabási, A.L.
    2001   "The physics of the web". *Physicsworld.com*. July 1, 2001. <http://physicsworld.com/cws/article/print/100>
    2002   *Linked: The new science of networks*. New York: Perseus Books.

Barabási, A.L. -- H. Jeong -- Z. Neda -- E. Ravasz -- A. Schubert -- T. Vicsek
    2002   "Evolution of the social network of scientific collaborations", *Physica A*. 311: 590-614.

Beal, Joan C.
    1999   *English pronunciation in the eighteenth century: Thomas Spence's grand repository of the English language*. Oxford: Oxford University Press.

Bernárdez, E.
    2004   *¿Qué son las lenguas?* 2nd ed. Madrid: Alianza Editorial. [1st ed. 1994].

Bravo, Antonio -- Fernando García -- Santiago Fernández-Corugedo (eds.)
    1991   *The Owl and the Nightingale: A critical text*. Oviedo: Universidad de Oviedo.

Conde-Silvestre, Juan Camilo -- Juan Manuel Hernández Campoy
    2004   "A sociolinguistic approach to the diffusion of Chancery written practices in late fifteenth-century private correspondence", *Neuphilologische Mitteilungen* 105: 133-152.

Dawkins, Richard
    1998   *Unweaving the rainbow: Science, delusion and the appetite for wonder*. Boston: Houghton Mifflin.

Goytisolo, Juan
    2001   "La defensa de las culturas amenazadas", *El País*. Madrid, 16th May. [English version available in <http://www.unesco.org/bpi/intangible_heritage/goytisoloe.htm>]

Granovetter, Mark
    1983   "The strength of weak ties: A network theory revisited", *Sociological Theory* 1: 201-233.

Guzmán-González, Trinidad
    1999   "Gender, grammar and poetry: Early 17th-century miscellanies in the light of historical sociolinguistics", in: *Proceedings of the 10th International Conference of SEDERI* ed. by María-Fuencisla García-Bermejo. 37-46. Salamanca: Universidad de Salamanca.
    2005   "Out of the past: a walk with labels and concepts, raiders of the lost evidence, and a vindication of the role of writing", *International Journal of English Studies*, ed. Juan Camilo Conde-Silvestre &

Juan Manuel Hernández-Campoy, 5: 13-31. Murcia: University of Murcia.

Guzmán-González, Trinidad -- Santiago González
2005 "'Why the furies were made female': An approach to gender assignment in 18th-century language treatises from sociolinguistic epistemology", in: *The margins of Europe: cultural and linguistic identities,* ed. Ewa Borkowska & M.J. Álvarez-Maurín. Katowice: University of Silesia, 81-109.

Lass, Roger
1987 *The shape of English.* London & Melbourne: J.M. Dent.

Lewens, Tim
2008 "Cultural evolution", in: *The Stanford encyclopedia of philosophy (Fall 2008 Edition),* ed. Edward N. Zalta. <http://plato.stanford.edu/archives/fall2008/entries/evolution-cultural/>.

Lightfoot, David
1999 *The development of language.* Malden, USA & Oxford, UK: Blackwell.

Menary, Richard
2007 "Writing as thinking", *Language Sciences* 29: 621-362.

Milroy, James
1992a *Linguistic variation and change.* Oxford: Blackwell.
1992b "Middle English dialectology", in: *CHEL II,* 156-206.

Milroy, Lesley
1987 *Language and social networks.* Oxford: Basil Blackwell.

Morala, José Ramón
2001 *Entre arrobas, eñes y emoticones.* Paper given at the Second International Conference on the English Language, Valladolid, October 2002.
<http://cvc.cervantes.es/obref/congresos/valladolid/ponencias/nuevas_fro nteras_del_espanol/4_lengua_y_escritura/morala_j.htm>

Moreno-Cabrera, Juan Carlos
2001 "Lengua escrita y lengua hablada", in: *La dignidad e igualdad de las lenguas: Crítica de la discriminación lingüística.* Madrid: Alianza Editorial, 161-182.

Page, Frederick (ed.)
1979 *Byron's poetical works.* Revised by John Jump. Oxford: Oxford University Press [1970].

Pattaro, Enrico
2005 "The law and the right", in: *A treatise of legal philosophy and general jurisprudence,* ed. Enrico Pattaro, Hubert Rottleuthner, Roger A. Shiner, Aleksander Peczeni & Giovanni Sartor. Volume 1. Heidelberg: Springer.

Ross, Don
2007 "*Homo sapiens* as ecologically special: what does language contribute?", *Language Sciences* 29: 710-731.

Spolsky, B. -- R.D. Lambert
2006 "Language planning and policy: Models", in: *Encyclopedia of language and linguistics,* ed. Keith Brown. 3: 561-574.

Sterelny, Kim
    2004   "The evolution and evolvability of culture", in: *Twenty-five years of spandrels,* ed. Dennis Walsh. Oxford: Oxford University Press. [Full text obtained from <http://www.victoria.ac.nz/phil/staff/documents/sterelny-papers/spandrels.pdf>]

Tieken-Boon Van Ostade, Ingrid
    1991   "Samuel Richardson's role as linguistic innovator: A sociolinguistic analysis", in: *Language, usage and description: Studies presented to N.E. Osselton on the occasion of his retirement,* ed. Ingrid Tieken-Boon van Ostade & J. Frankis. Amsterdam & Atlanta, GA: Rodopi, 47-57.
    1996   "Social network theory and eighteenth-century English: The case of Boswell", in: *English Historical Linguistics 1994,* ed. Derek Britton. Amsterdam & Philadelphia: John Benjamins, 327-337.

Trudgill, Peter
    2003   *A glossary of sociolinguistics.* Edinburgh: Edinburgh University Press.

Unesco World Report
    2005   *Towards knowledge societies.* UNESCO Publishing. <http//www.unesco.org/publications ISBN 92-3-204000-X>

The reflection of Pre-Old English sound changes in Pre-Old English runic inscriptions

Gaby Waxenberger (Munich, Germany)

Abstract

The emergence of a new /ɔ:/ in Pre-Old English brought about by common Germanic and Anglo-Frisian Compensatory Lengthening processes as well as the phonemic split of West Germanic /a:/ into Old English /æ:/, /a:/ and /o:/ and finally the development of Germanic /a/ are all mirrored in the Pre-Old English runic inscriptions (ca. 400-600). Scarce as the material may be, these inscriptions nevertheless provide new evidence for some of the sound changes not attested in early manuscripts but merely 'reconstructed' in grammar- and handbooks. Moreover, the chronology of these sound changes is reflected by the positions of the new runes in the Old English epigraphical *fuþorc*. After analyzing the Pre-Old English inscriptions, I have made an attempt to give the attested phoneme inventory of Pre-Old English. A complete list of Pre-Old English and Old English runic inscriptions is added in appendix 1.

1. Introduction

In Old English, linguistic evidence from manuscripts does not start before ca. 700 and therefore the sound changes before that time do not seem to be documented. However, manuscript evidence is not the only written evidence. While the Latin script was not designed for (Pre-)Old English and therefore had to be adjusted, the runes as a writing system for the Germanic languages[1] were in fact much better suited to the depiction of the phoneme inventory of Pre-Old English (Pre-OE). More importantly, runic inscriptions from Pre-OE times provide evidence of sound changes and their results in the time from the *adventus Saxonum* (ca. 400-450: see Hines 1990: 20f.) to the beginning of OE (ca. 650). The beginning of OE is marked by the completion of the Pre-OE sound changes of which phonemicization of *i*-umlaut is the last (see also Nielsen 1998: 87f.; Sauer & Waxenberger 2012: 346). Therefore OE is characterized by the emergence of new phonemes and as a consequence of this, at least in the runic script also new graphemes (= runes).

As traditional handbooks and OE grammars did not take these inscriptions into account, they could only reconstruct these sound changes.

1.1 Reconstructed sound changes and their chronologies

Luick's absolute chronology was later changed into a relative chronology by Campbell (1959: §255). In principle Campbell (1959: §255) follows Luick except for the fact that he posits a difference in time between the fronting of Gmc. long *$\bar{a}$

---

[1] The discussion about the origin of the runic script is in full swing. Although it is generally agreed upon that the runes were derived from another script (see e.g., Eichner 2006, Vennemann 2006, 2010), the original script is not at all clear. Undoubtedly, runic writing must have been adopted very early and thoroughly adjusted to the needs of the Germanic dialects, as the 'perfect fit' of the Older *fuþark* shows.

and fronting of short *a. Moreover, Campbell's time concept differs from Luick's inasmuch as his relative chronology starts later, at 450 (*adventus Saxonum*).

1.1.1 Absolute Chronology by Luick (1921)

Providing an absolute chronology, Luick (1921: §291) posits the following development, as shown in Table 1.

Table 1: Luick's chronology

I. **ca. 3rd – 4th cent.:** before the *adventus Saxonum*

1. Rounding of WGmc *a/ā before nasals and rounding of *ã developed by the common Gmc. and Anglo-Frisian lengthening processes.

2. Fronting of WGmc *a/ā in all other positions
2.1 WGmc *ai/ae > *æe > *æə > *æa > ā

3. Breaking and related processes
3.1 Breaking of palatal vowels before w, h, r, l
3.2 'Velarization' of æ/ǣ instead of breaking (e.g.: WS *gesawen* 'seen', WS *sāwon* 'they saw', Angl. *all* 'all')

4. Influence of velar vowels on *æ/ǣ (*caru* 'sorrow', *dagas* 'days').

II. **Probably before the 5th, certainly before the 7th cent.**
5. 'Re-organization' and further developments of WGmc *iu, *eo, *eu in PrOE.

III. **6th cent. (probably first half)**
6. *i*-umlaut

1.1.2 Relative Chronology by Campbell (1959: §255), starting at 450

Campbell's chronology is summarized in Table 2.

Table 2: Campbell's chronology

> 1. Anglo-Frisian development of nasal *ā/a;* and the development of $\bar{æ}$ /$\bar{e}$ from WGmc *$\bar{a}$
>
> 2. WGmc *ai > OE $\bar{a}$
>
> 3. Fronting of WGmc *a to OE æ
> The change *a > æ seems to have been later than that of *$\bar{a}$ to $\bar{æ}$ /$\bar{e}$ if we do not simply assume that OE, OFris. $\bar{æ}$/ $\bar{e}$ is derived directly from PrGmc. *$\bar{æ}$ [Campbell 1959: §131].
>
> 4. Breaking and the related processes of retraction
> The consonants which cause these early changes are
> 4.1 /l, r/, [x] + consonant: cause breaking
> 4.2 single [x] causes breaking
> 4.3 single /w/ is the reason for retraction (e.g.: *clawu* 'claw', *ġesawen* 'seen')
> Before these consonants and consonant groups front vowels are either retracted to whichever back vowel of the language is nearest in height (æ > a and occasionally e > o, i > u) or they undergo breaking [Campbell 1959: §139].
>
> 5. Restoration of *$\bar{a}/a$ before back vowels
>
> 6. *i*-umlaut

If the runic inscriptions are taken into account, it seems that these sound changes and their intermediary stages or results are in fact reflected in the early, that is, Pre-OE inscriptions.

2. The runic material

Before I can focus on the sound changes, it is important to provide some information on the runic corpus in Great Britain written in the (Pre-)*fuþorc*.

At present the Old English Runes Corpus (OERC) consists of 105 inscriptions that were written between ca. 400-1100 (see appendix 1: map no. 1 and also appendix 2). A relatively small sub-corpus of basically 9 early inscriptions dated between 400 and 600 (see appendix 1: map no. 2) will be analyzed for the early sound changes.

Due to the above-mentioned sound changes, the common Germanic *fuþark* was no longer sufficiently applicable to Pre-OE. Not only did this fact require the creation of new runes, namely
$\bar{o}s$ ᚩ = /o(:)/ and $\bar{a}c$ ᚪ = /a(:)/
but it also demanded internal shifts. The *ansuz*-rune ᚠ /a(:)/ of the Germanic *fuþark* (no. 4) adapted to the new sound value /æ(:)/, while the old *ōþil*-rune ᚫ (no. 24)

experienced a shift from /o(:)/ to /œ(:)/. This intermediary phase marks the transmission from the Common Germanic or Older *fuþark*² to the OE *fuþorc*.

Undoubtedly, complex processes must have been at work before the OE written vowel system known from manuscripts was established.

By the middle of the 7th century, however, the four runes

ᛢ = /œ(:)/,

ᚩ = /o(:)/,

ᚫ = /æ(:)/ and

ᚪ = /a(:)/ must have been established.

2.1 The pre-OE inscriptions (ca. 400-600)³

The early inscriptions (ca. 400-600) have a special status within the corpus of OE runic inscriptions as they grant us an insight into the changes of the system, a system that was only reconstructed by traditional grammars and handbooks as they did not take the runic data into account.

2.1.1 The early inscriptions in chronological order

The Pre-OE inscriptions are listed in chronological order. The attempts to date them are purely archaeological.
As can be inferred from the list of objects,⁴ the critical runes are marked in different colours. There has always been controversy on how to read, for example, the old rune *ansuz* ᚫ in the early inscriptions. Is it still /a(:)/ or is it already /æ(:)/? This insecurity has brought about different interpretations. As traditional grammars and handbooks do not consider the possibility of allophones, they are forced to see these sound changes as strictly consecutive events, that is, e.g., *ā* /a:/ changed to *ǣ* /æ:/.

---

² Generally, this rune row is called the 'Older *fuþark*'. I call it 'Common Germanic' because it is this rune row that was shared by all the Germanic tribes and because it was the basis for further developments, such as the Old English *fuþorc*.

³ Not counting the single-rune inscriptions, there are 11 early inscriptions in the OERC but only 9 can – at least partially – be deciphered. The non-decipherable Sarre Pommel (late 5th-6th cent. [Mitchell 1994: s.v. SarPo1], first half of the 6th cent. [Chadwick Hawkes 1967: 10], ca. 500-570 [Hines 2006: 194]) has been excluded. Additionally, the Ash-Gilton Sword Pommel (6th cent.) has not been included here because the decipherable sequence [...]**sigim**[...] does not contain any of the runes in question.
    Moreover, two 'borderline cases' (as far as dating is concerned) have also been excluded. Dating these objects is extremely difficult and therefore uncertain. These are the Boarley Brooch and the Sandwich Stone. Furthermore, both texts are only partially decipherable.

⁴ It has been argued that the Chessell Down Pail and also possibly the Undley Bracteate are imports from the Continent but this does not have an impact on my thesis.

Pre-Old English sound changes in Pre-Old English inscriptions 21

They tacitly assume a linear process, namely that a certain phoneme always directly became another phoneme. If allophonic stages are taken into consideration, however, one phoneme, e.g. WGmc */a:/ can have several allophones (Pre-OE [a:], [æ:], [ã:]: see also below figure 2) at a given time. Additionally, the intermediary allophonic phase may be potentially quite long. A phonemic split occurs only when these allophones become phonemes (OE /a:/, /æ:/, /o:/). This assumption brings about consequences for a phoneme-based writing system: while the individual allophones of one phoneme ([a:], [æ:], [ã:]) can be represented by a single character (rune *ansuz* ᚨ), in contrast to this, new phonemes (/a:/; /æ:/) require new characters (/a:/ = ᚪ; /æ:/ = ᚫ).[5]

2.1.1.1 List of early objects

Spong Hill Urn:	ca. 400-600 [Hines 1990: 443]	→	ᚨlu a/ælu
			(© Castle Museum Norwich)
Loveden Hill Urn:	ca. 400-600 [Hines 1990: 443, 1991: 65; Hills 1991: 54]	sᛋpᚦbᚠd siþa/æba/æd	||þi{c/u}w || [.]lᚠ[.] ||þi{c/u}w || [.]læ/a[.]
			(© The Trustees of The British Museum)

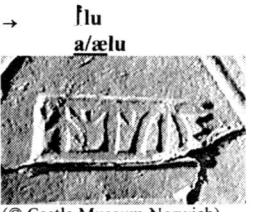

---

[5] The following graphic conventions are used in this article: Runes are transliterated in lower-case and bold letters. Roman characters are presented in upper-case letters. Uncertain runes are given in italics. Bind-runes are marked by an arc ⌒. Uncertain runes that allow for more than one interpretation are placed in braces { } and the individual interpretations are separated by slashes. Phonemes are put between slashes / / and square brackets [ ] are used for allophones. Graphemes are denoted by angled brackets < >. The symbol [k] is used for the velar allophone of /k/, whereas the symbol [k̟] is used for its palatal allophone. Subscript arrows before transliterations indicate the direction of writing and reading.

Caistor-by-Norwich Astragalus:	ca. 425-475 [Hines 1990: 442]	rᛇhᛇn [råɪxan] or possibly [råexan] (© Castle Museum Norwich)
Undley Bracteate:	ca. 450-500: [Hines 1990: 441]	ᛪᚷᛪ° m¹g¹ ° medu (© The Trustees of The British Museum)
Watchfield Purse Mount	ca. 500-550 [Scull 1986: 127]	hᛇribᚸ̂i : ᛇusᛇ ha/æribo/œki : wusa/æ (Drawing: Hines 1990:439)
Chessell Down Scabbard Mount:	ca. 525-550: [Chadwick Hawkes 1967: 17f.; Hines 1990: 439]	ᛇᛏᛇ : ᛇᚸᚱᛁ a/æko : cœri (© The Trustees of The British Museum)

Pre-Old English sound changes in Pre-Old English inscriptions 23

Welbeck Hill Bracteate:	ca. 500-570 [Hines 1990: 445]	← lᛇw **la/æw** (Photograph: IK no. 388a (p. 166), plate 165-166)
Chessell Down Pail:	ca. 520-570 [Hines 1990: 438]	[...]ᛚᛚᛚᛠ [...]ccca/æa/æa/æ (© The Trustees of The British Museum)
skanomodu coin (?OFris.):	ca. 575-610 [Blackburn 1991: 142]	sᛣnᛟmᛟdu (< Gmc. *skauna-* and < Gmc. **moda*-) skan*o*m*o*du

3. Pre-OE sound changes and Pre-OE runic inscriptions

In the following section the complex processes underlying these sound changes are discussed only briefly (for a detailed analysis, see Waxenberger forthcoming): A list of the relevant sound changes is given in table 3.

Table 3: Sound changes

Sound change	New phonemes/allophones in Pre-OE
1. The compensatory lengthening processes of *a + nasals as well as PrGmc. *$\bar{æ}$ + nasal led to	Pre-OE nasalized long /$\tilde{o}$:/
2. The phonemic split of WGmc long *$\bar{a}$ led to	Pre-OE /a:/ Pre-OE /æ:/
3. Phonemic split of Gmc. short *a led to	Pre-OE /a/ Pre-OE /æ/ Pre-OE [å]
4. The monophthongization of Gmc. *ai led to	Pre-OE /a:/
5. i-umlaut i-umlaut of Gmc. */a/ led to i-umlaut of Gmc. */o:/ led to	Pre-OE [ɛ] Pre-OE [œ:]

3.1 The sound changes in detail

3.1.1 The new phoneme /$\tilde{o}$:/ and the new rune o ᚩ (see Table 4)

In contradistinction to traditional grammars and handbooks which do not consider the possibility of allophones (see above), I wish to posit an allophonic phase, in which the sounds *[æ:], *[ɑ̃:] and *[a:] were in complementary distribution before they developed into phonemes (see below Figure 1).

Table 4: The new phoneme /ɔ̃:/

Sound change	New phonemes/allophones in Pre-OE	New Rune
The processes nos. 2-4 (see also below figure 1) led to Pre-OE nasalized long /ɔ̃:/ which finally fell together with OE ō (< PrGmc. *ō < IE *ā; IE *ō). 1. Common Gmc. compensatory lengthening: PrGmc. */a+ŋ+x/ > *[ã:] > /ɔ̃:/ > OE ō. 2. Anglo-Frisian compensatory lengthening: */a + m,n + f,s,θ/ > *[ã:] > /ɔ̃:/ > OE ō. 3. PrGmc. *ǣ+ nasal > *[ã:] > /ɔ̃:/ > OE ō	Pre-OE nasalized long /ɔ̃:/	Rune o ᚩ

Figure 1: Emergence of OE ō (the chronology of sound changes nos. 2, 3 and 4 is based on Luick 1921: §291)

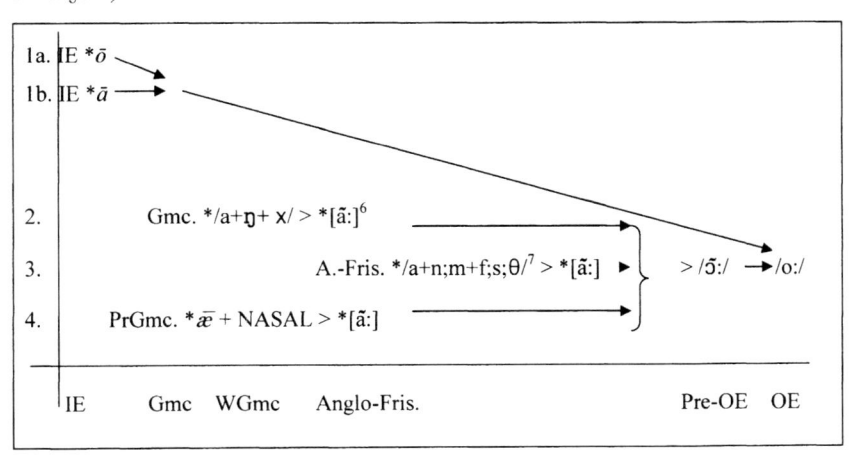

1a. IE *ō
1b. IE *ā

2. Gmc. */a+ŋ+ x/ > *[ã:][6]
3. A.-Fris. */a+n;m+f;s;θ/[7] > *[ã:] > /ɔ̃:/ → /o:/
4. PrGmc. *ǣ + NASAL > *[ã:]

IE   Gmc   WGmc   Anglo-Fris.   Pre-OE   OE

---

[6] This sound change is labeled as "Common Germanic Compensatory Lengthening Process".
[7] This sound change is known as "Anglo-Frisian Compensatory Lengthening Process".

3.1.1.1 Earliest Runic Evidence (for more attested runic forms see Waxenberger forthcoming)

The Undley Bracteate (ca. 450-500)
The first attestation of the new rune ᚫ is found on the Undley Bracteate (ca. 450-500) in the sequence ᚷᚫᚷᚷ ← g͡a g͡ō: g͡a or g͡æ g͡ō: g͡æ. At the time of Undley, the sound-value denoted by ᚫ should still have been /ɔ̃:/. If it had already fallen together with *o* < IE *ō/ā* we would expect the old rune o ᚨ. The new rune obviously denoted the new intermediate sound /ɔ̃:/.

In the following section it is necessary to group two sound changes together, as their interdependence brought about the Pre-OE phoneme /a:/ and /æ:/ - both sounds had been allophones ([a:]; [æ:]) prior to these sound changes.

*3.1.2 The monophthongization of Gmc. */aɪ/ and the phonemic split of WGmc long */a:/*

Table 5: Gmc. */aɪ/ > Pre-OE /a:/ and the phonemic split of WGmc */a:/

Sound change	New phonemes/allophones in Pre-OE	New Rune in Pre-OE
The monophthongization of Gmc. */aɪ/ led to	Pre-OE /a:/	Rune ᚫ[8]
The phonemic split of WGmc */a:/ led to	Pre-OE /a:/	Rune ᚫ
	Pre-OE /æ:/	ᚫ*fuþark* /a(:)/ > ᚫ*fuþorc* /æ(:)/

Nielsen (2000: 116) convincingly suggests that the phonemic split into *ǣ* and *ā* was triggered by the intrusion of the new monophthongized vowel *ā* (< Gmc. **ai*).
As I have already pointed out, I posit an allophonic phase, in which the sounds [æ:], [ã:] and [a:] were in complementary distribution. The situation before Gmc. */aɪ/ was monophthongized to Pre-OE /a:/ was as follows: WGmc */a:/ must have had three allophones ([æ:], [ã:], [a:], see Figure 2a):

---

[8] I am well aware of the fact that the first attestation of the new rune ᚫ is on the **skanomodu** coin which may be Frisian whereas the first attestation of the new rune ᚫ in OE is only on the Caistor-by-Norwich Brooch (ca. 610-650). However, the rune ᚫ must have been designed between ca. 425-475 (Caistor-by-Norwich Astragalus; see 3.1.2.3 below) and ca. 575-610 (**skanomodu** solidus), so the creation of the new rune ᚫ was in Pre-OE.

1. The development of */a:/ + nasal > *[ɑ̃:]
2. Fronting of */a:/ > *[æ:]
3. Retraction of */a:/ > *[ɑ:] before w.

*Figure 2a: Allophones of WGmc */a:/*

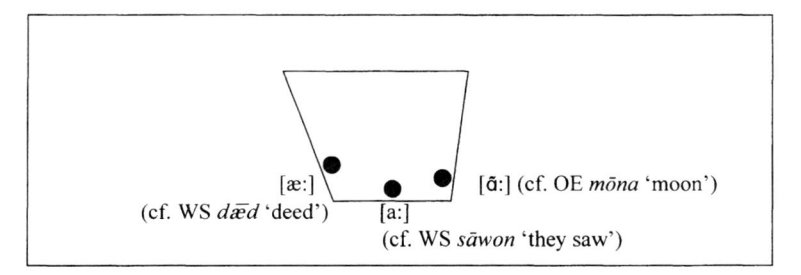

[æ:] (cf. WS dǣd 'deed')
[ɑ:] (cf. WS sāwon 'they saw')
[ɑ̃:] (cf. OE mōna 'moon')

The developments would have been like this:

The nasalized long open *[ɑ̃:] brought about as an allophone by both the Common Gmc. (see figure 1 no. 2) and the Anglo-Frisian (see Figure 1 no. 3) lengthening processes fell together with *[ɑ̃:] developed from WGmc */a:/ + nasal (see Figure 2b).

*Figure 2b: The allophone *[ɑ̃:] and its sources*

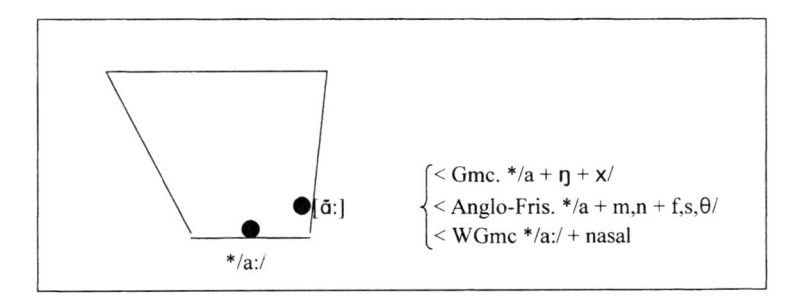

[ɑ̃:]
*/a:/
< Gmc. */a + ŋ + x/
< Anglo-Fris. */a + m,n + f,s,θ/
< WGmc */a:/ + nasal

The resulting long nasalized allophone *[ɑ̃:] was subject to rounding, finally becoming the phoneme /ɔ̃:/, which initially remained distinct from old /o:/ (see above figure 1 and Waxenberger forthcoming). That is why the new phoneme /ɔ̃:/ required a new grapheme and that was the new rune ᚩ (no. 4 in the OE fuþorc: see below appendix 3).

After the emergence of Pre-OE /a:/ < Gmc. */aɪ/, the allophone *[a:] of WGmc */a:/ (cf. OE *sāwon*: see figure 2a above) probably merged with the new phoneme /a:/ < */aɪ/ (see Figure 2c and also Nielsen 2000: 120).

*Figure 2c: The WGmc allophone *[a:] merged with */a:/ < */aɪ/*

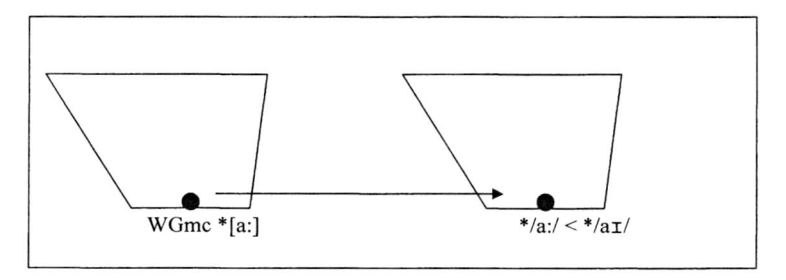

Figure 3 shows the situation after the phonemic split (/a:/ and /æ:/) and the merger of WGmc *[a:] and */a:/.

Figure 3: The new phonemes /a:/, /ɔ̃:/ and /æ:/

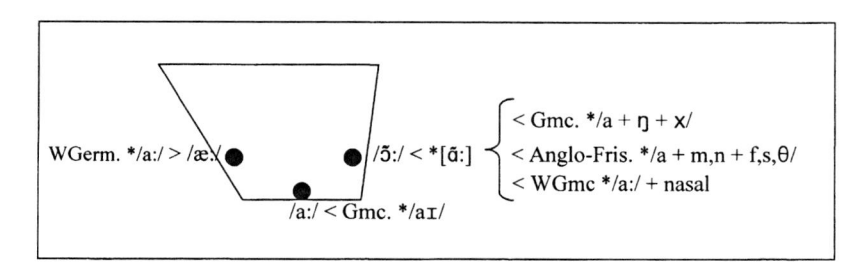

At this point the old rune *ansuz* ᚨ /a(:)/ must have been considered inadequate to express the new sound /ɔ̃:/. This was most likely the reason why a new rune, known as ᚩ *ōs*, was created.

3.1.2.1 The old rune ansuz ᚨ and the new rune āc ᚫ in the light of the emergence of the phoneme /æ:/ (< WGmc */a:/)

Fronting of WGmc */a:/ led to OE WS /æ:/ whereas WGmc */a:/ + nasal brought about Pre-OE /ɔ̃:/. As these sounds had become phonemes, it was necessary to represent them by two separate graphemes. While a new rune ᚫ was designed for the new sound Pre-OE /ɔ̃:/, the shape of the old rune *ansuz* was re-used and filled with a new sound value (= /æ:/), acquiring a new name in the process (*æsc*), cf. Figure 4.

Figure 4: The phonemic split of WGmc *ā and both the rune ᚨ and the new rune ᚫ

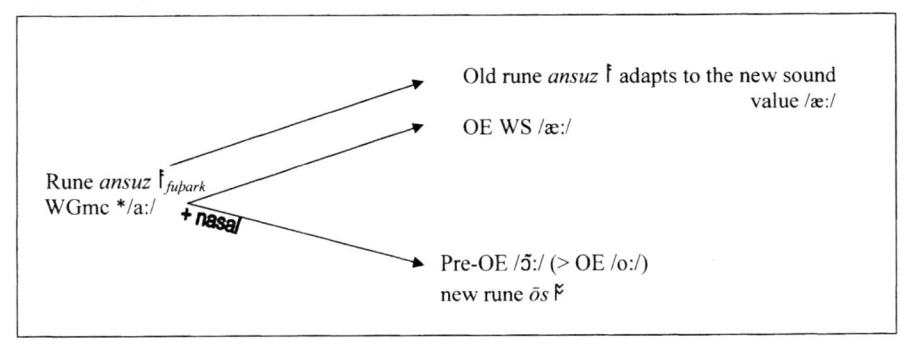

```
                                    → Old rune ansuz ᚨ adapts to the new sound
                                                                     value /æ:/
                                    → OE WS /æ:/
Rune ansuz ᚨ fuþark
WGmc */a:/      + nasal
                                    → Pre-OE /ɔ̃:/ (> OE /o:/)
                                      new rune ōs ᚩ
```

3.1.2.2 The development from Gmc. */aɪ/ to Pre-OE /a:/

Although it has been generally accepted that the new /a:/ phoneme came into existence by monophthongization of Gmc. */aɪ/ [Krupatkin 1970: 56f.; Nielsen 2000: 109; Bammesberger 2006: 179;[9] see also above], there are great differences not only in the chronology but also in the explanation of the development.

While Campbell (1959: §132) holds the view that WGmc *ai* became OE *ā* "by loss of the second element, accompanied by lengthening of the first", Luick (1921: §122) and Bammesberger (2006: 178) posit three intermediary stages before **ai* eventually became *ā*. Luick (1921: §122) assumes the following development: WGmc **ai/ae* > **æe* (fronting of the first element) > **æə* (dissimilation because the two components **æe* had become too close to each other) > **æɑ* (regressive assimilation) > *ā*.

---

[9] Unfortunately, Bammesberger's (2006: 179) "11.3. ᚨ" is due to an error in the character set and should therefore be replaced by the rune ᚫ.

Bammesberger (2006: 178) suggests the following stages: */aɪ/ > *[ae] (first element was not fronted) > *[åe] (first element was rounded in order to increase the distance between the two components)[10] > *[aə] > /a:/. Bammesberger (1996: 21) suggests that monophthongized /a:/ emerged around 500.

3.1.2.3 Runic evidence for Gmc. */aɪ/ > Pre-OE /a:/ (for the long /æ:/ see above 3.1.2)

1. The Caistor-by-Norwich Astragalus (ca. 425-475)
The monophthongization of *ai > ā had obviously not been completed at ca. 425-475 as -ᚠᛋ- in the word rᚠᛋhᚠn (Caistor-by-Norwich Astragalus) shows. The rune ᚠ must have denoted an intermediary stage of the first element of WGmc *ai. Eichner (1990: 322) posits -æe-, whereas Bammesberger (2006: 178) suggests either [âi] or [åe] for the combination -ᚠᛋ- (for more details see below 4.2 Caistor-by-Norwich Astragalus).

2. The **skanomodu** solidus (ca. 575-610)
Although probably Frisian, the **skanomodu** solidus (ca. 575-610) sheds light on the *terminus ante quem* of the creation of the rune ᚠ. Gmc. *au was monophthongized in Frisia, hence *skaun- developed to skān-, which is reflected in **skanomodu**.[11] Consequently, the rune ᚠ must have been designed between ca. 425-475 (= Caistor-by-Norwich Astragalus where it is not yet attested) and ca. 575-610 (**skanomodu** solidus). Since, however, there is reason to believe that the new rune ᚠ was in all probability contemporaneous with the new rune ᚠ, its emergence could not have been too long after 500, the latest possible date for the Undley inscription, on which the new rune ᚠ appears.

In the OE corpus proper the new rune ᚠ representing short /a/ was used for the first time in the inscription on the Caistor-by-Norwich Brooch (ca. 610-650: see below 3.2). As it was used here for /a/ in an unstressed position this means that it must have been well established by that time.

---

[10] Bammesberger (2006: 178) sees a parallel in the diphthong */au/ > *[ao] > *[æo] where fronting of the first element also resulted in an increase of the distance between the two elements of the diphthong.
[11] Looijenga (2003: 307) lists a vague example for *ai > ā in the Frisian corpus: **hada** (< *haið) but she also considers other more likely possibilities. As this would be the only case of *ai > ā in OFris., it does not concern us here.

3.1.3 Phonemic split of Gmc. short */a/ (see Table 6)

It is important to emphasize again that Campbell (1959: §131) considers the change *a* > *æ* to have been later than that of *ā* to *ǣ*, whereas Luick considers these changes to be simultaneous (see also above 3.1.2).

Table 6: Phonemic split of Gmc. short */a/

Sound change	New phonemes/allophones in Pre-OE	New rune in Pre-OE
3. Phonemic split of Gmc. short *a led to	Pre-OE /a/ Pre-OE /æ/ Pre-OE [å]	Rune ᚠ Rune ᚪ

3.1.3.1 Breaking and the related processes of retraction

1. The consonants /l, r/ [x] (+ consonant) cause breaking whereas
2. single /w/ which was not followed by *-i* or *-j* [SB 1965: §§50.2;87] is the reason for retraction (e.g.: *clawu* 'claw', *gesawen* 'seen': Campbell 1959: §139).
Campbell (1959: §139 footn. 1) holds the view that it was *æ* and not *a* that was the underlying sound for breaking (e.g.: OE *eald* 'old', *heard* 'hard', *eahta* 'eight') and he states that *æ* was retracted in OE (e.g.: *strawes* 'straw' (gen.sg.): see also Waxenberger forthcoming chapter 4). His hypothesis follows from the assumption that PrGmc. *a, if not followed by a nasal consonant, always became *æ* in OE. This assumption was made to account for the phenomenon of breaking: since *eo* and *io* arose from *e* and *i*, it is practically certain that *æa* (<ea>) arose from *æ*. That *æ* is a prior stage in the development of *a* in forms with retraction is not open to proof, but highly probable, in view of the similarity of the circumstances under which *a* and *ea* appear for PrGmc. *a [Campbell 1959: §139 footn. 1].

3.1.3.2 The necessity of restoration of a before back vowels

Luick (1921: §164) as well as Campbell argue against the hypothesis that OE *-a-* reflects WGmc *-*a*-. The interchange of *æ* and *a* in the phonological system of OE (*dæg* 'day' vs. *dagas* 'days') is, in their view, clearly due to the restoration of *a* before back vowels because breaking is regarded as a change affecting front vowels and from this it follows that OE *slēan* is developed from */slæxan-/.[12] For this reason Campbell concludes that "it is hardly conceivable that when PrGmc. */slaxan-/ was at the stage */slæxan/, PrGmc. *dragan- would not be at the stage

---

[12] */slæxan-/ was developed to *sleahan* by breaking and finally to *slēan* by contraction (*ea* + [x] + vowel > *ēa*).

drægan; from which it follows that OE *dragan* has restored *a* in its first syllable by later change" (see also below especially 3.1.3.3ff.).

3.1.3.3 The development of short Gmc. **a* > *æ*

While in Luick's opinion (see above 1.1.1 Table 1 no. I.1) the developments of short **a* and long **ā* took place at the same time, Campbell (1959: §132) posits the development of long *ā* first, followed by the monophthongization of **ai* and then by fronting of **a* (see above 1.1.2 Table 2 nos. 1 and 3).

Considering the old rune *ansuz* ᚫ in the inscriptions from approximately 400-600, it becomes obvious that the same rune must have been employed for different phenomena. As I have already emphasized, neither Luick nor Campbell took the possibility of an allophonic phase into consideration. Therefore they could only argue in favour of consecutive sound changes.

Bammesberger (1994: 18 and footn. 29; 1996: 16;20; 2006: 180) points out that the three allophones of Gmc. */a/ ([a] by retraction, [å] followed by a nasal, and [æ] by fronting) were in complementary distribution at an early stage and therefore the writing system did not need to differentiate as far as the short vowels [a], [å], and [æ] were concerned: the old rune ᚫ for *a* could have been used for these allophones over a certain period.

I suggest that more than three allophones must have belonged to Gmc. short */a/ and that the allophonic phase must have lasted throughout the entire period of the early inscriptions. This becomes obvious when the early runic inscriptions are analyzed. They hint at an allophonic phase by virtue of the fact that the allophones are all denoted by the same rune, a situation which would be highly unlikely if we were immediately confronted with phonemes in their own right, as was assumed by the traditional chronology. This assumption proceeded from the manuscript tradition, which shows the different spellings due to phonemicization having been completed. The earlier runic tradition shows that the phonemicization of the allophones of Gmc. */a/ was quite late, as it is not reflected in the Pre-OE runic spelling, whereas the other two developments, i.e. Pre-OE /ō:/ and the monophthongization of Gmc. */aɪ/ > Pre-OE /a:/ described above (see 3.1.2) had already reached phonemic status, documented by the development of the two new runes ᚩ and ᚪ. While the restriction of rune ᚫ to long /æ:/ had been brought about by the phonemic split of WGmc */a:/ into Pre-OE /ō:/ and /æ:/, the restriction of rune ᚫ to short /æ/ only came about by phonemicization of *i*-umlaut of Gmc. */a/. Three examples may suffice to illustrate the range of the *ansuz* rune at the Pre-OE stage.

The inscription on the Spong Hill Urn (ca. 400-600) reads ᚫlu and according to the rule of 'restoration of *a* before back vowels' (see below 3.1.3.4 no. 3 and table 7) the rune ᚫ must denote [a]. The *ansuz* rune ᚫ in the sequence -bᚫd (sᚦpᚫbᚫd) on the Loveden Hill Urn (ca. 400-600) must be deciphered as [æ] due to fronting of *a* > *æ* in monosyllables (see below 3.1.3.4 no. 2 and table 7). Rune ᚫ in

the sequence **hͰribX^i** on the Watchfield Purse Mount (ca. 500-550) appears in an *i*-umlaut environment and, therefore, can neither be the allophone [a] nor the allophone [æ] but ought to be [ɛ], that is the *i*-umlaut of the fronted allophone [æ] (see below 3.1.3.4 no. 5 and table 7).
It must be assumed that rune Ͱ denoted all the following allophones of Gmc. */a/ in the period from ca. 400-600.

*3.1.3.4 Allophones of Gmc. */a/*

1. Rune Ͱ must have been used for an allophone [å] when Gmc. */a/ was followed by a nasal   [see above 1.1.1 table 1 no. I 1].
2. Rune Ͱ must have denoted fronted [æ] in monosyllabic words[13] (OE *dæg*) and also in polysyllabic words when there was a palatal vowel (OE -*e* < (Pre-)OE -*i*, -*æ*, -*e*; OE *dæges*) or a syllabic ̥*l* or ̥*n* (OE *nægl* 'nail', *hræfn* 'raven') in the following syllable.
3. Rune Ͱ must have represented both
   retracted [a] before single /w/ [see above 1.1.1 table 1 no. I 3.2] and
   restored [a] when followed by a back vowel [see above 1.1.1 table 1 no. I 4].
4. Additionally, rune Ͱ must also have represented breaking of Gmc. */a/ + /l,r,x/ (+ Co) > [æa]
   */a/ + /x/ (+ Co) > [æa]
   */a/ + /r/ + Co   > [æa]
   */a/ + /l/ + Co   > [æa]
5. Finally, rune Ͱ must have rendered [ɛ] when the allophone [æ] of Gmc. */a/ was followed by /i,j/ [see above 1.1.1 table 1 no. III 6].

From a synchronic point of view, rune Ͱ thus most likely represented the following allophones, see table 7.

---

[13] Sievers' (1898: §49) definition is as follows: „In ursprünglich geschlossener silbe wird das kurze *a* normaler weise zu *æ*, wo nicht besondere umstände es verhindern: *dæg* tag (...). Dies *æ* bleibt auch da, wo die ursprünglich geschlossene silbe durch secundäre lautentwickelung im ags. offen wird wie in *nægl* nagel, *hræfn* rabe (mit silbenbildendem *l*, *n*) oder bei entwickelung eines secundären *e*, wie in *æcer* acker, *fæger* schön (...)."

Table 7: Overview over the allophones of rune ᚠ ([a] - [å] - [æ] - [ɛ] - [æa]) in the period between 400-600.[14]

[å]	[a]	[æ]	[ɛ]	[æa]
Gmc. */a/ + /m,n/ > [å]	1. Gmc. */a/ + /w-/ > [a] 2. Gmc. */a/ + /a,o,u/ > [a]	Gmc. */a/ + /e,æ,ɪ/ > [æ]	Gmc. */a/ + /i,j/ > [ɛ]	Gmc. */a/ + /x/ (+ Co) > [æa] Gmc. */a/ + /r/ + Co > [æa] Gmc. */a/ + /l/ + Co > [æa] in the later WS dialect

The phonological space of Gmc. */a/ must have been as shown in Figure 5.

*Figure 5: The phonological space of Gmc. */a/*

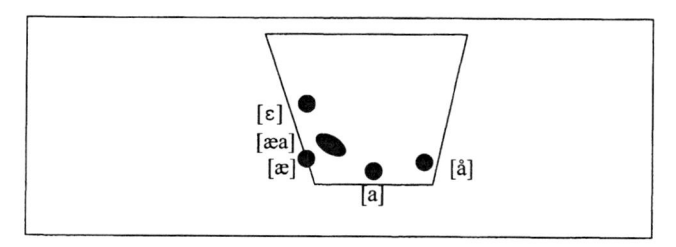

Due to the fact that the runic script does not differentiate between long and short quantities,[15] rune ᚠ denoted not only the allophones [a] - [å] - [æ] - [ɛ], but also [æ:] and [a:], although the latter only in the very early period, as the phonemic split of long */a:/ was earlier than that of its short counterpart (see also below 3.2).

Additionally, the same rune, I believe, rendered the first element of the diphthong Gmc. */aɪ/ and its later intermediary stages (see above 3.1.2.2) and must have represented the diphthong brought about by breaking (see above table 7).

3.1.3.5 How can this phenomenon be explained?

In my opinion, Luick (1921: §116), Campbell (1959: §139 footn.1), and SB (1965: §50 note 4) were absolutely right in assuming that Gmc. short */a/ was fronted in all positions (except before nasals).

---

[14] For Gmc. */a+ŋ+x/ and Gmc. */a + m,n + f,s,θ/ see above 3.1.1.

[15] The allophone [å] does not go through the same process as /ɔ:/ but remains an allophone and disappears in later stages of English.

Judging from the runic evidence, I propose that the allophone [æ] – originally limited to palatal environments (see table 7 above) – spread to velar environments as well and it was this 'opposite phonetic motivation' which was to make [æ] the 'primary allophone'. This allophone, in turn, was the prerequisite for both breaking and *i*-umlaut.

Table 8 demonstrates the development of Gmc. */a/ and its allophones in relation to the runes used for them. As can be seen, differentiation on the graphematic level does not set in until stage 6, when *i*-umlaut is phonemicized.

It must, however, be added here that Luick's absolute chronology cannot be proved by means of the runic material since the same rune is used throughout the early period (400-600).

Table 8: Gmc */a/ and its allophones

Development	Inventory at a given time: allophones/ phonemes	Rune	Inscription
1. The Gmc. phoneme */a/ had three allophones at some stage in Pre-OE:	[a], [æ], [å]	ᚠ*fuþark*	--
2. [æ] became the primary allophone by appearing before velar vowels (*dægas) as well. In this phase Gmc. */a/ only had two allophones. [æ] was the prerequisite for breaking [see also Campbell 1959: §139 footn.1].	[æ], [å]	ᚠ*fuþark*	--
3. Breaking before certain consonant groups and retraction before /-w-/ led to an increase in allophones.	[æ], [å] [æa], [a]	ᚠ*fuþark*	--
4. Restoration of [a] before velar vowels	[æ], [å] [æa], [a]	ᚠ*fuþark*	ca. 400-600: Spong Hill Urn ᚠlu = [a]lu ca. 400-600: Loveden Hill Urn -bᚠd = -b[æ]d
5. Allophonic phase of *i*-umlaut brought about 1. [æ] > [ɛ] and also 2. [å] > [æ]	[æ], [å] [æa], [a] [ɛ]	ᚠ*fuþark*	ca. 500-550: Watchfield Purse Mount hᚠribᚷ̂ i = [hɛri-] --
6. Phonemicization of *i*-umlaut	/æ/	ᚠ*fuþorc*	ca. 610-650: Caistor-

| and thus phonemic split of Gmc. */a/ into /a/ and /æ/. | /a/ | ᚠ | by-Norwich Brooch: ludᚠ gibœtᚠ sigilᚠ |

Figure 6 lists the complete set of possible allophones of the period between ca. 400-600 although not every allophone was continuously represented throughout the whole period (see also table 8).

Figure 6: The rune ᚨ *ansuz*

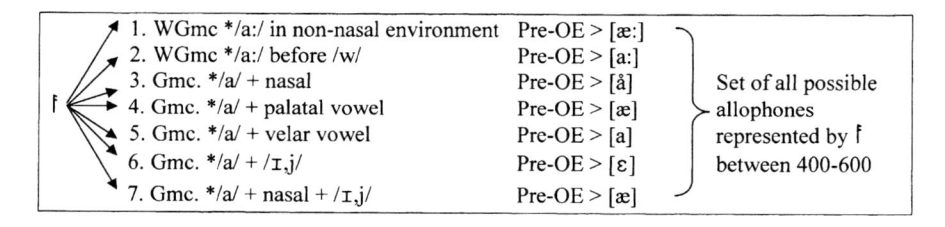

1. WGmc */a:/ in non-nasal environment	Pre-OE > [æ:]	
2. WGmc */a:/ before /w/	Pre-OE > [a:]	
3. Gmc. */a/ + nasal	Pre-OE > [å]	Set of all possible
4. Gmc. */a/ + palatal vowel	Pre-OE > [æ]	allophones
5. Gmc. */a/ + velar vowel	Pre-OE > [a]	represented by ᚨ
6. Gmc. */a/ + /ɪ,j/	Pre-OE > [ɛ]	between 400-600
7. Gmc. */a/ + nasal + /ɪ,j/	Pre-OE > [æ]	

Figure 7 shows the emergence of the new runes ᚩ *ōs* and ᚪ *āc*.

Figure 7: The rune ᚨ *ansuz and the emergence of* ᚩ *ōs and* ᚪ *āc*

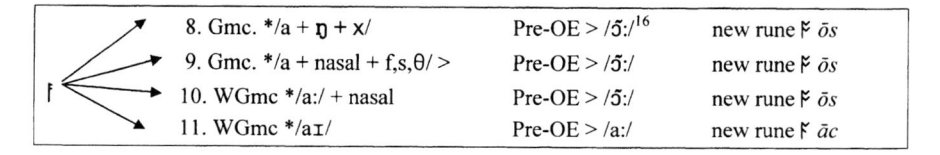

8. Gmc. */a + ŋ + x/	Pre-OE > /ṓ:/[16]	new rune ᚩ *ōs*
9. Gmc. */a + nasal + f,s,θ/ >	Pre-OE > /ṓ:/	new rune ᚩ *ōs*
10. WGmc */a:/ + nasal	Pre-OE > /ṓ:/	new rune ᚩ *ōs*
11. WGmc */aɪ/	Pre-OE > /a:/	new rune ᚪ *āc*

3.1.3.6 Reconstruction and concrete data

In the following I discuss the development of the rune ᚨ and the emergence of the rune ᚩ before 610-650 (= Caistor-by-Norwich Brooch: see below 3.2) in the corpus. Figure 8 shows the development of WGmc */a:/ until the phonemic split (ca. 500). Until then the rune ᚨ denotes the allophones [a:] and [æ:]. As was shown above, the same rune also renders the allophones [æ], [a], and [å] of Gmc. */a/. As can be inferred from the figure (and also from the early inscriptions: see table 8 above), the phonemic split of Gmc. */a/ was later than that of WGmc */a:/. The new rune ᚩ must have emerged around 500 although the first OE instance is only found on the Caistor-by-Norwich Brooch (c. 610-650). However, there is an earlier instance of

---

[16] For the intermediate stages of the nos. 8-10: see 3.1.1 particularly figure 1.

the rune ᚠ if the possibly OFris. **skanomodu** coin (ca. 575-610) is taken into account.

I wish to emphasize that Figure 8 demonstrates that the runic data supports both my own and also the traditionally reconstructed time-line of the phenomena in question, and the gaps between the reconstructed beginnings and the evidence put forward by the runic material are not irreconcilable (see also below section 4).

Figure 8: The runes ᚨ and ᚠ

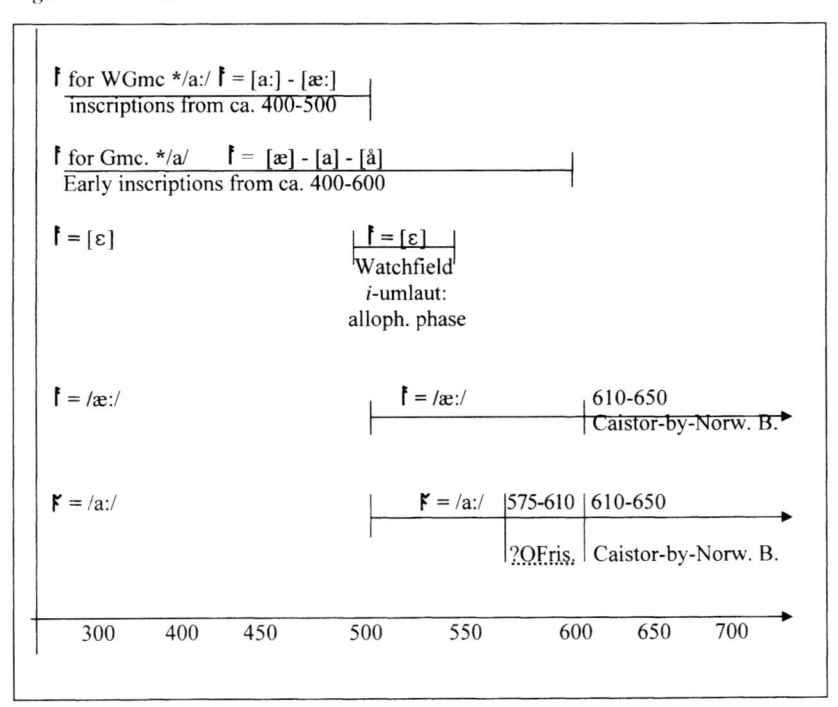

| ᚨ for WGmc */a:/ ᚨ = [a:] - [æ:] |
| inscriptions from ca. 400-500 |

| ᚨ for Gmc. */a/   ᚨ = [æ] - [a] - [å] |
| Early inscriptions from ca. 400-600 |

ᚨ = [ɛ]   ᚨ = [ɛ]
                           Watchfield
                           i-umlaut:
                           alloph. phase

ᚨ = /æ:/   ᚨ = /æ:/   610-650
                                             Caistor-by-Norw. B.

ᚠ = /a:/   ᚠ = /a:/   575-610 | 610-650
                                      ?OFris. | Caistor-by-Norw. B.

300   400   450   500   550   600   650   700

3.1.4 *i-umlaut in its allophonic phase*

It is to be assumed that the phonemicization of *i*-umlaut was preceded by an allophonic phase in which there was no need yet for new runes, as the triggering sound was still in place. This intermediary stage is shown in Table 9.

Table 9: i-umlaut in its allophonic phase

Sound change	New phonemes/allophones in Pre-OE	New Rune in Pre-OE
i-umlaut of Gmc. */a/ led to	Pre-OE [ɛ]	--

3.1.4.1 Runic evidence for the still allophonic i-umlaut [ɛ]
(for the allophonic phase of *i*-umlaut Pre-OE [œ:] see Waxenberger forthcoming).

1. The Watchfield evidence (ca. 500-550)
If the first element of HFRIBX^I is regarded as the forerunner of the later OE *here* 'army' (< Gmc. **harja*) and if Luick's and Campbell's chronologies are accepted, the -*a*- in **harja* would have developed to *-æ- by fronting and later to -*e*- by *i*-umlaut (cf. OE *here* 'army'; see also Waxenberger forthcoming). At the period of Watchfield (ca. 500-550), however, it must be assumed that *i*-umlaut was still in its allophonic phase otherwise rune F would not have been used. Therefore rune F*fuþark* denotes [ɛ] which would be the mutated form of -*æ*- in its allophonic phase. As a consequence, HFRI- in HFRIBX^I stands for [hɛrɪ], with rune F denoting the allophone [ɛ] of a phoneme Gmc. */a/.

3.2 Summary and conclusion for the sound changes and the runes

As shown above (see figures 5, 6, and 7), rune F covered a wide range of sounds between 400-600.
Around ca. 610-650, however, the picture changes completely: The Caistor-by-Norwich Brooch (**luda gibœtæ sigilæ** 'May Luda make amends/make compensation by means of the brooch') reveals the results of complex processes reshaping the OE rune-row.

Figure 9: Caistor-by-Norwich Brooch: ca. 610-650 [Hines 1991a: 6f.]

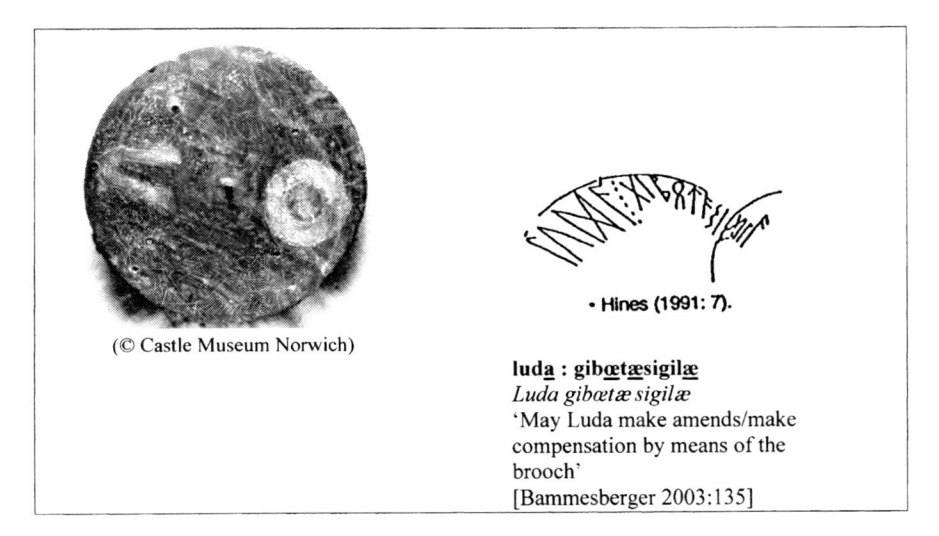

(© Castle Museum Norwich)

• Hines (1991: 7).

luda : gibœtæsigilæ
Luda gibœtæ sigilæ
'May Luda make amends/make compensation by means of the brooch'
[Bammesberger 2003:135]

This inscription marks the beginning of OE proper because all the new runes (ᚫ *æsc*, ᚪ *āc*, ᛟ *œþil*) and their sound values are used exclusively and consistently for the first time. The Caistor-by-Norwich text bears witness to the completion of all the sound changes which had been at work in Pre-OE. Thus a whole new set of runes had been established: rune ᚫ is found for the first time in OE denoting the phoneme /æ/. It represents both the verbal ending -æ (**gibœtæ** 'may make amends') and the nominal ending -æ (**sigilæ** dat.sg. of 'brooch'). It also bears witness to the new rune *āc* ᚪ = /a/ (**luda**)[17] and rune *œþil* ᛟ = mutated /œ:/. All the processes described above must have been completed at ca. 610-650. Undoubtedly, *i*-umlaut had a great impact on the vowel system of OE but there were also other phenomena at work which, in turn, triggered the "recasting" of the runes. As I have demonstrated, "recasting" started long before *i*-umlaut took effect and it was the long vowels /a:/, /æ:/ and /ō:/ which were the pivots for innovation. Therefore the opinion that *i*-umlaut reshuffled the system and was also responsible for the creation of new runes is only true in the case of the runes ᛟ /œ(:)/ and ᚣ /y(:)/ and short /æ/[18] whereas the new runes ᚩ /ō:/ (> OE /o:/) *ōs* and ᚪ /a:/ *āc* were created in the wake of sound changes appearing much earlier.

---

[17] Nielsen (2000: 117 footn. 52) regards the Selsey Gold Fragments as "the first runic item in England" showing the new rune ᚪ. I do not take this inscription into account here since neither its reading nor its date ("late 6th to 8th centuries": Hines 1990: 448) is certain. See also Waxenberger forthcoming.

[18] However, the rune ᚫ /æ:/ came about by the earlier split of *ā into /a:/ and /æ:/.

It seems to me that the period between approximately 400 and ca. 610-650 (Caistor-by-Norwich Brooch) was marked by turbulences in the phonological system. These turbulences and changes had come to an end at around the middle of the 7th century. The results are reflected in the manifestation of new phonemes and therefore a set of new runes.

Looking at the OE *fuþorc* as it appears on the London Thames *scramasax*, the order of the new runes can be analyzed as follows:

1. ᚩ *ōs* was the probably first of the new creations and took place 4.
2. Created approximately at the same time, ᚪ *āc* was added as the first new rune to the end of the rune-row.
3. Although originally created for the sounds /a(:)/, the rune ᚫ lost both its old name (*ansuz* > *ōs*) and its original sound value /a(:)/. This rune ᚫ, which now represented the fronted sound long /æ:/, lacked a name. Therefore this rune ᚫ must have been renamed *æsc* and shifted to position 26, that is to the end of the rune-row as it was at the time.
4. It was relatively late when the new phonemes resulting from *i*-umlaut were added. While the rune for the new sound /y(:)/ had to be added to the end of the row, the new sound /œ(:)/ could readily take over the slot of the old rune ᛟ /o(:)/. The same is true for rune ᚫ representing /æ/ which developed by *i*-umlaut of Gmc. */a/ whereas rune ᚫ had already represented long /æ:/.

In my opinion, the order of the OE epigraphical rune-row as it can be seen on the London Thames *scramasax* reveals the chronology of development (see Figure 10).

Figure 10: The London Thames scramasax

© The Trustees of the British Museum

To sum up, the following relative chronology can be given:

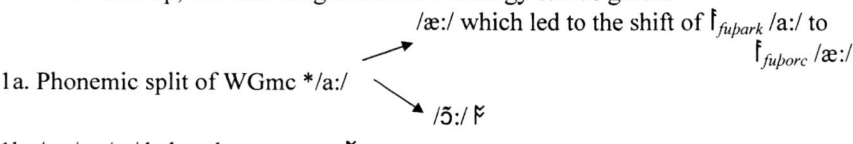

/æ:/ which led to the shift of ᚫ*fuþark* /a:/ to
ᚫ*fuþorc* /æ:/

1a. Phonemic split of WGmc */a:/

/ɔ:/ ᚩ

1b. /aɪ/ > /a:/ led to the new rune ᚪ

2. Gmc. */a/ and its allophones [æ], [å], [a], [æa], [ɛ] were represented by ᚠ until phonemicization of *i*-umlaut led to /æ/ (see Waxenberger forthcoming chapter 6.1.7 no. 2.4) and /a/. Then short /a/ was represented by ᚪ and /æ/ by ᚠ.
3. Phonemicization of *i*-umlaut brought about the runes ᛡ /y(:)/ and ᛟ /œ(:)/.

3.2.1 Luick's absolute chronology and runic evidence

Table 10 compares Luick's absolute chronology with the runic evidence. The sound changes not attested in the OERC are not considered in the table below (for more details see Waxenberger forthcoming for the complete list given by Luick).

Table 10: Luick's absolute chronology compared to the runic evidence

Chronology: Luick (1921: §291)	Runic evidence
IV. ca. 3rd – 4th cent.: before the *adventus Saxonum* 1. Rounding of WGmc *a/ā before nasals and rounding of *ã developed by the common Gmc. and Anglo-Frisian lengthening processes.	1. First attestation of the new rune as a result of WGmc *ā + nasal, the Common Gmc. and Anglo-Fris. Compensatory Lengthening processes: Rune o ᚩ (Undley Bracteate: 450-500).
2. Fronting of WGmc *a/ā in all other positions. 2.1 WGmc *ai/ae > *æe > *æə > *æa > ā.	2. Allophonic phase (ca. 400-600). 2.1 Gmc. */aɪ/ > OE /a:/ between 425-475 and 575-610. Gmc */aɪ/ occurs as ᛏᛋ (= [åɪ] or [åe]) on the Caistor-by-Norwich Astragalus (ca. 425-475). 2.1.1 First attestations of rune ā ᚪ: ?OFris. **skanomodu** solidus (ca. 575-610); OE Caistor-by-Norwich: 610-650. Reconstructed monophthongization of ā (< *ai) on the basis of the runic material: The rune ᚪ must have been created between ca. 425-475 (= Caistor-by-Norwich Astragalus) and ca. 575-610 (**skanomodu** solidus). Since, however, the new rune must have been contemporaneous with rune o ᚩ, its emergence could not have been too long after 500, the latest possible date for the Undley inscription (450-500)
3. Breaking and related processes 3.1 Breaking of palatal vowels (= æ) before *w, h, r, l*.	3.1 Since most of the inscriptions in the

3.2 'Velarization' of æ/ǣ instead of breaking (e.g.: *gesawen* 'seen', WS *sāwon* 'they saw', Angl. *all* 'all'; *warð* 'became')	OERC are Anglian, breaking of Gmc. *a is only attested in the very late Dover Stone inscription (9th-11th cent.): see also Waxenberger (forthcoming esp. chapter 4). 3.2 First attestations for *a*: 3.2.1 Allophonic phase [a] (ca. 400-600): Spong Hill Urn (ca. 400-600); Chessell Down Scabbard Mount (ca. 525-550). 3.2.2 Velarization of Gmc. */a/ is attested relatively late: Auzon/FC (ca. 720): **warþ**; Whitby Comb (657 - ?second half of 9th cent.): a̅luwaluda̅.

4. The Pre-OE inscriptions: Archaeological dating and linguistic consequences

4.1 Loveden Hill Urn (400-500 or 500-600)

sᛊᚦᛁᛒᛁd || þi{c/u}w || [.]|ᛁᚠ[.]

In the period between ca. 400-600, as has been shown, rune ᚠ must have denoted the allophones [æ], [a], and [å] of Gmc. */a/. Since Hills (1991: 54) considers the time between 450 and 500 for the production of the urn,[19] the rune ᚠ may also render Gmc. */a:/ as the character ᚪ can only have been created after 500 (see above 3.1.2.3). Although Hines (1991: 65) takes the later 5th century into account, he concludes that the "balance of probability [for Loveden] must lie in the sixth": in the latter case, rune ᚠ would have ceased to represent /a:/ (see also Waxenberger forthcoming).

4.1.1 sᛊᚦᛁᛒᛁd

sᛊᚦᛁ- has generally been accepted (see also Waxenberger forthcoming) as the successor of *sinþa-. Nedoma (2004: 436) lists the development as "*senþa > *sinþa- > *sīþ-" but does not mention the intermediary stage *sĩþ*- brought about by Anglo-Frisian compensatory lengthening (*i* + nasal + *þ*). In my opinion, it is this intermediary stage that is represented by the *yew*-rune ᛊ (see also below no. 4.2 Caistor-by-Norwich Astragalus). If this is true, we must posit a phoneme /i:/ (< Gmc. */i:/: see Waxenberger forthcoming) and a phoneme /ĩ:/ (<

---

[19] The production date is equal to the date of inscribing the urn because it is generally assumed [Page 1973: 20, 184; Bammesberger 1991: 125; Hills 1991: 44; Nedoma 1991-1993: 115; Mitchell 1994: s.v. Lov1; Parsons 1999: 55] that the runes must have been cut before firing the clay.

*/ɪ+nasal+{f,s,θ}/: see Waxenberger forthcoming). Nedoma (2004: 437) posits *æ* < *a* for rune ᚠ and comments: "In der Kompositionsfuge ist der 'Bindevokal' *æ* < *a* nach schwerer Silbe noch erhalten"; he quotes Luick (1921: §§303, 350) according to whom the connecting vowel was lost at the end of the 6th cent.
Various suggestions have been made for -**b**ᚠ**d**:
1. -*bad* < *baðu [Odenstedt 1980: 29, 18; 1990: 76; 1991: 373] and -*bad* < Gmc.
*-*baduz* [Nedoma 1991-1993: 121; 2004: 437],
2. -*bad* < Gmc. *baðwa-, 'battle' [Parsons 1999: 55f.] or
3. in its feminine variation -*bæd* < PrGmc. *badwō 'battle, war' [Looijenga 1997: 166].
Nedoma (2004: 437) lists all the possibilities mentioned above for the second element: *-*badu* masc., *badwō fem.; *-*baduz* masc. "als Schwundstufenvariante neben *-*badwaz*" ('variant derived from zero-grade beside *-*badwaz*').

It should be pointed out that the reading -*bæd* is problematical in two ways: the masc. name was hardly used as a second element in OE [see Müller 1913: §70] and the fem. variant is not at all attested as a second element [see Boehler 1930: 34].

The sequence in question is also seen as -**bld** with the vowel omitted before *ld* by Page (1968: 134) and also Looijenga (1997: 166) who reads it as the nom.sg. masc. *a*-stem "-*bald*, OE *beald* 'bold'". Admittedly, the shape of the rune ᚠ is different from the one in s**ᛋ**ᚦᚠ- but this may be due to a damaged tool rather than to the inscriber's lack of care and precision (see below 4.1.3 and Waxenberger forthcoming 1). If, however, such a reading is undertaken, the sequence should be seen as **bald** in case of Anglian provenance, whereas it should be seen in the light of breaking (although in its allophonic phase) if Kent. or WS provenance is assumed, although I think the latter possibility is rather unlikely.

4.1.2 [.]|ᛁᚠ[.]

The first character of the sequence [.]|ᛁᚠ[.] is commonly seen as an unusual **h** and the last character of the sequence is thoroughly unclear.
After a new autopsy of the Loveden Hill inscription with a microscope camera in 2012, I do not think that the first rune of the last sequence is an unusual form of **h** (for more details see Waxenberger forthcoming 1).

[.] | a/æ   [.]
© The Trustees of the British Museum

The sequence [.]lᛁ[.] has been seen as *hlāf* 'bread' [Odenstedt 1980: 30], *hlāw* 'tomb; mound' [Nedoma 2004: 435]; *hlǣ* 'grave' [Bammesberger 1991: 127; see also Eichner 1990: 325] and as a "perhaps incomplete" personal name "*Hlǣ*" [Bammesberger 1994: 17 quoting Robinson (personal correspondence: 18.2.1992)]. It should be pointed out that the readings [a:] and [æ:] as in *hlāf, hlāw*, and *hlǣf* are only possible if Loveden Hill is dated before ca. 500.

4.1.3 Conclusion

Beside the fact that the runes may have been cut with a two-pointed object[20] and are therefore difficult to decipher, the pivotal point is the dating of the urn. If an early date is assumed, the rune ᚠ denotes not only [a], [æ] but also [æ:] and [a:]. This circumstance has a great impact on the first and even more so on the third sequence. For as a consequence, [.]lᛁ[.] might be seen either as *hlǣ̄ w* which may be interpreted as the allophonic phase of the *i*-umlaut of *ā* [see Campbell 1959: §636; SB 1965: §288], but it may as well render non-mutated *hlāw* [see Bammesberger 1990: 69].

If a later date is accepted, the sequence [.]lᛁ[.] can neither be *hlāw* nor *hlǣw* because /a:/ would have been rendered by the new rune ᚪ and subsequently also its *i*-umlaut, because this would have been in its allophonic phase [æ:] in the 6th cent. There has been some controversy over the third character in *þi{c/u}w* as to which rune it depicts. If it were intended as **c**, it would be retrograde (ᚲ) and if it were meant to be **u** (ᚢ), it would lean towards the left:[21] → ᚦ / ᚱ ᛈ

© The Trustees of the British Museum

Bammesberger's (1991: 128) reading 'Sīþæbæd' ‖ 'female servant' ‖ 'tomb' is one plausible explanation. However, in my opinion, there are too many variables involved to allow an unequivocal interpretation.[22]

---

[20] The general opinion, however, is that they are not carefully cut [Page 1973: 184; Odenstedt 1980: 25; Nedoma 1991-1993: 115; Looijenga 1997: 165; Parsons 1999: 55]; Nedoma (1991-1993: 115) points out the irregularities of the size and shape of the runes as well as the distances between the individual characters.

[21] Parsons' observation (1999: 56f.) that the character is not in full height which he regards as a point counting "against reading it as an obliquely angled **u**". However, his argument is not completely convincing with regard to difficulty in writing on a convex surface (see also the height of **d**).

[22] For the different readings see Waxenberger (forthcoming).

4.2 Caistor-by-Norwich Astragalus (ca. 425-475)

rᚠᛋhᚠn
[råɪxan] or possibly [råexan]
Although it can be assumed that the sequence -ᚠᛋ- in rᚠᛋhᚠn proves that Gmc. *ai had not been monophthongized at approximately 425-475, the quality of -ᚠᛋ- is difficult to determine. See Waxenberger (forthcoming) for Eichner's four phases of the development */aɪ/ > /a:/.

Surprisingly, the *yew*-rune ᛋ is used instead of the *īs*-rune | for the second element of the diphthong. The *yew*-rune is a problematic character (see Waxenberger forthcoming), because its sound value is not clear. It can, however, be stated that ᛁ, ᛋ originally denoted a high front vowel, presumably /i(:)/. Obviously, the *yew*-rune must have been in competition with the *īs*-rune at some stage but before this was to happen, the *yew*-rune may have denoted a slightly different *i*-sound. The inscription on the Loveden Hill Urn may reveal the solution: as I emphasized above, the Loveden Hill Urn still represents the nasalized intermediary stage /ĩ:/. Due to its character as a kind of "floating signifier", the *yew*-rune would have been a good choice to express the nasalized /ĩ:/. Undoubtedly, nasalization must still have existed at the time of the Loveden Hill Urn. If ᛋ was used to mark the nasalization of *ī*, the *yew*-rune may also have been employed to represent a possible nasal quality of the second part of the diphthong <ᚠᛋ>, i.e [ĩ]. This nasal quality was derived from the first element of the diphthong, if Bammesberger's theory is accepted. Thus, the *yew*-rune could be seen as another piece of evidence for Bammesberger's theory.

To conclude, I agree with Bammesberger in reading the sequence as a genitive '(this is) Raiha's (piece)', or 'roe's (< *raih-an-az)* piece' because the ending -ᚠn is in full agreement with < **raih-an-az*.

4.3 Undley Bracteate (ca. 450-500)

ᚷᚹᚷ° mᛁgᛁ ° meduᚨ
The object has been dated by archaeologists to ca. 450-500.
The inscription is seen as a sequence of three words marked by a word-divider °. The first and the third bind-runes consist of the runes **g** ᚷ + *ansuz* ᚠ. The bind-rune in the middle combines the runes **g** ᚷ + **o** ᛟ. The direction of reading is from right to left.
ᚷᚹᚷ° mᛁgᛁ ° meduᚨ

On the template of the discussed phonemes and allophones, I would like to analyze the sounds possible for the period between 450-500.

The second sequence contains two *ansuz* runes ᚨ
mᚨgᚨ
For the reasons listed under 3.1.3.6 above (see also figure 8), the old rune *ansuz* ᚨ in the sequence **mᚨgᚨ** may have represented the allophones [æ] and [a] of Gmc. */a/. If a date not too close to 500 is assumed, it could still have denoted [a:] and [æ:]; after this, the new rune *ā* ᚪ would have been used for /a:/, whereas rune ᚨ would still have denoted /æ:/ (see above 3.1.2.1 especially figure 4).

Theoretically, the following words (in the cases listed) could be represented by the sequence **mᚨgᚨ** (see table 11 and also Waxenberger forthcoming):

Table 11: Possible Old English words for **mᚨgᚨ**

1. For the phoneme short *a* 1.1 OE *maga* (inflected cases of *magu* 'son, youth') masc. *u*-stem in the following cases: gen.sg.; dat.sg.; nom.pl.; gen.pl.; acc.pl. 1.2 OE *maga* 'stomach': masc. *n*-stem: nom.sg. 1.3 OE *maga* 'powerful': masc. weak adjective
2. For the long WGmc *ā* 2.1 OE *mǣġ* 'woman, kinswoman': fem. *ō*-stem in the following cases: gen.sg.; dat.sg.; acc.sg. 2.2 OE *mǣg* 'relative': masc. *a*-stem in the dat.sg. *mǣgæ* as well as in the gen.pl. *mǣga*
3. For the long WGmc *ā* if the inscription was written not too close to ca. 500 3.1 OE *māga* 'son, descendant, young man': masc. *n*-stem: nom.sg. 3.2 OE *māge* 'female relative' fem. *n*-stem: nom.sg.

I fully agree with Nielsen (2006: 211f.) who transliterates **mᚨgᚨ** as **mægæ** and regards it as the "predecessor of OE *mǣgæ* (dsm. *a*-st.) 'for kinsman'".

Theoretically, the following words would qualify as underlying readings for the second sequence **medu**.
1. OE *medu* 'mead' masc./neut. *u*-stem: either nom.sg. or acc.sg. [Campbell 1959: §614]
2. OE *mēd* 'reward, pay, price, compensation' (< Gmc. *$\bar{e}^2$ [SB 1965: §19; Nielsen 2000: 109]): fem. *ō*-stem. The nom.sg. of the Undley bracteate would have been **mēdu*.
3. OE (*ge*)*mēde* neutr. -*es*; 'consent, good-will, pleasure' [BT 1898: 415; BTS 1921: 634]. The nom. sg. of the Undley bracteate would have been **mēdu*.
4. (*ge*)*mēde* 'agreeable, pleasant, suitable'[23]

---

[23] OE *mēd* 'meadow' [< PrGmc. **mē-dwō-* (*o*-stem)/**mēdu* (*u*-stem): Bammesberger 1990: 118] can be excluded on semantic grounds.

After examining the four possible candidates for **medu**, it becomes clear that only two fulfill the formal requirements (see Waxenberger forthcoming chapter 3 for the detailed discussion):
1. OE *medu* 'mead' (masc./neutr. *u*-stem): nom.sg. or acc.sg.
2. OE *mēd* 'reward, pay, price, compensation' (fem. *ō*-stem).
Undley: nom.sg. *mēdu (nom.sg. -*u* < Gmc. *- *ō* (< IE *-*ā*; see Waxenberger 1996: 71).
To sum up: At present, I cannot analyze the first sequence ᛉᛝᛉ but **mᛝgᛝ** would best be rendered as *mǣgæ* dat.sg. of *mǣg* 'relative'.
Both OE *medu* 'mead' in the nom.sg. or acc.sg. and the nom.sg. of OE *mēd* 'reward, pay, price, compensation' would be possible readings for **medu**.
Therefore I propose the following possibilities:

ᛉᛝᛉ ° *mǣgæ* ° *medu/mēdu*
ᛉᛝᛉ ° 'to the relative' ° 'mead' (nom. or acc.sg.)/ 'reward, compensation' (nom.sg.)
1. $\widehat{ga(:)}$ $\overline{go:}$ $\widehat{ga(:)}$
   [ɣa(:) ɣɔ̄: ɣa(:)]
2. $\widehat{gæ(:)}$ $\overline{go:}$ $\widehat{gæ(:)}$
   [jæ(:) ɣɔ̄: jæ(:)]

The inscription would then be parsed as: 'ᛉᛝᛉ (is) the reward/mead to the relative'.
For semantic reasons, I prefer 'reward' to 'mead' and translate therefore:
'ᛉᛝᛉ (is) the reward to the relative'.

4.4 Chessell Down Scabbard Plate (ca. 525-550)

ᚠᛁᚠ : ᚠᛇᚱᛁ

For two reasons, the Chessell Down inscription has been seen as a problematic text: Firstly, rune no. 4 has been interpreted as **s, f, w** and **l**. From a runological and linguistic point of view none of these suggestions is satisfactory (see Waxenberger forthcoming) and secondly, a possible Scandinavian provenance or influence has been repeatedly advocated.

Regarding rune no. 4, the form **s** = ᛌ, is only used in the 7th-9th cent. (see Waxenberger forthcoming). With the exception of the Chessell Down inscription, the s-rune forms of the 5th-6th cent. belong to the so-called 'diagonal type' [see Waxenberger 2000: 99] with three, four or more strokes (ᛌ; ᛊ; ᛋ). Therefore I consider rune no. 4 to be a **k**, analyzing it as a variant ('inverted rune') of type 3 ᚳ or type 4 ᚺ (see Waxenberger forthcoming).[24]

As rune no. 5 ᛉ is used in an *i*-umlaut environment, I assume that **k** was palatal, compared to a velar variant ᛣ in ᛠᛣᚠ. If taken as **k**, the sequence would read **cœri**. This could reflect a noun, only attested in ON in the meaning 'sword' [see Egilsson & Jónsson 1957: 368: *kǫri*: 'a tent, probe; **poet. a sword**'].

The rune ᚠ in the sequence ᛠᛣᚠ can only denote a rounded back vowel, consequently rune ᚫ ought to represent the retracted allophone [a] (see above 3.1.3.4). The neighbouring rune ᛣ may give an additional hint on how to read ᚫ? Admittedly, the evidence for ᛣ in the 5th and 6th cent. is extremely scanty but it shows that ᛣ may have been used before velar vowels (e.g.: **skanomodu** coin: sᛣᚠnᛉmᛣdu).[25] Nevertheless, it leaves the question open whether or not it was used after velar vowels as well. The only other identifiable **k** in this early period occurs in ᚺᛠᚱᛁᛒᛉ^ᛁ on the Watchfield Purse Mount (ca. 500-550); it has the shape ^ and stands in a palatal environment. All this may be sheer coincidence, but should the data reflect runic practice, the sequence should be transliterated as **ako**.

As I have stated above, the rune ᚠ must have been created between ca. 425-475 (= Caistor-by-Norwich Astragalus) and ca. 575-610 (**skanomodu** solidus). As the new rune ᚠ was presumably contemporaneous with rune ᚠ, its emergence could not have been too long after 500 (= the latest possible date for the Undley inscription). Being inscribed at ca. 525-550, the sequence in question ought to reveal either a very late state of the diphthong *ai (if a date around 525 is assumed), or in the more likely case of a monophthong, we would expect the new rune ᚠ. Neither possibility is evident in the text. For this reason I propose short */a/, although its positional variant – [a] or [æ] (see above table 8) – is not completely clear, as I could only provide a relative chronology in table 8. Therefore the question arises, as to whether the attested use of the rune ᚫ belongs to phase no. 2 in the table (in which [æ] was the primary allophone) or if it belongs to phase no. 4 (restoration of [a] before velar vowels).

Logically, the personal name ᛠᛣᚠ should be in the genitive, so that the phrase should be: 'Ako's sword'. As has been shown for OE, the gen.sg. of the OE *n*-stems could not have been derived from the regular suffix IE *-*en*- or possibly *-*n*-, but must have been replaced by IE *-*on*- > Gmc. *-*an*- [Bammesberger 1990: 165ff.; see also Waxenberger 1996: 101]. Hence, the ending for the gen.sg. IE *-*on-os* > Gmc. *-*anaz* would have been PrOE *-*an* and therefore would have been denoted by the rune ᚫ. Hence this possibility is ruled out here.

If, however, the rune ᚠ is here used to denote a masc. name inflected according to the OE weak declension pattern, it could only be in the nom.sg. In this

---

[24] Interestingly, Seebold (1991: 457f.) observes the late forms "ᚣ, ᚠ "(vereinzelt ᛣ)" in Scandinavia from ca. 500 onwards, although these forms seem not to appear in Denmark (see Seebold 1991: 459).
[25] See also Waxenberger forthcoming.

case ᛣᛟ could be seen as the sword's name. The nom.sg. ending PrGmc. *-$\tilde{o}$ is thinkable for the OE ending -*a* according to Bammesberger (1990: 167).[26] For the Undley Bracteate, Nielsen (2006: 211) assumes the state -ɔ rather than -*a* for the unstressed vowels (see above) and in his footnote 9, Nielsen (2006: 211) adds a comment by John Hines: "the unaccented final vowel of **ako** (-ᛟ) in the legend of the sixth-century Chessell Down scabbard plate (...) might bear out this point." I agree with Hines. The first evidence of -**a** represented by the new rune ᛟ in the nom.sg. ending of a weak noun (**luda**) appears only at ca. 610-650 on the Caistor-by-Norwich Brooch.

For the reasons discussed above, I read and translate the inscription:
ako : cœri
'Aka : sword'
In Classical OE the ending of the nom.sg. **ako** would be -*a*.

4.5 Watchfield Purse Mount (ca. 500-550)

hᛁribᚷ^i : ᚹusᛁ
For the personal name **ᚺᛁᚱᛁᛒᚷ^ᛁ hᛁribœki** (OE *here* 'army'; OE *bōc* 'beech-tree': see also Waxenberger forthcoming chapter 2 no. 86) I follow Page (1986: 126) in interpreting **wusᛁ** also as a personal name. When compared to the nom.sg.masc. *n*-stem **ako** on the Chessell Down Scabbard Mount (ca. 525-550), a nom.sg.masc. *n*-stem is hardly to be expected. A nom.sg.fem. *n*-stem would, however, be in complete congruence with the rune ᛁ. Bammesberger (1990: 167) argues that OE -*e* cannot be explained from PrGmc. *-$\tilde{o}$ (< IE *-*ōn*) and therefore holds the view that feminine nouns in WGmc must have applied the ending *-$\acute{o}$. In my opinion, rune ᛁ confirms Bammesberger's thesis. I propose the following reading:

hᛁribœ^i : wusᛁ
[hɛribɵ:ki] : [wusæ]
'To Haribok : Wuse'

5. The attested phoneme inventory of Pre-OE

In the following, I made an attempt to list the phonemes that are attested in the Pre-OE inscriptions listed above. When it was possible I also listed their allophones.

---

[26] See also Waxenberger (1996: 101) on the discussion of possible suffixes.

50 Gaby Waxenberger

Table 12: The attested phoneme inventory of Pre-OE
The **skanomodu** coin is excluded here as it may be Old Frisian.

Incription	Time-Frame	Rune	Phoneme(s) in Pre-OE	Status in the inscription
Spong Hill Urn: ← ᚠᛚᚢ → alu	ca. 400-600			
		Rune *ansuz* ᚠ *fuþark*	/a/	[a]
		Rune l	/l/	
		Rune u	/u/	
Loveden Hill Urn: sᛇᚦᚨᛒᚨᛞ ‖ þi{c/u}w ‖ [.]lᚨ[.]	ca. 400-600			
sᛇᚦᚨᛒᚨᛞ		Rune s	/s/	
		Rune ᛇ	/iː/	
		Rune þ	/θ/	
		Runes ᚨ; ᚨ	/a/	[æ]; [æ]
		Rune b	/b/	
		Rune d	/d/	
þi{c/u}w		Rune þ	?/θ/	
		Rune i	/i(ː)/	
		Rune c or rune u	?/k/ or ?/u(ː)/	
		Rune w	?/w/	
[.]lᚨ[.]		Rune l	/l/	
		Rune *ansuz* ᚠ *fuþark*	/a/	
Caistor-by-Norwich Astragalus rᚨᛇhᚨn	ca. 425-475			
		Rune r	/r/	
		Runes ᚨᛇ		[åɪ] or possibly [åe]
		Rune h	/x/	
		Rune *ansuz* ᚠ *fuþark*	/a/	[a]
		Rune n	/n/	
Undley Bracteate ᚷᚷᚷ° mᛚgᛏ° **medu**	450-500			

ᚷᚫᚷ	450-500	Bindrune ᚷ (Rune *ansuz* ᚠ*fuþark* + rune g)	/ɣ/ + /a(:)/	[ɣ] + [a(:)] or [j] + [æ(:)]
		Bindrune ᚷ (Rune ᚠ + rune g)	/ɣ/ + /õ:/	[ɣ] + /õ:/
		Bindrune: ᚷ (Rune *ansuz* ᚠ*fuþark* + rune g)	/ɣ/ + /a(:)/	[ɣ] + [a(:)] or [j] + [æ(:)]
mᵃgᵃ		Rune m	/m/	
		Rune *ansuz* ᚠ*fuþark*	/a(:)/	Probably [æ:]
		Rune g	/ɣ/	Probably [j]
		Rune *ansuz* ᚠ*fuþark*	/a(:)/	Probably [æ]
medu		Rune m	/m/	
		Rune e	/e(:)/	
		Rune d	/d/	
		Rune u	/u/	
Watchfield Purse Mount hᛚribᚷ^i : wusᚠ	ca. 500-550			
hᛚribᚷ^i		Rune h	/x/	
		Rune *ansuz* ᚠ*fuþark*	/a/	[ɛ]
		Rune r	/r/	
		Rune i	/i/	
		Rune b	/b/	
		Rune ōþil ᚷ*fuþark*	/o:/	[œ:]
		Rune ^	/k/	[k̟]
		Rune i	/ɪ/	
wusᚠ		Rune w	/w/	
		Rune u	/u(:)/	
		Rune s	/s/	
		Rune *ansuz* ᚠ*fuþark*	/a/	[æ]
Welbeck Hill Bracteate ←lᚠw	ca. 500-570			
		Rune l	/l/	

		Rune *ansuz* ᚠ*fuþark*	/a(:)/	
		Rune **w**	/w/	
Chessell Down Scabbard Mount **ako : cœri** **ako**		Rune *ansuz* ᚠ*fuþark*	/a/	[a]
		Rune ᚲ	/k/	[k̟]
		Rune **o**	/ɔ/	
cœri		Rune ᚳ	/k/	[k̟]
		Rune *ōþil* ᛟ*fuþark*	/o/	[œ]
		Rune **r**	/r/	
		Rune **i**	/ɪ/	
Chessell Down Pail [...]ᚳᚳᚳᚠᚠ	ca. 520-570	Rune ᚲ (3x)	/k/ (3x)	
		Rune *ansuz* ᚠ*fuþark* (3x)	/a(:)/ (3x)	

5.1 The consonant system of Pre-OE

Table 13 shows Hogg's (1992: 101) reconstructed "Pre-OE" phoneme inventory while in table 14 the inventory attested by the Pre-OE inscriptions is listed.

Table 13: Hogg's reconstructed phonemes of Pre-OE

The phonemes of Pre-OE according to Hogg (1992: 101)			
	Labial	Dental	Palatal	Velar
Voiceless stops	/p/	/t/	-	/k/
Voiced stops	/b/	/d/	-	-
Voiceless fricatives	/f/	/θ/	-	/x/
Voiced fricatives	-	-	-	/ɣ/
Sibilants	-	/s/	-	-
Nasals	/m/	/n/	-	-
Liquids, approximants	-	/l, r/	/j/	/w/

With the exception of /p/, /f/, /t/ and /j/, the Pre-OE inscriptions confirm Hogg's reconstructed phoneme system.

Table 14: The attested phonemes of Pre-OE

The attested phonemes of Pre-OE				
	Labial	Dental	Palatal	Velar
Voiceless stops	not attested	not attested	-	/k/
Voiced stops	/b/	/d/	-	-
Voiceless fricatives	not attested	/θ/	-	/x/
Voiced fricatives	-	-	-	/ɣ/
Sibilants	-	/s/	-	-
Nasals	/m/	/n/	-	-
Liquids, approximants	-	/l/, /r/	not attested	/w/

5.2 The stressed vowels of Pre-OE

As runic writing does not mark quantity, it is difficult to determine vowel length. The vowels shown in table 15 can be given with certainty. Table 16 shows short monophthongs in unstressed position.

Table 15: Monophthongs and diphthongs in stressed position

MONOPHTHONGS		DIPHTHONGS
SHORT	LONG	
	/iː/	The Gmc. diphthong */aɪ/ is presented at the stage [åɪ] or possibly [åe].
	/oː/	
/a/	/ɔ̄ː/	
The phonemes /e(ː)/ and /u(ː)/ are also attested but their quantities cannot be determined. For /e(ː)/ see above 4.3 **medu**.		

Table 16: Short monophthongs in unstressed position

/ɪ/		/u/
		/ɔ/
	/a/	

6. Conclusion

I have made an attempt to analyze the Pre-OE sound changes as they are reflected by the Pre-OE runic inscriptions. Moreover, it was also possible to establish a relative chronology of these sound changes (see above 3.2). Furthermore, Pre-OE runic writing sheds light on the hitherto only reconstructed phoneme inventory of Pre-OE.

Appendix 1: Maps

MAP 1: OE runic inscriptions

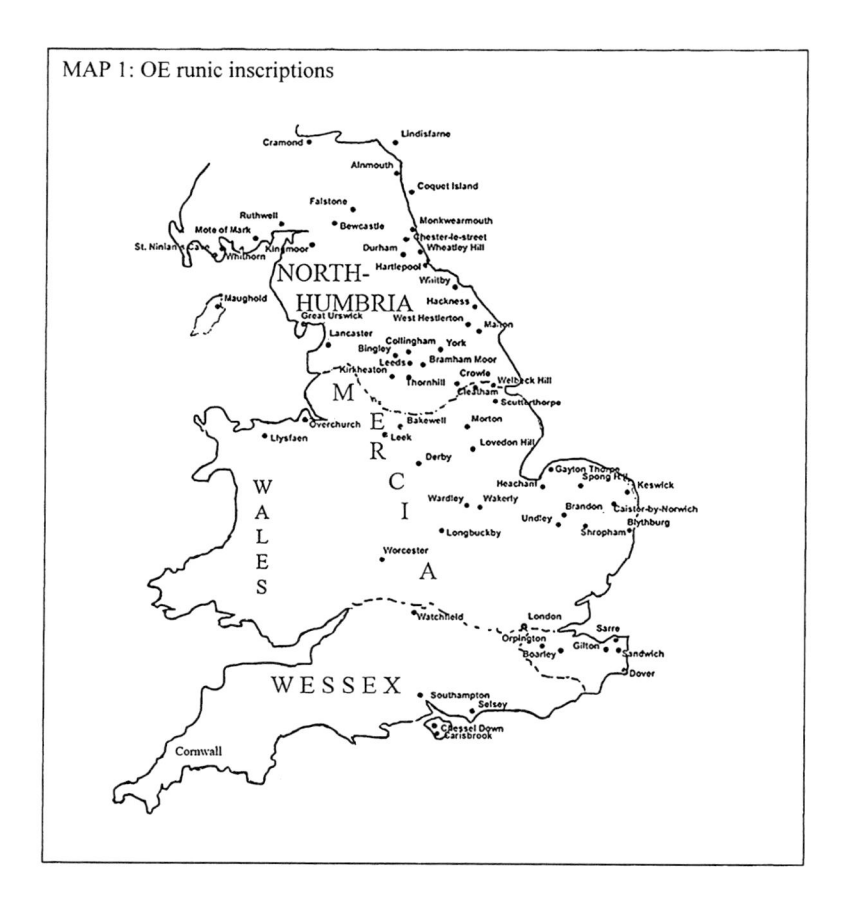

Map 2: Pre-OE runic inscriptions

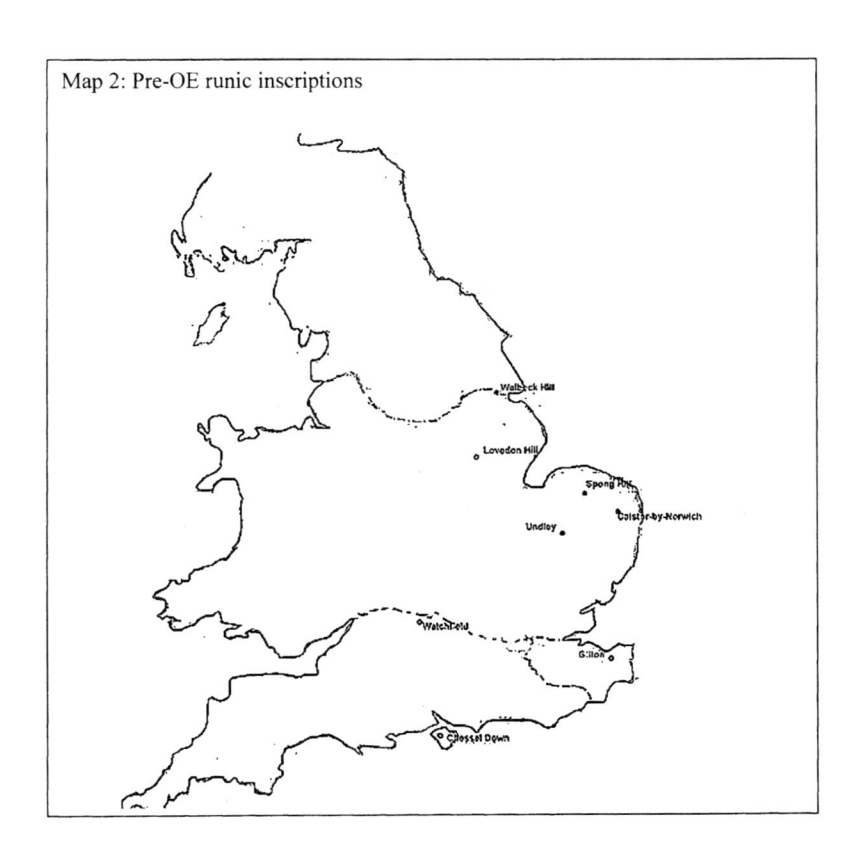

Appendix 2: Alphabetical list of Pre-OE and OE runic inscriptions

1. **THE ALNMOUTH STONE** [Great North Museum: Hancock, Newcastle-upon-Tyne: reg. no: 1958.8.N]
2. **ASH-GILTON RUNIC POMMEL** [National Museums & Galleries on Merseyside: Liverpool Museum: accession no: M6402].
3. **AUZON CASKET / FRANKS CASKET**
[Three panels and the lid: London: The British Museum, Department of Prehistory and Europe: 1867, 1-20,1. Right panel: Florence: Museo Nazionale del Bargello, Carrand Collection no. 25]

4. **BACONSTHORPE PAGEHOLDER/PAGETURNER** [Norwich Castle Museum: found in 2009]
5. **BAKEWELL STONE** [Sheffield City Museum and Art Gallery; accession no: J931385]
6. **BEWCASTLE CROSS** [Churchyard of the Parish Church of St Cuthbert, Bewcastle, Cumberland [Page 1959: 180]).]
7. **BINHAM BRACTEATE NORFOLK** [British Museum under the Treasure Act process]
8. **BLYTHBURGH WRITING TABLET** [London: The British Museum, Department of Prehistory and Europe: 1902, 3-15.1]
9. **BOARLEY BROOCH** [Private possession: Parsons 1992: 8, 1999: 46; Flowers 1999: 7; Looijenga 2003:278]
10. **BRAMHAM MOOR RING** [Copenhagen: National Museum, no. 8545]
11. **BRANDON ANTLER HANDLE** [Castle Museum Norwich, Norfolk]
12. **BRANDON PINHEAD** [Castle Museum Norwich, Norfolk]
13. **BRANDON TWEEZERS** [Castle Museum Norwich, Norfolk]
14. **BRISTOL/LINSTOCK CASTLE AGATE RING** (= Linstock Castle (Cumberland/Cumbria: Page 1998: 291ff.; 1999: 30; 228) [London: The British Museum, Department of Prehistory and Europe: 1873, 2-10, 3]
15. **CAISTOR-BY-NORWICH ASTRAGALUS** [Castle Museum Norwich, Norfolk: N 59]
16. **CAISTOR-BY-NORWICH BROOCH (= HARFORD FARM BROOCH)** [Castle Museum, Norwich, Norfolk]
17. **CARRISBROOK (ISLE OF WIGHT) RUNIC MOUNT (= DORSET STRAP END)** [London: The British Museum, Department of Prehistory and Europe: 1999.4-1.1]
18. **CHESSELL DOWN PAIL** [London: The British Museum, Department of Prehistory and Europe: 67.7-29.136]
19. **CHESSELL DOWN SCABBARD MOUNT/PLATE** (= Chessel Down II: Looijenga 1997: 162, 2003: 276) [London: The British Museum, Department of Prehistory and Europe: 67.7-29.150]
20. **CHESTER-LE-STREET STONE** [Chester-le-Street (Durham): Upper room of Anchorage].
21. **CLEATHAM HANGING BOWL** [Scunthorpe Museum & Art Gallery, Oswald Road, Scunthorpe, North Lincolnshire DN15 7BD, GB]
22. **COLLINGHAM STONE** [North aisle of Collingham Church (W. Yorkshire) [Mitchell 1994:Col]
23. **CRAMOND RING** [Museum of Scotland (Early People Section), Chambers Street, Edinburgh EH1 1JF: Reg. No: X.NJ19]
24. **CROWLE STONE** [St. Oswald's Church, Crowle, N. Lincolnshire]
25. **DERBY(SHIRE) BONE PLATE** [London: The British Museum, Department of Prehistory and Europe: M & LA 1890.8-10.5]
26. **DOVER BROOCH** [London: The British Museum, Department of Prehistory and Europe: 1963 11-8 583]
27. **DOVER STONE** [Dover Museum]
28. **EYE** [Location unknown]
29. **FALSTONE HOGBACK** [Great North Museum: Hancock, Newcastle-upon-Tyne: accession no. 1814.23]
30. **GANDERSHEIM/BRUNSWICK CASKET** [Braunschweig, Lower Saxony, Germany: Herzog Anton Ulrich-Museum Braunschweig: accession no: MA 58.]
31. **GAYTON THORPE WHORL (= NORFOLK SPINDLE WHORL)** [Present location: unknown]
32. **GREAT URSWICK STONE** [South aisle of Great Urswick Church, Lancashire]

33. **HACKNESS STONE** [South aisle of St. Peter's Church, Hackness (Hackness Parish Church, North Yorkshire)]
34. **HARTLEPOOL STONE I** [St. Hilda's Church, Hartlepool, Co. Durham]
35. **HARTLEPOOL STONE II** [Great North Museum: Hancock, Newcastle-upon-Tyne: accession no. 1845.7]
36. **HEACHAM TWEEZERS** [Castle Museum, Norwich, Norfolk]
37. **KESWICK RUNIC DISC** (= **THE RIVER YARE NEAR NORWICH DISC**) [Present location is not known as it was sold by its finder: Hines 1997-1998: 14f.]
38. **KINGMOOR AMULET RING** (= GREYMOOR HILL RING) [London: The British Museum, Department of Prehistory and Europe: Ring Cat 1840A 10262]
39. **KIRKHEATON STONE** [Tolson Museum, Huddersfield, Ravensknowle Park, HD5 8D5]
40. **LANCASHIRE (MANCHESTER) RING** [The British Museum: Department of Prehistory and Europe: SL 64, ring cat. no 181.]
41. **LANCASTER CROSS** [London: British Museum, Department of Prehistory and Europe: 68,10-4,3]
42. **LEEDS STONE** (lost since the 19th century: Page 1973: 31)
43. **LEEK STONE** [South of the church in the churchyard of St. Edward the Confessor's, Leek, Staffordshire.]
44. **LEICESTERSHIRE PIECE** (?pair of tweezers) [The British Museum under the Treasure Act process]
45. **LINDISFARNE STONE I** [Lindisfarne Priory Museum: No. 81077015]
46. **LINDISFARNE STONE II** [Lindisfarne Priory Museum: No. 81077019]
47. **LINDISFARNE STONE III** [Lindisfarne Priory Museum: No. 81077022]
48. **LINDISFARNE STONE IV** [Lindisfarne Priory Museum: No. 81077018]
49. **LINDISFARNE STONE V** [Lindisfarne Priory Museum: No. 81077017]
50. **LINDISFARNE STONE VI** [Lindisfarne Priory Museum: No. 81077024]
51. **LLYSFAEN RING** [London: Victoria and Albert Museum, Jewellery Gallery: Case 32 Board H, Catalogue No: 627-1871.]
52. **LONDON NATIONAL PORTRAIT GALLERY BONE** [Museum of London, no. NPG 97]
53. **LONDON ROYAL OPERA HOUSE BONE** [Museum of London, no. ROP 95]
54. **LONDON THAMES FITTING MOUNT** [London: The British Museum, Department of Prehistory and Europe: 1869,6-10,1]
55. **LONDON THAMES RING** [London: Museum of London; London Wall; London EC2Y 5HN; Acc. No: TEX 88 [+] <1330>]
56. **LONDON THAMES SCRAMASAX** [London: The British Museum, Department of Prehistory and Europe: 1857,6-23,1]
57. **LONG BUCKBY STRAP-END, NORTHAMPTONSHIRE** (= **Northamptonshire**) [London: The British Museum, Department of Prehistory and Europe: 56217. T. 261.]
58. **LOVEDEN HILL URN** [London: The British Museum, Department of Prehistory and Europe: 1963, 10-1,14.]
59. **MALTON PIN** (= Vale of Pickering disc: Page 2006: 219) [The British Museum, London, Department of Prehistory and Europe: 56217-T.261 (2000 5-8).]
60. **MARCH PLAQUE** [Castle Museum Norwich, Norfolk]
61. **MAUGHOLD STONE I** [Shelter in Maughold Churchyard, Isle of Man]
62. **MAUGHOLD STONE II** [Shelter in Maughold Churchyard, Isle of Man]

63. **MONKWEARMOUTH STONE I** [London: The British Museum, Department of Prehistory and Europe: 1880,3-13,1]
64. **MONKWEARMOUTH STONE II** [Sunderland Museum]
65. **MONTE SANT' ANGELO (= GARGANO) GRAFFITI**
[West facade of the gallery leading to the sacred Grotto of the Archangel beneath the church of St. Michael at Monte Sant' Angelo: Page 1994:180; Mitchell 1994:s.v. GG1; inscription E is found in the inside: Düwel 2008: 83].
66. **MORTAIN CASKET** [Mortain, Normandy, France]
67. **MORTON RUNIC STRAPEND (= HOOKED TAG FROM LINCOLNSHIRE)** [London: The British Museum, Department of Prehistory and Europe]
68. **MOTE OF MARK BONE** [National Museums of Scotland: Museum of Scotland (Early People Section), Chambers Street, Edinburgh EH1 1JF; Reg. No. X1997.291]
69. **ORPINGTON SUNDIAL** [All Saints' parish church, Orpington (Kent)]
70. **OVERCHURCH STONE** [Williamson Art Gallery and Museum, Birkenhead, Liverpool]
71. **ROME CATACOMBS AD DUAS LAUROS GRAFFITI** [Basilica S. Petrus (Exorcista) and S. Marcellinus, Via Labicana]
72. **ROME CIMITERO DI COMMODILLA GRAFFITO** [Cimitero di Commodilla on the Via Ostiense, Rome, Italy: Derolez 1987: 15; Page 1999: 224]
73. **ROME BRONZE FRAGMENT** (= Rome pot; fragment of Roman bronze vessel: Parsons 1999: 82; Moore-Bronze: Seebold 1991: 511)
[The David and Albert Smart Museum University of Chicago: accession no. 1967.115.538 (UC 538-B37)]
74. **RUTHWELL CROSS** [Ruthwell Church, Dumfries (Dumfries and Galloway), Scotland]
75. **SALTFLEET BY LINCOLNSHIRE SPINDLE WHORL** [Castle Museum, Norwich, Norfolk]
76. **SANDWICH STONE** [Royal Museum Canterbury]
77. *SKANOMODU* SOLIDUS (= London Solidus: Beck 1981: 74; London gold solidus: Nielsen 2000: 93) [The British Museum, London, Department of Coins and Medals]
The inscription may be OFris.
78. **SCOTTERTHORPE LEAD FRAGMENT** [Scunthorpe Museum]
79. **SELSEY FRAGMENTS** [London: The British Museum, Department of Prehistory and Europe: 1878.3-15.4]
80. **SHROPHAM LEAD PLATE/PLAQUE** [Castle Museum, Norwich]
81. **SOUTHAMPTON BONE I** (= Hamwih Bone) [Sea City Museum, Southampton: Sou 39.7]: OE or possibly OFris
82. **SOUTHAMPTON BONE II** (= Southampton Bone Plaque) [Sea City Museum, Southampton]
83. **SPONG HILL URN STAMP** [Castle Museum, Norwich, Norfolk]: on all three urns
84. **ST BENET LEAD PLATE** [Castle Museum, Norwich, Norfolk]
85. **ST CUTHBERT'S COFFIN** [Durham Cathedral Treasury]
86. **ST NINIAN'S CAVE STONE** [Whithorn Priory Museum (Ministry of Works Museum) Wigtownshire]
87. **THORNHILL STONE I** [St. Michael's Church, Thornhill, West Yorkshire]
88. **THORNHILL STONE II** [St. Michael's Church, Thornhill, West Yorkshire]
89. **THORNHILL STONE III** [St. Michael's Church, Thornhill, West Yorkshire]
90. **UNDLEY BRACTEATE** [London: The British Museum, Department of Prehistory and Europe: 1984, 11-1,1]
91. **WAKERLEY BROOCH** [Northampton Central Museum (Looijenga 2003: 287)]

92. **WARDLEY METAL PLATE (= LEICESTERSHIRE FIND)** [Present location unknown]
93. **WARWICKSHIRE ?AMULET** [Castle Museum, Norwich, Norfolk]
94. **WATCHFIELD PURSE MOUNT** [Oxfordshire Museum, Woodstock, registration no. 1985.89]
95. **WELBECK HILL BRACTEATE** [In private hands: Page 1973: 182; Looijenga 1997: 128; Flowers 1999: 42; Parsons 1999: 70]
96. **WEST HESLERTON BROOCH** [in the hands of the excavator: Looijenga 1997: 164; 2003: 279]
97. **WHEATLEY RUNIC RING** [London: The British Museum, Department of Prehistory and Europe: MME 1995,9-2,1]
98. **WHITBY BRACTEATE** [London: British Museum, Department of Prehistory and Europe: W31]
99. **WHITBY COMB** [Whitby Literary and Philosophical Society's Museum]
100. **WHITBY DISC** [London: The British Museum, Department of Prehistory and Europe: W.396]
101. **WHITHORN STONE I** [Whithorn Priory Museum (Ministry of Works Museum) Wigtownshire]
102. **WHITHORN STONE II** [Whithorn Priory Museum (Ministry of Works Museum) Wigtownshire]
103. **WORCESTER SHERD, DEANSWAY** [present location unknown]
104. **YORK SPOON** [Yorkshire Museum, York]

New Finds 2012
105. **IPSWICH BELT BUCKLE** [Pre-Construct Archaeology Ltd., London]
106. **IPSWICH WHALE BONE FRAGMENT**

N.B. With some of the recently discovered objects, especially those kept at the Norwich Castle Museum, it is not quite clear who actually owns them.

Appendix 3: The Old English fuþorc

THE GERMANIC fuþark

ᚠ	ᚢ	ᚦ	ᚨansuz	ᚱ	ᚲ	ᚷ	ᚹ	ᚺ	ᚾ	ᛁ	ᛃ	?	ᛈ	ᛇz(R)	ᛋ	ᛏ	ᛒ	ᛖ	ᛗ	ᛚ	ᛜ	ᛞ	ᛟōþil
f	u	þ	a	r	k	g	w	h	n	i	j		p	z	s	t	b	e	m	l	ŋ	d	o
1	2	3	4	5	6	7	8	9	10	11	12	13	14	15	16	17	18	19	20	21	22	23	24

ᚩ /ō:/

PRE-OE INNOVATIONS

ᚪ ᚫ
/o:/ /a:/ /æ:/
[œ(:)] [æ(:)]
[a(:)]
[ɑ̃(:)]
[ɛ(:)]

THE EARLY OE fuþorc

ᚠ	ᚢ	ᚦ	ᚩ	ᚱ	ᚳ	ᚷ	ᚹ	ᚻ	ᚾ	ᛁ	*	ᛡi/ ᛄ[ç]	ᛈpeorþ	⟨x⟩[x]eolhx	ᛋsigel	ᛏ	ᛒ	ᛖ	ᛗ	ᛚ	ᛝ	ᛞ	ᚪ	ᚫ	ᚣ
f	u	þ	o	r	c	g	w	h	n	i	j		p		s	t	b	e	m	l	ŋ	d	œ	æ	y
1	2	3	4	5	6	7	8	9	10	11	12	13	14	15	16	17	18	19	20	21	22	23	24	25	26	27

feoh þorn rād ġiefu hæġl ī̆s ēoh/īh peorþ eolhx sigel tīr beorc man lagu ing dæġ āc æsc ȳr
ūr ōs cēn wynn nīed ġē(a)r æþil

Dictionaries

BT
    An Anglo-Saxon Dictionary, by Joseph Bosworth and T. Northcote Toller. Oxford: Oxford University Press, 1898; *Supplement*, by T. Northcote Toller, 1921; *Enlarged Addenda to the Supplement*, by Alistair Campbell, 1972.
    <http://beowulf.engl.uky.edu/~kiernan/BT/Bosworth-Toller.htm>

Hall, J. R. Clark
1960   *A concise Anglo-Saxon dictionary.* 4th edition with a supplement by H. D. Meritt. Cambridge: Cambridge University Press.

Egilsson, Sveinbjörn -- F. Jónsson
1957   *An Icelandic-English dictionary*, 2nd ed., Oxford.

References

Bammesberger, Alfred
1990   *Die Morphologie des urgermanischen Nomens*, Indogermanische Bibliothek, Untersuchungen zur vergleichenden Grammatik der germanischen Sprachen 2, Heidelberg: Winter.
1991   "Three Old English runic inscriptions", in: *Old English runes and their Continental background*, ed. A. Bammesberger. Anglistische Forschungen 217, Heidelberg: Winter, 125-136.
1994   "The development of the runic script and its relationship to Germanic phonological history", in: *Language change and language structure, Older Germanic languages in a comparative perspective*, eds. T. Swan; E. Mørck & O.J. Westvik. Trends in Linguistics 73, Berlin: Mouton de Gruyter, 1-25.
1996   "Frisian and Anglo-Saxon runes: From the linguistic angle", *Amsterdamer Beiträge zur Älteren Germanistik* 45: 16-23.
2003   "The *Harford Farm* brooch runic inscription", *Neophilologus* 87: 133-135.
2006   "Das Futhark und seine Weiterentwicklung in der anglofriesischen Überlieferung", in: *Das fuþark und seine einzelsprachlichen Weiterentwicklungen*, eds. A. Bammesberger & G. Waxenberger. Ergänzungsbände zum Reallexikon der Germanischen Altertumskunde 51, Berlin & New York: Mouton de Gruyter, 171-187.

Blackburn, Mark
1991   "A survey of Anglo-Saxon and Frisian coins with runic inscriptions", in: *Old English runes and their Continental background*, ed. A. Bammesberger. Anglistische Forschungen 217, Heidelberg: Winter, 137-189.

Boehler, Maria
1930   *Die altenglischen Frauennamen*, Germanische Studien 98, Berlin: Ebering.

Brunner, Karl
1965   *Altenglische Grammatik: Nach der angelsächsischen Grammatik von Eduard Sievers*, 3. Aufl., Sammlung kurzer Grammatiken germanischer Dialekte, Hauptreihe 3, Tübingen: Niemeyer.

Campbell, Alistair
   1959   *Old English Grammar*, Oxford: Clarendon Press.

Eichner, Heiner
   1990   "Die Ausprägung der linguistischen Physiognomie des Englischen anno 400 bis anno 600 n. Chr. ", in: *Britain 400-600: Language and history*, eds. A. Bammesberger & A. Wollmann. Anglistische Forschungen 205, Heidelberg: Winter, 307-333.

   2006   "Zu den Quellen und Übertragungswegen der germanischen Runeninschrift – Ein Diskussionsbeitrag", in: *Das fuþark und seine einzelsprachlichen Weiterentwicklungen*, eds. A. Bammesberger & G. Waxenberger. Ergänzungsbände zum Reallexikon der Germanischen Altertumskunde 51, Berlin & New York: de Gruyter, 101-108.

Hawkes, Sonya – Ray Page
   1967   "Swords and runes in South-East England", *The Antiquaries Journal* 47: 1-26.

Hills, Catherine
   1991   "The archaeological context of runic finds", in: *Old English runes and their continental background*, ed. A. Bammesberger. Anglistische Forschungen 217, Heidelberg: Winter, 41-59.

Hines, John
   1990   "Philology, archaeology and the *adventus Saxonum vel Anglorum*", in: *Britain 400-600: Language and history*, eds. A. Bammesberger & A. Wollmann. Anglistische Forschungen 205, Heidelberg: Winter, 17-36.

   1991   "Some observations on the runic inscriptions of Early Anglo-Saxon England'", in: *Old English runes and their continental background*, ed. A. Bammesberger. Anglistische Forschungen 217, Heidelberg: Winter, 61-83.

   1991a   "A new runic inscription from Norfolk", *Nytt om Runer* 6: 6-7.

   2006   "The early runic inscriptions from Kent and the problem of legibility", in: *Das fuþark und seine einzelsprachlichen Weiterentwicklungen*, eds. A. Bammesberger & G. Waxenberger Ergänzungsbände zum Reallexikon der Germanischen Altertumskunde 51, Berlin & New York: de Gruyter, 188-208.

Hogg, Richard
   1992   *A grammar of Old English*, Vol. 1 Phonology, Oxford: Blackwell.

Krupatkin, Y.B.
   1970   "From Germanic to English and Frisian", *Us Wurk* 19: 49-71.

Looijenga, Tineke
   1997   *Runes: Around the North Sea and on the Continent AD 150-700, Texts and Contexts*, Diss. University Groningen: SSG Uitg.

   2003   *Texts & contexts of the oldest runic inscriptions*, The Northern World 4, North Europe and the Baltic c. 400-1700 AD, Peoples, Economics and Cultures, Leiden & Boston: Brill.

Luick, Karl
   1921   *Historische Grammatik der englischen Sprache:* Band 1., 1. Abteilung, Leipzig: Tauchnitz.

Mitchell, Mark
   1994   *Corpus of English runes*, Basle [unpublished MS].

Müller, Rudolf
  1901 *Untersuchungen über die Namen des nordhumbrischen Liber Vitae*, Palaestra 9, Berlin: Mayer & Müller.
Nedoma, Robert
  1991-1993 "Zur Runeninschrift auf der Urne A.11/251 von Loveden Hill", *Die Sprache* 35: 115-124.
  2004 *Personennamen in südgermanischen Runeninschriften*, Studien zur altgermanischen Namenkunde I,1,1, Indogermanische Bibliothek, 3. Reihe, Heidelberg: Winter.
  2006 "Schrift und Sprache in den südgermanischen Runeninschriften", in: *Das fuþark und seine einzelsprachlichen Weiterentwicklungen*, eds. A. Bammesberger & G. Waxenberger. Ergänzungsbände zum Reallexikon der Germanischen Altertumskunde 51, Berlin & New York: de Gruyter, 109-156.
Nielsen, Hans Frede
  2000 *The early runic language of Scandinavia: studies in Germanic dialect geography*, Indogermanische Bibliothek, Erste Reihe, Heidelberg: Winter.
  2006 "The vocalism of the Undley runes viewed from a North-Sea Germanic perspective", in: *Das fuþark und seine einzelsprachlichen Weiterentwicklungen*, eds. A. Bammesberger & G. Waxenberger. Ergänzungsbände zum Reallexikon der Germanischen Altertumskunde 51, Berlin & New York: de Gruyter, 209-215.
Odenstedt, Bengt
  1980 "The Loveden Hill runic inscription'", *Ortnamnssällskapet i Uppsala Årskrift*, 24-37.
  1990 *On the origin and early history of the runic script: Typology and graphic variation in the older Futhark*, Acta Academiae Regiae Gustavi Adolphi 59, Stockholm: Almqvist & Wiksell.
  1991 "A new theory of the origin of the runic script: Richard L. Morris's book *Runic and mediterranean epigraphy*", in: *Old English runes and their continental background*, ed. A. Bammesberger. Anglistische Forschungen 217, Heidelberg: Winter, 359-387.
Page, Ray
  1968 "The OE rune *eoh, ih* 'yew tree'", *Medium Ævum* 37: 125-136.
  1973 *An introduction to English runes*, London: Methuen.
  1986 "The runic inscription", ed. Ch. Scull, "A Sixth-Century Grace Containing a Balance and Weights from Watchfield, Oxfordshire, England'", *Germania* 64: 125-126.
Parsons, David
  1999 *Recasting the runes, The reform of the Anglo-Saxon Futhorc*, Runrön 14, Uppsala: Institutionen för Nordiska Språk.
Sauer, Hans -- Gaby Waxenberger
  2012 "Old English dialects", in: *Historical linguistics of English*, ed. Alexander Bergs & Laurel Brinton. Handbücher zur Sprachwissenschaft 34.1 [HSK 34.1], Berlin & New York: Mouton de Gruyter, 340-361 = chapter 22.
SB = Brunner (1965)

Scull, Christopher
   1986   "A sixth-century grave containing a balance and weights from Watchfield, Oxfordshire, England" with contributions by D. Nash, B. Odenstedt & R.I. Page, and a Technical Appendix by S. Pollard, *Germania* 64: 105-138.

Seebold, Elmar
   1991   "Die Stellung der englischen Runen im Rahmen der Überlieferung des älteren Fuþark", in: *Old English runes and their continental background*, ed. A. Bammesberger. Anglistische Forschungen 217, Heidelberg: Winter, 439-569.

Sievers, Eduard
   1898   *Angelsächsische Grammatik*, 3rd ed., Sammlung kurzer Grammatiken germanischer Dialekte 3, Halle: Niemeyer.

Vennemann, Theo, gen. Nierfeld
   2006   "Germanische Runen und phönizisches Alphabet", *Sprachwissenschaft* 34: 367-429.
   2010   "Griechisch, lateinisch, etruskisch, karthagisch? Zur Herkunft der Runen", eds. E. Glaser, A. Seiler, M. Waldispühl, *LautSchriftSprache*, Beiträge zur Vergleichbaren historischen Graphematik, Medienwandel – Medienwechsel – Medienwissen 15, Zurich: Chronos, 47-82.

Waxenberger, Gaby
   1996   *Die Zuordnung der altenglischen Substantive zu den Flexionstypen untersucht am Buchstaben D*, Frankfurt am Main: Peter Lang.
   2000   "The inscription on the Gandersheim Casket and the runes in the Old English Runes Corpus (Epigraphical Material)", ed. R. Marth, *Das Gandersheimer Runenkästchen*, Internationales Kolloquium Braunschweig, 24.-26. März 1999, Kolloquiumsbände des Herzog-Anton-Ulrich-Museums 1, Braunschweig: Limbach Druck und Verlag, 91-104.
   Forthcoming 1   *Towards a phonology of the Old English runic inscriptions and a catalogue of graphemes* [originally habilitation thesis, University of Munich (LMU)].
   Forthcoming 2   "Graphs and our interpretations of them", Paper at Script and Sound, September 2013.

Middle English evidence of the elimination of velar fricatives:
a prose corpus study

Jerzy Wełna (Warsaw, Poland)

Abstract
The paper examines how changes in spelling mirrored the process of the elimination of word-final velar fricatives from Middle English dialects. The new spellings with final <-ow, -u, -f> sporadically or permanently replaced the conservative traditional spellings with <–h> or, later, <-gh> in the word-final position. To reduce the amount of words with the above structure and achieve the consistency of source data, the study exploits samples of three lemmata (THROUGH, THOUGH, ENOUGH) from a single source, i.e. the Innsbruck Middle English Prose Corpus. Of 158 texts in the corpus only 36 were found to contain forms showing modified spellings of the abovementioned three words indicating the transformation of the original velar fricative to vocalic segments or <f>. The study has shown that scribes continued to use unmodified archaic spellings with <h, ʒ> until the end of the 15th century, especially in the South, although certain texts from the North (Liber de Diversis Medicinis) and the West Midland (Gesta Romanorum, Le Morte d'Arthur) already demonstrate prevalence of spellings with <-ow>. In the East Midland, a best-documented area, conservative and advanced spellings show a lot of variation depending on region. The retention of <-gh> spellings in the London writers in the 14-15th centuries may testify to spelling standardisation in the capital, the place where the written standard was born.

1. Preliminaries

The question of the loss of the velar [χ] has so far enjoyed wide popularity among English historical linguists, as testified, apart from the standard classic works by Jordan (1925/1974), Luick (1940), and Brunner (1962), by a host of scholars, to mention only Ekselius (1940), Bonebrake (1979), Lauttamus (1981), Nieuwint (1981), Lutz (1991) and the relatively recent, brief, but highly informative study by Knappe (1997).

There has been a general agreement that the process belongs to the Middle English period, more precisely, to its latter half, although traces of the change can be found in the early 13th century, as is evidenced especially by place names and proper names from various areas of England. The loss of /χ/ was effected in three ways:

(1) (a) Labialisation of [χ] in the cluster [-χt(-)], involving the insertion of [u] before the fricative to yield the sequence [uχ], followed by the loss of the fricative, as in *boht-* > *bout*, spelt <bout(e), bought(e)> 'bought'.

(b) The change of final [-χ] to [-f], as in *ynough* > *enoff* 'enough'. The labial fricative sometimes also appears before [t], e.g. *draht* > *draught* [dra:ft], also spelt <draft>. The latter change seems confirmed by rhymes like *dohter: softe* (392) or *dohter: ofte* (699 etc.) in *King Horn*.

(c) Vocalisation of [γ], the allophone of /χ/ which, when between back vowels, merged with the semivowel [w], as reflected in the spelling <w>, sometimes <u>, as in *boga* > *bowe* 'bow'.

The data in the studies referred to above are rather selective and are adduced to illustrate the authors' claims concerning the process of the modification of the fricative. The reader is usually offered single instances of spelling indicating that change in progress. The only study which offers a relatively comprehensive account, Ekselius (1940), is confined to the sequences *aht/oht/ōht*, i.e. where the fricative [χ] is followed by the dental plosive [t], as in *brought, ought, sought, taught, thought* etc.; see (2a). His account does not include data concerning words like *bough, dough, though, through*, now with vocalic codas (see 2b), nor does it deal with items where the word-final voiceless velar fricative [x], usually represented by the digraph <gh>, yields the labial fricative [f], as in contemporary English *cough, enough, rough, tough* and a few other words.

(2) (a) brought, ought, sought, taught, thought /ɔːt/

(b) bough, dough, though, through /aʊ/ or /əʊ/ or /uː/

(c) cough, enough, rough, tough; dwarf /ɒf/ or /ʌf/ or /ɔːf/

As regards spellings which correspond to velar fricatives discussed in Dietz's recent study (2006) of relationships between orthography and pronunciation, they include, among others, single graphs, i.e. < h, ȝ>, *gh*-digraphs and their allographs, i.e. <gh, ȝh, hȝ, ch>, all matching the relevant velar fricatives.

Although Dietz's comprehensive and detailed study is also concerned with the late Middle English graphemes which replace OE <h>, i.e. yogh <ȝ> or clusters with yogh and <h>, it does not contain a discussion of their subsequent developments leading to spellings like <ow, ou> or <f>. In short, Dietz's data rather testify to the survival of archaic spellings than to their evolution reflecting vocalisation or change to [f] of the velar fricative. Very helpful are the data in McIntosh et al. (1986), *A Linguistic Atlas of Late Mediaeval English* (*LALME*), which contains several maps recording relevant spellings from the post-1350 period of English.

Thus, the goal of the present brief study is to examine reflection in spelling of the evolution of items with word-final velar fricatives which modified their codas, producing, to use Knappe's (1997) terminology, either "vocalic results" or "consonantal results". Consequently, the paper does not cover changes in words containing the original sequence <ht>, like e.g. *bought, brought*, etc. For lack of space, also excluded are fully lexical items (lexical words) like *bough, cough, dwarf, laugh, tough, trough* and several other less frequent words as they deserve a separate treatment.

The three words selected for the examination are THROUGH, THOUGH (both yielding a vocalic result, ModE /θruː/, /ðəʊ/) and ENOUGH (consonantal result, ModE /ɪˈnʌf/), all of which are high frequency items. The Old English form of *through* and the Old English conjunction *þēah* (later replaced by its Scandinavian cognate *though*) hold very high positions on the Old English word frequency list (Healey & Venezky 1980). The highest ranking belongs to

THROUGH (OE *þurh*, ranked 46th with 7,548 tokens). As regards the current form *though* it is not a direct continuation of OE *þēah*, the item ranked 90th, with 3,373 tokens. A conjunction and adverb of Scandinavian origin, *though* was registered in the *Ormulum* as *þohh*, soon replacing in the standard speech forms like *þeih* or *þauh*, which later survived in dialects. The third item, ENOUGH (OE *ʒenōh*, with 221 tokens) is ranked among the second thousand of words on the Old English frequency list, a position which may be nevertheless regarded as relatively high, because all other words with a final voiceless velar fricative, except a few preterites like *ʒeseah*, *astāh* and *slōh*, enjoy lower ranking on the frequency list, see Table 1:

Table 1: *through, though, enough*

	Old English form	Number of tokens	Ranked
THROUGH	þurh	7,528	46th
THOUGH	þēah	3,373	90th
ENOUGH	ʒenōh	221	1199th

With reference to Table 1 it should be emphasised that the number of the tokens of THOUGH indicates the frequency of a proto-form of the Middle English forms with [ei] and [au], but considering a similar grammatical and semantic function of the loanword *þoh* this statistics may be helpful in establishing the approximate frequency of THOUGH in later Middle English. As regards ENOUGH it should be remembered that apart from the consonantal result [f] in its coda it also had a variant form *enow*, with a vocalic result. This form, now pronounced [i'nau], was derived from the inflected forms of the adjective and functioned as the plural of the adjective ENOUGH until the 18th century, later surviving in dialects and in Scottish writers (cf. *ODEE* s.v.).

The 35 texts selected from the *Innsbruck Corpus of Middle English Prose* were (a) those in manuscripts with established localisation, (b) containing examples of at least two of the three lemmas above and (c) exhibiting modification in the evolution of the Old English source forms (this constraint allowed me to eliminate those Middle English texts which contained practically unchanged Old English forms of the three words examined).

Considering the question of correspondences between Middle English spellings and sounds occupying the coda position in words, the method chosen involved the following principles [brackets enclose capitalised letters representing the five types]:

(3) (a) <h, ʒ> represent voiceless velar fricative /x/ (early period) [H]

(b) <gh, ʒh, hʒ, ch> stand for voiceless velar fricative /x/ (later period) [GH]

(c) <wh, wʒ> indicate rounded voiceless velar fricative /w/ [WH]

(d) <o(w), (o)u> indicate complete vocalization of the velar fricative [OW]

(e) <f> testifies to the completion of the change [x] > [f] [F]

It is not the aim of the present study to solve the problem whether the employment of the grapheme <f> for the earlier <h, ʒ, gh> etc. symbolises a sound change or a replacement, an issue widely debated in the literature on the subject. Rather the goal of the paper is to offer some statistical data concerning the evolution of spellings first used to render velar fricatives and then representing their transformations in the coda position until the end of Middle English. The relevant data, arranged according to dialects, are presented in chronological order.

As regards the distribution of texts in particular dialects, their vast majority come from the East Midland (25), while other dialects are represented by relatively few sources: three texts from the Southwest, three from the West Midland, three from the North and only one from Kent. But, as was already mentioned, a certain number of early texts from the western areas contain forms not differing from those in Old English. It is not surprising that the highest number of tokens come from the East Midland, a region which preserved numerous works of literature. Finally, I would like to emphasise that many of the texts examined do not belong to the group of widely exploited standard written sources and as such they offer some fresh material.

2. North

The evidence from the Northern prose texts which represent a late period of Middle English (15th century) is scant. In addition, the Northern provenance of the *Mirror of St. Edmund* is uncertain. All three texts which come from MS Thornton, Lincoln Cathedral Library, show the following distribution of spellings, see Table 2. Examples are: *thurgh(e)*, *þof(e)* (*Mirror*), *thurgh(e)*, *thorow(e)* (Gaytryge), *enoghe*, *ynowghe* (*Liber*).

Table 2: Northern prose texts from the 15th century

		THROUGH	THOUGH	ENOUGH
The Mirror of Saint Edmund (c1440)	GH	47		1
	F		2	
Dan Jon Gaytryge's Sermon (c1450)	GH	13		1
	OW	3		
Liber de Diversis Medicinis (1422-54, Yks)	GH	3		6
	OW	45		

The evidence extracted from such a limited number of texts, all coming roughly from the same period, i.e. the middle of the 15th century, does not allow one to formulate far reaching conclusions concerning the situation in the North. Nevertheless, as regards THROUGH it is evident that the vocalisation of the velar fricative in the coda position is almost completed in *Liber de Diversis Medicinis*, which is reflected in the predominating OW spellings. But the same text contains no examples of OW for ENOUGH, which is thus represented by *gh*-forms. Of interest is the presence of two forms of *though* with final <f> in *The Mirror of Saint Edmund*, which, however, retains the conservative GH spelling of THROUGH (47 instances).

Although data for the present study come from prose texts, it is worth emphasising that the most famous poetic composition of the earlier period produced in the North, the *Cursor Mundi* (ca. 1300), contains both GH and OW forms of THROUGH (*thurgh* vs. *thorw, thoru, thoro*), ENOUGH (*inogh* vs. *inow, inou*) and both OW and F forms of THOUGH (*þou* vs. *þof, þowf*).

3. West Midland

As said earlier, the data from texts like *Hali Meiþhad* (AB-language, northern Herefordshire/southern Shropshire from around 1200) are disregarded here, because they exhibit only conservative H forms, with no spelling variation (*þurh* 22, *þah* 35 and *inoh* 4). Another document from a somewhat later period, *The English Text of the Ancrene Riwle* (c1220, BL, Cotton Titus D. XVIII, fol. 14-105), classified as close to the AB-language, contains analogous H forms exclusively (*þurh* 165, *þah* 108 and *inoh* 20). Variation of forms and signs of phonological change in prose texts from that dialect can only be observed in 15th century manuscripts. The most striking variation of spellings is found in *The Brut or the Chronicles of England* (c1400, Oxford, Bodleian Library, MS Rawlinson B 171). The two other texts are *The Gesta Romanorum* (BL MSS Harley 7333 & Add. 90) and *Le Morte d'Arthur* (Caxton's edition), with the following distribution (forms of *through* with and without metathesis are treated together), see Table 3. Examples are: *prouȝ, þurgh, throw, ynow* (*Brut*), *thorow, þoȝ* (*Gesta*), *thorou, though* (*Morte*).

The scribe of *Brut or the Chronicles of England* appears to have been very conservative as he fondly employed the archaic yogh <ȝ> in the forms of THROUGH, testifying to the survival of the fricative in the word-final position, while the modernised spelling with <gh> is found in roughly 20 per cent of the forms of that preposition. As regards the conjunction THOUGH, *Brut* only offers continuations of OE *þēah*, which appear as two different dialectal forms, *þeiȝt* (1 token) and *þauh* (3 tokens). The texts from the later period, *Gesta Romanorum* and *Le Morte d'Arthur* (MSS from around 1440 and later) exhibit the prevalence of the vocalised codas of THROUGH.

To sum up, an increasing number of OW spellings in prose texts from the West Midland confirm an evident tendency in the dialect to eliminate the velar fricative in the coda position from the middle of the 15th century.

Table 3: West Midland prose texts from the 15th century

		THROUGH	THOUGH	ENOUGH
Brut (c 1400)	H	369		1
	GH	75		3
	WH			1
	OW	4		7
Gesta Romanorum (c1440)	H	8	8	
	GH	7		3
	OW	33		4
Le Morte d'Arthur (c1450)	H	3		8
	GH	28	31	17
	OW	49		2

4. East Midland

The Innsbruck Corpus offers a very rich selection of successfully localised prose texts from the East Midland. As their number is much higher than that of texts from other dialects, the East Midland texts are here split into three groups, i.e. those produced in (a) the southern East Midland, including London, (b) the eastern East Midland, including Norfolk, and (c) in the rest of the region.

(a) The first two texts, both from Essex, offer only tokens of THROUGH and ENOUGH, but contain only one form of the loanword THOUGH. These texts, *Vices and Virtues* (BL, MS Stowe 240; 13th century) and *Ancrene Riwle* (Cambridge, Magdalene College, MS Pepys 2498; 14th century), employ the dialectal form *þeih* of THROUGH descending from Old English, with 13 tokens in *Vices* and as many as 102 in *Ancrene Riwle*. As regards the forms surviving into the later periods, they are listed in Table 4. Examples are: *þurh, inohȝ* (Vices), *þorouȝ, ynouȝ* (*Ancrene Riwle*).

Table 4: East Midland prose texts from Essex

		THROUGH	THOUGH	ENOUGH
Vices and Virtues (a1225)	H	13		
	GH	1	1	
	WH			1
Ancrene Riwle (14ct.)	H	182		8
	WH			1
	OW	1		

Although the manuscripts of both texts are separated by the span of more than one hundred years, they show archaic traits with the final velar fricative prevailing, while single occurrences of forms apparently indicating rounding may have no phonological significance. From some precisely unidentified areas of the southern East Midland come three texts produced before the end of the 14th century. One is a scholarly treatise *Macer Floridus de Viribus Herbarum* (ed. G. Frisk), while the remaining two texts are translations from Latin as *The Three Kings of Cologne*: 1. Cambridge University Library MS. Ee 4. 32, f. and 2. BL MS Royal 18 A x. f 87.); see Table 5. Examples are: *þorow, þouȝ* (*Macer Floridus*), *þorwe, þow(e)* (*Kings*, C), *þorow, þow, ynow* (*Kings*, L)

Table 5: Southern East Midland prose texts from the late 14th century

		THROUGH	THOUGH	ENOUGH
Macer Floridus (late 14ct.)	H	3	10	
	GH	8	4	
	OW	5		
Three Kings of Cologne (Camb.)	H	3		
	OW	42	12	
Three Kings of Cologne (Lond.)	H	1		
	WH	2		
	OW	48	5	1

The south East Midland texts with imprecise localisation, especially both versions of *The Three Kings*, show a high degree of the vocalisation of the velar fricative, which is reflected in H spellings being only occasionally employed. Especially characteristic in this respect is the use of the grapheme <w> in MS Royal, which is attached at the end of all the three key words.

Very important are texts from London, where the new written standard began to materialise in the 14-15th centuries. Spelling regularity is seen in works of Chaucer, Gower and Caxton, see Table 6. Examples are: *ynough* (Caxton *RPG*), *þough* (*Birgitta*), *though* (*Dicts*), *though* (*Boece*), *thorw* (*Astrolabe*).

The texts from London offer some surprises. For instance, Chaucer's *Astrolabe* contains prevalent OW forms of THROUGH, while *Boethius* only has the conservative GH spellings. The two texts by Caxton (late 15th century) only contain 'conservative' forms, which should rather be called standard forms since Caxton was one of the writers who contributed to the creation of the standard spelling system. But Caxton's and other writers' choice of GH forms as standardised spellings makes tracing of pronunciation changes difficult.

Archaic H spellings are also found in the *Complaint of Our Lady*, *Speculum Sacerdotale*, while the scribe of *English Mediaeval Lapidaries* had problems with deciding whether to employ traditional or innovative phonetic spelling, as he uses all possible variants. Quite ambiguous is the spelling of THOUGH in the *Revelations of St. Birgitta* with 34 GH standard and 21 phonetic F spellings. This apparently indicates that it is the labial fricative [f] which is concealed under GH for TOUGH.

(b) A very important area which supplied quite a number of written sources, East Anglia, especially Norfolk, was linguistically most influential in the Central and East Midlands. Here lived and worked such important writers as Mandeville and Capgrave as well as the Paston family, renowned for leaving numerous pieces of letter correspondence, see Table 7. Examples are: *thow* (Paston), *þoruȝ* (Ermyte), *thorw* (Mandeville), *þouȝ* (Ermyte, Capgrave), *thorw* (Capgrave).

Unlike their colleagues in London, the writers (or rather scribes) from Norfolk show a preference to use the phonetic spelling OW, which is evident in Mandeville and Capgrave. But the latter still uses yogh to indicate the retention of the velar fricative of THOUGH in *Lives of St. Augustine and St. Gilbert*, while *Mandeville* consistently indicates vocalisation of the velar fricative as he employs OW forms for all the three key words. The *Paston Letters* offer rather confusing evidence, while Ermyte's *Pater Noster* sticks to the traditional graphemes thorn and yogh to render the initial and final consonant in THROUGH.

Table 6: Texts from London from the late 14th & 15th centuries

		THROUGH	THOUGH	ENOUGH
Complaint of Our Lady (c1375)	H	19		8
	GH	1		
A Treatise on the Astrolabe (a1420)	GH	1	1	
	OW	11		
Chaucer's *Boethius* (c1420)	GH	14	12	
The Tale of Melibeus (c1420)	GH	4	14	
	OW			3
Speculum Sacerdotale (early 15ct.)	H	131	36	
	WH	2		
	OW	1		
Dicts and Sayings (c1450)	GH	6	52	1
Revelations of St. Birgitta (a1475)	GH	2	34	
	OW	2		
	F		21	
Caxton's *Right Plesaunt and Goodly* (c1489)				
	GH	62	24	45
	OW			3
Caxton's transl. of *Reynard the Fox* (late 15ct.)	GH	1	54	
	OW			1
English Mediaeval Lapidaries (15ct.)	GH	12	1	2
	WH	5	1	1
	OW	5	2	

Table 7: Prose texts from East Anglia, late 14th &15th centuries

		THROUGH	THOUGH	ENOUGH
Mandeville's *Travels* (1350-1420)	OW	9	11	4
The Paston Letters (1420-1500)	GH	2	6	3
	WH		1	
	OW	1	5	23
Capgrave's *Abbreuiacion of Cronicles* (1420-50)				

	H		1	
	OW	23	3	2
Capgrave's *Lives of St. Augustine and St. Gilbert* (1440)				
	H		57	
	OW	30	1	
Pater Noster of Richard Ermyte (early 15ct.)				
	H	109		
	GH	2		
	HW			1
	OW			1

(c) The last group of texts are those from the East Midland, which lack more precise localisation, see Table 8. Examples are: *þof* (*Deonise*), *þorow* (*Cloud*), *thowff, enow* (*Cely*), *þoru, þouȝ* (*Lollard*).

Table 8: East Midland prose texts from the late 14th & 15th centuries

		THROUGH	THOUGH	ENOUGH
Deonise Hid Diuinite (late 14ct.)	OW	16		1
	F		28	
The Cloud of Unknowing (c1400)	H	1	7	1
	WH			3
	OW	16		
The Lanterne of Liht (a1415)	H	14	29	
	OW	2		
Revelations of Divine Love (1420-1500)	GH	2		1
	WH		13	1
	OW	2		
Cely Letters (1472-78)	GH			1
	WH	6		
	OW	9	5	13
	F		2	
Lollard Sermons (15ct.)	H	24	63	2
	GH		1	
	WH		1	
	OW	109	13	14
Arderne's *Fistula in Ano* (15ct., Rutland)	H	20		7
	OW	1		
	F		10	

Spellings in several texts in this group, especially *Deonise* and *Fistula in Ano*, indicate the completion of the change from a velar to a labiodental fricative in the coda position, the employment of the grapheme <f> in these texts leaving no doubts that the change must have taken place. In addition, *Deonise* reveals fricative vocalisation, hidden under numerous OW spellings for the renderings of THROUGH. At the same time the conservative spelling with yogh still holds in

The Lanterne of Liht and *Fistula in Ano*. Contrasting spellings characterise *Lollard Sermons*, with more than one hundred OW spellings, and no consonantal digraph spellings, but simultaneously retaining yogh, especially in THOUGH. Finally, *Cely Letters*, as could be expected considering the authorship of different family members, show much variation, but the very few instances of the three key words do not allow for any far-reaching generalisations.

5. Southwestern

It is common knowledge that the Southwestern dialect exhibits striking phonological similarities to the southern West Midland, which is not necessarily true as regards the present small corpus of words.

Although the *Innsbruck Corpus* offers adequately localised manuscripts, those from the early 13th century Southwest prevailingly contain Old English H forms and thus fail to offer much variation as regards the three words debated here. Their only interesting feature is the use of the non-standard *a*-forms of THOUGH, i.e. *þauh* (*Ancrene Riwle* BL MS Cotton Nero A XIV) and *þah* (*Hali Meidenhad*, Oxford, Bodleian Library MS Bodley 34), while *Ancrene Wisse* (Cambridge, Corpus Christi College, 402) contains the standard form *though*, a loanword from Scandinavian.

The fifteenth century texts investigated include *The Book of Foundation of St. Bartholomew's Church* (BL MS Cotton Vespasian B ix from Buckinghamshire), some fragments from Wyclif, and Pecock, see Table 9. Examples are: *thorowgh, thow* (*The Book of the Foundation*), *þouȝ, ynowe* (Wyclif), *þoruȝ, þouȝ* (Pecock)

Table 9: Southwestern texts from the 15th century

		THROUGH	THOUGH	ENOUGH
The Book of the Foundation (c 1400)	GH	2	2	
	WH		2	
	OW	4	4	
Wyclif (15ct.)	H	5	131	1
	WH			19
	OW	4		18
Pecock (a 1450)	H	38	125	31

The data from the Southwest reveal the conservative character of the dialect, which continues the tradition of Old English West Saxon. This conservatism is especially evident in Pecock who consistently uses the grapheme yogh instead of the digraph in all the three key words. Equally conservative is the Wyclif scribe in his employment of the forms of THOUGH, which also retains the yogh word-finally. The last text, *The Book of Foundation*, supplies very limited evidence, with much variation in the spelling of the three types, and cannot be treated as a reliable source.

As regards Kentish, the only localised text from that region, *Ayenbite of Inwyt* (1340), contains only archaic forms with H in the coda (e.g. *þorʒ, ynoh*) and the dialectal *a*-variant *þah* of OE *þēah*.

6. Conclusions

On the basis of the above, the following tentative conclusions can be formulated with reference to the process of the elimination of the velar fricative in the coda position in Middle English.

1. The employment by the scribes of the single symbols <h> and <ʒ> in word-final position continued long after Old English, the grapheme yogh still being retained in the 15th century. These facts confirm that the velar fricative was not completely eliminated before Early Modern English. At the same time a competition between H or GH types and the new OW type indicate that now the one, now the other pronunciation was reflected in spelling variation even in the same text.

2. As regards the dialectal distribution of the change, the GH : OW alternation is found in Northern texts from the middle of the 15th century, except in *The Mirror of Saint Edmund*, which exhibits consistent GH spellings. The West Midland (*Brut*) preserves the conservative H spellings and also GH spellings, both indicating the retention of the velar fricative. But a vocalisation tendency is seen in other texts from the area (*Gesta Romanorum, Le Morte d'Arthur*). The Southwestern scribes seem to continue the tradition of their pre-Conquest colleagues, using conservative spellings quite consistently (especially Pecock).

3. In the texts from the Southern East Midland, scribes from Essex use conservative H spellings, but other southern texts from the region reveal a multitude of OW forms indicating the completion of vocalisation (*The Three Kings of Cologne*, 2 versions). The London writers still employ archaic H and modified GH graphemes around 1400 (Chaucer). The retention of GH in Caxton, who almost completely ignores OW spellings (except for ENOUGH), shows that the famous printer used the old spellings as a sign of standardisation of written English. At the same time East Anglian writers, particularly those from Norfolk (Mandeville, Capgrave, but not Richard Ermyte), show preference for the 'phonetic' spelling OW.

Sources

Healey, Antonette DiPaolo – Venezky, Richard L.
    1980   *A microfiche concordance to Old English: publications of the dictionary of Old English.* Toronto: Centre for Medieval Studies.

Markus, Manfred (ed.)
    1999   *Innsbruck computer archive of machine-readable English texts.* (CD-ROM version). University of Innsbruck.

LALME	*A linguistic atlas of Late Mediaeval English*, ed. Angus McIntosh, M. K. Samuels & M. Benskin. Aberdeen: Aberdeen University Press. 1986.

Dictionaries

ODEE	*The Oxford Dictionary of English Etymology*, ed. Charles T. Onions with the assistance of G. W. S. Friedrichsen and Robert W. Burchfield. Oxford: Oxford University Press, 1966 [many reprints].

References

Bonebrake, Veronica
1979 — *Historical labial-velar changes in Germanic: A study of the counter-directional sound changes in English and Netherlandic.* Umeå: Acta Universitatis Umensis.

Brunner, Karl
1960 — *Die englische Sprache: Ihre geschichtliche Entwicklung.* Vol.1. 2nd. ed. Tübingen: Niemeyer.

Dietz, Klaus
2006 — *Schreibung und Lautung im mittelalterlichen Englisch: Entwicklung und Funktion der englischen Schreibungen ch, gh, sh, th, wh und ihrer kontinentalen Entsprechungen.* Heidelberg: Winter.

Ekselius, Paul
1940 — *A Study on the development of the Old English combinations aht/oht in Middle English.* Uppsala: Appelberg.

Jordan, Richard
1974 — *Handbook of Middle English grammar: Phonology.* Translated and revised by Eugene J. Crook. The Hague: Mouton [original German edition: 1925].

Knappe, Gabriele
1997 — "*Though* it is *Tough*: On regional differences in the development and substitution of the Middle English voiceless velar fricative [x] in syllable coda position", in: *Language in time and space: studies in honour of Wolfgang Viereck on the occasion of his 60th birthday,* ed. Heinrich Ramisch & Kenneth Wynne. Stuttgart: Steiner, 139-163.

Lauttamus, Timo
1981 — "A note on the development of Old English [x] to Middle English [f]", *Neuphilologische Mitteilungen* 82: 1-4.

Luick, Karl
1940 — *Historische Grammatik der englischen Sprache.* Vol. 2. Stuttgart: Tauchnitz.

Lutz, Angelika
1991 — *Phonotaktisch gesteuerte Konsonantenveränderungen in der Geschichte des Englischen.* Tübingen: Niemeyer.

Nieuwint, P. J.
1981 "What happened to Middle English /(u)(x)/?", *Neophilologus* 65: 440-467.

Part II. Words and phrases

The chain-mail coat terminology in Old English and the dating of *Beowulf*

Carla Morini (Perugia, Italy)

Abstract

While much attention has been focused on the sword from an historical, archaeological and linguistic point of view, it has been very different for body armour, the other weapon favoured by the Anglo-Saxon warrior. This essay tries to fill this gap and to give an historical and linguistic appraisal of the use of the corselet in Anglo-Saxon England, comprising a look at its reproduction in manuscripts, by collecting, analyzing and comparing all the Old English terms for 'corselet' as they occur in their context. The aim of this research is to define which was the type of 'corselet' used in Anglo-Saxon England, and also at which time it was in use. On the basis of the evidence, the corselet depicted on the Anglo-Saxon manuscript drawings, and mentioned in Old English texts, proves to be *a chain-mail coat*, with the same technical features as those discovered in Scandinavia. From the analysis of the Old English documents and their comparison with Old Norse texts and Old Norse archaeological finds, it may be concluded that the chain-mail coat described in the Anglo-Saxon sources could only have been body armour of Scandinavian origin, which could be known in Anglo-Saxon England only after the Viking invasion. Such a conclusion would confirm a late dating of *Beowulf*.

1. OE terms for 'corselet' and their occurrences in Old English poetry[1]

The oldest literary reference to body armour in Old English texts is Aldhelm's Latin *Lorica* (*Aenigmata* 33), the Anglo-Saxon translation of which (*Riddle* 35; ed. ASPR 6, 209) is preserved in an eighth-century version written in the Northumbrian dialect and preserved in a tenth-century version in Late West Saxon.[2] The body armour, subject of the riddle, speaks, using the prosopopeia, in its own person describing itself, as an object 'made of iron' and as being protection for heroes. The very nature of this composition itself, just a riddle, gave no indication of its subject's name, and this did not help to define the features of the armour.

But in the Old English texts,[3] both in prose and in poetry, simple nouns usually occur for the concept of 'body armour'[4] as well as various compounds and circumlocutions.[5]

---

[1] For historical and archaeological references and documents on this armour, see Morini 2006: 155-162.
[2] Quotations from *Beowulf* are from Klaeber 2008; all other quotations from OE poetry are from the ASPR.
[3] In this paper, I follow the system of short titles for OE texts proposed by Mitchell et al. 1975; 1979; Healey 1980.
[4] There is no mention of the corselet in Cramp 1957; it is just mentioned in Webster 1998: 190 and in Hooper 1989: 191-202. More detailed is Brooks 1978: 94-96; Brooks 1991. See now Morini 2006: 160-164. From the linguistic point of view but related only to *Beowulf*, see Brady

1.1 *byrne* 'corselet, coat of mail'

The Old English term for 'body armour', *byrne* 'corselet, coat of mail', is probably a Germanic loan-word from Celtic,[6] or from Latin:[7] Gothic *brunjo*, OHG *brunne*, MHG *brünne*, Gmc *brunne*, *brunnia*, ME *brunie*, *brynie*, ON *brynja* < Gmc **brunja* < IE **bhreu-s*; see also OIr *bruínne* 'breast'. OE *byrne* 'coat of mail' occurs frequently in heroic, religious and judicial contexts.[8] In many instances, it indicates a piece of real defensive armour, while more rarely, as well as for example in *Salomon and Saturn* 444, it defines symbolic armour, the *lorica fidei*.[9]

In *Judith* the anonymous poet, unlike his source, presents the biblical story as a heroic conflict between opposing armies,[10] Assyrian and Jews, both equipped with corselets. Judith, in her speech to the Jews, lists the *byrne* among the Jewish weapons and armour. To define it, the poet uses *byrnhomas* 'corselet garment' as synonym of *byrne*:[11]

> syððan frymða God,
> arfæst Cyning, éastan sende
> léohtne léoman berað linde forð,
> bord for breostum and byrnhomas
> scíre helmas in sceaðena gemong. (*Judith* 189b-193, ed. ASPR 4)
>
> [When the God of beginnings, the merciful King, has sent
> the shining light from the east, go forth bearing shields,
> the bucklers before your breasts and the mail-coats
> and shining helmets into the foe's midst.]

Then the corselet (OE *byrne*) is also quoted among the booty captured from the Assyrians by the Jews:

> Ða seo cneoris eall,
> mægða mærost, anes monðes fyrst,

1979: 110-21; of no importance, very different from what it seems from his title, Mc Guinness 1989.
[5] See only for *Beowulf* Brady 1979: 110-21.
[6] Holthausen 1934; Kluge 1995.
[7] De Vries 1960: 72. For a contrasting opinion see Grimm 1882-1836: iii, § 443 who remarks that the armour and the word are of Germanic origin, relating the term to Gmc **brinnan* 'to shine'; cf. also Shetelig & Falk 1937: 403.
[8] See diPaolo Healey-Venezky 1980, *s. v.*; Crandell Amos et al. 1991; Roberts et al. 2000, 13.02.08.03.01.04, 606, "coat of mail/ corselet".
[9] Since the occurrences of *byrne* in the allegorical sense of Christian armour are not useful to this investigation, they shall not be examined in this study.
[10] Godden 1991: 220.
[11] Unless otherwise indicated, the translations are usually mine.

> wlanc wundenlocc wægon and læddon,
> to ðære beorhtan byrig Bethuliam,
> helmas and hupseax, hare byrnan,
> guðsceorp gumena golde gefrætewod,
> mærra madma þonne mon ænig
> asecgan mæge searoþoncelra. (*Judith* 324b-331, ASPR 4)
>
> [Then, all the nation,
> most famous of races, proud, curled-locked, bore and conveyed
> for the duration of one month to the beautiful city of Bethulia,
> helmets and hip-swords, grey corselets,
> and men's battle dress decked with gold, treasure more glorious
> than any man among ingenious men can tell.]

It is remarkable that the corresponding biblical text (*Jud*, ch. 15, 4-8) does not mention any corselet or weapon. The Anglo-Saxon poet neither makes any reference to corselets when he describes the battle nor does he give any indication about the type of body armour worn by the Assyrians.

In *The Fight at Finnsburg* the term *byrne* is mentioned only once without specifying which kind of armour it is:

> Ða gewat him wund hæleð on wæg gangan,
> sæde þæt his byrne abrocen wære,
> heresceorp unhror, and eac wæs his helm ðyr[e]l.
> (*Finnsb.* 43-45, ed. Klaeber 2008)
>
> [Then a hero came walking away wounded;
> a man of action in his military trappings,
> he said that his corselet was hacked to pieces and his helmet was holed too.]

From the evidence of these contexts, where there is no reference to the type of corselet, it appears clear that *byrne* is a noun meaning 'corselet' in a general sense with no characterizing connotations.

Despite this, while in *Elene* the corselet is generally mentioned as *byrne* or *hildeserce* 'shirt of war' (l. 234), the adjective *brogden* (l. 257) in the same poem leads one to deduce that the armour was 'woven', a 'coat of mail':

> Ðær wæs on eorle eðgesyne
> brogden byrne ond bill gecost,
> geatolic guðscrud, grimhelm manig,
> ænlic eoforcumbul (*Elene* 256-59, ed. ASPR 2)

[There the woven armour was conspicuous on the earl and the excellent sword,
the wonderful battle-dress, many masked helmets,
adorned with the magnificent image of the boar.]

In this poem, in contrast to its source, *Acta Apocrypha S. Quiriaci*,[12] which does not mention any weapon or armour, the *byrne*, worn by Roman warriors at the moment of their departure to the Holy Land, is to be considered as an innovation introduced by Cynewulf.

Now, analyzing *Beowulf*, it is evident that the term *byrne*, always defined in the whole poem as a 'coat of mail', occurs 20 times as a simple noun and three times as base of compounds.[13] While there is frequent use of compounds with *gar, æsc, daroð, lind, bord, rand* and *scyld*, those with *sweord, helm* and *byrne*,[14] (which always characterized the *byrne* as a chain-mail coat), are rarer.[15]

It is well known that the vocabulary used to describe body armour in Anglo-Saxon poetry was very varied with synonyms and circumlocutions, also further expanded by the introduction of compounds. In this application, *byrne*, considered as a basic term indicating the concept of 'corselet', is preceded by a noun, usually taken from the semantic field relating to war: *guðbyrne* (*Beo* 321); *heaðubyrne* (*Beo* 1552[16]); *herebyrne* (*Beo* 1443).[17] It is also used as the first term in compounds formed with *wigan* 'to fight' and *wiga* 'fighter' as the first term of the compound[18], which are to be considered as kennings for 'warrior, lord': *byrnwigend* (*Jud* 17); *byrnwigende* (*El* 235; *Jud* 39 and 224); *byrnwiga* 'corseletted warrior' (*Beo* 2918; *Wand* 94).

1.2 OE *serce, syrce* and *syric* 'shirt'[19]

OE *serc, syrce* and *syric* literally means 'shirt'.[20] It was, however, very rarely used in a war context in the sense of 'corselet'. It only occurs three times as a simple word in *Beowulf*: *syrcan hrysedon* 'shirts shook' (*Beo* 226), *græge syrcan* 'gray shirt' (*Beo* 334) and *sawtfah syrce* 'a blood stained shirt' (*Beo* 1111), also a kenning for 'chain-mail'. This noun also occurs six times as a base of compounds: *licsyrce* (*Beo* 550), *heresyrce* (*Beo* 1511), *hioroserce* (*Beo* 2539), *beaduserce* (*Beo*

---

[12] "...tunc congregans et ipsa moltitudinem exercitus profectus est.", *Acta Apocrypha S. Quiriaci*, i, 3, *AA. SS.*, col. 450.
[13] Cf. Brady 1979: 110-128.
[14] See Lansfield Keller 1905: 268-69 and Brady 1979: 110-21.
[15] Marquardt 1938: 240.
[16] It occurs also in *The Gifts*, l. 61.
[17] See Brady 1979: 110-14.
[18] In these compounds it is not clear if the base is a substantive or a participle. *BT* uses *wigend* both as substantive and participle, Clark Hall only as a participle.
[19] diPaolo Healey & Venezky 1980, *s.v.*; Roberts & Kay 2000: 606.
[20] OE *serce* is an interpretamentum of Latin words for cloak as well as *colobium, tunicam, armilausia, suppar, interula*, see Stroebe 1904: 59-61; Lansfield Keller 1967: 268-69.

2755), *leoðosyrce* (*Beo* 1505 and 1890), *hildeserce* (*El* 234), and *leoðusyrce*, *leoðuserce* (*Beo* 1505 and 1890).[21] All these compounds have been considered as 'kennings' for *byrne*.[22] Because this Germanic word occurs very often in Old Norse sources (ON *serkr*) in a war context, it has been suggested[23] that *serce* in the meaning 'corselet' could probably be a loan word or a calque (loan meaning) from Old Norse.

Besides OE *serce*, other clothing nouns, which have been considered as 'kennings' for *byrne*[24] and for 'warrior', are used in Old English texts as base terms of compounds in a war context:

- OE *pad* 'coat', 'covering':[25] *herepad* 'war dress', thus 'coat of mail' (*Beo* 2258);[26]
- OE *hrægl* 'dress'[27]: *beaduhrægl* 'war garment', thus 'coat of mail' (*Beo* 552) and *fyrdhrægl* 'war garment, thus 'coat of mail' (*Beo* 1527);
- OE *hom, homa* 'covering': *byrnhom* (*Jud.* 192); *fyrdhom* (*Beo* 1504)'war dress', thus 'coat of mail',[28]
- OE *wæd* 'dress':[29] *herewæd* (*Beo* 1897), *heoðowæd* (*Beo* 39) 'wardress', thus 'coat of mail'; *herewæda* 'warrior' (*Jud* 126);
- OE *scrud*[30] 'clothing, dress', which assumes the meaning of body armour: *beaduscrud* 'battle dress' (*Beo* 453), *guðscrud* 'war dress' (*El* 258).

It is interesting to note that some compounds with an Old English term related to the material of the *byrne* (OE *nett* 'net', OE *iron*, OE *isern* 'iron' and OE *hring* 'ring') as a base, such as *breostnet* (*Beo* 1548), *herenet* (*Beo* 1553), *hringiren* (*Beo* 1889 and 2754), *searonet* (*Beo* 406), even specify, unequivocally, that the body armour concerned is a coat of ring mail. They are to be considered neither as 'kennings' nor as descriptions, but only as variations, or 'kend heiti',[31] because its

---

[21] As the basic text for my investigation, and the one from which quotations are taken, I used Klaeber 2008. See Brady's classification of the simplex word and of his compounds, Brady 1979: 110-128.
[22] Marquardt 1938: 230. See also Watanabe 1972: 1-18; Molinari 1983: 29-52.
[23] See Sarrazin 1886: 173; for a contrasting opinion see Sievers 1886: 355-6; Sievers 1887: 171-2. On the much-debated etymology of this word, see more recently Breeze 1993: 91-3, who suggests that ON *serkr* is a loan word from Old English, which derives from OIr *seirch*; Anderson 1990 affirms that the OE word comes from Gothic.
*serik- < L *serica*.
[24] Marquardt 1938: 111 and 116; see also Stroebe 1904: 60.
[25] Stroebe 1904: 47-48.
[26] On OE *pad*, see Stroebe 1904: 47-49.
[27] Stroebe 1904: 75.
[28] See Lansfield Keller 1905: 268-69; Marquardt 1938: 220.
[29] Stroebe 1904: 82.
[30] This last compound has not been cited among the list of dress compounds by Marquardt 1938: 320. See also Stroebe 1904: 81.
[31] See Molinari 1983: 35 who refers to Arthur Gilchrist S. Brodeur, *The Art of Beowulf* (Berkeley: University of California Press, 1959) 247.

meaning is always *byrne*.[32] In spite of them, OE *wælnet* 'deathnet' (*Ex* 202) could be considered a kenning for 'corselet', because there is no term for the corselet in either element of this compound nor any clear allusion to the corselet in it:

> Forþon wæs in wicum. wop up ahafen,
> atol æfenleoð, egesan stodon,
> weredon wælnet, þa se woma cwom.   (*Ex* 200-203, ed. ASPR 1)
> [Because of this it happened that in the encampment was raised the sound of weeping,
> a hideous evensong; fears loomed,
> the deadly meshes (mail coats) trapped them, as the tumult advanced.]

1.3. *hlence* 'links, chain-mail links'

OE *hlence* 'link, chain-mail links, chain-mail coat' is thus considered to be a 'bahuvrihi'. It is a hapax legomenon in Old English (*Ex* 218)[33] and it does not exist in any other Germanic languages apart from Old Norse, *hlekkr*, 'ring', bracelet'.[34] Moreover, there is an Old English compound *wælhlence* 'a battle shirt twisted from iron rings' (*Ex* 176),[35] a new and unique formation (< *hlencan* 'to twist (the rings)'), which is to be considered a 'kenning' for 'chain-mail':

> Him þær segncyning   wið þone segn foran,
> manna þengel,   mearcþreate rad,
> guðweard gumena,   grimhelm gespeon
> cyning cinberge,   cumbol lixton,
> wiges on wenum,   wælhlencan sceoc
> het his hereciste   healdan georne
> fæst fyrdgetrum.   (*Ex* 172-178, ed. ASPR 1)
> [There, hard by the royal standard rode the bannered king,
> prince of men, ahead with his contingent;
> the warriors' warlord fastened his visored helmet,
> the king his cheek-guard, to make ready for the battle, the standards shone forth.
> He shook his chain-mail and bade his troops of chosen men zealously hold firm their
> battle array.]

---

[32] Marquardt 1938: 220-21.
[33] See *BT*; Hall 1960: 185.
[34] Cf. Jónsson 1931: 261; Cleasby & Vigfusson 1957: 270.
[35] This compound is not mentioned by Roberts & Kay 2000: 607.

>   wæccende bad,
> eall seo sibgedriht, somod ætgædere
> maran mægenes, oð Moyses bebead,
> eorlas on uhttid ærnum bemum
> folc somnigean, frecan arisan,
> habban heora hlencan, hycgan on ellen,
> beran beorht searo, beacnum cigean,
> sweot sande near.   (*Ex* 211-220, ed. ASPR 1)
>
> [Watchful, the whole company of kinsfolk assembled together and waited the onset of the superior military force, until at daybreak Moses commanded the leaders to summon the folk at to sound of brazen trumpets, the warriors to get up, to put on their chain-mail coats, to set their minds on courageous conduct, to take up their bright armour and by signal band together the army close to the shore.]

Wælhlenca occurs also in *Elene* during the description of the battle scene:

>   Wæron hwate weras,
> gearwe to guðe garas lixtan,
> wriðene wælhlencan wordum ond bordum
> hofon herecombol.   (*El* 22-25, ed. ASPR 1)
>
> [The proud warriors were ready to fight:
> the spears and the twisted coats of mail shone.
> (Acclaiming) by cries and by shield, they raised up the banner].

1.4. *hring* 'ring, circle'

OE *hring*[36] occurs widely with the meaning of 'ring', 'circle' or 'diadem' in all the Germanic languages.[37] It is, however, found rarely in Old English as a simple noun in the sense of 'sword' (*hringmæl* 'sword adorned with rings') and of 'coat of ring mail', synecdoche for an object 'made of rings' or with 'rings'. But these lost particular meanings of *hring* find a large Old Norse correspondence in the poetic language of the skalds.

---

[36] Cf. diPaolo Healey & Venezky 1980: *s.v.*; Roberts-Kay, 2000: 607.
[37] Cf. *BT*, s.v. *hring*.
For different meanings of the compound *wopes hring* 'eye's circle', 'raindrop' (*El* 1131, *Christ* 537, *Andr* 1277, *Gu* 1338, *Riddles* 48 and 59), see Brooks 1948-49; Gradon 1977, 67. For a contrasting opinion ('eye's sound') see Grein 1912 and Okasha 1993: 64.

As 'ring mail coat', *hring* is used twice as a noun by the poet of *Beowulf* (1503, 2206) and often as a first member of compounds: *hringiren* 'iron rings (of the coat)' (322b) and *hringnet* 'coat of mail' (1889b, 2754b). Four metaphorical compounds for *byrne* are 'bahuvrihi', because the adjective is indispensable to the identification of the base term containing a dress word: *goldhama* (*El* 991) and *grǣghama* (*Fin* 7), *grǣge syrcan* (*Beo* 334), *irenbyrne* (*Beo* 2986), *isernbyrne* 'iron coat' (*Beo* 671).

While there are few doubts about the meanings of the first and the second component of the compound *hringa fengel* (*Beo* 2345) or 'lord of the coats',[38] the second compound is more problematical: *hringa þengel* (*Beo* 1507), a unique appellation for Beowulf, where the base has been interpreted as 'prince' ('the ring mailed prince'[39]) or as a past participle of *þeon* 'thrive', 'to be successful in arms'. Thus the entire compound could mean 'the one that went on in staying alive by means of the rings'.[40] Lastly, the epithet *Hringdena*,[41] used three times by the poet of *Beowulf*, has been interpreted as a proper name:[42] it has also been claimed that the epithet was introduced for reasons of alliterative device (/h/), either because of the context,[43] or for aesthetic purposes.[44] It is remarkable that this compound might indicate that the Dane warriors possessed ring-corselets.

The OE verb **hringan* 'to ring' derives from the same root of OE *hring*, and describes the sound produced by the rings of the coat when the warrior moved (*Beo* 2615, 327 and *Sol* 258).

It is also necessary to shed light on some adjectives referring to *byrne* or *serce*, which characterized it as a chain-mail coat: *hringed*, which explains that *byrne* is 'made of rings' (*Beo*, 1245, and 2615)[45]; *locen*, derived from *lucan* 'to link'; *brogden*, derived from *beowian* 'to knit, to weave'; *seowed*, derived from *seow(i)an* 'to sew', but in this context 'to link, to put together'.

---

[38] See Marquardt 1938: 241. For *Hring* with the meaning of 'ornament', see Klaeber 2008, Glossary, *s.v. hring*.

[39] Heaney translates in this way. See Marquardt 1938: 241; *Ead, Anglia* 68 (1936): 393-94; Heyne-Schücking 1949: 198; 59.

[40] Brady 1979: 239.

[41] Gewat ða neosian, syþðan niht becom, / hean huses, hu hit Hring-Dene æfter beorþege / gebun hæfdon (*Beo* 115-16); Com þa to Heorote, ðær Hring-Dene / geond þæt sæld swæfun (*Beo* 1279-80a); Swa ic Hring-Dena hund missera / weold under wolcnum ond hig wigge beleac / manigum mægþa geond þysne middangeard, / æscum ond ecgum þæt ic me geond þæt ænigne, / under swegles begong gesacan ne tealde (*Beo* 1769-73). See *BT (Supplement), s. v. Hring-Dene,* 'The Danes; The mailcoated (?) Danes'.

[42] Cf. Klaeber 2008: s.v. *Dene*.

[43] "...in most instances the epithets forming folk-name compounds were most happily chosen by the poet with especial reference to the specific situation in which they are used.", Bryan 1929: 122-23.

[44] See Storm 1957: 8-12.

[45] Klaeber 2008, Glossary, *s. v.*; Okasha 1993: 64.

2. The corselet in the Old English laws and in the wills

Body armour (OE *byrne*), which was so costly and valuable that only the highest-ranking aristocrats could afford it,[46] is mentioned, for the first time, in *King Ine's Laws*, as comprising *wergild*. Therefore, it was valuable enough to be considered a form of compensation for injury:

> Gif hine man gylt, ðonne mot he gesyllan an þæra hyndenna gehwylcere monna byrnan an sweord on þæt wergild, gif he ðurfe [47] (*Ine*)
>
> [And if wergild is paid, than he may give in each of the hundreds (of the wergild) a slave, and a coat-of-mail, and a sword, if he need.] (cf. Whitelock 1955: 370)

While no mention of the corselet could be found in the judicial dispositions on *wergild* promulgated by King Alfred, it is listed among the military equipment of the *eorlas* and *ðegnas*, according to the new dispositions on *heregeatu* ('heriot', that is, the return on death of war equipment and other valuable objects they had received from their lord on entering his following) promulgated by king Æthelred and later by king Cnut.[48] In the legal text known as *Northleoda Laga*, probably written by archbishop Wulfstan and laid down by Æthelred, two new elements, the byrne, together with the helmet, were included in the equipment of the warrior:

> 10. And þeah he [ceorlicsc man] geþeo, þæt hæbbe helm and byrnan and golde fæted sweord, gif he þæt land nafað, he bið ceorl swa þeah[49]
>
> [10. And even if he prospers so that he possesses a helmet and a coat of mail and a gold-plated sword, if he has not the land, he is a *ceorl* all the same.] (cf. Whitelock 1955: 433)

The *Anglo-Saxon Chronicle* D preserved under the year 1008 an entry relating to the warriors' equipment. King Æthelred ordered the building of ships from men who owned three hundred hides and also ordered men who owned eight hides to find a *helm* and a *byrne*, a new element:

> Mille.viii. Her bebead se cyng þæt man sceolde ofer eall Angelcyn scypu fæstlice wyrcan, þæt is þonne of þrym hund hydum, and .x. be tynum, anne scægð, and of .viii. hydum, helm and byrnan [50]
>
> [1008. In this year the king gave orders that ships should be speedily built throughout the whole of England: namely [one large warship was to be provided from every] three hundred 'hides' and a cutter from every ten 'hides', while every eight 'hides' were to provide a helmet and a corselet.] (Garmonsway 1967: 138)

---

[46] Ashdown 1925: 11-12; Brooks 1978: 90-2.
[47] Text quoted from Liebermann 1903: 114.
[48] See Brooks 1987: 90-91.
[49] Text quoted from Liebermann 1903: 458.
[50] Text quoted from *MS D*, ed. Cubbin 1966: 54.

King Cnut's Laws also confirmed that the heriot of the nobility had to be paid in weapons and armour:

> [70] Be hergeate: eorles. [71a] Eorles swa ðærto gebyrige, þæt syndon viii hors, iiii gesadelode and iiii unsadelode, and iiii helmas and iiii byrnas and viii spera and eallswa fela scylda and iiii swurd and twa hund mances goldes. [71.1] and syððan cingces þegnas, þe him nyhste syndan: iiii hors, ii gesadelode and ii unsadelode, and ii swurd and iiii spera and swa feala scylda and helm and byrnan and I mances goldes.   (ii, 70-71)[51]

> [And heriots are to be so determined as befits the rank:

> 71a. an earl's as belongs thereto, namely eight horses, four saddled and four unsaddled, and four helmets and four coats of mail and eight spears and as many shields and four swords and 200 mancuses of gold;

> 71.1. and next, the king's thegns, who are closest to him: four horses, two saddled and two unsaddled, and two swords and four spears and as many shields, and a helmet and coat of mail and 50 mancuses of gold;] (Whitelock 1955: 429)

A *byrne* 'mail coat' could be acquired through booty, through payment to the owner's lord, or as a gift from him, or as inheritance.[52] In some *wills*,[53] drawn up between the end of the tenth century and the first part of the eleventh, body armour is more frequently mentioned as a bequest to the testator's lord:

> ...he becwað his laford his beste scip and þa segelgeræda ðarto and lx. healma and lx. Beornena (*The Will of Archbishop Ælfric*, ca. 1003-1004, ed. and trans. Whitelock 1930: 52-53)

> [...he bequeathed to his lord his best ship and the sailing tackle with it, and sixty helmets and sixty coats of mail]

> ... and þære byrnan þe mid Morkære is. (*The Will of the ætheling Æthelstan*, ca. 1014-1015, ed. Whitelock 1930: 58-59)

> [and the coat of mail which Morcar has.]

> '... and mine brother bern here owen lond. and .ii. hors mid sadelgarun and .i. brinie and on hakele'. *(The Will of Wulfsige,* ca. 984-1016, ed. Whitelock 1930: 74-75)

> [...and my brother's children their own land, and two horses with harness, and one coat of mail and one cloak.]

or as part of the heriot:

---

[51] Text quoted from Liebermann 1903: 356-358.
[52] The heriot (*wargear*), usually paid in arms, was to be returned to the owner's lord as payment for the equipment received on entering his service.
[53] Whitelock 1930: x, xviii, xx, xxvii, xxxi, xxxiv. See also Napier & Stevenson 1895, no. 10; Sawyer 1968, no. 1492. Brooke's List 1978: 88 mentions the will of Æthelmær, of Wulsige, of Thurstan, and of Ketel only.

And ic becweðe minum cynehlaforde to heregeatuwum iii beagus on ðrym hund mancesum goldes and iiii sweord and viii hors feower geræedode and iiii ungerædode and iiii helmas and iiii byrnan and viii speru and viii scyldas. (*The Will of the ealdorman Æthelmær* † 983, ed. Whitelock 1930: 26-27)

[And I bequeathe to my lord as my heriot four armlets of three hundred mancuses of gold, and four sword and eight horses, four with trappings and four without, and four helmets and four coats of mail and eight spears and eight shields.]

And ic an kynelouerd .ii. hors and Helm and brinie and an Swerd and a goldwrecken spere. (*The Will of Wulfsige,* ca. 984-1016, ed. Whitelock 1930: 74-75)

[And I grant to my royal lord two horses and a helmet and a coat of mail, and a sword and a spear inlaid with gold.]

And ic an mine kinelouerd for mine Hergete to marc goldes and to hors. and sadelfate and Helm and brinie and Suerd and to scheldes and to speren. (*The Will of Thurstan,* ca. 1045, ed. Whitelock 1930: 80-81)

[And I grant to my royal lord as heriot two marks of gold and two horses with trappings, and a helmet and a coat of mail and a sword and two shields and two spears.]

...and gif ic ongein ne cume, þan an ic him [Herlinge Stigand Archebisscop] to min heregete an helm and a brenie. and hors. and gereade. and sverd and spere. (*The Will of Ketel,* ca.1052-66, cf. Brooks 1978: 87-90)

[...and if I do not come back again, I grant to him as my heriot a helmet and a coat of mail and a horse with harness and a sword and a spear.]

This obligatory practice, coded at the time of king Æthelered and of king Cnut, has been well described by the poet of *Beowulf*. Before facing Grendel in combat, the hero requests that, in the case of his death, his coat of ring mail should be sent to his lord, King Hygelac:

Onsend Higelace, gif mec hild nime,

beaduscruda betst, þæt mine breost wereð,

hrægla selest; þæt is Hrædlan laf,

Welandes geweorc.   (*Beo* 452-55a)

[If the battle takes me, send back this breast-webbing

that Weland fashioned and Hrethel gave me, to Lord Hygelac.][54]

Before fighting Grendel's mother, Beowulf also decides to send the king the treasure he has received from Hrothgar:

---

[54] Translation by Heaney 1999.

swylce þu ða madmas, þe þu me sealdest,

Hroðgar leofa, Higelace onsend.   (*Beo* 1482-83)

[And be sure also, my beloved Hrothgar, to send Hygelac the treasures I received.][55]

3. The chain-mail coat in Old English glosses and glossaries

In the Old English Glosses[56] OE *byrne* is the common term generally found to translate each type of Latin *lorica* 'body armour' with the exception of the *lorica hamata* 'hauberk of mail':

> lorica: *byrne* (*DurRitGl*)[57]
> torace: *byrne* (*DurRitGl*)[58]
> lorica: *byrne* (*ÆGl*)[59]
> lorica vel torax vel squama: *byrne* (*AntGl*).[60]

Despite this, for Latin *lorica hamata* the compilers of the glossaries used OE *hring/ hringan/ hringed* only:

> hamis, circulis lorice, *hringum* (*Prud.Gl*)
> lorica anata: *hringedu byrne* (*ClGl*1).[61]

The compiler of the glosses to Prudentius's *Psychomachia* (MS London, British Library, Cotton Cleopatra viii, f. 32r, Christ Church, Canterbury, X-XI centuries)[62] was the first to use properly the term *hring* for the Latin gloss *circulis lorice* to *hamis*, which appeared in the Latin text (l. 675):

> dum stipata pedem iam tutis moenibus infert,
> excipit occultum Vitii latitantis ab ictu
> mucronem laeuo in latere, squalentia quamuis
> texta catenato ferri subtegmine corpus
> ambirent sutis et acumen uulneris **hamis**

---

[55] Translation by Heaney 1999.
[56] For an overview of the recent research see Derolez 1992 and Lendinara 1999.
[57] "Fratres nos qui diei sumus sobrii simus induti *lorica salutis* et galea salutis broð ve ða ðe dæges ve aron gigearwad byrne sie gileafes and broðerlufu", Lindelöf 1927: 15.26.
[58] "Induent sancti pro torace iustitiam ..: gigeruað halga ua/fore/byrne soðfæstinnisse", Lindelöf 1927: 121.3.
[59] Zupitza 1880: 317.
[60] Kindschi 1955: 394; also published by Wright & Wülker 1884: 142, 5.
[61] The gloss is found on f. 44 of the manuscript, cf. Stryker 1951: 273; also published by Wright & Wülker 1968: 434.
[62] Gneuss 1981: 324.

respuerent, rigidis nec fila tenacia nodis
inpactum sinerent penetrare in uiscera telum. [63]

[just as she [Concord] is setting foot within the safety of the ramparts, receives a treacherous thrust in her left side from the stroke of a lurking Vice, albeit the stiff fabric of iron chain-mail covered her body and with its links repelled the deadly point, and the firm, hard-knotted strands did not suffer the weight of the blow to reach the flesh.]
(Translation by Thomson 1962: 327)

In the first Cleopatra Glossary (MS London, British Library, Cotton Cleopatra iii, tenth century)[64] the entry *lorica anata* is referred to 1 *Kings* 17.5 *Et cassis aerea super caput ejus, et lorica hamata induebatur*. The occurrence of the 'varia lectio' *hamata/anata* 'hooked' against *squamata* 'scaled' of the *Vulgate* seems to have been introduced in Anglo-Saxon manuscripts on the basis of Bede's Commentary: *si lorica hamata quae sit inquiris, lege in Virgilio: loricam consertam hamis, auraque trilicem.*[65]

All these entries give a particular interpretation with respect to the ordinary one (*byrne*), on the basis of the Latin sources and on the Latin gloss to them, which give a much more specific meaning. It is well known that the compiler of the glossary was free to deviate from the sources available at his monastery, by adding or eliminating terms, updating its vocabulary. Therefore the compilers of the glossaries quoted above might have introduced the new meaning of *hring/hringed*, against the well-known *byrne*, because of the real spread of this armour exactly at that time: he probably knows only one type, only this kind of armour.

4. The chain-mail coat in Anglo-Saxon illuminated manuscripts

Drawings of chain-mail coat also first appeared in Anglo-Saxon manuscripts between the tenth and the eleventh century. The *Harley Psalter* (MS London, British Library, Harley 603, f. 73v, Christ Church, Canterbury XI-XII centuries)[66] is a well known, important source for understanding the development of illustration, script, and book-making during the 'golden age' of Anglo-Saxon art. In the *Utrecht Psalter's* drawings the warriors had shields, spears and helmets; in the *Harley Psalter* no figure wears any type of body armour except in one of the latest illustrations of the manuscript, on f. 73v. Here Goliath is wearing a Danish-style helmet[67] and a corselet, which seems to be a chain-mail coat, is positioned over the

---

[63] *Prudentius*, ed. Cunningham 1966; see Napier 1900, n° 50, l. 216, 50.
[64] See Ker 1959: 143, art. A; also Lendinara 1999: 22-6.
[65] PL 93, col. 611; for this suggestion cf. Stryker 1951, note 130.
[66] This manuscript is the only surviving copy in England of the three Anglo-Saxon copies of the *Utrecht Psalter* (Reims 815-835), see Gneuss 1981: 422; Wormald 1952: 69; Backhouse 1984: 98; for a contrasting opinion see Dodwell 1914: 1-3, who believes that the manuscript was produced at St Augustine's Church. See also Noel 1995.
[67] Cramp 1957: 61.

text of Psalm 143 written by master-scribe Eadui Basan.[68] The image does not, however, illustrate this psalm, but I *Kings* 17. 4-5, where the *lorica hamata* is mentioned: "...et egressus est vir spurius de castris Philisthiarum nomine Goliath de Geth, altitudinis sex cubitorum et palmo et cassis aerea super caput eius et *lorica hamata (squamata)* induebatur..." Lat. *hamata* 'hooked' is a variant gloss of the Vulgate *squamata* 'scaled' as already mentioned. Artist F, who illustrated Harley Psalter ff. 63-73 deviating, simplifying from his exemplar, introduced details of objects and artefacts from his own contemporary world.[69] Artist F did not depict scaled body armour, but drew instead a shirt of chain-mail. This innovation cannot be attributed to a literal evocation of the text because the accompanying psalm is not complementary to the illustration. It is reasonable to suggest the artist has deliberately introduced a picture of an item of war-dress very familiar to him from his contemporary life.[70] This mail-shirt is similar to the Norman chainmail portrayed on the *Bayeux Tapestry*; the regular depiction of a kite-shaped shield reveals a certain familiarity with the shields depicted on the *Bayeux Tapestry* also.

The *Ælfric Hexateuch* (MS London British Library, Cotton Claudius B. iv,[71] first half of XI century) contains more than four hundred drawings, many of which are illustrations of war. One of the artists adopted a new graphic language, depicting what is unequivocally a coat of ring mail on f. 24; he was inspired by *Genesis* 14.1, *quatuor reges adversus quinque* which text was translated into Old English by Ælfric in this way: "iiii. < cyningas wið .v > cyningas, oð ðæt hi comon to feohte".[72] In this drawing of the campaign of the four kings, only one is wearing a coat of ring mail.[73]

A close relationship has been noted between the drawings in these manuscripts and the iconography patterns of *The Bayeux Tapestry*,[74] where both Norman and Anglo-Saxon warriors wear chain-mail coats, conical helmets and kite-shaped shields.[75] Artist F of the *Harley Psalter*, working between 1025 and

---

[68] The famous scribe Eadui, surnamed Basan, monk of Christ Church (Canterbury), wrote the psalm 143 on fol. 73v. He also produced the so-called *Eadwig Gospels* and the *Eadwig Psalter*, see Backhouse, Turner & Webster 1984, n°. 56 and 57. See also Heslop 1990.

[69] Gameson 1995.

[70] Carver 1986 lists three different reasons for an iconographic innovation: 1, the literal evocation of the related text; 2, a geometrical abstraction; 3, the influence of contemporary life.

[71] See Ker 1959: 142; Gneuss 1981: 315. The manuscript contains 394 illustrations. See Dodwell & Clemoes 1974: 71-73.

[72] Crawford 1922: ch. xiv, 119, 2-9.
There is an anomaly between the illustration and the OE text, because the picture illustrated an incorrect translation of the Latin text (*quatuor reges adversus quinque*), only a later sixteenth-century hand added *cyningas wið .v*.

[73] See Morini 2006: pl. 12.

[74] For the arms and armour depicted in the *Tapestry* see Wilson 1985: 219-25, and below, Appendix, Picture 4. On *The Bayeux Tapestry*, a source for describing war equipment during the late eleventh century and very close to the drawings in the manuscripts of the same period, see Oakeshott 1960: 174.

[75] See Morini 2006: 164-66.

1050, and the artist of the *Ælfric Hexateuch*, working before the Norman Conquest, depicted mail-coats in advance of *The Bayeux Tapestry*. It seems possible that these manuscripts reflect the tradition of a single school of iconography, probably the *scriptorium* of Christ Church, at Canterbury.[76] The school came under Scandinavian influence[77] and these manuscripts were probably produced when there was a second influx of "Scandinavian taste", identifiable mainly in isolated ornamental details.[78] Thus, the innovative motif of the coat of ring mail seems to represent a foreign and a new code, defined by the recent creative context and by models that were more accessible to a contemporary audience. It is very remarkable, finally, that the same kind of iconographic innovation may also be observed in the *Book of Maccabees* (MS Leiden, Bibliotheek der Rijksuniversiteit, Cod. Perizoni 17), which was compiled in St. Gall at the beginning of the tenth century.[79] The illustrations follow late Carolingian traditions but introduce a new iconographic canon with respect to its source, the *Psalterium Aureum*. It is reasonable to think that the artist depicted on fol. 45v and 46r a group of horsemen wearing mail-coats, oval shields and Scandinavian helmets. Hand mail is depicted in this manuscript instead of the scaled armour of the sources and this innovation could be suggested as an expression of the new reality, a reflex of the spreading of a new corselet, familiar to everybody through its use by Scandinavian raiders and invaders.[80]

5. Anglo-Saxon and Scandinavian finds of chain-mail coats

It is generally accepted that the Romans acquired their chain-mail (*lorica hamata*) from the Celts and that they wore it from before the 2nd century BC onwards.[81] Roman-style body armour, an exclusive privilege of military leaders, became more popular in the North Germanic area and in Scandinavia only from the fourth century AD onwards. It was probably part of the equipment supplied by the Roman army to the chiefs of its German confederates,[82] but may also have been acquired as spoils of war or through commercial channels.[83] While finds of this armour are extremely uncommon during the early Middle Ages in central and southern Europe, it only rarely comes to light in Germanic-settled central and northern Europe,[84] and dates from not earlier than the third century AD (Hagenow, Öremölla, etc).[85] A complete Roman mail coat has been discovered in England at the Roman fort of

---

[76] Brooks & Walker 1978.
[77] Wieland 1997: 185.
[78] Frank 1987: 339.
[79] See Morini 2006: 166.
[80] See Morini 2006: pl. 10 and 11.
[81] See Morini 2006: 160.
[82] Krüger 1983: 643-51; Liebeschuetz 1990: 7-85; Todd 1992: 60-1.
[83] Todd 1992: 43.
[84] Todd 1992: 41-45; Junkelmann 1986: 166; Rasmussen 1995: 84-86.
[85] Rasmussen 1995: 86; Todd 1992: 95-6; Morini 2003.

Arbeia (Tyne);[86] some fragments at Chester,[87] at Carlingwark Loch (Scotland) and at Newstead (Scotland), the rings of these mails were alternately riveted and punched.[88]

Early medieval historical sources on the Goths, Franks, Lombards and Saxons attest that body armour was a privilege restricted to military leaders, kings and nobles. But no characterizing connotations are given of the kind of body armour concerned. However a "curtain" of mail was applied to the helmets for protecting the neck and the back of the head, as rare finds have shown, e.g. the helmet from Benty Grange, Derbyshire, 8th-9th century, or that from Copperdale (York),[89] which is probably from a bit later.[90] Apart from that, no archaeological find of a chain-mail coat or any type of coat has been discovered during excavations in Anglo-Saxon sites,[91] with the exception of the rusted, flattened and inextricable fragment of ring mail coat found at Sutton Hoo.[92] Its rings of about 8-mm diameter are linked together by hand, using a combination of closure techniques, involving riveting with copper rivets and punching, which are typically Scandinavian.

Between the end of the sixth and the beginning of the seventh century in Anglo-Saxon England,[93] the custom of burying warriors or individuals of some social standing[94] with their weaponry seems to have fallen into disuse, probably because of the spread of Christianity.[95] But it did not disappear so early in Scandinavia. The sole type of corselet found in the Scandinavian area was the chain-mail,[96] which is the unique armour described in the literary sources. It was different from the Roman ring mail corselet (*lorica hamata* or *catenata*) in manufacturing technique, appearance and weight rendering its finds easy to distinguish.[97] The Germanic chain-mail coat may have looked like a tunic draped

---

[86] Croom 1995. The links of mail are 7 mm in diameter made of ca. 1mm wire, other details are not clear.

[87] Croom & Griffiths 1996.

[88] Robinson 1975: 172.

[89] The mail of the curtain of the helmet from Coppergate was made of iron welded, lapped and riveted rings, see O'Connor 1992: 999, 1057 and 1171.

[90] O'Connor 1992: 1082.

[91] Webster 1998: 190.

[92] It has been shown that the fragment of linked rings found at Benty Grenge could not have come from a coat of ring mail; see Bateman 1861: 32 and especially Bruce-Mitford et al. 1978: ch. IV, 232-39; Care Evans 1994: 41.

[93] Härke 1990: 32; Härke 1992: 160-64.

[94] Male infants and young boys were also buried with their weapons: Härke 1992: 153.

[95] Only some spears, axes, arrows and, more rarely, swords have been found complete or in part in the graves of Anglo-Saxon males from before the seventh century, see Cramp 1984; Härke 1990: 30-4; Härke 1992: 156-57.

[96] "Die Annahme, dass es auch Waffenhemden aus Leder oder dickem Zeugstoff mit aufgenähten Ringen (oder Metallplatten) in der Sagazeit gegeben hat, ist unhaltbar."; "Die Ring Brünne scheint noch im 11. Jahrhundert im Norden der einzige gebräuchliche Leibharnisch gewesen zu sein.", Falk 1912: 176 and 179. See Morini 2006: 155-157 on the diffusion of the Celtic chain-mail in Germanic culture.

[97] Roman ring mail corselets weighed about 12-15 kilograms, see Morini 2006: 157-158.

over the wearer's body; it was not close fitting. The links that make up the coats are of two types: a) riveted and b) punched. Riveted links are assembled open and subsequently closed by the insertion of an iron or copper rivet. In contrast, the punched variety comprises groups of four closed links, obtained by punching a thin sheet of iron, inserted into an opened link that was then closed with a rivet. The technique is always identical, indicating the same workmanship for each find.[98] Thus, entire coats of chain-mail, or fragments of them, dating from as late as the ninth and tenth centuries have been found over the entire Norwegian Scandinavian area, as is confirmed by the poetical descriptions of corselet given by the skalds:[99] chain-mail of Holtefjeld, Bakke, Eiker, Buskerud; of Holtene, Sannidal, Telemark; of Søndena, Vikeland, Rogaland;[100] of Romol, Melhus, Sør Trøndelag; one chain-mail of Verdal, Nord Trøndelag,[101] chain-mail of Gjermundbu.[102]

6. Old Norse terms for corselet: *brynja*, *hringabrynja*, *bryniarring*, *hringserkjar*

The Old Norse vocabulary, used in the poetic language of the skalds,[103] is very rich in terms, mostly compounds, for the 'ring mail coat'. ON *brynja* 'coat of ring mail',[104] the common Germanic word for 'corselet', occurs frequently in Sturluson's *Heimskringla*, which refers to and quotes the Skaldic poetry of the ninth and tenth centuries as the source for the narrated events. In contrast with contemporary Anglo-Saxon sources, the Old Norse ones very often mention armour among the components of the military equipment of kings, their *jarlas* and brave warriors. For example it is mentioned four times in the description of Storð'battle (960 AD) in Eynindr Skáldaspillir's *The Hákonarmál:*[105]

> 39. Broður fundu þær Bjarnar
>
> í brynju fara
>
> [They found Björn's brother / to tuck his armour]

---

[98] "Die Brünnen der Wikingerzeit waren aus eisernen Ringen geflochten, wie die der älteren Eisenzeit... jeder Ring ist hier in vier andere gesteckt; teils sind sämtliche Ringe genietet, teils jeder zweite, während die übrigen zusammengeschmiedet sind.", Falk 1912: 175. See also Morini 2006: 160.
[99] See further, § 6.
[100] Grieg 1947: n° 2, 4, 7 and 9.
[101] Grieg 1933: 315-17, where other finds are listed in notes; see also Grieg 1947: 19, no. 10 and 14.
[102] Grieg 1947: 17-8. He also lists and describes all the Norwegian archaeological sites from the Viking period in which numerous fragments of ring mail body armour or entire corselets have been found, 18-19. Subsequently, the author traces the history of the coat of mail in Norway before and during the Viking period, 48-51.
[103] I will restrict my discussion to compounds and kennings only with base *brynja*, *serkr* and *hring*.
[104] With this meaning the term is defined by Egilsson 1931: 68; Cleasby & Vigfusson 1957: 85.
[105] Text quoted from Sturluson 1941-51: ch. 30, 186. For the translations, cf. Kershaw 1922.

41. Hrauzk ór hervöðum,
hratt á völl brynju
vísi verðungar,
áðr til vígs tœki.

[He ripped off his armour, he threw his chain-mail coat down, the king of the people, before beginning his fighting.]

46. Sötu þá döglingar
með sverð of togin,
með skarða skjöldu
ok skotnar brynjur.

[Then, the princes crumpled with drawn swords, with broken shields, with shot corselets]

54. Hjalm ok brynju
skal hirða vel.

[The helmet and the armour must be well guarded.]

Two compounds, *hringabrynja*[106] and *brynjuhringr*,[107] clarify that the body armour mentioned in the Old Norse works was made of 'knit of rings'. No other type of corselet was described in the Old Norse sources. For this reason the substantive *brynja* is always considered as 'ring mail coat'.[108]

There is a great number of compounds with *brynja* as the first element: *brynjaðr* adj. 'wearing a coat of mail, warrior';[109] *brynnir*, 'warrior'; *brynjumeiðð* 'warrior'; *brynþorn* 'warrior';[110] *brynjuhálsbjörg* 'a hauberk';[111] *brynhosa* 'coat's hose';[112] *brynstakkr* 'a mail jacket'; *brynjurokkr* 'a coat of mail'; *brynjumeistari* 'a smither of chain-mail coat';[113] *brynjulauss* adj. 'without a coat of mail'.[114] Lastly, the use of the verb *brynja* 'cover with a coat of mail' in Old Norse should be emphasised.[115]

---

[106] Cleasby & Vigfusson 1957: 285.
[107] Cleasby & Vigfusson 1957: 85.
[108] "Die alte Bedeutung von *brynja* schimmert noch durch im neunorw. *brynja* 'Gürtel aus eisernen Ringen', Falk 1912: 175.
[109] Egilsson & Jónsson 1931: 68; Cleasby & Vigfusson 1957: 85.
[110] Egilsson & Jónsson 1931: 69.
[111] Cleasby & Vigfusson 1957: 85.
[112] Egilsson & Jónsson 1931: 68.
[113] Cleasby & Vigfusson 1957: 85.
[114] Egilsson & Jónsson 1931: 68; Cleasby & Vigfusson 1957: 85.
[115] Cleasby & Vigfusson 1957: 85.

What is also interesting is that, besides the already mentioned *rokkr* 'coat', *stakkr* 'jacket', *hose* 'hose', other dress terms were used by the skalds for the formation of compounds like ON *serkr* and *skirta* 'shirt' which occur only in compounds as a base and as a referent: *hringserkr* 'ring mail coat'; *serkrhringskúr* 'warrior';[116] *hringserkr* 'a shirt of ring mail';[117] *hringskyrta* 'a shirt of ring mail'.[118]

In Old Norse *hringr* and its pl. *hringar* do not mean only 'a ring', 'a circle', but also (in poetical language) 'the rings in a coat of mail' and 'sword'.[119] Besides *brynjuring* other compounds also exist with base *hringr*: *hrigofinn* 'woven with rings';[120] *hringberandi* 'lordly man who wears a chain-mail coat';[121] *hringsköð* 'warrior'.[122]

7. The chain-mail coat in Old Norse poetry

It is interesting to note that Danish and Norse kings, chief captains, warriors and the skalds wore a chain-mail coat, as is shown by some Old Norse texts. If we are to believe the words of Þorbjörn Hornklofi (855-920) in *The Hrafnsmál* (*Haraldskvæði*),[123] the skalds were equipped with chain-mail coats:[124]

Á gerðum sér þeira

ok á gollbaugum,

at eru í kunnleikum við konung,

feldum ráða rauðum,

ok vel fagrrenduðum,

sverðum silfrovöfðum,

serkjum hringofnum,

gyltum andfetlum

ok gröfnum hjölmum,

hringum handbærum,

es þeim Haraldr valði.

[Their intimacy with the king can be seen from their apparel, and from their rings of gold; they wear red mantles with glittering hems, they carry swords with silver-wrought

---

[116] Egilsson & Jónsson 1931: 283; Cleasby & Vigfusson 1957: 285.
[117] Egilsson & Jónsson 1931: 282; Cleasby & Vigfusson 1957: 285.
[118] Egilsson & Jónsson 1931: 283; Cleasby & Vigfusson 1957: 285.
[119] Egilsson & Jónsson 1931: 282; Cleasby & Vigfusson 1957: 268
[120] Egilsson & Jónsson 1931: 282; Cleasby & Vigfusson 1957: 285.
[121] Egilsson & Jónsson 1931: 281; Cleasby & Vigfusson 1957: 285.
[122] Egilsson & Jónsson 1931: 283.
[123] The poem was composed shortly after the battle of Hrafrsfjörðr (c. 875 AD). Handed down without a title, it was preserved in part by Snorri Sturloson in *The Haraldssaga ins hárfagra* and in *The Fagrskinna* in an unabridged form.
[124] Text quoted from Jónsson 1912: 24f.

knobs, coats of ring mail, golden baldrics, engraved helmets and armlets, all given to them by Harold.]

According to Snorri, Saint Olaf, king of Norway (†1030) also wore a chain-mail coat:[125]

Óláfr konungr var svá búinn, at hann hafði hjálm gylltan á höfð, en hvítan skjöld ok lagðr á með gulli kross inn helgi. Í annarri hendi hafði hann kesju þá, er nú stendr í Kristskirkju við altára. Hann var gyðr sverði því, er Hneitir var kallat, it bitrasta sverðr ok gulli vafiðr meðalkaflinn. Hann hafði hringabrynju. Þess getr Sigvatr skáld:

146. Öld vann Óleifr fellda,

öflgan sigr, enn digri,

gekk sóknþorinn sœkja

sinnióR framm i brynju.

[The king Olaf was armed thus: he wore on his head a helm of gold and in his hand held a white shield on which was a golden holy cross. In his other hand, he brandished a spear that can still be found today by the altar in the Church of Christ. At his waist hung a very sharp sword wrought with knolls of gold, called Hnieter, the sharpest. He also had a coat of ring mail. Thus Sigvatr the skald says: ...Olaf the Fat struck down the men, the valiant lord pushed forward on the attack, wearing his coat of mail, to win a crushing victory.]

Haakon, according to Tindr Hallkelsson, removes his chain-mail coat in battle:

ok svá mikill vápnaburðr var at Hákoni jarli, at brynja hans var slitin til ónýts, sva at hann kastaði af sér. Þess getr Tindr Hallkelsson:

139. Gerðr bjúglimum herða,

gnýr óx Fjolnis fúra,

farlig sæing jarli,

þás hringfôum Hanga

hrynserk, viðum brynju

hruðusk riðmarar Róða

rastar, varð at kasta.[126]

[So many spears were thrown at Jarl Haakon that his corselet had been torn until it became unserviceable, so he threw it away. Till Hallkensson says: The ring-linked coat of strongest mail could not withstand the iron hail, though sewed with care and elbow bent, by Norn, on its strength intent. The fire of battle raged around, Odin's steel shirt flew all unbound! The earl his ring-mail from him flung, its steel rings on the wet deck rung;][127]

---

[125] Sturluson 1941-51a: ch. 223, 367.
[126] Sturluson 1941-51: ch. 40, 281.
[127] Laing 1907: i, 164.

Haakon's followers wear a chain-mail corslet too, as is confirmed by Hallföðr Ottarsson in *The Oláfsdrapa*, composed on the death of king Olaf Tryggvason

> ... fákhalaðendr frœknir / farligs at vin jarla / húfs með hamri þœfðar / hringskyrtur framm gingu.[128]
>
> [When the valiant warriors from the decorated ship brought forward with the hammer-worked ring mail corselets against the friend of the jarls (king Olaf)...]

The armour is also worn by the warriors of the king of Norway, Saint Olaf:

> Óláfr konungr hafði á sínu skipi hundrað manna, ok höfðu allir hringabrynjur ok valska hjálma.... Jarl hafði lið meira, en konungr hafði einvalalið á sínu skipi, þat er honum hafði fylgt í hernaði, ok búit svá forkunnliga, sem fyrr var sagt, at hverr maðr hafði hringabrynju. Urðu þeir ekki sárir. Svá segir Sigvatr:
>
> 41. Teitr, sák okkr í ítru
>
> allvalds liði falla,
>
> gerðisk harðr, of herðar,
>
> hjördynr, svalar brynjur,
>
> en min at flug fleina —[129]
>
> [King Olaf had one hundred men on his ship, all with ring mail corslets and Welsh helmets ...The jarl had more men but the king (Olaf) had on his ship an elite company that had followed him in the battle; above all, they were so superbly equipped, as has been said before, that each man had a coat of ring mail so that he could not be wounded. Thus Sigvatr says: Glad, I saw slip our cold armours behind our shoulders while we were in the brave troops: the fight became hard.]

On the basis of the examined texts, it appears quite clear that ON *hringarbrynju*[130] 'chain-mail' is referred to as being worn by both Danes and Norwegians, and as belonging to kings and leaders, but also to their numerous followers.

Lastly, a significant passage in *Óláfs Saga Helga* (c. 1015-1030) should be mentioned, in which it is stated that a chain-mail coat cannot protect the warrior from an enemy's spear as appears in the well-known passage of *The Battle of Maldon*:

> Þá lagði Þórir hundr spjóti til hans. Kom lagit neðan undir brynjuna ok renndi upp í kviðinn.[131]

---

[128] Jónsson 1912: i, 9, 152.
[129] Sturluson, *Heimskringla*, ii, *Óláfs Saga Helga*, ch. 49.
[130] Cleasby & Vigfusson 1957: *s. v.*, 285.
[131] Sturluson 1941-51a: ch. 228, 385.

[Then Thor the Dog struck him (OLAF) with his spear, and the blow penetrated his coat of mail and ran into his stomach.]

8. The chain-mail coat in Anglo-Saxon poetic texts

Only in *Beowulf* (226: *syrcan hrysedon* 'the shirts creaked' and 284b: *seo byrne sang* 'the corselet sang') and in *Exodus* (176), quoted above (see section 1), are there references to the noise made by the rings of the mail coat. But it is especially the poet of *Beowulf* who describes the corselet, worn by both Geats and Danes, with such particulars that it is quite clear that it is a chain-mail coat. It is called *hring-nett* (*Beo* 551, 1889, 2754) 'a net of rings'; *hond-locen* 'joined together by hands'; or *here-byrne hondum locen* (*Beo* 1443) 'by hand (made) corslet of the (war) army'; *locene leoðosyrcan* 'linked corselet' (*Beo* 1505 and 1890), *brogden* 'woven, knitted' (*Beo* 1243, *El* 257).

Four compounds (*Beo* 550-53) change the chain-mail coat one after another because they give more accurate definitions, in a multiple variation, introduced by the poet to describe carefully the best defense of the hero:

þær me wið laðum   licsyrce min
heard hondlocen,   helpe geferemede,
beadohægl broden,   on breostum læg
golde gegyrwed.   (*Beo* 550-53)
[My armour helped me to hold out;
my hard-ringed chain-mail, hand-forged and linked,
a fine, close-fitting filigree of gold.]

The anonymous poet provides detailed descriptions of body armour with specific indications of the type involved and its characteristics and recalls, in its description, the manufacture and the ring-linking technique used in the exemplars of mail coats found in Scandinavia. The body armour in *Beowulf* is the work of skilled, or even legendary, metalworkers:

Beowulf maðelode - on him byrne scan,
searonet seowed smiþes orþancum (*Beo* 405-6)
[Beowulf spoke out – on him the mail-coat shone,
an intricate mesh linked together by the ingenious arts of the smith.][132]

   þæt is Hrædlan laf,

---

[132] This and the following translations have been taken from Bradley 1982.

> Welandes geweorc (*Beo* 454b-55a)
>> [it is an heirloom from Hrethel,
> the work of Weland.]

When the warrior sits down it sounds:

> bugon þa to bence, byrnan hringdon
> guðsearo gumena (*Beo* 327-29b)
> [Then they seated themselves on a bench;
> their mail-coats, the men's battle-equipage]

because it is soft and long. It jingles to the warriors' steps:

> Guðbyrne scan
> heard hondlocen, hringiren scir
> song in searwum (*Beo* 321b-23a)
> [battle corslet shone, tough, with rings interlocked by skillful hands;
> shining iron link jangled in their mail-coats.]

> þam æt sæcce wearð,
> wræcca(n) wineleasum Weohstan bana
> meces ecgum, ond his magum ætbær
> brunfagne helm, hringde byrnan, ealdsweord etonisc (*Beo* 2612b-16a)
> [of which friendless, banished man Weohstan had been the killer, by the sword's edges, and had carried off to his kinsmen the burnished, gleaming helmet, the ring-linked mail-coat and the ancient sword forged by giants.]

it is sturdy and impenetrable, with closely intertwined rings:

> þær me wið laðum licsyrce min
> heardhondlocen helpe gefremede;
> beadohrægl broden, on breostum læg (*Beo* 550-52)
> [There my mail-shirt, tough, with rings interlocked by skilful hands, afforded me help against adversaries; the meshed battle-garment decorated with gold covered my breast.]

of a grey color:

> Hwanon ferigeað ge fætte scyldas,
> græge syrcan, ond grimhelmas,

heresceafta heap? (*Beo* 333-335a)

[From where do you come conveying gold-ornamented shields, grey mail-coats and vizored helmets, and that heap of war-spears?]

iron made:

Þenden reafode rinc oðerne,

nam on Ongenðio irenbyrnan,

herad swyrd hilted, ond his helm somod (*Beo* 2985-87).

[Meanwhile the warrior stripped his opponent; he took from Ongentheow his iron mail-coat, his tough hilted sword and his helmet as well,]

The garment swathes and protects the wearer's body and it is woven:

hring utan ymbbearh,

þæt heo þone fyrdhom ðurhfon ne mihte,

locene leoðosyrcan laþan fingrum (*Beo* 1503b-05)

[on the outside, chainmail shielded it about so that she was unable to poke her loathsome fingers through his soldier's armour, the corslet of interlocked rings.]

forming a tight net of rings:

Beowulf maðelode - on him byrne scan,

searonet seowed smiþes orþancum (*Beo* 405-06)

[Beowulf spoke out – on him the mail-coat shone, an intricate mesh linked together by the ingenious arts of the smith:]

Him on eaxle læg,

breostnet broden (*Beo* 1547b-48a)

[Across his shoulder lay the meshed mail-shirt:]

The corselet, intertwined by hand, protects Beowulf from a deadly attack by killer whales (see above, the quotation from *Beo* 550-553a) and from Grendel's mother:

Him on eaxle læg

breostnet broden; þæt gebearh feore,

wið ord ond wið ecge ingang forstod.

Hæfde ða forsiðod sunu Ecgþeowes

under gynne grund, Geata cempa,

nemne him heaðobyrne helpe gefremede,

herenet hearde (*Beo* 1547b-54; see also *Beo* 1502b-05)

[Across his shoulder lay the meshed mail-shirt: it saved his life and resisted penetration by point or edge. Ecgtheow's son, the Geatish campaigner, would have perished then down in the vast deep, had not his battle-corslet, his sturdy soldier's mail-coat, afforded him help;]

The poet of *Exodus* defines the body armour as *wælhlenca* 'battle coat of mail'(176) and as *walnet* 'battle net' (202), giving with these terms the information that it is made from twisted element, and that it is a net.

It is remarkable that, in *The Battle of Maldon,* only the Danes are equipped with a corselet. The chain-mail coat, as the poet wrote, offers no protection to a Danish warrior against the impact of the spear of Byrhtnoð:

ða he oþerne   ofstlice sceat,
þæt seo byrne tobærst;   he wæs on breostum wund
þurh ða hringlocan,   him æt heortan stod
ætterne ord.   (*Maldon* 143-46, ed. ASPR 6)

[Then, he hastily hurled another, so that the coat of mail burst; he was wounded in the breast through the linked rings of coat, the poisonous spear stood at his heart.]

But, the chain-mail coat protects the wearer from Byrhtnoð's sword during hand-to-hand combat and it is exactly in this circumstance that the poet refers to it as made with rings:

Eode þa gesyrwed   secg to þam eorle;
he wolde þæs beornes   beagas gefecgan,
reaf and hringas   and gerenod swurd.
þa Byrhtnoð bræd   bill of sceðe,
brad and bruneccg,   and on þa byrnan sloh.   (*Maldon* 162-63, ed. ASPR 6)

[Then an armed warrior went to the earl; he wanted to take the valuables of the man, the corselet, and rings, and ornamented sword. Then Byrhtnoth drew the sword from sheath, broad and gleaming of blade, and struck at the corselet.]

It is interesting to note from the textual evidence that the *byrne* occurrences appear only in poems with a Scandinavian setting, such as *Beowulf* and *The Battle of Maldon,* or in others with other foreign historical settings (*Judith, Elene, Exodus*). Also, the only warriors who wear a corselet in the Anglo-Saxon texts are, without exception, foreigners. The Assyrian warriors are described as 'combatants (armoured) with a corselet'; Holophernes is *byrnewiggende* 'corseted warrior' and *byrnwigena brego* 'lord of the corselet warriors' in *Judith* (l. 17 and 39); the 'Roman' warriors are *byrnwiggendra* in *Elene* (l. 224); *byrnwiga* is referring to Hygelac in *Beowulf* (l. 2918). In two cases there is no reference to the nationality of the *byrnwiga* (*The Wanderer*, l. 94) and it is not clear if the warrior with body armour (*Finnsburg Fragment*, 1. 43) is Frisian or Danish, in any case he is a foreigner.[133] On the other hand, it is noteworthy that chain-mail coat is not mentioned among the weapons of Anglo-Saxons in *The Battle of Brunanburh*, in which only *scyld*, *gar*, and *sweord* are named.

9. The chain-mail coat in Anglo Saxon England, the Vikings' influence and the dating of *Beowulf*

It has been suggested that the typically Scandinavian fashion of a royal eulogy following a victory could have inspired the composition of *The Battle of Brunanburh*,[134] of *The Conquest of the Five Boroughs*, and of *The Panegyric of Athelstan*, which has survived both in Latin and in English.[135] *Exodus*, which was probably composed later than *Beowulf*, and certainly postdates the Scandinavian invasions,[136] exhibits a number of stylistic peculiarities of Skaldic origin, such as the introduction of repeated 'kennings',[137] in particular in the area of weapons, including sword and shield. The same stylistic features are also present in *The Battle of Brunanburh*.[138] It seems that the preferences of the Anglo-Saxon audience "were not immune to Norse taste has as its springboard the fact that certain lines of Old English verse are extraordinarily responsive to a Skaldic' reading".[139] In the early tenth century, in fact, the Old Norse and Anglo-Saxon cultures experienced a phase of interaction. The affinity of heroic style and ethics that united Anglo-Saxons and Scandinavians as part of their common Germanic heritage seems to have been reinforced by these new contacts.[140] The alliances and familiarity between Anglo-Saxons and Danes that grew up during the reign of Athelstan (924-939), called *Anglosaxonum Denorumque gloriosissimus rex*,[141] contributed to the creation of a high level of culture. Nor should we underestimate the influence of the

---

[133] 'Then a hero came walking away wounded; a man of action in his military trappings, he said that his mail coat was hacked to pieces and his helmet was holed too'. It appears probable that the wounded man who 'goes away' is a Frisian warrior. For arguments to the contrary, see Bugge 1899: 28.

[134] Niles 1987: 359.

[135] See Poussa 1981: 277-78 and 280-81.

[136] Frank 1988; lastly the drawings preserved on the Anglo-Saxon manuscripts, which depicted a body armour; Frank 1987: 342; Klaeber 1918.

[137] "Anglo-Saxon authors seem to have had two distinct lexicons at their disposal, that of poetry and that of prose. The two discourses are separated from each other by a semantic shift as far-reaching as any sound change. Sometimes the Old Norse cognate of an English word seems to help in establishing the latter's meaning in *Beowulf*', Frank 1987: 344 and 348-51; "Nothing in the bits and pieces of information extracted from Skaldic verse was found incompatible with a date for Beowulf in the late ninth century or the first half of the tenth century; and some facts were more compatible with this period than with any other." Frank 1981: 137.

[138] Niles 1987: 359-63.

[139] Frank 1987: 339; see also Frank 1979: 13.

[140] Bugge 1899 believed that a part of *Edda* could have been composed in Anglo-Saxon England; see now Smith 1928-36: 221.

[141] Stenton 1988: 348, notes.

presence at king Athelstan's court[142] of a large number of nobles of Scandinavian origin, the future King of Norway, Haakon,[143] and of the warrior-Skald, Egill Skallagrimsson (900-992) with his followers.[144] It has been claimed that the heroic and religious ideals evinced in *Beowulf*, in *Judith*, in *The Battle of Maldon* and in *The Battle of Brunanburh* would have been inconceivable any earlier than the tenth century,[145] when

> the Danes in England were working hard to be more Christian and English than the English. [...] An Old English poem about northern heathens and northern heroes, opening with the mythical figure of Scyld from whom the ruling houses of both Denmark and England were descended, fits nicely with the efforts of Alfred and his successors to promote an Anglo-Danish brotherhood, to see Dane and Anglo-Saxon as equal partners in a united kingdom.[146]

Although it is very difficult to suggest a dating for the composition of *Beowulf*, it seems, in the light of historical evidence, that a poem like *Beowulf* could not have been composed, copied, or "chanted",[147] before or during the first Viking raids.[148] Moreover

> a post Alfredian date... explains the poet's and audience's apparent acquaintance with Norse literary genres, his ability to manipulate Scandinavian legend and myth, and theirs to follow what he was doing.[149]

---

[142] Stenton 1988: 347.
[143] Haakon was in England when his father Harald died (933), see Sturluson 1941-51: 42-45.
[144] *Egils saga Skalla Grímssonar*, which dates from about 1230, perhaps composed by Snorri, tells of his sojourn at the court of Ethelstan, and of his participation in the Battle of Brunanburh (937), see Nordal 1933-55: ch. 50-55.
[145] Frank 1982: 62.
[146] Frank 1982: 64.
[147] "As long as Viking raids continued in England, no Anglo-Saxon *scop* in his right mind would chant the opening lines of Beowulf before a live, beer-drinking audience... If no Anglo-Saxon poet would create the poem, no *scop* recite it, and no audience listen to it, why would ninth and tenth century scribes copy it? The usual scribes of the time were the same monks whose rich monasteries were prime targets of the Vikings." Kiernan 1986: 200.
[148] "Those who propose a 7th or 8th century provenance for the poem neglect to discuss how it passed through all of the Anglo-Saxon kingdoms, including Alfred's, during the Viking Age of the 9th and 10th centuries. ...If it is hard to conceive of an Anglo-Saxon poet in these centuries who would have composed *Beowulf*, it is just as hard to conceive of scriptoria throughout these centuries that would repeatedly engage scribes to copy a poem praising the people who were ravaging their country. It is even harder to imagine receptive audiences in Northumbria, Mercia, Wessex, or Kent, but these are the dialect areas that supposedly contributed the mixture of forms in the course of the poem's transmission.", Kiernan 1981: 21. Recently Davis (2006: 129) dates the poem to the time of the latter part of King's Alfred reign, because "in the 10th century Alfred's heirs evince no special interest at all in this old ethnic lore", of the mature King Alfred.
[149] Frank 1981: 137; see also Frank 1987: 343-47; Frank 1979: 1-19; Poussa 1981: 281.

The poet's memory also embraces the paganism of the invaders,[150] their ship burials,[151] their history and place names presupposing the existence of an audience that was probably familiar with Danish history (*ACr* 937, ll. 29b-32), and Scandinavian lands.[152]

The poet of *Beowulf* created various compounds and circumlocutions for varying the concept of chain-mail coat, classifiable as 'kennings', 'heiti', 'kendi heiti' and 'bahuvrihi' for *byrne* for an audience which may have been familiar with the chain-mail coat 'kennings' typical of Old Norse poetry. Although it has been claimed that *Beowulf*'s style is independent of that of the Skalds, there is still a significant presence of 'kennings' for weapons and armour. The poet of *Beowulf* described the shield and the sword with a wide range of metaphors,[153] similar to those used by the Skalds for the same weapons,[154] and did the same with the chain-mail, referring to it in terms reminiscent of the Skaldic one. According to the literary evidence just presented, it is interesting to note that OE *wælhlence* 'a shirt twisted from iron rings' is a 'kenning' for chain-mail which stands alone in Old English poetry and finds relatives only in Old Norse poetry. There are also rare 'kennings' for 'warrior' as *byrnwigend, byrnwigende, byrnwiga* and *herewæda*, which is an hapax legomenon in Old English and another 'warrior' kenning very similar to the old Norse creations, as well as the 'shield' compound, used by the poet of *Exodus,* too (*Ex, randwiga* 'shield warrior', 126 and 134, *randwigend*, 436) and *Beo, randwiga*, l. 1298 and l. 1793. It is also relevant that some Germanic words occur with the same meaning only in Old English and in Old Norse poetry and do not exist in other Germanic languages (such as for example *hlence* or *hring, -serce* in the meaning 'coat of mail'). The use of *hring* and of its 'chain-mail coat' compounds is found only in the Old English poetry, their only relatives exist in Old Norse Skaldic poetry. Adjectives like *locen* 'linked', *hondlocen* 'linked by hand' and *brogden* 'knitted', *handgewipan* 'twisted, woven by hand', *seowed* 'knitted together, linked', qualifying in *Beowulf* that the *byrne* is formed from rings joined and twisted together by hands as are the mail coats of the Scandinavian finds. Thus, on the linguistic and stylistic evidence of similarity between *Beowulf* and the poetry of the Skalds, it seem possible to assume that the audience of *Beowulf* was probably, as has been suggested for those of *Exodus*,[155] very used to the chain-mail coat poetic vocabulary of the Skaldic metalangue or at the least was "not immune to Norse taste".[156]

---

[150] Poussa 1981: 281.
[151] Poussa 1981: 284-5.
[152] Poussa 1981: 279.
[153] See Marquardt 1938 and Frank 1987: 343.
[154] Schücking (1917) was the first scholar who believed that the poem could be composed into the cultural backdrop of the Danelaw, even if he had in mind the post Alfredian time (9th century). See now Frank 1987: 340
[155] Frank 1987: 338-339.
[156] Frank 1987: 339.

10. Conclusion

Thus, the use of such elaborate and refined vocabulary for a 'chain-mail coat' by the poet of *Beowulf* would be further proof in favour of the recent dating of the poem. There is, in fact, no archeological evidence for the existence of such body armour either at the time of the migration of the Angles,[157] or in the centuries preceding the Scandinavian invasions. The mention and especially the precise description of the chain-mail coat in Anglo-Saxon England during the tenth century cannot be attributed to any historical folk memory.[158] The drawings of armour which appear in manuscripts from the same period and the description of it in Old English texts such as *Beowulf* and *The Battle of Maldon* suggest that it was the chain-mail coat and that it was worn by enemies only. Anglo-Saxon warriors were not in fact equipped with byrnies to defend themselves from their enemies before the end of tenth century: the corselet is never mentioned among the weapons of Anglo-Saxon warriors in *The Battle of Brunanburh* (937 AD), in which only *scyld* 'shield', *gar* 'spear' and *sweord* 'sword' are named, or in the *Battle of Maldon* (991 AD). The promulgation of the heriot's code by King Æthelred and King Cnut, and the first mention of the byrne as a valuable element of military equipment, at the time of Æthelred (1008), could be considered as the first confirmation of an already widespread custom and of the necessity that also Anglo-Saxon warriors should be equipped with armour, like their enemies. Thus, in accordance with the evidence we have just examined, it seems possible that the chain-mail coat, and the use of the substantive *hring* in its meaning, could only have been known by the Anglo-Saxons through the Vikings, the only people who until the 10th and 11th century made, used and described it in their texts. On the basis of the evidence, the corselet depicted on the Anglo-Saxon manuscripts' drawings, and mentioned in OE texts, proves to be *a chain-mail coat*, of the same technical features as those discovered in Scandinavia. From this analysis and the comparison with Old Norse texts and Old Norse archaeological finds, it may be concluded that the chain-mail coat described in the Anglo-Saxon sources could only have been body armour of Scandinavian origin and, further, that it had spread into Anglo-Saxon England only with the invading Vikings. Such a conclusion could confirm a late dating of *Beowulf*.

It is in the light of this kind of cultural, historical and literary evidence regarding chain-mail coat, that it is important to reintroduce the issue, so relevant today, of the dating of *Beowulf* and of *Elene*. It seems possible to assume that the poet of *Beowulf* too could not have lived before the Viking invasion, probably at the time of Athelstan, or of his son Edmund (939-946),[159] when Old Norse and

---

[157] In accordance with the inexistence of finds of Angle chain-mail coat, it has been suggested that the Angles lacked the relevant manufacturing techniques, see Rose 1906: 53-54.
[158] Stjerna 1912: 347.
[159] "Any monastically-educated second or third-generation Anglo-Dane of good family is a potential Beowulf-poet...Anyone born in the Danelaw as late as 930 could probably have remembered at least one pagan grandparent, and known many respected old people who had been

Anglo-Saxon cultures experienced a phase of interaction. There is no doubt that the description of the chain-mail coat which has been given by the poet of *Beowulf* corresponds to the armour found in Scandinavian finds from the third century BC to the eleventh century AD, and also to that of the fragment found in the Sutton Hoo ship burial, which is also of Swedish origin (seventh century).[160] Other Anglo-Saxon texts, such as *Exodus, Judith* and *Elene*,[161] also mentioning chain-mail coat, as has been demonstrated, concur in dating the spread of body armour in Anglo-Saxon England to the tenth century, in any case after the beginning of Viking raids.[162]

Appendix: Illustrations

The illustrations show what the chain-mail looks like, and how it was made.

Picture 1 (from Rose 1906: 51; for details see also Morini 2006) illustrates two construction types, showing in detail how the rings were put together.

Picture 2 shows the chain-mail from Vimose (Denmark), the oldest completely preserved chain-mail coat from Northern Europe (ca. 3rd century A.D.). For the permission to reproduce it here we thank the Nationalmuseet in Copenhagen, especially Roberto Fortuna, Kira Ursem, and Lone Klint Jacobsen.

Picture 3 show a recent reconstruction (2012) of a chain-mail coat, made in Germany.[163] For the permission to reproduce it here, we thank Unter freyem Banner www.unter-freyem-banner.de.vu; Unter-freyem-banner@gmx.de

Picture 4 is from the Bayeux Tapestry (after 1066). It depicts the scene with King Harold's death. It shows that the Anglo-Saxon defenders and the Norman attackers wore the same kind of chain-mail coat. It is also clear from other parts of the Bayeux Tapestry that only the more aristocratic fighters wore a chain-mail coat, whereas the common soldiers did not have this kind of protection and were accordingly much more vulnerable. For the permission to reproduce this picture we thank the City of Bayeux.

---

brought up as pagans....Information about Geatish history was available in England at the turn of the ninth and tenth centuries, as the Leyden MS of the Latin *Liber Monstrorum*, which refers to the last raid of Hygelac, was copied in England at this period.": Poussa 1981: 281.

[160] See Morini 2006: 166.

[161] On the basis of the metrical principles, it has been recently suggested that *Elene* may have been composed between the end of the 9th and the beginning of the 10th century, or during the 10th century, see O'Connor who also affirms how important it is to first examine the traditional dating of other poems than *Beowulf* (2001: 23).

[162] At the end of this article I wish to remember my friend Prof. Antonio Piccolini (†), University of Catania, with whom I shared the connections I found between Anglo-Saxon and Old Norse Literature. I also wish to thank Kevin Kiernan for reading the first draft of this article.

[163] This modern reproduction of a chain-mail coat was displayed in the window of a bookshop opposite the editors' office, so that they could admire it every day while working on the present volume. See also p. 345 below.

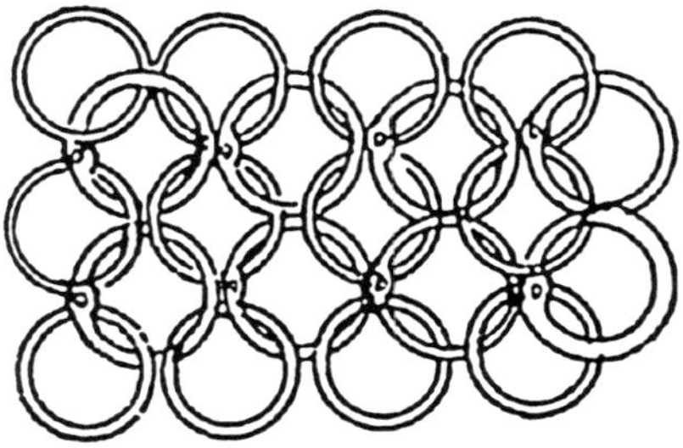

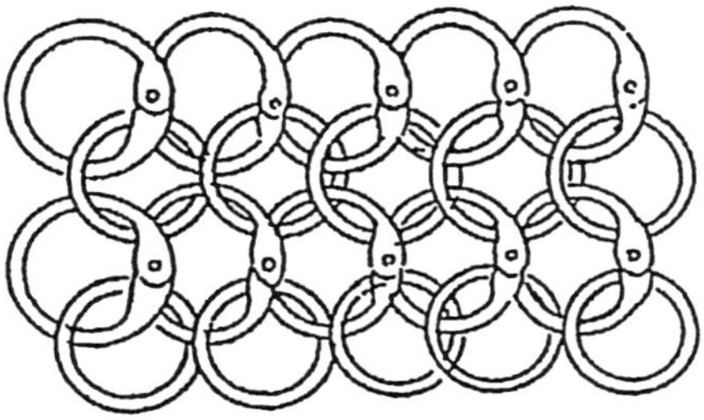

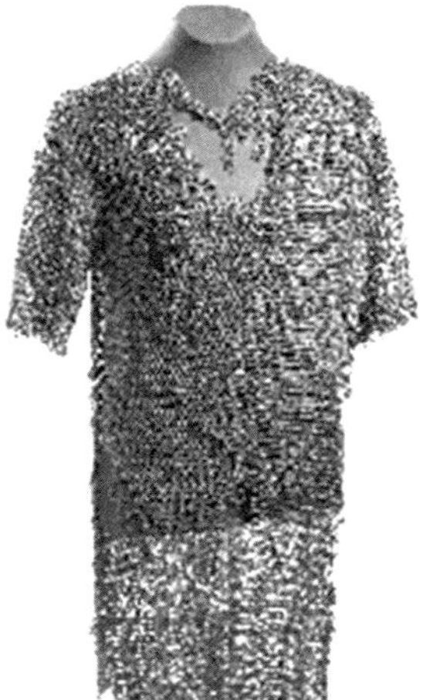

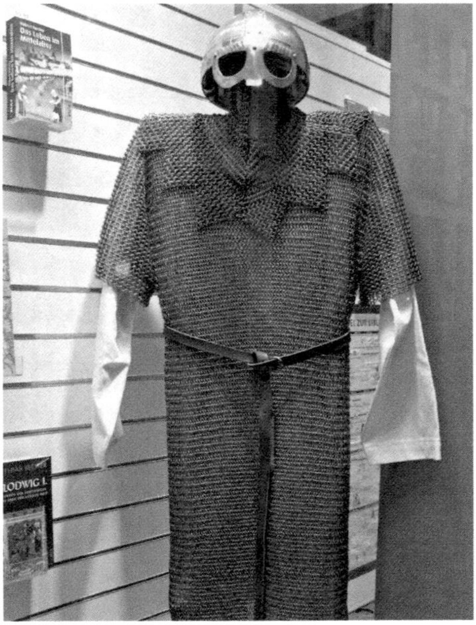

Picture 4: Chain-mail coats on the Bayeux Tapestry (© The City of Bayeux)

Sources

ASPR 1	*The Junius Manuscript*, ed. George Philip Krapp. New York: Columbia University Press, 1931.
ASPR 2	*The Vercelli Book*, ed. George Philip Krapp. New York: Columbia University Press, 1932.
ASPR 4	*Beowulf and Judith*, ed. Elliot v. Kirk Dobbie, New York: Columbia University Press*,* 1953.
ASPR 6	*The Anglo-Saxon Minor Poems*, ed. Elliot v. Kirk Dobbie. New York: Columbia University Press, 1942.
Bradley, S. A. J. (ed. & transl.)	
1982	*Anglo-Saxon poetry. An anthology of Old English poems in prose translation*. London: Dent.
Crawford, Samuel John (ed.)	
1922	*The Old English version of The Heptateuch, Ælfric's treatise on the Old and New Testament and his preface to Genesis*", Early English Text Society, o.s. 160. London: Oxford University Press [repr. with an appendix by Neil R. Ker, 1969].
Cubbin, Geoffrey P. (ed.)	
1966	*MS D: a semidiplomatic edition with introduction and indices*. The Anglo-Saxon Chronicle: a collaborative edition vi. Cambridge: Brewer.

Cunningham, Maurice P. (ed.)
1966 *Aurelii Prudentii Clementis Carmina. CCSL* 126. Turnhout: Brepols.
Dodwell, Charles Reginald -- Peter Clemoes
1974 *The Old English illustrated Hexateuch, BM Cotton Claudius B iv*, Early English Manuscripts in Facsimile 18. Copenhagen: Rosenkilde & Bagger.
Garmonsway, George N.
1967 *The Anglo-Saxon Chronicle*. London: Dent.
Gradon, Pamela O.E. (ed.)
1977 *Cynewulf's Elene*. Exeter: University of Exeter.
Heaney, Seamus (ed.)
1999 *Beowulf: A new verse translation*. London: Faber.
Heyne-Schücking
1949 *Beowulf*, 3. *Glossar*, 15th edition by Else von Schaubert. Paderborn: Schöningh.
Jónsson, Finnur (ed.)
1912 *Den norsk islandske skjaldedigtning*, i. Copenhagen: Gyldendal [repr. Rosenkilde & Bagger, 1973].
Kershaw, Nora (ed. & transl.)
1922 *Anglo-Saxon and Norse poems*. Cambridge: Cambridge University Press.
Kindschi, Lowell
1955 *The Latin-Old English glossaries in Plantin Moretus MS. 32 and British Library MS. Additional 32246*, Diss. Stanford: Stanford University [repr. Ann Arbor: Umicrofilms International, 1986].
Klaeber, Frederick (ed.)
2008 *Klaeber's Beowulf and the Fight at Finnsburg*. 4th ed. by Robert D. Fulk, Robert E. Bjork & John D. Niles. Toronto: University of Toronto Press. [1st ed. 1922].
Laing, Samuel (transl.)
1907 Snorri Sturluson, *Heimskringla: A History of the Norse Kings*, 2 vols., rev. by Rasmus B. Anderson. London: Norroena Society.
Liebermann, Felix (ed.)
1903 *Die Gesetze der Angelsachsen*, vol. 1. Halle: Max Niemeyer [repr. Aalen: Scientia, 1960].
Lindelöf, Uno (ed.)
1927 *Rituale ecclesiae Dunelmensis: The Duhram Collectar*, a new and ren. Edition Publications of the Surtees Society. Durham: Andrews & Co.
Napier, Arthur S. -- William Henry Stevenson (eds.)
1895 "The will of Bishop Ælfwold (aa. 1008-1012)" in *The Crawford collection of early charters and documents now in the Bodleian Library*. Oxford: Clarendon Press.
Napier, Arthur S.
1900 *Old English glosses*, Anecdota Oxoniensia, Medieval and Modern Series, 11. Oxford: Clarendon [repr. Hildesheim: Olms, 1969].

Nordal, Sigurdur (ed.)
 1933-55   *Egils Saga Skalla-Grímssonar.* Íslenzk Fornrit 2. Reykjavik: Íslenzka Fornritafélag.
Sturluson, Snorri
 1941-51   *Heimskringla,* i, *Hákonar Saga Góda,* ed. Bjarni Aðalbjarnarson, Íslenzk fornrit 26. Reykjavík: Íslenzka Fornritafélag.
 1941-51a   *Heimskringla,* ii, *Óláfs Saga Helga,* ed. Bjarni Aðalbjarnarson, Íslenzk fornrit 26. Reykjavík: Íslenzka Fornritafélag.
Stryker, W. G.
 1951   "The Latin-Old English glossary in MS. Cotton Cleopatra A.iii", Diss. Stanford: Stanford University.
Thomson, H. J. (ed./transl.)
 1962   *Prudentius. With an English translation.* Volume 1. Loeb Classical Library. London: William Heinemann.
Whitelock, Dorothy
 1930   *Anglo-Saxon wills.* Cambridge: Cambridge University Press [repr. Holmes Beach: Graunt, 1986].
Whitelock, Dorothy (ed./transl.)
 1955)   *English historical documents,* c. 500-1042. Oxford: Oxford University Press.
Wright, Thomas -- Richard Paul Wülker
 1884   *Anglo-Saxon and Old English vocabularies.* 2nd ed. London: Trübner & Co. [repr. Darmstadt: Wissenschaftliche Buchgesellschaft, 1968].
Zupitza, Julius (ed.)
 1880   *Ælfrics Grammatik und Glossar.* Berlin: Weidmann [4th ed. with an introduction by Helmut Gneuss, Hildesheim: Weidmann, 2003].

Dictionaries

BT   *An Anglo-Saxon Dictionary,* by Joseph Bosworth and T. Northcote Toller. Oxford: Oxford University Press, 1898; *Supplement,* by T. Northcote Toller, 1921; *Enlarged Addenda to the Supplement,* by Alistair Campbell, 1972.
         <http://beowulf.engl.uky.edu/~kiernan/BT/Bosworth-Toller.htm>
Cleasby, Richard -- Gudbrand Vigfusson
 1957   *An Icelandic-English dictionary,* 2nd ed. with a supplement by William A. Craigie. Oxford: Clarendon Press.
diPaolo Healey, Antonette -- Richard L.Venezky
 1980   *A Microfiche Concordance to Old English,* The Dictionary of Old English Project, Centre for Medieval Studies, University of Toronto. Toronto: Toronto University Press [repr. 1985].
DOEWC   *Dictionary of Old English Web Corpus,* eds. Antonette diPaolo Healey, John Price Wilkin & Xin Xiang. Toronto, 2009.
         <http://www.doe.utoronto.ca/pages/pub/web-corpus.html>
Egilsson, Sveinbjörn -- Finnur Jónsson
 1931   *Lexicon poeticum antiquae linguae septentrionalis.* Ordbog over det Norsk-Islandske Skjaldesprog. Copenhaven: Lynge & Søn [repr. 1966].

Grein, Christian Wilhelm
   1912   *Sprachschatz der angelsächsischen Dichter*, new ed. by Johann Jakob Köhler & Ferdinand Holthausen, Germanische Bibliothek, i, iv, 7. Heidelberg: Winter.
Hall, J. R. Clark
   1960   *A Concise Anglo-Saxon Dictionary*. 4th edition with a supplement by H. D. Meritt. Cambridge: Cambridge University Press.
Holthausen, Ferdinand
   1934   *Gotisches Etymologisches Wörterbuch*. Heidelberg: Winter.
Kluge, Friedrich
   1995   *Etymologisches Wörterbuch der deutschen Sprache*, 23rd ed. Berlin: De Gruyter.
Roberts, Jane -- Christian Kay -- Lynne Grundy (eds.)
   2000   *A Thesaurus of Old English*, 2 vols. Amsterdam-Atlanta: Rodopi.

References

Ashdown, Charles Henry
   1925   *Armour and weapons in the Middle-Ages*. London: Harrap.
Anderson, Earl R.
   1990   "The etymology of OE *serc, syrce, syrc* ON *serkr*", *Neophilologus* 74: 635-37.
Backhouse, Janet
   1984   "The making of the Harley Psalter", *Journal of the British Library* 10: 97-113.
Backhouse, Janet -- D.H. Turner -- Leslie Webster
   1984   *The golden age of Anglo-Saxon art*. London: British Museum Press.
Bateman, Thomas
   1861   *Ten years' diggings in Celtic and Saxon grave hills: in the counties of Derby, Stafford and York*. London: J.R. Smith.
Brady, Caroline
   1979   "Weapons in *Beowulf*: An analysis of the nominal compounds and an evaluation of the poet's use of them", *Anglo-Saxon England* 8: 79-141.
Breeze, Andrew
   1993   "Celtic etymologies for OE *cursung* 'curse', *gafeluc* 'javelin', *stær* 'history', *syrce* 'coat of mail' and ME *clog(ge)* 'block', 'wooden shoe', *cokkunge* 'striving', *tirven* 'to flay', *warroke* 'hunchback', *N&Q* 40: 287-97.
Brooks, Kenneth R.
   1948-49   "Old English *wopes hring*", *English and German Studies* 2: 68-74.
Brooks, Nicholas P.
   1978   "Arms, status and warfare in later-Saxon England", in: *Ethelred the Unready: Papers from the Millennary Conference*, ed. David Hill, British Archaeological Reports 59. Oxford: British Archaeological Reports. 81-103.

1991	"Weapons and armour", in: *The Battle of Maldon. AD 991*, ed. Donald Scragg. Oxford-Cambridge: B. Blakwell in Ass. with the Manchester Centre for Anglo-Saxon Studies. 215-217.

Brooks, Nicholas -- Harold Earle Walker
1978	"The authority and interpretation of the Bayeux Tapestry", *Proceedings of the Battle Conference, Anglo-Norman Studies* 1: 1-34.

Bruce-Mitford, Rupert et al. (eds.)
1978	*The Sutton Hoo Ship-Burial*, vol. 2: *Arms, Armour and Regalia*. London: British Museum Press.

Bryan, William Frank
1929	"Epithetic compound folk-names in *Beowulf*", in: *Studies in English philology: A miscellany in honour of Fredrick Klaeber*, eds. Kemp Malone & Martin B. Ruud, 120-34. Minneapolis: University of Minnesota Press.

Bugge, Sophus
1899	*The home of the Eddic poems*, Grimm Library 1. London: D. Nutt.

Care Evans, Angela
1994	*The Sutton Hoo Ship Burial*. London: British Museum Press.

Carver, Martin
1986	"Contemporary artefacts illustrated in late Saxon manuscripts, *Archaeologia* 108: 117-46.

Cramp, Rosemary
1957	"Beowulf and archaeology", *Mediaeval Archaeology* 1: 57-77.
1984	"Anglo-Saxon settlement", in: *Settlement in North Britain: 1000 BC-AD 1000, Papers Presented to George Jobey*, eds. John Charles Chapman & Harold C. Mytum, 263-79. British Archaeological Reports, 118. Oxford: BAR.

Croom, Alexandra T.
1995	"A hoard of Roman military equipment from South Shields", *The Arbeia Journal* 4: 45-54.

Croom, Alexandra T. -- W.B. Griffiths
1996	"A fragment of ring-mail from Chesters", *Arma* 8.1-2: 3-4.

Davis, Craig R.
2006	"An ethnic dating of *Beowulf* at the time of the mature King Alfred", *Anglo-Saxon England* 35: 111-129.

Derolez, René (ed.)
1992	*Anglo-Saxon glossography*. Brussels: koninklijke Academie voor Wetenshappen, Letter en Schone Kunsten.

De Vries, Jan
1960	*Kelten und Germanen*, Bibliotheca Germanica, 9. Bern-München: Francke.

Dodwell, Charles Reginald
1914	*The Canterbury School of Illumination 1066-1200*. Cambridge: Cambridge University Press.

Falk, Hjalmar
1912	*Altnordische Waffenkunde*. Kristiania: J. Dybwad.

Frank, Roberta
1979	"Old Norse memorial eulogies and the ending of *Beowulf*", in: "The Early Middle Ages", *Acta* 6: 1-19.

1981	"Skaldic verse and the date of *Beowulf*", in: *The Dating of Beowulf*, ed. Colin Chase, 123-39. Toronto-Buffalo-London: Toronto University Press [repr. in *Beowulf: Basic readings*, ed. Peter B. Baker. New York: Garland, 1995, 155-180.]
1982	"The Beowulf poet's sense of history", in: *The wisdom of poetry. Essays in Early English literature in honour of Morton W. Bloomfield*, eds. Larry D. Benson & Siegfried Wenzel, 53-65. Kalamazoo: Medieval Institute Publications, Western Michigan University.
1987	"Did Anglo-Saxon audiences have a skaldic tooth?" *Scandinavian Studies* 59: 338-55.
1988	"What kind of poetry is *Exodus?*", in: *Germania: Comparative studies in the Old Germanic languages and literatures*, eds. Daniel G. Calder & Craig Christie, 191-205. Woodbridge, Suffolk: D.S. Brewer.

Gameson, Richard
1995 *The role of the art in the late Anglo-Saxon church*, Oxford: Clarendon Press.

Gneuss, Helmut
1981 "A preliminary list of manuscripts written or owned in England up to 1100", *Anglo-Saxon England* 9: 1-60.

Godden, Malcom
1991 "Biblical literature: The Old Testament", in: *The Cambridge companion to Old English literature*, eds. Malcom Godden & Michel Lapidge. Cambridge: Cambridge University Press. 206-26.

Grieg, Sigurd
1933 *Middelanderske byfund fra Bergen og Oslo*. Oslo: A. W. Brøggers.
1947 *Giermundbufunnet. En høvdingegrav fra 900-. ärene fra Ringerike*, Norske Oldfunn 8. Oslo: J. Griegs.

Grimm, Jacob
1819-1837 *Deutsche Grammatik*, 4 vols. Göttingen: Dieterich [repr. London-New York: Roy Harris, 1999].

Härke, Heinrich
1990 "Warrior graves? The background of the Anglo-Saxon weapon burial rite", *Past and Present* 126: 22-43.
1992 "Changing symbols in a changing society: The Anglo-Saxon weapon burial rite in the seventh century", in: *The age of Sutton Hoo. The seventh century in North-Western Europe*, ed. Martin O. H. Carver, 149-65. Woodbridge: Boydell Press.

Heslop, T. A.
1990 "The production of *de luxe* manuscripts and the patronage of King Cnut and Queen Emma", *Anglo-Saxon England* 19: 151-95.

Hooper, Nicholas
1989 "The Anglo-Saxon at war", in: *Weapons and warfare in Anglo-Saxon-England*, ed. Sonia Chadwick Hawkes, Oxford University Committee for Archaeology 21, 191-202. Oxford: Oxford University Committee for Archaeology.

Junkelmann, Marcus
  1986 *Die Legionen des Augustus: der römische Soldat im archäologischen Experiment*, Kunstgeschichte der antiken Welt 33. Mainz: von Zabern.

Ker, Neil R.
  1957 *Catalogue of Anglo-Saxon manuscripts*. Oxford: Clarendon [repr. 1990].

Kiernan, Kevin S.
  1981 *Beowulf and the Beowulf manuscript*. New Brunswick: Rutgers [repr. with a foreword by Katherine O'Brien O'Keefe. Ann Arbor: Michigan University Press, 1996].
  1986 "The legacy of Wiglaf", *The Kentucky Review* 6: 27-44 [repr. Baker 1995, 195-238].

Klaeber, Friedrich
  1918 "Concerning the relation between *Exodus* and *Beowulf*", *Modern Language Notes* 33: 218-24.

Krüger, Bruno (ed.)
  1983 *Die Germanen: Geschichte und Kultur der germanischen Stämme in Mitteleuropa*, i. Berlin: Akademie, 241-63.

Lansfield Keller, May
  1905 *Anglo-Saxon weapon names treated archaeologically and etymologically*. Anglistische Forschungen 15. Heidelberg: Winter [repr. Amsterdam: Swets-Zeitlinger, 1967].

Lendinara, Patrizia
  1999 *Anglo-Saxon Glosses and Glossaries*. Aldershot-Brookfield: Ashgate.

Liebeschuetz, John Hugo Wolfgang Gideon
  1990 *Barbarians and bishops: Army, church, and state in the age of Arcadius and Chrysostom*. Oxford: Clarendon Press.

Marquardt, Herta
  1938 *Die altenglischen Kenningar: ein Beitrag zur Stilkunde altgermanischer Dichtung*, Schriften der Königsberger Gelehrten Gesellschaft, Geisteswiss. Kl, 14.3. Halle.

Mc Guinnes, Daniel
  1989 "Beowulf's Byrnes", *English Language Notes* 26.3: 1-3.

Mitchell, Bruce -- Christopher Ball --Angus Cameron
  1975 "Short titles of Old English texts", *Anglo-Saxon England* 4: 207-21.
  1979 "Short titles of Old English texts: Addenda and Corrigenda", *Anglo-Saxon England* 8: 331-33.

Molinari, Maria Vittoria
  1983 "Per un'analisi tipologica della Kenning anglosassone", *Annali dell'istituto universitario orientale di Napoli*, sez. Fil. Germanica 26: 29-52.

Morini, Carla
  2006 "OE Hring: Anglo-Saxon or Viking armour?", *Anglo-Saxon Studies in Archaeology and History* 13: 155-172.

Niles, John
  1987 "Skaldic technique in *Brunanburh*", *Scandinavian Studies* 59: 356-66.

Noel, William
1995 *The Harley Psalter*, Cambridge Studies in Palaeography and Codicology 4. Cambridge: Cambridge University Press.

O'Connor, Patrick
2001 "On dating Cynewulf", in: *The Cynewulf reader*, ed. Robert E. Bjork, 23-55. New York & London: Routledge.

O'Connor, Sonia A.
1992 "Technology and dating of the mail and the mail curtain", in: *The Anglian Helmet from Coppergate*, ed. Dominic Tweddle, The Archaeology of York, small finds 17. York: York Archaeological Trust for the Council for the British Archaeology.

Oakeshott, Ewart
1960 *The archaeology of weapons: Arms and armour from prehistory to the age of chivalry*. London: Lutterworth Press.

Okasha, Elisabeth
1993 "Old English *hring* in Riddles 48 and 59", *Medium Aevum* 63: 61-69.

Poussa, Patricia
1981 "The Date of *Beowulf* reconsidered: The tenth century?", *Neuphilologische Mitteilungen* 82: 276-88.

Rasmussen, Birgit M.
1995 "Brokaer. Ein Reichtumszentrum der römischen Kaiserzeit in Südwestjutland", *Acta Archaeologica* 66: 39-109.

Robinson, Henry Russel
1975 *The armour of imperial Rome*. London: Arms and Armour Press.

Rose, Walther
1906 "Römische-germanische Panzerhemden", II. "Germanische Panzerhemden", *Zeitschrift für historische Waffen- und Kostümskunde* 4: 40-55.

Sarrazin, Gregor
1886 "Der Schauplatz des ersten Beowulfliedes und die Heimat des Dichters", *Beiträge zur Geschichte der deutschen Sprache und Literatur* 11: 159-83.

Sawyer, Peter H. (ed.)
1968 *The Anglo-Saxon charters: An annotated list and bibliography*. London: Royal Historical Society.

Schücking, Levin L.
1917 "Wann entstand der *Beowulf*? Glossen, Zweifel und Fragen", *Beiträge zur Geschichte der deutschen Sprache und Literatur* 42: 347-410.

Shetelig, Haakin -- Hjalmar Falk
1937 *Scandinavian Archaeology*, transl. by E V. Gordon. Oxford: Clarendon Press.

Sievers, Eduard
1886 "Die Heimat des Beowulfdichters", *Beiträge zur Geschichte der deutschen Sprache und Literatur* 11: 354-62.
1887 "Altnordisches im Beowulf?", *Beiträge zur Geschichte der deutschen Sprache und Literatur* 12: 168-200.

Smith, Alexander H.
1928-36 "The early literary relations of England and Scandinavia", *Saga-Book of the Viking Society for Northern Research* 11: 215-32.

Stenton, Frank M.
1971 *Anglo-Saxon England.* 3rd ed. Oxford: Clarendon Press [many reprints].

Stjerna, Knut
1912 *Essays on questions connected with the Old English poem of Beowulf*, trans. from Swedish by John R. Clark Hall, Viking Club Extra Series, III, published for the Viking Club: Society for Northern Research. Coventry: Curtis & Beamish.

Storm, Gustav
1957 *Compounded names of peoples in Beowulf: A study in the diction of a great poet.* Utrecht-Nijmegen: Dekker en Van de Vegt.

Stroebe, Lilly L.
1904 *Die altenglischen Kleidernamen: Eine kulturgeschichtlich-etymologische Untersuchung,* Diss. Leipzig: Noske.

Todd, Malcom
1992 *The early Germans.* Oxford: Blackwell.

Watanabe, Kazuso
1972 "The kennings of *Beowulf*", in: *Collected essays by members of the faculty* 14: 1-18.

Webster, Leslie
1998 "Archaeology and Beowulf", in: *Beowulf: An edition with relevant shorter texts,* eds. Bruce Mitchell & Fred C. Robinson. Oxford: Clarendon Press. 183-93.

Wieland, Gernot R.
1997 "The origin and development of the Anglo-Saxon Psychomachia illustrations", *Anglo-Saxon England* 26: 169-186.

Wilson, David M.
1985 *The Bayeux Tapestry.* London: Knopf.

Wormald, Francis
1952 *English drawings of the tenth and eleventh centuries.* London: Faber and Faber.

Old English *geweald habban/āgan* as a stylistic set phrase, compared with Old High German and Old Saxon cognates

Kousuke Kaita (Munich, Germany & Tokyo, Japan)

Abstract

This paper shows that OE *geweald habban/āgan* 'to have power', denoting the mightiness of the subject, is a stylistic set phrase, and it examines whether this phrase has anything related to auxiliation when a *to*-infinitive follows. Through the comparison with OS *giwald hebbian/êgan* in *Heliand*, it is shown that verse texts prefer *āgan*, sometimes with a genitive phrase accompanying *geweald*, whereas some prose texts show deviation from either verb in this phrase. The OS *Heliand* employs *hebbian* rather than *êgan* in combination with *giwald*, showing the linguistic difference between cognate languages. Unlike the structure of ModE *have to* or *ought to*, the *to*-infinitive cannot be used with the possessive verb in *geweald habban/āgan*, as *geweald* is not the object of the infinitive. OE *geweald habban/āgan* remains a set phrase rather than a candidate for an auxiliary of possibility, where *āgan* is a verb more restricted in syntax than *habban*.

1. Introduction

In the historical research on older English there is the problem of whether idioms existed in the modern linguistic sense.[1] We can certainly find some set phrases in Old English. For example, Capek (1970: 359, fn. 9) points to the combination OE '*geweald* + *habban* + *to* + inflected infinitive' in *Genesis B* (280b-281a): *Ic hæbbe geweald micel / to gyrwanne*, 'I have great power to adorn'.[2] According to Capek, this phrase "does not occur in OE outside *Genesis B*" (p.359, fn. 9), whereas Capek finds the same construction in several Old Saxon texts[3] and calls them "formulaic".[4] Semantically, the OE phrase *geweald habban* 'to have power' seems to express the notion of possibility (as in OE *magan*) and, if negated, impossibility (as in OE *ne magan*) or prohibition (as in OE *ne mōtan*). This claim can be supported when both this verb phrase and apparently corresponding preterite-present verbs can take a *to*-infinitive or a bare infinitive. From the various versions of the *Gospels*,[5] which enable us to compare the use in various translations

---

[1] I will not enter into the detailed discussion of the notion of 'idiom' itself in this paper. For the analysis of 'idiom' from a ModE linguistic view point, see, e.g., the discussion by Nunberg et al. (1994).
[2] In the examples cited, underlinings and translations are mine unless otherwise noted. The short titles of OE texts are based on *The Dictionary of Old English, Web Corpus* (henceforth *DOEWC*).
[3] The lines are: *Genesis* 200b-201a, *Heliand* 2162b-2163a, 2327b-2328a, 2696a-2698a, and 4516b-4518a. Sugawara (1984: 3) cites the lines 2163, 2328, and 4518 and considers OS *geweald hebbian* accompanying *te*-infinitive as a use like a modal auxiliary.
[4] Capek (1970: 358), following Parry, defines "formula" as "a group of words which is regularly employed under the same metrical conditions to express a given essential idea" (Parry 1930: 80).
[5] Examples garnered from the various versions of the *Gospels* are Mt 7.29-Mk 1.22, **Mt 9.6-**Mk 2.10-*Lk 5,24, *Lk 12.5, Lk 19.17, **Jn 10.18 (two examples), *Jn 19.10 (two examples), Jn 19.11, and Mt 20.25-Mk 10.42-Lk 22.25. Hyphenated passages indicate that they have similar contents. Passages with a single asterisk are occurrences of Latin *potestatem habere* with infinitive, and those with double asterisks are those of Latin *potestatem habere* with gerund. The

chronologically and comparatively among Germanic languages, Tuso (1968: 96, 103) gives statistical data which show that OE *anweald* or *mæht* can correspond to Latin *potestas*. In Mt 7.29, for instance, we find such correspondence as Latin *potestatem habens*, OE (*Li*) *mæht hæfde*, OE (*WSCp*) *anweald hæfde*, OHG (*Tatian* 43.4) *giuualt habenter*, and OS (*Heliand* 1832) *geuuald habde*. Ono (1989: 66-67), citing Liebermann (1903-1916, I: 30 and s.v. *nagan*) and Mitchell (1969: 375-376 and 1985: §933), mentions that OE *nage ... to bebycganne* 'ought not to sell' in *LawAfEl* 12.1 corresponds to Latin *Exodus* 21.8 *uendendi non habebit potestatem* 'he will have no power of sending'. In the OE *Heptateuch* (Crawford 1922: 264) the part is rendered as *ne mot ... syllan* '(he) is not allowed to sell'. In this cursory examination, OE *geweald habban* (or its synonym *āgan*) can be a set phrase or an auxiliary when followed by a *to*-infinitive. In this paper I focus on the phrase *geweald habban* or *āgan* meaning 'to have power' in OE texts by comparing it with OS and OHG cognate expressions. I intend to argue that OE *geweald habban* or *āgan* should be regarded as a set phrase, and to discuss whether this phrase has some relation to auxiliation, when an inflected infinitive follows.

2. The use without *to*-infinitive in OE

The phrases dealt with here are OE *gew(e)ald/anw(e)ald/onw(e)ald/w(e)ald* + *habban/āgan* (with *to*-infinitive), and OS *giwald* + *hebbian/êgan* (with *te*-infinitive). I regard these phrases in the respective languages as morphological variants and represent them as OE *geweald habban/āgan* and OS *giweald habban/êgan*.

The *OED* defines the (now obsolete) English word *weald* as 'control'.[6] The *DOE* also mentions the phrase *weald* with genitive noun and *habban* or *āgan*.[7] The accompanying verb can vary according to each text. In the *DOEWC* I found the following distributions in OE verse and prose as shown in Tables 1 and 2. The verb *āgan* is more frequent in verse than *habban* (*āgan* 28: *habban* 14), whereas in prose (Ælfric, *Anglo-Saxon Chronicle* etc.) *habban* is more frequent (*āgan* 69: *habban*

---

last three passages are the examples where Latin uses not only *potestatem habere*, but also another wording. See example (6) in section 2.

[6] *OED*, s.v. †*wield*, *sb. Obs.*:
1. Command, control; possession, keeping; *occas.* hold, grasp: chiefly in phr. **at, in, on** (one's) *w.*; **to have in** *w.*, to have command or control of, to possess, have; **to** *w.*, in or into one's possession. (See also 4a.) (First example: *c*893, Last example: 1567)
4. In phr. *aʒen* (*owen*) *awold*, also *aʒen* or **haven wold** (**wald, weld**), representing OE. *on* (*ʒe-*) *wealde habban*, and *ʒeweald áʒan* or *habban* with genitive
a. To have in control or possession, possess. (First example: *Beowulf*, Last example: *a*1300)

[7] *DOE*, s.v. *āgan*:
I.A.5.f.i.a.: with *geweald* qualified by a genitive: (not) to have power (over something).
I.A.5.f.i.a.i.: *geweald agan* with *geweald* qualified by a genitive and with reflexive pronoun: to have power (over something).

102). In OS *Heliand*, *giwald* with *hebbian* shows 32 occurences, while *giwald* with *êgan* has only 4.[8]

Table 1: *OE geweald + habban/āgan in verse*[9]

	GenA,B	Sat	And	Dream	El	ChristA,B,C	GuthA,B	Gifts	Wid
habban	3	0	0	0	0	1	0	0	0
āgan	2	6	1	1	1	1	2	1	1

	Rid	Beo	PPs	Met	MSol	Rewards	KtHy	GDPref	MEp	Total
habban	0	3	2	2(1)	1	1(1)	1	0	0	14(2)
āgan	1(1)	2	0	6(1)	1(1)	0	0	1	1	28(3)

The phrase *geweald habban* or *āgan* is not found in *Genesis A*, but in *Genesis B*. This seems to be one of the features that show that *Genesis A* and *Genesis B* were originally different poems.

Table 2: *OE geweald + habban/āgan in prose (Ælfric's works, Orosius, Boethius, and Chronicle)*

2a	ÆCHom	ÆLS	ÆHom	ÆHex	ÆAbusMor	ÆAbusWarn	ÆCreat
habban	10(1)	8	10	4	0	0	2
āgan	3(2)	2(2)	4	0	1(1)	1(1)	0

	ÆLet	ÆGram	ÆGenPref	ÆJudgEp	Total
habban	3	0	0	1	38(1)
āgan	1(1)	1(1)	1(1)	0	14(9)

2b	Or	Bo	ChronA	ChronF	ChronC	ChronD	ChronE	Total
habban	22(1)	40(12)	0	0	0	1	1	64(13)
āgan	2	3(1)	11	3	12	13	11	55(1)

As shown in the *OED* and the *DOE geweald habban/āgan* with genitive nouns are found often, for example in (1). Table 3 shows the distribution of occurrences in verse texts classified according to the genitive modifiers.[10]

---

[8] They are the lines 70, 763, 842, and 5573.
[9] Negative is indicated in small-bracketed numbers in the Tables 1 and 2.
[10] Another form found concerning *geweald habban/āgan* is the collocation with the prepositions *to* or *on* with *geweald* found in *Christ and Satan* 412-413 (with *āgan*) and *Kentish Hymn* 13 (with *āgan*), respectively, and much more frequently in prose texts.

(1) *Beowulf* 1724b-1727

Wundor is tō secganne,

hū mihtig God manna cynne

þurh sīdne sefan snyttru bryttað,

eard ond eorlscipe;hē āh ealra geweald.

[It is a wonderful thing to tell how mighty God distributes estate and rank to the race of men through great mind; he has the power of everything.]

Table 3: OE geweald habban/āgan with genitives

noun (phrase)	pronoun	*eall*	*dom*	nothing	Total
17	7	6	3	9	42

Cook (1900: 222) suggests the attribution of *ealra* to *geweald* rather than to *Fæder* in *Christ* 1647 (see (2)): "*geweald* requires a dependent gen. and a governing verb". Cook's claim seems justified considering that *geweald* with genitive and *āgan* in OE texts can qualify as a set phrase where *āgan* is more preferable than *habban*.

(2) *Christ* 1647b-1648

Fæder ealra geweald

hafað ond healdeð   haligra weorud.

[(the) Father shall have power of all and keep the host of the holy (ones).]

Cook (1902:18) and Clubb (1925:61) have provided notes for some examples of *geweald habban/āgan* with *eall* and *dom* in the genitive case.[11]

In OE prose texts, especially in *Boethius*, there seems to be no difference as to the choice of *habban* and *āgan*. Example (3) shows a co-occurrence of the two verbs, while in the corresponding verse text *habban* is converted to *āgan* for alliteration.

---

[11] The texts with *eall* (in genitive case) are *Christ and Satan* **55, **107, ***117, *Christ* 1647, *Beowulf* **1727, *Paris Psalter* 118.91 (with *habban*), and *The Metrical Epilogue to MS. 41* 28. The lines with a single asterisk are referred to by Cook (1902: 18), those with double asterisks are by Clubb (1925: 61), and those with triple asterisks are by both. Cook (1902: 18) refers to these passages with *Dream of the Rood* 107, *Elene* 725, and *Gifts of Men* 27 (occurrences with *dom*) in order to compare these with *The Metrical Preface to Wærferth's Translation of Gregory's Dialogues* 22, *se þe āh ealles rīces geweald* "who rules the whole kingdom" (Cook's translation on p.16). Clubb exemplifies the lines to state their similarity with each other. *Beowulf* 1727 and *Dream of the Rood* 107 are cited in *OED*. See footnote 6.

(3) *De Consolatione Philosophiae* MS.B, f.41^{v12}

[S]e[a] þe wille fullice <u>anweald agan</u>, he sceal tiligan ærest þæt he <u>hæbbe anweald</u> his agenes modes,

[He who wishes fully to have power, must try first that he has power of his own mind,]

(4) *The Metres of Boethius* 16.1-3a

[S]e þe wille <u>anwald agon</u>, ðonne sceal he ærest tilian

þæt he his selfes   on sefan <u>age</u>

<u>anwald</u> *i*nnan,

[He who wishes to have power, then he must try first that he has power of himself in mind inside,]

In *The Anglo-Saxon Chronicle* there is a frequent collocation of '*āgan* + *welstowe* + *geweald*' throughout *A*, *F*, *C*, *D*, and *E* especially in the texts for the 800s (see example (5) and Table 4).[13]

(5) *The Anglo-Saxon Chronicle A* 833[14]

Her gefeaht Ecgbryht cyning wiþ .xxxv. sciphlæsta æt Carrum, 7 þær wearþ micel węl geslægen, 7 þa Denescan <u>ahton węlstowe gewald;</u>

[In this year king Egbert fought against 35 ship-crews at Carhampton, and there great slaughter was made, and then the Danes had the battlefield in their power.]

Table 4: *Occurrence of geweald āgan according to the year of the Chronicle*

Year	ChronA (11)	Chron F (3)	Chron C (12)	Chron D (13)	Chron E (11)
800s	7	1	7	7	7
900s	2	1	3	2	1
1000s	2	1	2	4	3

This phrase is cited and defined in Hall (1960: s.v. *wælstōw* f.) as "to obtain possession of battlefield, conquer". Noteworthy is that *wælstōw* in the genitive always occurs in this phrase in the *Chronicle*, according to Plummer's glossary (1892). The translation of *Orosius* also usually uses the combination with *geweald* and *habban*, while one example (Or 3 7.64.23 in *DOEWC*) with *welstowe* shows the collocation with *āgan*.

Other relevant texts are the versions of the *Gospels*. We have seen in the introduction that *geweald* or *mæht habban*, not with *āgan*, is a usual way of

---

[12] Texts from *Boethius* are based on Griffiths (ed.) (1994). Italics in the edition.
[13] In the *Anglo-Saxon Chronicle* '*habban* + *anweald*' is found in *D* 1067, '*habban* + *wælstōwe* + *geweald*' in *E* 1025, '*āgan* + genitive + *geweald*' in *D* 1010 and *E* 1066, and '*āgan* + *wælstōwe* + *geweald*' is found in the other examples.
[14] Text from Bately (ed.) (1986: 42).

rendering Latin *potestatem habere*. Considering that *geweald habban*[15] can also be found in non-religious poems, this phrase may not have been influenced. Mt 20.25 presents two noteworthy points: (a) Latin *potestatem exercere* is not always consistently rendered into Old English where only *WSCp* uses *geweald habban*, and (b) there is one example using *geweald* with *āgan* in *Ru1* for Latin *dominor*. The other corresponding parts use some other means of expression.[16]

(6) Mt 20.25

Latin: iesus autem uocauit eos ad se et ait scitis quia principes gentium <u>dominantur</u> eorum et qui maiores sunt <u>potestatem exercent</u> in eos

OE (*WSCp*): þa clypode se hælend hig to him 7 cwæð; Wite ge þæt ealdor-menn <u>wealdað</u> hyra þeoda. 7 þa ðe synt yldran <u>habbað anweald</u> on him.

OE (*Ru1*): hælend þa ceigde þæm to him 7 cwæþ ge cunun þæt ðeoda aldormenn <u>agun gewald</u> [*Li*: <u>ricsað</u>] þara ł heora 7 þa þe mare sindun <u>mæhte begæþ</u> ofer heo

The comparison of three passages in several OE versions tells us that OE *geweald habban* can be used not only for *potestatem habere* and that *geweald āgan* is avoided for rendering *potestatem habere*. In either case the phrase *geweald habban/āgan* in the *Gospels* has the literal meaning 'to have power' denoting the power of the subject. The difference of the two verbs lies in the style of the texts, where *geweald* (or *mæht*) *habban* is the Old English phrase used for rendering Latin *potestatem habere*.

3. The use without *te*-infinitive in the OS *Heliand*

In the OS *Heliand*, *hebbian* and *êgan* seem to show no difference of meaning. As a type of set phrase, the use in *ef-* or *sô*-clause is found in lines 1065b (*ef*-clause with *hebbian*), 1832b (*sô*-clause with *hebbian*, corresponding to Mt 7.29, see the introduction), 3983b (*sô*-clause with *hebbian*), and 5573b (*ef*-clause with *êgan*). In the last example *êgan* is governed by *sculan*, as *êgan* itself in *Heliand* can be governed by *skulan* (22%, 8 instances), *môtan* (19%, 7 instances), and *willian* (11%, 4 instances) with 36 instances, whereas *hebbian* occurs less frequently. This kind of parenthetical or conditional use is found in OE verse only once as far as I have found: *swa hit wolde gif hit geweald ahte*: / *þeah bið* ... in *The Metres of Boethius* 22.36-37, which is missing in the corresponding prose version (*swa hit wolde. 7 þeah bið* ...). From the comparison with two OE versions of *Boethius*, we can say that OS *giwald hebbian/êgan* in an *ef-* or *sô*-clause is a parenthetically employed method for metrical purpose.

---

[15] A cursory inspection showed that *miht habban* can be found in verse twice: *se weard <u>hafað miht</u> and strengðo* in *Genesis A* 949b-950a and *meotod <u>hæfde miht</u> and strengðo* in *Christ and Satan* 2, which are similar with each other.

[16] E.g. *wealdan* (in Mt 20.25 and Lk 22.25 in *WSCp* and Mk 10.42 in *Li* and *Ru1*) and *ricsian* (in Mk 20.25 and Lk 22.25 in *Li*).

Another tendency not found in OE *geweald habban/āgan* is the poetical variation of *giwald* with *megin*: *he sulic megin êhta, / giuuald an thesaro uueroldi* (*Heliand* 841-842a) 'he [= God's own child] had such power, the power over this world'. Here *megin* is reworded as *giwald* in the next line, showing the synonymy of these two nouns.[17]

4. OE *geweald habban* with *to*-infinitive and OS *giwald hebbian* with *te*-infinitive

In the investigation so far, OE *geweald habban/āgan* and OS *giwald hebbian/êgan* are set phrases within verse texts which express the power of the subject. For the lexical choice of the possessive verbs of OE *geweald habban/āgan* and its OS counterpart, as shown in Table 1, OE verse texts prefer *āgan* to *habban* in the set phrase. In *Heliand*, on the other hand, *giwald* with *hebbian* is more prevalent, whereas the semantic differences between *habban/hebbian* and *āgan/êgan* are slight, if any. In this section the syntactic difference of these two lexemes (*habban/hebbian* and *āgan/êgan*) with *geweald/giwald* is illustrated according to the combination with the *to-/te*-infinitive. I have already mentioned, in the introduction, Capek's claim that this use in OE is limited to *Genesis B*. I can add one more example as in (7), where the verb used is *habban*, not *āgan*,[18] likewise in *Genesis B*.

(7) *The Rewards of Piety* 35-37a[19]

Ceapa þe mid æhtum   eces leohtes,

þy læs þu forweorðe,   þænne þu hyra geweald nafast

to syllanne.

[Buy with your possessions the eternal light, lest you should perish, when you have no power over them to give them away.]

In addition OS *Heliand* uses *hebbian* with *te*-infinitive four times according to Capek (see footnote 3), as in (8), but not *êgan*.

---

[17] Similar rewording can be found in *maht* (with *hebbian*) by *geuuald* in the lines 2070-2071. It is also noteworthy that in the line 2286 in *Heliand maht* and *craft* show manuscript variants. Compare the textual variation in the OE *Gospels* of *geweald* and *mæht* by Tuso (1968). Also in OHG *Evangelienbuch* V.17.9 three nouns *máhti, giwalt* and *krefti* share the meaning 'power'. According to Ushida (1986: 128) these OHG nouns correspond to Latin *virtus* in *Acts of the Apostles* 1.8. The distribution of these lexemes will be a further research problem.

[18] Ono (1989: 77), discussing the use of *āgan* + (object) + *to*-infinitive, points out that "there is no example of *āgan* + infinitive in poetry".

[19] Text from Robinson (ed.) (1994: 188).

(8) *Heliand* 2161b-2163a[20]

Kristes uuârun thô

uuord gefullot: hi geuuald habda

te *tôgeanna* têcan,

[Christ's words were then filled: he had the power to show tokens,]

In prose texts and glosses OE *geweald habban* with a *to*-infinitive is limited to the versions of the *Gospels* as far as the present research covers. The *Gospels* show another verbal collocation with an inflected infinitive modifying *geweald*, telling that the *to*-infinitive belongs to the noun.[21] When Latin *potestatem habere* takes a verbal complement belonging to *potestatem*, it can be either an infinitive or a gerund. We should note that Mt 9.6 and Mk 2.10 employ *dimittendi* and Lk 5.24, *dimittere*, sharing the same content, whose OE (*WSCp*) counterparts are all *to*-infinitives.[22] These examples explain that *geweald* with *habban* can be used for expressing 'to have power' as a usual verb phrase, rather than an auxiliary. Therefore the two OE texts based on *Exodus* 21.8, which we have seen in the introduction, are semantically expanded renderings of *uendendi non habebit potestatem*. Although Old English uses auxiliaries, the contexts alone are insufficient to conclude that *geweald habban* with the *to*-infinitive should be regarded as an auxiliary. The sense as an auxiliary for negative permission, that is, prohibition, should be read contextually rather than syntactically. Another remarkable context is Jn 19.10-11, a dialogue between Pilatus and Jesus, where Latin *potestatem habeo crucifigere té et potestatem demittere té ... non haberes potestatem* is rendered in OE (*WSCp*) as *ic hæbbe mihte þe to honne. 7 ic hæbbe mihte þe to forlætene; ... Næfst þu nane mihte*. Here *potestatem habere* denotes legal power, so that the literal meaning of 'power' is easily entailed.

The OE *habban* + object + *to*-infinitive construction is the precursor of ModE semi-auxiliary *have to*.[23] The object in Lk 7.40 can belong to either *habban* or *to secgenne* in *WSCp*. According to the definition of the *OED2*, Lk 7.40 is cited under 7a,[24] whereas the use as an auxiliary is distinguished under 7c. On the other

---

[20] The text from *Heliand* is based on Behaghel (1933: 76-77). Italics in the edition.

[21] Callaway (1918: 171-173) refers to the infinitive modifying the noun object in the *Lindisfarne Gospels* by citing some passages including Lk 5.24, Lk 12.5, and Jn 19.10.

[22] Lk 5.24 is similar to OS *Heliand* 2327-2728 *ik geuuald hebbiu / sundea te fargebanne* and OHG *Tatian* 54.7 *mannes sun habet giuualt in erdu zi furlazenne sunta*, both using an infinitival modifier.

[23] E.g. Lk 7.40: Latin *habeo tibi liquid dicere*, OE (*WSCp*) *ic hæbbe þe to secgenne sum ðing*, and ModE (*AV*) *I haue somewhat to say vnto thee*.

[24] *OED*, s.v. *have* v.:
2b. With complement or adverbial extension, particularizing the relation of the object or expressing some qualification, condition or limitation thereof. (First example: c1000, Last example: 1891)

hand OE *habban* + *geweald* with a *to*-infinitive cannot be qualified as the candidate for the use of auxiliary in that *geweald* is not the object of the *to*-infinitive. The ModE auxiliaries *ought to* and *have to* are alike in that both can denote obligation. OE *āgan* with a *to*-infinitive, however, is limited to the rendering of Latin *debere* in the *Lindisfarne Gospels*.[25] On this basis OE *āgan* can be said to be more limited in its collocation or textual distribution than *habban*. This tendency may be the same in OS and OHG because OS *ēgan* is rarely found with *giwald*, and OHG *Tatian* uses *giwalt* with *haben*, not *eigun* for Latin *potestatem habere*. OE *āgan*, OHG *eigun*, and OS *ēgan* seem to be rather limited in their occurrences compared to *habban*, *haben*, and *hebbian*.

5. Conclusion

OE *geweald habban/āgan* is difficult to read as an idiom, because the meaning 'to have power' is entailed in its components. Instead it can qualify as a frequent collocation or a set phrase. The distribution of *habban* and *āgan* varies according to the genre of the texts. In OE verse *āgan* is a metrically preferable candidate for a set phrase for denoting the mightiness of the subject (e.g. God). OE *āgan* seems to be more limited in its occurrence than *habban*.

When we consider this phrase with the infinitive with respect to the question of auxiliation, OE *geweald habban*, and incidentally OS *giwald hebbian*, too, is a phrasal unit. OE *habban* with an object and a *to*-infinitive is at the first stage of auxiliation. They are different, however, from the original structure of ModE *have to*, so that syntactically they should be regarded as the use of a main verb phrase, even if they are semantically closer to the auxiliary 'can'. The occurrences in parenthetical clauses show the use as a main verb rather than the ellipsis of infinitival complement. Each given text should be examined stylistically, structurally, and contextually as well as semantically when we consider auxiliation. On this basis *āgan* is a more restricted verb than *habban*. This paper confirms the importance of examining the distribution of set phrases in Old English and Old Saxon texts.

7a. To possess as a duty or thing to be done. With object and dative inf. expressing what is to be done by the subject. (This is in origin a particular case of 2 b.) (First example: 971, Last example: 1892)
7c. With infinitive: To be under obligation, to be obliged; to be necessitated *to do something*. It forms a kind of Future of obligation or duty. (First example: 1579, Last example: 1892)
[25] E.g. Lk 7.41: Latin *unus debebat denarios quingentos*, OE (*Li*) *an ahte to geldanne penningas fif hūnd*, and ModE (*AV*) *the one ought fiue hundred pence*.

Sources

Bately, Janet M. (ed.)
    1986 — *The Anglo-Saxon Chronicle: A collaborative edition. Vol. 3: MS A.* Cambridge: D. S. Brewer.

Behaghel, Otto (ed.)
    1933 — *Heliand und Genesis.* 5th edition. Halle (Saale): Max Niemeyer.

Clubb, Merrel D. (ed.)
    1925 — *Christ and Satan. An Old English poem.* New Haven: Yale University Press.

Cook, Albert S. (ed.)
    1900 — *The Christ of Cynewulf: A poem in three parts.* Boston: Ginn & Company [repr. New York: AMS Press, 1973].

Crawford, Samuel J. (ed.)
    1922 — *The Old English version of the Heptateuch.* EETS, o.s. 160. London: Oxford University Press.

Griffiths, Bill (ed.)
    1994 — *Alfred's Metres of Boethius*, 2nd ed. Pinner: Anglo-Saxon Books.

The Holy Bible, King James Version: A reprint of the edition of 1611
    2005 — Peabody: Henderickson Publishers.

Klaeber, Frederick (ed.)
    2008 — *Klaeber's Beowulf and the Fight at Finnsburg.* 4th ed. by Robert D. Fulk, Robert E. Bjork & John D. Niles. Toronto: University of Toronto Press. [1st ed. 1922].

Liebermann, Felix (ed.)
    1903-1916 — *Die Gesetze der Angelsachsen.* 3 vols. Tübingen: Niemeyer [Repr. Aalen: Scientia, 1960].

Plummer, Charles. (ed.)
    1892 — *Two of the Saxon Chronicles parallel: with supplementary extracts from the others. A Revised Text.* 2 vols. Oxford: Clarendon Press [repr. 1952].

Sievers, Eduard (ed.)
    1892 — *Tatian.* Paderborn: Ferdinand Schöningh [repr. 1966].

Skeat, Walter W. (ed.)
    1871-1887 — *The Gospel according to St. Matthew, St. Mark, St. Luke and St. John.* Cambridge: Cambridge University Press. [Repr. in 2 vols. Darmstadt: Wissenschaftliche Buchgesellschaft, 1970].

Dictionaries

DOE — *Dictionary of Old English*, eds. Angus Cameron, Ashley Crandell Amos & Antonette diPaolo Healey. 2009 University of Toronto Press. <http://www.doe.utoronto.ca/>

DOEWC — *Dictionary of Old English Web Corpus,* eds. Antonette diPaolo Healey, John Price Wilkin & Xin Xiang. Toronto, 2009. <http://www.doe.utoronto.ca/pages/pub/web-corpus.html>

Hall, J. R. Clark
1960 — *A concise Anglo-Saxon dictionary*. 4th edition with a supplement by H. D. Meritt. Cambridge: Cambridge University Press [many reprints].

OED2 — *The Oxford English Dictionary*, 2nd edition in 20 volumes, ed. John A. Simpson & Edmund S. C. Weiner. Oxford: Oxford University Press, 1989 [incorporates the *Supplement* in 4 vols. ed. Robert W. Burchfield, 1972-1986].

References

Callaway, Morgan
1918 — *Studies in the syntax of the Lindisfarne Gospels*. Baltimore: Johns Hopkins Press.

Capek, Michael J.
1970 — "A note on formula development in Old Saxon", *Modern Philology* 67: 357-363.

Cook, Albert S.
1902 — "An unsuspected bit of Old English verse", *Modern Language Notes* 17: 13-20.

Mitchell, Bruce
1969 — "Postscript on Bede's *Mihi Cantare Habes*", *Neuphilologische Mitteilungen* 70: 369-380.
1985 — *Old English syntax*. 2 vols. Oxford: Clarendon Press.

Nunberg, Geoffrey -- Ivan A. Sag -- Thomas Wasow
1994 — "Idioms", *Language* 70: 491-538.

Ono, Shigeru
1989 — *On Early English syntax and vocabulary*. Tokyo: Nan'un-do.

Parry, Milman
1930 — "Studies in the epic technique of oral verse-making. I. Homer and Homeric Style", *Harvard Studies in Classical Philology* 41: 73-147.

Robinson, Fred C. (ed.)
1994 — *The editing of Old English*. Oxford: Blackwell.

Sugawara, Kazutake
1984 — "Der Infinitiv und die Präposition *te* Heliad", *Bulletin of Miyagi University of Education* 19: 1-7 [in Japanese].

Tuso, Joseph F.
1968 — "An analysis and glossary of dialectal synonymy in the *Corpus*, *Lindisfarne*, and *Rushworth Gospels*", *Linguistics* 43: 89-118.

Ushida, Kounin
1986 — "Zur Übersetzungsgeschichte von lat. 'Virtus' im Althochdeutschen", in: *Chukyo University Bulletin of the Faculty of Liberal Arts* 27: 117-143 [in Japanese].

An etymological analysis of shell nouns

Annette Mantlik (Heidelberg, Germany)

Abstract

This paper presents a collation and systematic analysis of the etymology of shell nouns and relates the results to the etymology of the overall Present-Day English lexicon. The primary question in this investigation is whether shell nouns, some of which belong to the most frequently used items in Present-Day English across registers and discourse domains (cf. Schmid 1999: 111; 2000: 42; Davies and Gardner 2010), deviate from the overall etymological composition of Present-Day English vocabulary, thus forming a sub-set, or whether the group of 670 shell nouns mirrors the overall etymological composition of the English lexicon. It will be shown that shell nouns do indeed form a sub-set of the lexicon in which borrowed material (77 percent of the 670 shell nouns) is strongly overrepresented in comparison to the overall etymological composition of the English vocabulary. This supports the claim made in Mantlik (forthcoming) that shell-noun-constructions are an instance of structural borrowing which slowly became integrated into the English language from around 1220 onwards. The first part of this paper briefly defines shell nouns; the second part presents the results of the etymological analysis, discussing both prototypical and doubtful cases in the data taken from the *Oxford English Dictionary Online (OED3)*; the third part of this study compares the results of the etymological survey on shell nouns to Scheler's (1977) study on the overall composition of the Present-Day English lexicon. The most important aspects are summarized in the conclusion.[1]

1. Introduction: shell nouns

The study of shell nouns (such as *problem, thing, issue, idea* used in a particular syntactic environment) first appeared in the late 1990s (term first used in Schmid 1998, 1999) and has risen in number in recent years.[2] This newly devoted attention is partly due to the high frequency of use[3] and the multi-functionality of shell nouns.[4]

---

[1] I would like to thank Hans Sauer, Gaby Waxenberger and Beatrix Busse for their invaluable comments on an earlier version of this paper.

[2] E.g. Hunston and Francis 2000; Ungerer and Schmid 2006; Aijmer 2007; Aktas and Cortes 2008; Caldwell 2009; Mihatsch 2009.

[3] Cf. Schmid 1999: 111, 2000: 42; Davies and Gardner 2010.
In their *Frequency dictionary of contemporary American English* (2010), Davies and Gardner list lexemes according to their frequency, including all word classes. In the following, the most frequently used abstract nouns are listed. The number in front of the noun indicates its rank in Davies and Gardner's frequency list, and the number following the noun counts its rank in a frequency list of abstract nouns only: (52)*time*(1), (84)*way*(2), (97)*thing*(3), (171)*problem*(4), (178)*part*(5), (181)*place*(6), (186)*case*(7), (197)*question*(8), (212)*point*(9), (231)*area*(10), (236)*fact*(11), (240)*right*(12), (244)*job*(13), (247)*business*(14), (248)*issue*(15), (272)*power*(16), (277)*line*(17), (312)*idea*(18), (315)*information*(19), (347)*art*(20), (355)*result*(21), (357)*change*(22), (360)*reason*(23), (369)*moment*(24), (387)*age*(25), (389)*policy*(26), (414)*plan*(27), (417)*interest*(28), (421)*experience*(29), (428)*effect*(30), (452)*role*(31), (455)*effort*(32), (718)*concern*. Compare these American English data to those of Schmid's British English in the *Bank of English*: (1)*time*, (2)*way*, (3)*place*, (4)*part*, (5)*thing*, (6)*business*, (7)*case*, (8)*power*, (9)*point*, (10)*fact*, (11)*problem*, (12)*right*, (13)*job*, (14)*line*, (16)*interest*, (17)*area*, (18)*policy*, (21)*information*, (23)*idea*, (26)*moment*, (27)*age*, (29)*question*, (42)*result*, (43)*reason*,

Shell nouns are abstract nouns used in a particular syntactic environment and are thus functionally defined:

> Shell nouns make up an open-ended functionally defined class of abstract nouns that have, to varying degrees, the potential for being used as conceptual shells for complex, proposition-like pieces of information (Schmid 2000: 4).

In his corpus study in the British section of the *Bank of English* (COBUILD) – at the time of data retrieval amounting to 225 million words – Schmid identifies 670 abstract nouns as being used as shell nouns (cf. Schmid 2000: 41). What makes these 670 abstract nouns shell nouns is the simple fact that they can be inserted in one or more of the following constructions:

Type A)

(1) abstract noun + BE + *that*-clause

The Elizabethan's chief **concern was that** the present would soon merge in the past and be gone. (s.v. *will*, v^1., *OED3*, 1918, *Cornh. Mag.* June 569, emphasis AM)

(2) abstract noun + BE + *to*-infinitive clause

The first **decision** we took **was to** ask individual viewers and listeners for their opinions. (s.v. *viewer*, n., *OED3*, 1977, Rep. comm. *Future of Broadcasting* i. 3, emphasis AM)

Type B)

(3) abstract noun + *that*-clause

Mr. Justice Stephen's recent **decision that** cremation is a legal proceeding has stirred the Cremation Society of England to be up and doing (s.v. *cremation*, n., *OED3*, 1884, *Pall Mall Gaz.* 7 Mar. 3/2, emphasis AM)

(4) abstract noun + *to*-infinitive clause

He made a feeble **attempt to** restrain the intolerant zeal of the House of Commons. (s.v. *attempt*, n., *OED3*, 1849, Macaulay, *Hist. Eng.* I. 177, emphasis AM)

The crucial point about these constructions is that a link of 'experiential identity', defined as "two or more separate linguistic elements contribut[ing] to the formation of one thought" (Schmid 2000: 29), is established between the shell noun and the shell content, i.e. between the noun and the postmodifying clause. In type A), the grammatical link between the shell noun and the complementing clause is established by a form of the copula (cf. Schmid 1999: 114). In type B), "[...] the

---

(44)*change*, (46)*experience*, (49)*issue*, (50)*effect*, (56)*art*, (58)*plan*, (111)*effort* (cf. Schmid 2000: 383-407).

[4] Cf. Schmid 2000: 301-376; 1999: 117-129; Furthmann 2006; Rundell 2010.

shell content is expressed by a clause that functions syntactically as a postmodifier which stands in what has traditionally been called an appositive relation to the head of the NP realized by the shell noun" (Schmid 1999: 114). Shell-noun-constructions of type B) are more difficult to identify than their type A) counterparts since they need to be distinguished from, for example, uses with relative *that*-clauses, etc. The criterion for testing a type B) construction for its shell-nounhood is the insertability of a form of the copula BE between shell noun and complementing clause: if this insertion renders a grammatical sentence without altering its meaning, the construction classifies as a shell-noun-construction (cf. Schmid 2000: 343, Mantlik forthcoming).

There have been various investigations on the functions of shell nouns,[5] on their semantics (cf. Schmid 2000: 308-328), but hardly any on the historical development of shell nouns.[6] The present paper aims at partly filling this gap in respect to the etymological exploration of shell nouns.

2. Methodology

While it holds true that "[o]ne of the most obvious characteristics of Present-Day English is the [...] mixed character of its vocabulary [...] [and] more than half of its vocabulary is derived from Latin" (Baugh and Cable 2002: 11), a question unanswered yet is whether this statement also holds true for shell nouns. Apart from tracing the etymology of shell nouns per se, the interesting question about this enterprise is thus whether and to what extent shell nouns mirror the etymological composition of the overall Present-Day English lexicon. A first step is hence the collation of etymological information on shell nouns; in a second step the etymology of shell nouns is compared to the etymological composition of the English lexicon as such.

In order to explore the origins of shell nouns, etymological information was retrieved from the *Oxford English Dictionary Online* (henceforth *OED3* <http://www.oed.com>) for the complete set of 670 abstract nouns identified as shell nouns in Schmid (2000: 41). The etymological information was retrieved from the etymology section in the entry of the respective noun; in those cases where two or more entries exist for one form, all the entries were checked and listed. In some of these cases, an entry/ entries could be excluded: entries which refer to a concrete entity/ concept, and entries that designate an entity/ concept the use of which is obsolete (for they cannot be the source of the noun which in Present-Day English is used as a shell noun). Here are the instances in which either case was encountered:

---

[5] Cf. e.g. Schmid 2000: 301-376; 1999: 117-129; Furthmann 2006; Rundell 2010; J. Flowerdew 2010, L. Flowerdew 2004, 2008; Mahlberg 2005.

[6] As exceptions, Schmid 1997, on the historical development and present-day use of the noun *idea*, and Mantlik (forthcoming), a full-scale survey and analysis of the diachrony of 670 shell nouns, have to be mentioned.

- entries referring to a concrete entity/ concept (45):

> adage(2)[7] art(2) case(3) cheek(2) cure(5, 6) deal(3) fear(2) folly(2) gall(3) gamble(2) gripe(2) hope(2) law(3) line(1, 4) link(3) marvel(2) pain(2) part(2) permit(2) place(2) point(3) power(2) pressure(2) pride(2) race(2, 3, 4, 7) retort(1) room(3) rule(2) rush(2) scheme(2) scope(3) shock(1, 2, 5) snag(2, 3, 4) spot(2) stand(2) step(2) stipulation(2) tactic(2) target(2) test(2, 3, 4) theory(2) thing(2) thrill(4) twist(3) wish(2)

- entries the use of which is obsolete (41):

> betting(2) catch(2, 3) cure(2, 3, 4) demand(2) doubt(2) dream(1) gripe(3, 4, 5) insight(2,3) job(3) law(2) line(3) longing(2) manoeuvre(1) maxim(2, 3) need(2) occasion(2) outcome(2) ploy(1) point(2) prize(3) proviso(2) query(1) quest(2) race(5) reading(2) reason(2) relief(1) request(2) scope(1) shock(4) site(1) skill(2) solace(2) space(2) spot(2) stance(1) symbol(2) tip(6) twist(2) warning(2) way(2)

These entries are not taken into consideration for the analysis. It has to be mentioned explicitly that the etymological information provided in the *OED3* is the basis in the present study.

3. Results

In the first step of the etymological analysis four categories – because this is what the etymology sections of the nouns in the *OED3* feature – are established: nouns of Germanic origin, loanwords, word-formation products, and, as a fourth group containing the remainder, 'undetermined' as the 'catch-all' category for those cases which do not fit in one of the other categories and/ or remain unspecified in the *OED3*. This preliminary categorization of the 670 shell nouns in four classes yields the following results, as shown in Table 1:

Table 1: Etymological survey of 670 shell nouns: four categories

category	number of nouns	percentage
Germanic origin	48	7.16 %
loanword	450	67.16 %
word-formation product	135	20.15 %
undetermined	37	5.52 %

As the table shows, the proportion of native nouns with nearly 7.2 percent is very low; 5.5 percent of the nouns remain 'undetermined'; word-formation products account about 20 percent of the material while the lion's share – more than two-

---

[7] The number in brackets specifies which of the entries in the *OED3* is referred to. In this study, the numbering of the *OED3* is retrained throughout and provided directly after the respective noun in brackets.

thirds of the nouns (67 percent) – is supplied by loanwords. The vast amount of shell nouns are thus loanwords.

This categorization can be further refined by drawing up sub-categories of the four classes, particularly for the class of loanwords and the class of word-formation products. The aim of the next sections is to, first, discuss the members of the four different categories, and, second, to classify the word-formation products according to their root/base/morphemes[8] so as to distribute them to the classes 'Germanic origin' and 'loanword' (and, if necessary 'undetermined') in order to get a full-scale picture of the etymological distribution of shell nouns.

3.1 Germanic origin

The 48 nouns of Germanic origin amongst the 670 shell nouns include the following 41 nouns that are clearly labelled 'Germanic' in the *OED3*:

answer belief bitterness burden cheek clout(1) dream(2) fear(1) freedom gall(1, 2) gossip ground guilt heart hope(1) hurdle key law(1) longing(1) need(1) oath right room(1, 2) shame sin sorrow spot(1) step(1) strength tale thing(1) thought threat time truth twist(1) warning(1) way(1) wisdom wit wonder

Problematic cases are *dream(2)* which is "not recorded in OE; but pointing to an OE word" (s.v. *dream*, n.[2], *OED3*), and *twist(1)* which is attested in Old English but is only supposed to have a Germanic stem (s.v. *twist*, n.[1], *OED3*). The following forms are included in the class as well: a direct loan from Scandinavian: *snag(1)*; direct loans from Old Norse: *anger, skill(1)*; and a direct loan from (Middle) Low German: *luck*. The nouns *flaw(1, 2), link(1, 2)*, and *knack(1, 2)* are also included: *flaw(1)* is Old Norse while *flaw(2)* is "not found until the 16th century, possibly < OE" (s.v. *flaw*, n.[2], *OED3*) but is nevertheless likely to be Germanic; for *link(1, 2)* it is the other way round: its first entry is Germanic, its second entry Old Norse; finally, *knack(1)* is of "Germanic 'echoic origin'" according to the *OED* etymologists (s.v. *knack*, n.[1], *OED3*) while the origin of *knack(2)* is obscure but the noun is nevertheless attested in Old English.

3.2 Loanwords

In the category 'loanword', several sub-categories emerge that can be distinguished according to their path of borrowing: some of the loanwords prove to be direct loans (from French, Latin, Italian, Ancient Greek or other languages), others display a history of borrowing via two or more languages as, for example, the noun *problem* which is ultimatley an Ancient Greek word that was borrowed into Latin, French and English consecutively (s.v. *problem*, n., *OED3*). Thus, in the category 'loanword' different cases have to be accounted for (cf. Durkin 2009: 132-140). It is important to note that the etymological analysis presented here goes back as far

---

[8] For the terminology see e.g. Schmid 2011: 47.

as possible and classifies a loanword according to its ultimate origin (and not according to its immediate origin, i.e. the language from which English borrowed the lexeme).[9]

A first sub-category of loanwords consists of direct loans (e.g. *bonus* < Latin, *offer* < French, *hypothesis* < Ancient Greek, *scenario* < Italian), i.e. cases in which English borrowed the noun directly from another language.

The following groups of direct loans can be distinguished:

– direct loans from Latin (89):

absurdity(1; 2 via French) agenda anxiety area aspect assumption audacity bonus caveat compensation complication concept confidence connection consensus conspiracy context conviction corollary credo crux decency delusion demonstration dictum difficulty directive distortion edict effect equation era estimate expectation explanation fact fallacy fate formula foundation frustration ideal impact imperative impetus implication impulse incentive indicator indignation infererence injunction innovation instinct invitation irritation joke justification lament limitation mandate manifestation nerve norm notion part(1) passion potential prediction presupposition pretext priviledge project propensity prospect proviso(1) rationale(1, 2) recipe sensation signal significance speculation stamina stipulation(1) success supposition temerity tenet testimony

– direct loans from French (55):

account achievement advantage agreement amendment annoyance appeal appointment arrangement assurance campaign claim cliché comfort constraint coup courage courtesy debacle delight demand(1) disadvantage doubt(1) duty effort effrontery enterprise excuse failure folly(1) franchise grief grievance incapacity judgement novelty nuisance offer plan pleasure procedure proof punishment purpose request(1) reward role routine ruse shock(3) surmise surprise technique trouble view

– direct loans from Ancient Greek (7):

catastrophe characteristic criterion hypothesis nous orthodoxy thesis

Other direct loans from less strongly represented donor languages include direct loans from Italian (*gambit, scenario*). The Celtic element in shell nouns is minute which is also true for the overall lexicon (cf. Sauer 2000: 153): Gaelic *slogan*, and Scots *gumption* are the only two Celtic cases amongst shell nouns.

In a few other cases of direct borrowing it is not clear which language English borrowed from: a loan from Latin or Greek (*myth*), a loan from French or Italian (*disgust*), a loan from Spanish or French (*guarantee*). In a number of cases it is not clear whether the noun was borrowed from French or from Latin:

---

[9] For an approach that follows this principle see, e.g., Scheler 1977: 73.

An etymological analysis of shell nouns 139

- loans from French or Latin (16):

> *anticipation declaration determination gratitude importance interpretation news*[10] *pretence projection site(2) situation solution specialty version vision vocation*

The total number of direct loans is 172. A second sub-category of loanwords contains indirect loans, i.e. cases where the item was borrowed via two or more languages (e.g. *affirmation*: Latin > French > English, *problem*: Ancient Greek > Latin > French > English).
The groups in which one 'intermediate' language was involved are:

- loans from Latin via French (218):

> *ability accident accusation act action adage admission advice affirmation age allegation alternative ambition announcement application appreciation apprehension argument art(1) assertion asset assignment authority bargain beauty benefit brief calculation capacity case(1, 2) cause certainty challenge chance change charge charm choice coincidence comment commission complaint compromise compulsion conception concession conclusion condition confession confirmation conjecture consequence consideration consolation contention contract(1) contradiction contribution convention courage crime crusade cure(1) curiosity custom danger deception decision declaration decree defence definition description desire determination destiny difference disposition distinction doctrine effect error essence event evidence example exception experience extent facility factor faith fault feature fiction flexibility function fury grace habit illusion image impression improvement inclination indication initiative inspiration instruction intelligence intent intention intimation intuition issue joy legacy legend lesson licence manoeuvre(2) marvel(1) maxim(1) measure merit message miracle mission moment motion motive necessity notice notification objection objective obligation observation obsession obstacle occasion(1) offence opinion opportunity option order pain(1) permission perspective persuasion petition pity plea pledge position possibility power(1) precaution precept predicament preface preference prejudice premise premonition preoccupation pressure(1) presumption principle priority probability proclamation promise proposition proverb provision provocation question rage reality reason(1) recognition(1, 2) recollection reflection region remedy reservation resistance resolution response restriction revelation revolution ritual rule(1) rumour satisfaction secret sentiment sequel sign solace(1) space(1) stage subject suggestion superstition suspicion task temptation terror test(1) tradition trick triumph verdict virtue vow*

This class includes two cases which are slightly problematic: 1) cases in which the Latin assumed source is not attested, e.g. "*bargain* < Old French *bargaine*, [...] pointing to a late Latin form **barcāne-um, -a*" (s.v. *bargain*, n.,

---

[10] On *news*, the *OED3* says: "Etymology: Spec. use of plural of *new*, n., after Middle French *nouvelles* (see *novel*, n.), or classical Latin *nova* new things [...]" (s.v. *news*, n., *OED3*). It could thus convincingly be argued that *news* is a loan formation (personal communication, H. Sauer).

OED3), or *coincidence* "< French *coïncidence*, Latin type **coincidentia*" (s.v. *coincidence*, n., *OED3*), and in which it is not entirely clear whether a specific Latin root can be assumed or whether only principles were imitated,[11] e.g. for *courage*: "a common Romanic word, answering to a Latin type" (s.v. *courage*, n., *OED3*), similarly e.g. for *trick* (s.v. *trick*, n., *OED3*); 2) cases, in which it is unclear whether they have been borrowed from Latin via French or directly from Latin (*declaration, promise, crusade, superstition, task*).

– loans from Ancient Greek via Latin (22):

allegory analysis anomaly basis diagnosis dilemma drama energy enigma ethos idea irony method paranoia phenomenon place(1) prognosis scheme(1) tactic(1) theory(1) topic zeal

Two intermediate languages are involved in the following cases:

– loans from Ancient Greek via Latin and French (19):

analogy aphorism axiom disaster dogma fantasy logic metaphor pact paradox period philosophy policy(1, 2) problem prophecy scandal symbol(1) theme tragedy

There are a number of other indirect loans with one or two intermediate language(s) which are so few in number that they are grouped according to the language which provided the ultimate source:

– Ancient Greek loans via different paths:

  (a) loans from Ancient Greek via French: *stereotype strategy*

  (b) loan from Ancient Greek via Italian: *scope(2)*

Latin loans via different paths:

  (a) loan from Latin via Italian: *motto*

  (b) loan from Latin via Italian via French: *travesty risk attitude compliment*

  (c) loans from French and Latin: *deduction quest(1) recommendation*

  (d) loan in sense I and II from Latin, in sense III from Latin via French: *programme*[12]

– Romance loanwords (French, Italian, Spanish):

  (a) loan from Italian via French: *contrast disgrace stance(2)*

  (b) loan from French via Italian: *compliment*

  (c) loan from Latin in branch I), and from French in branch II): *perception*

---

[11] Arguably, these instances could be seen as cases of *Lehnbildung* (cf. Gneuss 1955: 1, 31-37).
[12] For reasons of space, the different meanings for *coup, mystery, perception, programme,* and *story* are provided in Table 6.1 in the appendix.

Finally, there are two nouns that were borrowed twice in the history of the English language:

- borrowed twice via different paths:

    (a) in Old English: Ancient Greek via Latin, in Middle English: Latin via French: *talent*

    (b) in early use: Ancient Greek via Latin, in modern use: French or directly Latin: *symptom*

For other nouns, their entries in the *OED3* have to be accounted for individually: one form is a direct loan while the other is an indirect one (*mystery(1)*: L < Gr, *mystery(2)*: L; *story(1)*: F < L, *story(2)*: L; *coup(1)*: F, *coup(3)*: F < L < Greek.

The number of indirect loans is 278, and is thus much higher than the number of direct loans (172). Taking all loanwords together, the total number is 450 which accounts for 67.16 percent of the shell nouns.

3.3 Word-formation products

3.3.1 Classification according to word-formation process

The focus is now on word-formation products which are, in a first step, regarded as the third major class but will be further refined below. The members of this class are grouped according to the type of word-formation process they are formed by (conversion,[13] suffixation, prefixation, compounding), yielding several subgroups of which suffixation and conversion are the most frequent. Two examples of cases where two or more word-formation processes were at work are: (1) *yearning*: *yearn*(noun) < *yearn*(verb) + *–ing*(suffix), classified as suffixation in the *OED3*; (2) *unwillingness*: OE *willende*(adjective) + *un-*(prefix), then *unwilling*(adjective) + *-ness*(suffix), classified as suffixation in the *OED3*. Such cases are – in this initial categorization – categorized according to the last word-formation process that was at work.

- conversion from the verb (40):

aim approach attempt bid call catch(1) concern dread drive endeavour fight gamble(1) grumble guess hint mistake move permit(1) practice praise protest puzzle remark(1) reply resolve result retort(2) stand(1) struggle talk thrill(3) trend urge whisper wish(1) worry whinge

Other cases of conversion include conversion from the adjective (*pride(1)*, *attribute*), and conversion from both the verb and the adjective (*disquiet*).

---

[13] For the terminology and discussion of different approaches to the word-formation process of conversion see e.g. Schmid 2011: 183-200.

- compounding (10):

> *breakthrough catchphrase downside drawback leeway nightmare payoff standpoint viewpoint willpower*

- prefixation (23):

> *counterclaim countermeasure disinclination forecast foresight inability insight(1) misapprehension miscalculation misconception misfortune misjudgement misperception nonsense outcome(1) preconception precondition presentiment reaction reassurance uncertainty unknown upshot*

- suffixation (59):

> *acknowledgement amazement assessment astonishment awareness betting blessing business capability commitment denial disappointment disclosure discovery*[14] *discrepancy eagerness feeling finding generalization happiness inconcistency inducement inevitability inkling insistence keenness knowledge likelihood motivation oddity peculiarity pronouncement proposal quibble readiness reading(1) realization reasoning reckoning refinement refusal reluctance reminder requirement resentment responsibility ruling sadness statement teaching tendency thinking truism understanding undertaking unwillingness weakness willingness yearning*

Other cases of nouns that underwent a word-formation process are: ploy(3) (clipping from *employ*, *ploy(2)* is probably a variant of *plea, n.*) and two cases in which two word-formation processes intermingled: *grudge* (conversion from verb or variant of *grutch*, n.²), *hunch* (sense 1) conversion from verb, 2) reduced from 'hunch-backed').

These 135 word-formation products can now be further segmented and then distributed to the categories 'Germanic origin' and 'borrowing' (and, if necessary, 'undetermined') once segmented into affixes and base (for suffixation)/root (for prefixation), and morphemes (for conversion and compounding).

3.3.2 Classification according to root/base/morphemes

In order to answer the question of whether the word-formation products consist of native or borrowed material, a segmentation and consecutive classification of the elements involved has been conducted. In the classification, the origin of the root/base/morphemes are decisive, not the origin of the affixes. The results of this analysis are summarized in Table 2; Tables 6.3 to 6.6 in the appendix contain the

---

[14] *Discovery* is, according to the *OED3*, derived from the verb: "< *discover* v., apparently after the analogy of *recover*, *recovery*. [...] Compare *deliver-y*, also *battery*, *flattery*, which associate themselves with *batter*, *flatter*, though not actually derived from these" (s.v. *discovery*, n., *OED3*). However, in this paper, it is treated as a quasi-suffixation with a suffix-like item –*y*, since, to treat *discovery* as conversion (no alteration of form) is even less plausible.

information retrieved from the *OED3* according to which the classification has been conducted.

Table 2: Origins of the roots/bases/morphemes involved in the word-formation processes

	Germanic	loanword	undetermined	overall	percentage
conversion	15	20	5	40	29.63 %
compounding	4	1	5	10	7.4 %
prefixation	5 + 1(ON[15])	17	0	23	17.04 %
suffixation	22 + 2(ON) +1(Scand.)	29	5	59	43.7 %
other	0	2	1	3	2.22 %
in sum	46 + 3(ON) +1(Scand.)	69	16	135	
overall	50	69	16	135	
percentage	37.04 %	51.11 %	11.85 %		99.99 %

3.3.2.1 Conversion

An etymological analysis of the verbs from which the 40 nouns referred to above are derived, shows that in thirteen cases, the noun is derived from a verb of Germanic origin. These nouns are:

> *bid call drive fight gamble(1) hint stand(1) trend whisper wish(1) worry whinge*; *guess*[Scandinavian]

Another seventeen nouns are derived from verbs that are loanwords, predominantly of Latin origin:

> *aim approach attempt catch(1) concern endeavour move permit(1) practice praise protest remark(1) reply resolve result retort(2) urge*

In five instances, two or more processes took place before the noun was derived from the verb: *pride*(n) is derived from the adjective *proud*(adj.) which is a Latin

---

[15] ON stands for Old Norse, Scand. for Scandinavian.

loanword that was borrowed into English via French; *attribute*(n) is either derived from the respective adjective or, possibly, directly borrowed from Latin or from Latin via French; *disquiet*(n) is derived from either the adjective or the verb with the adjective *disquiet* being a word-formation product (prefix *dis-*, of Latin origin) with the adjective *quiet* as a loanword from Latin via French; the respective verb *disquiet* is apparently either a Latin loan or a derivative of the adjective; *thrill*(n^1) is derived from *thrill*(v^1) which is derived from *thirl*(v^1) which is of Germanic origin; *mistake*(n), finally, is derived from the verb *mistake*(v) which is a word-formation product (prefixation) and said to be 'partly after Scandinavian'. Five nouns in the class 'deverbal noun' remain in the category 'undetermined', these are: *dread*, *grumble*, *puzzle*, *struggle*, *talk*. In the class of conversion, there are fifteen Germanic, twenty borrowed, and five undetermined elements.

3.3.2.2 Compounding

Four of the ten compounds (*breakthrough, drawback, leeway, nightmare*) are of Germanic origin, that is, all their constituents are Germanic. *Breakthrough* and *drawback* are furthermore compounds from phrasal verbs. Another phrasal verb is *payoff*, combining a Latin base (*pay*) with a Germanic affix (*off*), thus a member of the class 'undetermined'. Three other compounds remain in the category 'undetermined' as well because they also combine Germanic and loan elements (i.e. are hybrid formations) and additionally have experienced a word-formation process (*viewpoint*: *view(n)*: F < L, *point*(n): F < L, 'probably also partly < *point*(v^1); *standpoint*: *stand*(n): Germanic, *point*(n): F < L, 'probably also partly < *point*(v^1); *willpower*: *will*(n): Germanic, *power*(n): F < L). For one noun (*downside*) it is unclear how it was derived. One noun consists of borrowed material altogether (*catchphrase*: < *catch*(v): F < L, and *phrase*: L < Greek) and thus belongs to the class of 'loanwords'.

3.3.2.3 Prefixation

A survey of the prefixes involved yields the following results: of the eleven prefixes, five are Germanic (*mis-, up-, fore-, out-, un-*), and six are Latin prefixes (*non-, dis-, re-, counter-, pre-, in-*). A survey on the distribution and number of occurrence of the different prefixes supplies eighteen cases consisting of borrowed material, and six cases consisting of native material. Typically, borrowed prefixes are attached to borrowed roots (e.g. *reassurance*: *re-*: F < L, *assurance*(n): F; *countermeasure*: *counter-*: F < L, *measure*(n): F < L; *nonsense*: *non-*: F < L, *sense*(n): F < L), but there are also cases in which a prefix and a root of different origin are combined (e.g. *mis-*: Germanic,[16] in six compounds: *misapprehension, miscalculation, misconception, misfortune, misjudgement, misperception*, in all of which the root is a Latin loan borrowed via French). Another case of mixed

---

[16] Germanic *mis-* was later reinforced from French *mes-*.

material are the prefixations with *in-*[17], and *un-*, where the Latin *in-* represents Germanic *un-* (*inability, insight(1)*), while Germanic *un-* (*uncertainty, unknown*) coexists. Both prefixes combine with native and with borrowed material: *in-*: Latin, *ability*(n): F < L; *sight*(n): Germanic; *un-*: Germanic, *unknown*: *know*(v): Germanic; *certainty*(n): F < L. The other Germanic prefixes (*up-, fore-, out-*) combine with native roots: *unknown, upshot, foresight, forecast, outcome*. The Latin prefixes (*pre-, counter-, re-, dis-, non-*) combine with borrowed roots (e.g. *conception, condition, sentiment; sense; inclination*: all F < L). Of the prefixations, six are hence classified as Germanic and seventeen as borrowed material.

3.3.2.4 Suffixation

With the results of suffixation, the composition of Germanic versus loan elements is less pronounced: there are twenty-five cases in which the base is Germanic:

> *acknowledgement awareness blessing business feeling finding happiness keenness knowledge likelihood oddity readingess reading(1) reckoning reminder sadness teaching thinking truism understanding weakness willingness yearning*; including two Old Norse cases (*undertaking, likelihood)* and one Scandinavian (*oddity*)

There are twenty-nine words containing borrowed material:

> *assessment capability commitment denial disappointment disclosure discovery discrepancy eagerness generalization inconsistency inducement inevitability insistence motivation peculiarity pronouncement proposal quibble realization refinement refusal reluctance requirement resentment responsibility ruling statement tendency*

Generally, borrowed suffixes combine with borrowed lexemes while Germanic suffixes combine with Germanic lexemes in the instances at hand. Five cases are undetermined because they contain several different processes or are simply of unkown origin: two suffixations with suffix *–ment*: *amazement, astonishment* (e.g. *amazement*: < *amaze*(v); *amaze*(v): prefixation "< *a-* prefix? intensive + *maze* n."; *a-* prefix: Germanic; *maze*(n): "Probably < the same base as *amaze* v.; further etymology uncertain" [s.v. *maze*, n. and *amaze*, v., *OED3*]); three suffixations with suffix *–ing*: *betting, inkling, reasoning* (e.g. *inkling*: < *inkle*(v) – 'Origin unascertained' [s.v. *inkle*, v., *OED3*]). Overall, in the class of suffixations, there are twenty-five Germanic, twenty-eight borrowed, and five undetermined items.

---

[17] On *in-* prefix[3] the *OED3* says: "the Latin *in-*, cognate with Greek α-, αν-, Common Germanic *un-* [...]" (s.v. *in-* prefix[3], *OED3*), while on *un-* prefix[1] it states: "Etymology: Representing Old English *un-*, [...] Latin *in-* (*im-, il-, ir-, i-*)" (s.v. *un-* prefix[1], *OED3*)". 'Representing', which appears to be the crucial aspect here, is thus likely to mean 'semantically equivalent' and will be understood this way in the present paper.

3.3.2.5 Other word-formation processes

Three nouns, having experienced other word-formation processes, are classified as loans (*ploy(3)*, *grudge*) and undetermined (*hunch*).

3.4 'Undetermined'

Having dealt with the clear-cut cases, there still remains a considerable number of nouns that are 'undetermined', i.e. their etymology is somewhat dubious.[18] Nevertheless, some general tendencies can be made out, so as to arrive at different sub-groups in the class of 'undetermined' items.

Some nouns cannot be assigned to any of the categories mentioned above (i.e. Germanic origin, loanword, word-formation product) since they incorporate different strands of development and/ or contain different sources in their etymology. Cases in this category are:

acceptance command criticism information object point(1) qualification regret relief(2) report reposte similarity tip(1, 2, 3, 4, 5) venture[19]

These nouns either consist partly of loan elements and are partly the product of a word-formation process, e.g. *acceptance* for which the *OED3* claims "probably partly F[rench], partly word-formation < verb" (s.v. *acceptance*, n., *OED3*), or *qualification* for which the information is "F < L and word-formation < verb" (s.v. *qualification*, n., *OED3*), or consist of Germanic material in combination with a word-formation process (*deal(1)*, *lie(1)*, *rush(1)*).

Another prominent subgroup of the class of 'undetermined' contains nouns which are explicitly labeled 'undetermined' (although not in this terminology) by the *OED* etymologists with phrases like 'of unknown origin; attested in OE' for *curse* (s.v. *curse*, n., *OED3*), or "Origin lost" for *conundrum* (s.v. *conundrum*, n., *OED3*), or "Origin unknown" for *plot* (s.v. *plot*, n., *OED3*). This type of unspecificity applies for the following nouns:

bet boast blow(1) clue conundrum critique curse goal gripe(1) handicap job(2) plot subtext target(1)

Yet another group of 'undetermined' comprises cases in which a noun is a variant or respelling of another lexeme which, in many cases, is a loanword. This is the

---

[18] Compare Scheler 1977: 71 and Durkin 2009: 69-73 for dealing with lexemes the etymology of which remains doubtful.
[19] For the exact etymology of these nouns see Table 6.2 in the appendix.

case with, e.g. *query(2)* which is described as "Respelling of *quaere,* n., after the spelling conventions of English (in forms in *-y* perhaps after words in *-y* suffix[4])" (s.v. *query,* n[2]., *OED3*), while the etymology of *quaere* is "< classical Latin *quaere,* imperative singular of *quaerere* (in post-classical Latin also *querere*) to ask, inquire (see *queer,* v.[1]). For later spellings of the word see *query,* n.[2] and discussion at that entry" (s.v. *quaere,* n., *OED3*). Similar notes are found for *prize(1, 2), interest.* Another special case is *line(2),* which consists of two words that have coalesced, a Germanic and a Romanic stem (s.v. *line,* n.[2], *OED3*), also *race* which is Scandinavian (entry 1) and an Italian loan borrowed via French (entry 6). In sum, there are thirty-seven nouns in the category 'undetermined' plus sixteen items added from the word-formation products.

3.5 Summary of the results

The overall results of the etymological survey of all 670 shell nouns according to the information from the *OED3* are summarized in Table 3.

Nearly eight percent of the shell nouns remain undetermined in terms of etymology. Almost fifteen percent are Germanic nouns. More than seventy-seven percent of the 670 shell nouns are loanwords or consist of borrowed bases/roots/morphemes. The major proportion of shell nouns therefore consists of borrowed material. In fact, the proportion of borrowed material is five times as high as that of native material. This certainly is a noteworthy feature of the phenomenon of shell nouns.

Table 3: Etymological survey of 670 shell nouns: three categories

category	number of nouns	percentage
Germanic origin	98	14.62 %
loanword/ borrowed base/ root/ morphemes	519	77.46 %
undetermined	53	7.91 %

4. Comparison with the English lexicon

In his seminal analysis of the English vocabulary, Scheler (1977) draws on statistical analyzes conducted by Finkenstaedt, Wolff and Leisi (1973) "Ordered Profusion – Studies in Dictionaries and the English Lexicon" which is an etymological scrutiny of the *SOED* (1964), the data being saved in the *CD (The Computer Dictionary),* and compares them to the etymological data retrieved from the *ALD (The Advanced Learner's Dictionary of Current English* [1963]), and the

GSL (*A General Service List of English Words* [1953]). Scheler (1977) compares the percentage of material of Germanic, Romance, Latin, Ancient Greek, Celtic, and Anglo-Celtic origin, and that originating in other European and non-European languages in these sources (cf. Scheler 1977: 70-74).[20] In the etymological analysis of shell nouns, some of Scheler's categories do not emerge (other European, non-European languages and proper names) and are thus neglected; the Celtic element in shell nouns is minute so that this category can be neglected as well. The classes still relevant in comparison to Scheler's are hence: Germanic, Romance, Latin, Ancient Greek, and zero-etymology. Scheler's zero-etymology roughly equals what is called 'undetermined' in this paper:

> Da sind [...] die etym. nicht bestimmbaren Wörter, die unter dem Nenner Null-Etymologie zusammengefaßt [sind.] [...] Hinzu kommen die unsicheren oder nicht eindeutig bestimmbaren Etymologien [...] Dazu rechnen auch Fälle, bei denen wegen morphologischer und semantischer Identität die genaue Zuweisung innerhalb einer Sprachfamilie Schwierigkeiten bereitet. [...] Bei gelehrten Wörtern lat. Provenienz kann, falls Parallelformen im Französischen (*mots savants*) existieren, statt Direktentlehnung aus dem Lateinischen auch Entlehnung über das Französische in Frage kommen (Scheler 1977: 71).
>
> [There are those words whose etymology cannot be determined. They are subsumed under the label 'zero etymology'. [...] There are furthermore words with unascertained or not unambiguously determinable etymologies. [...] The latter include cases in which a clear-cut attribution to one branch of language is difficult due to the morphological and semantic identity of the words. [...] For learned Latin words for which French forms exist in French (*mots savants*) borrowing via French could have been possible instead of direct borrowing from French. (Scheler 1977: 71, translation AM)]

For the case last mentioned (direct or indirect loan from Latin or from Latin via French), Scheler adds: "Bei der Subsumierung unter der Sammelbezeichnung Germanisch bzw. Romanisch-Lateinisch verlieren solche Fälle ihre Problematik" (Scheler 1977: 71). ["Such cases become unproblematic when subsumed under the collective term 'Germanic' or 'Romance-Latin'." (Scheler 1977: 71, translation AM)]. In this paper, cases as these are listed separately but subsumed in the category 'loanword' and hence do not pose a problem either. As in Scheler (1977), forms borrowed from Scandinavian or Old Norse are merged in the category 'Germanic' (cf. Scheler 1977: 72). Romance, Latin and Ancient Greek have been subsumed in the category 'loanwords' in this paper.

The following table summarizes Scheler's (1977) findings on the etymological composition of the Present-Day English lexicon:

---

[20] For the exact differentiation and categorization see Scheler 1977: 72.

Table 4: Etymology of the English lexicon (figures taken from Scheler 1977: 72, classification slightly adapted and simplified)

	CED	%	ALD	%	GSL	%
Romance		30.23		37.49		38.20
Latin		28.29		22.05		9.59
Ancient Greek		5.32		1.59		0.25
Germanic		26.28		31.83		50.89
Celtic		0.43		0.32		0.025
other[21]		9.45		7.03		1.03

Added up, the overall percentage of loanwords (including 'Romance', 'Latin', and 'Greek' in Scheler's table) is 63.8 percent in the *CED*, 61.1 percent in the *ALD*, and 48 percent in the *GSL* (cf. Scheler 1977: 73). The Germanic part is 26.3 percent in the *CED*, 32 percent in the *ALD*, and 51 percent in the *GSL* (cf. Scheler 1977: 73). These percentages serve as a basis of the overall etymological composition of the Present-Day English lexicon and are compared to the etymological findings on shell nouns.

In the etymological analysis of 670 shell nouns it was shown that 77 percent of the shell nouns are loanwords, while only 15 percent of the nouns are of Germanic origin, and almost 8 percent remain undetermined.

Table 5: Comparison Present-Day English lexicon – shell nouns

	Present-Day English lexicon[22]			shell nouns
	CED	ALD	GSL	
loanwords	63.8 %	61.1 %	48 %	77.46 %
Germanic	26.28 %	31.83 %	50.89 %	14.62 %
undetermined/other[23]	9.88 %	7.35 %	1.055 %	7.91 %

---

[21] This category comprises what is split up in 'other European languages', 'non-European languages', 'zero-etymology', and 'proper names' in Scheler (1977: 72).

[22] The figures for Present-Day English are taken from Scheler 1977: 73. The column 'loanword' summarizes Scheler's Romance, Latin, and Ancient Greek.

[23] In columns 'CED', 'ALD', and 'GSL', 'undetermined' comprises what is split up in 'other European languages', 'non-European languages', 'zero-etymology', 'proper names' and 'Celtic' in Scheler 1977: 72.

In comparison to the overall etymological composition of Present-Day English, in the group of shell nouns, borrowed material is strongly overrepresented while native material is strongly underrepresented. It can thus be concluded that shell nouns form a sub-set of the Present-Day English lexicon with regard to their origin and etymology.

5. Conclusions

The etymological analysis of 670 shell nouns presented in this paper has shown that the vast majority of shell nouns, including an analysis of the roots/bases/morphemes involved in the 139 word-formation products, are loanwords/ contain borrowed material (77 percent), while only around fifteen percent of the nouns are of Germanic origin, and nearly eight percent remain undetermined. If these percentages are compared to the percentages on the overall etymological composition of the Present-Day English lexicon, it is striking that the group of shell nouns does not mirror the etymological composition of the Present-Day English vocabulary: it deviates considerably. In comparison to the overall etymological composition of Present-Day English, in the group of shell nouns, borrowed material is strongly overrepresented while native material is strongly underrepresented. It can thus be concluded that shell nouns form a sub-set of the Present-Day English lexicon with regard to their origin and etymology with a strong tendency to be non-native in origin. The etymological composition of the group of shell nouns corresponds to the dates of first attestation (in the *OED3*) of the 670 nouns (cf. Mantlik forthcoming). In Mantlik (forthcoming) it is argued that the phenomenon of shell-noun-constructions is a development starting in the Middle English period in the aftermath of massive foreign influence on the English language. All relevant factors indicate that shell-noun-constructions are an instance of structural borrowing from the Romance tradition (cf. Mantlik forthcoming). It is thus not surprising that the lion's share of shell nouns should consist of non-native material.

6. Appendix: Additional tables on word-formation
6.1 Nouns with different etymological strands

noun	different senses/etymology
coup(1)	"**Etymology:** In sense 1, < Old French *coup*, *cop*, *colp* blow: see *coup*, n.[3] (s.v. *coup*[1], n., *OED3*). Only sense 2 in this entry referring to an abstract notion: 'A fall, upset, overturn. Sc.'" (s.v. *coup*[1], n., *OED3*).
coup(3)	"**Etymology:** French *coup* /ku/ blow, stroke < Old French *colp* , *cop* = Provençal *colp*, *cop*, Italian *colpo* < late Latin *colpus* (Salic Law), *colapus* (Law of the Alemanns) blow, stroke, for Latin *colaphus* blow with the fist, cuff, < Greek κόλαφος cuff, buffet. Adopted in Middle English in a literal sense, and naturalized in pronunciation (see *coup*,

	n.¹); re-introduced in the 18th cent. in fig. sense, as a non-naturalized word, with modern French pronunciation (exc. that in English the vowel is made long); it also occurs in many French phrases and expressions borrowed in English." (s.v. *coup³*, n., *OED3*).
mystery(1)	"**Etymology:** < classical Latin *mystērium* secret, (plural) secret rites, in post-classical Latin also mystical or religious truth (Vetus Latina), (plural) Christian rites (late 2nd cent. in Tertullian), the Eucharist, the elements used in the Eucharist (4th cent.) < ancient Greek *μυστήριον* mystery, secret, (plural) secret rites, implements used in such rites, in Hellenistic Greek also secret revealed by God, mystical truth, Christian rite, sacrament, in Byzantine Greek also the elements used in the Eucharist (4th cent.), probably (compare also *μύστης mystes*, n.) < the base of *μύειν* to close (the lips or eyes), probably of imitative origin + *-τήριον*, suffix forming nouns. Influenced in sense also by Middle French *mistere* mystical significance (1174 in Old French; superseded by form *mystère* from the 18th cent. onwards), religious truth (*c*1240), Christian sacrament (13th cent.), secret rite of an ancient religion (15th cent.), something inexplicable or beyond human comprehension (1452)." (s.v. *mystery*¹, n., *OED3*).
mystery(2)	"**Etymology:** < post-classical Latin *misterium* duty, office, service (from 11th cent. in British sources), occupation, trade (from 13th cent. in British sources), guild (from 14th cent. in British sources), altered form of classical Latin *ministerium ministry*, n. by confusion with *mystērium mystery*, n.¹ (see discussion at that entry)." (s.v. *mystery*², n., *OED3*).
perception	"**Etymology:** In branch I. < classical Latin *perceptiōn-, perceptiō* action of receiving, collecting, action of taking possession, apprehension with the mind or senses, in post-classical Latin also receiving of the sacrament (4th or 5th cent.), levy, payment (14th cent. in British sources) < *percept-* , past participial stem of *percipere*, perceive, v. + *-iō, -ion*, suffix¹; in later use perhaps also partly < French *perception* action by which a subject takes note of objects through the senses (1611 in Cotgrave in this sense) < classical Latin *perceptiōn-, perceptiō* (see above). In branch II. probably via Middle French, French *perception* collection of revenue from land, property, etc. (*c*1370 in Middle French; earlier in Old French in sense 'receiving the Holy Spirit' (12th cent. in an isolated attestation) and in sense 'receiving the elements of the Eucharist' […]." (s.v. *perception*, n., *OED3*).
programme	"**Etymology:** In senses 1 and 2 < post-classical Latin *programma*, n. (in spec. use in sense 2 after German *Programm* (early 19th cent.; now obsolete in this sense)). In sense 3 (from which all the later senses have developed) < French *programme* (in education) descriptive notice of a course of study, etc. (1677), descriptive notice of any formal proceedings (1762), (in politics) prospectus of a party or individual (1789), plan (1831 or earlier) < post-classical Latin *programma*, n." (s.v. *programme*, n., *OED3*).
story(1)	"**Etymology:** < Anglo-Norman *estorie* (Old French *estoire*, later in semi-learned form *histoire*) < Latin *historia*: see *history*, n. Compare Italian *storia*, medieval Latin *storia*." (s.v. *story*¹, n., *OED3*).

story(2)	"**Etymology:** First in Anglo-Latin form *historia*; hence probably the same word as *story*, n.[1], though the development of sense is obscure. Possibly *historia* as an architectural term may originally have denoted a tier of painted windows or of sculptures on the front of a building" (s.v. *story*[2], n., *OED3*).

6.2 Etymology for 'undetermined' nouns (group 1)

noun	etymology
acceptance	probably partly F, partly WF < V (*accept*, v. + *-ance* suffix)
command	F or WF < V
criticism	WF from *critic* or L
information	F < L and partly WF < V (*inform*, v. + *-ion* suffix)
object	branch I) < adj. / L; branch II) L
point(1)	I) F < L; II) F < L; III) WF < V
qualification	F < L and WF < V (*qualify*, v. + *-ation* suffix)
regret	F and WF < V
relief(2)	F and WF < V
report	F and WF < V
reposte	alteration of *riposte*, n. or F; *riposte*: F < It.
similarity	WF suffixation or F
tip(1, 2, 3, 4, 5)	*tip(1)*: German, Dutch, Frisian; *tip(2, 3, 4, 5)*: WF < V; *tip(2, 3)* < v(2), *tip(4, 5)* < v(1)
venture	F and perhaps WF < V

6.3 Conversion:

conversion from verb (i.e. verb into noun)			
noun	etymology	noun	etymology
aim	two verbs confounded 1) F < L 2) F < L	*praise*	F < L
approach	F < L	*protest*	F < L
attempt	F < L	*puzzle*	undetermined
bid(1)	Germanic	*remark(1)*	F; WF in French: prefixation
call	Germanic	*reply*	F < L
catch(1)	F < L	*resolve*	L
concern	L + F < L	*result*	L

An etymological analysis of shell nouns 153

dread	undetermined – "not found in Old English; probably aphetic < *adreden*" (*OED3*)	*retort(2)*	L
drive	Germanic	*stand(1)*	Germanic
endeavour	< F; WF pref in French	*struggle*	undetermined
fight	Germanic	*talk*	Undetermined
gamble(1)	Germanic	*thrill(3)*	< *thirl(1)* < Germanic
grumble	undetermined	*trend*	Germanic
guess	Scandinavian	*urge*	L
hint	< *hent* (obsolete) Germanic	*whisper*	Germanic
mistake	WF pref, partly after Scandinavian	*wish*	Germanic
move	F < L	*worry*	Germanic
permit(1)	L	*whinge*	Germanic
practice	L and F		

conversion from verb/ adjective (i.e. verb or adj. into noun) + process of borrowing

noun	etymology
attribute	WF < adj. or L or F < L; adj.: L
disquiet	WF < adj. / V; verb: WF pref; *dis-*: L; *quiet*: L / WF < adj.; adj.: WF pref; *quiet*: F < L
pride	WF < adj.; *proud*(adj.): F < L

6.4 Compounding:[24]

noun	etymology
breakthrough	phrasal verb; *break*(v): Germanic; *to break through*. "*Through* is here originally a preposition, and the analysis is *to break through-a-fence*, not *to break-through* a fence, but the prep. tends to attach itself to the vb. as in Latin *perfringĕre*, and is sometimes used absol. as an adverb." (*OED3*); *through*(prep. and adv.): Germanic
catchphrase	*catch*(v): F < L; *phrase*: L < Ancient Greek
downside	phrase or adjective or clipping – undetermined

---

[24] Alternatively, *breakthrough*, *drawback* and *payoff* could be seen as conversions from phrasal verbs rather than as compounds (personal communication from H. Sauer).

drawback	phrasal verb; *draw*(v): Germanic; *back*(adv): Germanic
leeway	*lee*(n): Germanic; *way*(n): Germanic
nightmare	*night*(n): Germanic; *mare*(n): Germanic
payoff	phrasal verb; *pay*(v): F < L; *off*(adv., prep., n, and adj.): Germanic
standpoint	*stand*(v): Germanic; *point*(n): branch I) F < L; II) F < L; III) 'probably also partly < *point*, v1' – undetermined
viewpoint	< *view*(n); *view*(n): F; *point*(n): branch I) F < L; II) F < L; III) "probably also partly < *point*, v.[1]" (*OED3*) – undetermined
willpower	< *will*(n); *will*(n): Germanic; *power*(n): F < L

6.5 Prefixation:

prefix	origin	number of occurrences	nouns
counter-	F < L	2	*counterclaim countermeasure*

counterclaim: *claim*(n) < F

countermeasure: *measure*(n) < F < L

dis-	L (related to Greek)	1	*disinclination*

disinclination: *inclination*(n) < F < L

fore-	Germanic	2	*forecast foresight*

foresight: *sight*(n) Germanic

forecast: *cast*(v) < Old Norse

in-	L (representing Germanic *un-*)	2	*inability insight(1)*

inability: *ability*(n) < F < L

insight: *sight*(n) Germanic; 'in' in *insight* is, strictly speaking, not the prefix *in-* but the adverb *in* (Germanic) (s.v. *insight*, n., *OED3*)

mis- (prefix[1])	Germanic	6	*misapprehension miscalculation misconception mistfortune misjudgement misperception*

misapprehension: *apprehension*(n) < F? < L

miscalculation: *calculation*(n) < F < L

misconception: *conception*(n) < F < L

misfortune: *fortune*(n) < F < L			
misjudgement: *judgement*(n) < F < L			
misperception: *perception*(n) I) < L II) < F < L			
non-	F < L	1	*nonsense*
nonsense: *sense*(n) < F < L			
out-	Germanic	1	*outcome(1)*
outcome: *come*(n) < Germanic			
pre-	< L	3	*preconception precondition presentiment*
preconception: *conception*(n) < F < L			
precondition: *condition*(n) < F < L			
presentiment: *sentiment*(n) < F < L			
re-	F < L	2	*reaction reassurance*
reaction: *action*(n) < F < L			
reassurance: *assurance*(n) < F			
un-	"Representing Old English *un-*" (OED3) – Germanic	2	*uncertainty unknown*
uncertainty: *certainty*(n) < F < L			
unknown: *know*(v) Germanic			
up-	Germanic	1	*upshot*
upshot: *shoot*(v) Germanic			

6.6 Suffixation:

suffix	origin	number of occurrences	nouns
-ance	< F –*ance* < L –*ant-ia*, -*ent-ia*, -*ent-ia*	1	*reluctance*
reluctance: *reluctant*(adj) < L			

-ancy	< Latin –antia	1	discrepancy
discrepancy: discrepance(n) < F < L			
-al	representing L –al-em (-alis, -ali, stem -ali-)	3	denial proposal refusal
denial: deny(v) – F			
proposal: propose(v) – F < L			
refusal: refuse(v) – F < L			
-ation	"the particular form of the compound suffix –t-ion (-s-ion, -x-ion), which forms nouns of action from Latin pples. in –at-us of vbs. in –are, French vbs. in –er, and their English representatives." (OED3) < L	3	generalization motivation realization
generalization: generalize(v) < general(adj) + -ize suffix, general(adj): < F < L			
motivation: motive(v) < motive(n); motive(n): F < L			
realization: realize(v) < real(adj) + -ize suffix; real(adj): < F < L			
-ence	< French –ence, < Latin –entia	1	insistence
insistence: insist(v) – L			
-ency	< Latin –entia	2	inconsistency tendency
inconsistency: inconsistence(n) < inconsistent(adj) + -ence suffix; inconsistent(adj): in- prefix + consistent(adj); consistent(adj) < L			
tendency: tendence(n) < L			
-er	Germanic	1	reminder
reminder: remind(v); remind(v): re- prefix + mind(v); mind(v): < mind(n); mind(n): Germanic			
-hood	Germanic "Middle English – hod (-hode) < Old English – had" (OED3)	1	likelihood
likelihood: likely(adj) – Old Norse			
-ing	Germanic	14	betting(1) blessing feeling finding inkling reading(1) reasoning reckoning ruling teaching thinking

An etymological analysis of shell nouns 157

| | | | understanding | undertaking |
| | | | yearning | |

betting: *bet*(v) < *bet*(n): "Of uncertain origin; nor is it clear whether the n. or the vb. was the starting-point" (*OED3*)

blessing: *bless*(v) – Germanic

feeling: *feel*(v) – Germanic

finding: *find*(v) – Germanic

inkling: *inkle*(v) – 'Origin unascertained'

reading: *read*(v) – Germanic

reasoning: *reason*(v) – partly < French and partly < Latin and partly directly < *reason* n.[1]

reckoning: *reckon*(v) – Germanic

ruling: *rule*(v) – F < L

teaching: *teach*(v) – Germanic

thinking: *think*(v[2]) – Germanic

understanding: *understand*(v) – Germanic

undertaking: *undertake*(v); *undertake*(v): *under-* prefix + *take*(v) < Old Norse

yearning: *yearn*(v[1]) – Germanic

| -ism | "Repr. French –*isme*, Latin –*ismus*, < Greek –*ισμός*" (*OED3*) | 1 | *truism* | |

truism: *true*(adj) – Germanic

| -ity | F < L < French –*ité*, classical Latin –*itat-*, *-itas*) | 5 | *capability inevitability oddity peculiarity responsibility* |

capability: *capable*(adj) – F < L

inevitability: *inevitable*(adj) – L

oddity: *odd*(adj) – early Scandinavian

peculiarity: *peculiar*(adj) – L

responsibility: *responsible*(adj) < *responsable*(adj) or directly < F < L

| -lec (OE) | | 1 | *knowledge* |

knowledge: *know*(v) + late OE *–lec*; *know*(v): Germanic

| -le | "The form –*el* suffix[1] is retained where phonetic law or orthographical convention does not permit the change | 1 | *quibble* |

	into -le'. 'A suffix of various function and origin." (OED3); general: Germanic		
quibble: *quib*(n) < L			
-ment	F < L	12	*acknowledgement* *amazement* *assessment* *astonishment* *commitment* *disappointment* *inducement* *pronouncement* *refinement* *requirement* *resentment* *statement*

acknowledgement: *acknowledge*(v) – prefixation *ac-* + *knowledge*(v) < *knowledge*(v) (obsolete) – Germanic

amazement: *amaze*(v) – prefixation "< *a-* prefix? intensive + *maze* n" (*OED3*); *a-* prefix: Germanic; *maze*(n): "Probably < the same base as *amaze* v.; further etymology uncertain" (*OED3*)

assessment: *asses*(v) – F < L

astonishment: < *astonishingness*(n) "Formed as *astonishingly* adv. + *-ness* suffix" (*OED3*); *astonishingly*(adv): < *astonishing*(adj) + *ly* suffix; *astonishing*(adj): "Formed as *astonishing* n. + *-ing* suffix" (*OED3*); *astonishing*(n): "Formed as *astonisher* n. + *-ing* suffix" (*OED3*); *astonisher*(n) < *astonish*(v) → undetermined

commitment: *commit*(v) < L

disappointment: < *disappoint*(v) + *-ment* suffix; *disappoint*(v): < F, prefixation < *des-* + *appointer*; *dis-* prefix: L, related to Greek; *appoint*(v): < F

inducement: *induce*(v) < L

pronouncement: *pronounce*(v) < F < L

refinement: *refine*(v) – prefixation: *re-* prefix + *fine*(v³); *re-* prefix: < F < L; *fine*(v): < *fine*(adj); *fine*(adj): < F < L

requirement: *require*(v) – partly F and partly L

resentment: *resent*(v) – F < L

statement: *state*(v) < *state*(n); *state*(n): partly < F < L, partly direct adaptation from the Latin source

-ness	Germanic	10	*awareness* *business* *eagerness* *happiness* *keenness* *readiness* *sadness* *unwillingness* *weakness* *willingness*

awareness: "Formed as *awaredom*(n) + *-ness* suffix" (*OED3*); *awaredom*(n): < *aware*(adj) + *-dom* suffix; *aware*(adj): Germanic
business: *busy*(adj) – Germanic
eagerness: *eager*(adj.) – F < L
happiness: *happy*(adj); *happy*(adj): < *hap*(n) + *-y* suffix; *hap*(n): < Old Norse; *-y* suffix: "Descending from the Old English adj. suffix *-ig*" (*OED3*)
keenness: *keen*(adj) – Germanic
readiness: *ready*(adj); *ready*(adj): Germanic
sadness: *sad*(adj.) – Germanic
unwillingness: *unwilling*(adj) – Germanic
weakness: *weak*(adj) – Old Norse
willinness: *willing*(adj) – Germanic
-ure
disclosure: *disclose*(v) – F < L
special case: *discovery* – see footnote 14; *discover*(v): F < L

Dictionaries

ALD	*The Advanced Learner's Dictionary of Current English*, eds. Albert S. Hornby, Edward V. Gatenby and H. Wakefield. 2nd ed. 1963. 3rd ed. 1974. London: Oxford University Press.
CED	*A Chronological English Dictionary, Listing 80 000 Words in Order of their Earliest Known Occurrence*, eds. Thomas Finkenstaedt, Ernst Leisi and Dieter Wolff. 1970. Heidelberg: Winter.
Davies, Mark -- Dee Gardner 2010	*A frequency dictionary of contemporary American English*. London: Routledge.
GSL	*A General Service List of English Words with Semantic Frequencies and a Supplementary Word-List for the Writing of Popular Science and Technology*. 1953. Compiled and edited by Michael West. London: Longman, Green and Co.
ODEE	*The Oxford Dictonary of English Etymology*, ed. Charles T. Onions with the assistance of G. W. S. Friedrichsen and Robert W. Burchfield. Oxford: Oxford University Press, 1966 [many reprints].
OED3	*The Oxford English Dictionary*, 3rd edition, also known as the *OED online*. In progress 2000- <http://www.oed.com> or <http://dictionary.oed.com>
Rundell, Michael 2010	*Macmillan collocations dictionary*. Oxford: Macmillan Education.

SOED *The Shorter Oxford English Dictionary.* 1964. Prepared by William Little, H.W. Fowler and Jessie Coulson. Revised and edited, with an appendix by Charles T. Onions: Oxford: Clarendon Press.

References

Aijmer, Kari
    2007   "The interface between discourse and grammar: *the fact is that*", in: *Connectives as discourse landmarks*, ed. Agnès Celle & Ruth Huart. Amsterdam: Benjamins, 31-46.

Aktas, Nur -- Viviana Cortes
    2008   "Shell nouns as cohesive devices in published and ESL student writing", *Journal of English for Academic Purposes* 7: 3-14.

Baugh, Albert C. -- Thomas Cable
    2002   *A history of the English language.* 5th ed. London: Routledge.

Caldwell, Candice
    2009   *Lexical vagueness in student writing: Are shell nouns the problem?* Saarbrücken: VDM Verlag Dr. Müller.

Durkin, Philip
    2009   *The Oxford guide to etymology.* Oxford: Oxford University Press.

Flowerdew, John
    2010   "The use of signalling nouns across L1 and L2 writer corpora", *International Journal of Corpus Linguistics* 15: 36-55.

Flowerdew, Lynn
    2004   "The problem-solution pattern in apprentice vs. professional technical writing: an application of appraisal theory", in: *Corpora and language learners*, ed. Guy Aston. Amsterdam: Benjamins, 125-135.
    2008   *Corpus-based analyses of the problem-solution pattern: A phraseological appraoch.* Amsterdam: Benjamins.

Furthmann, Katja
    2006   *Die Sterne lügen nicht: Eine linguistische Analyse der Textsorte Pressehoroskop.* Göttingen: v&r unipress.

Gneuss, Helmut
    1955   *Lehnbildungen und Lehnbedeutungen im Altenglischen.* Berlin: Erich Schmidt.

Hunston, Susan -- Gill Francis
    2000   *Pattern Grammar: a corpus-driven approach to the lexical grammar of English.* Amsterdam: Benjamins.

Maaß, Christiane
    2010   *Diskursdeixis im Französischen.* Berlin: Beihefte zur Zeitschrift für romanische Philologie, 355.

Mahlberg, Michaela
    2005   *English general nouns: A corpus theoretical approach.* Philadelphia: Benjamins.

Mantlik, Annette
    Forthcoming   *The historical development of shell nouns: A diachronic study of abstract noun constructions in English.* PhD thesis University of Munich (LMU).

Mihatsch, Wiltrud
 2009 "Nouns are THINGS: evidence for a grammatical metaphor?", in: *Metonymy and metaphor in grammar*, ed. Klaus-Uwe Panther, Linda L. Thornburg & Antonio Barcelona. Amsterdam: Benjamins, 75-97.

Sauer, Hans
 2007 "Sprachwissenschaft", in: *Einführung in die Anglistik und Amerikanistik.* 2nd ed., ed. Uwe Böker & Christoph Houswitschka. München: Beck, 89-165.

Scheler, Manfred
 1977 *Der englische Wortschatz.* Berlin: Erich Schmidt.

Schmid, Hans-Jörg
 1997 "The historical development and present-day use of the noun *idea* as documented in the *OED* and other corpora", *Poetica: An International Journal of Linguistic-Literary Studies* 47: 87-128.
 1998 "Constant and ephemeral hypostatization: *thing, problem* and other shell nouns", in: *Proceedings of the 16th International Congress of Linguistics (Paris, July 22-25, 1997)*, ed. Bernard Caron. With CD-ROM. Amsterdam: Elsevier.
 1999 "Cognitive effects of shell nouns", in: *Discourse studies in cognitive linguistics,* ed. Karen van Hoek, Andrej A. Kibrik & Leo Noordman. Amsterdam: Benjamins, 111-132.
 2000 *English abstract nouns as conceptual shells: From corpus to cognition.* Berlin: de Gruyter.
 2011 *English morphology and word-formation.* 2nd ed. Berlin: Schmidt.

Ungerer, Friedrich -- Hans-Jörg Schmid
 2006 *An introduction to cognitive linguistics.* 2nd ed. Harlow: Pearson/Longman.

Secondary agent constructions from a diachronic perspective

Naděžda Kudrnáčová (Brno, Czech Republic)

Abstract
This paper traces the emergence of secondary agent constructions (transitive causative constructions with verbs of self-agentive locomotion, exemplified by *John walked Harry to the station*) in the historical development of English and looks into the factors that underlie their relatively late formation. Secondary agent constructions involving coercive force on the part of the causer (*John marched Harry to the bathroom*) and constructions endowed with very specialized meanings (*John walked a young hound*) represent a yet later development. The later emergence of secondary agent constructions may be explained by appealing to their elaborate causal structure and to the semantics of the verbs admitted into them.

1. Introduction

The present paper deals with certain diachronic aspects of the formation of transitive causative constructions with verbs of self-agentive locomotion, exemplified by sentences of the type *John walked Mary to the station, John walked the bicycle up the hill* or *John jumped the horse over the fence*.[1] These constructions, termed here "secondary agent constructions" (henceforth "SA constructions"), express the external causation of self-agentive locomotion: the causer acts upon the causee, in this way inducing him to carry out a given movement (Levin (1993) treats SA constructions under the heading of "induced action alternations"). The term was inspired by the "secondary agent" used in Langacker (1991: 412-413) to designate a causee that is "secondary in the sense of being downstream from the original energy source, yet agentive in the sense of having some initiative role".

In these constructions, the direct object position may be taken up by a causee (*John danced Mary around the ballroom, John swam the cattle across the river*) or by a patientive causee (*John walked the bicycle up the hill*). In the former case, the participant acts as a self-agentive (co-)executor of the motion encoded in the verb, i.e. represents a second energy source.[2] In the latter case, the participant does not execute the movement independently of an external energy source (represented by the causer). Nevertheless, this participant also represents a second energy source because it is, on account of its properties, actively involved in the execution of the movement.

SA constructions employ verbs designating the basic, most neutral types of motion: *run, walk, swim, march, dance* and *waltz*. SA constructions with birds as

---

[1] A terminological remark: The term 'transitive' may either be used to refer to the use of verbs (cf. representative descriptive grammars like Quirk et al. (1985) or Huddleston and Pullum (2002), following the tradition established by Sweet (1898) or Jespersen (1949)), or it may be used to refer to a type of construction.
[2] See, e.g., Davidse & Geyskens (1998) or Shibatani & Pardeshi (2002).

causees employ the verb *fly* and corresponding constructions with horses employ the verbs *trot, canter, pace, jump, leap, prance* and *gallop*. The largely restricted repertory of verbs appearing in SA constructions is an outcome of two factors. The first factor is a pragmatic one: there is a strong tendency to reserve these constructions for the expression of more or less prototypical motion situations (hence the difference in the repertory of verbs representing caused movements of humans and those of animals, especially horses). The second factor is a semantico-syntactic one: the verbs must designate wholly intentional movements (cf. the unacceptability of **John staggered Harry to the door* or **John strutted Harry to the door*). This means that all the aspects of the movement that are encoded in the verb must fall under the scope of the operation of the mover – only in this way is it possible to admit this participant into the direct object position, reserved for participants which are included in the event "in their entirety", so to say.[3]

Whenever a self-agentive locomotion verb enters into a transitive causative construction and, at the same time, loses (to some extent at least) reference to a specific, concrete manner of motion (i.e. whenever the verb gains in the generality of its reference), it is a signal that a given SA construction encodes pragmatic meanings that diverge, to varying degrees, from the skeletal kinetic frame. For example, the sentence *He trotted them around* means 'He showed them around' or the sentence *John ran (/marched) Harry to the bathroom* means 'John forced Harry to walk (probably quickly) to the bathroom' – it should be realized that this shift in the verb's meaning is, in actual fact, a necessary prerequisite for the expression of additional meanings like 'coercion'.

Apart from SA constructions, there is another type of transitive causative construction into which some of the verbs from the category under consideration may enter, namely, a construction with the direct object position occupied by a fully-fledged patient (i. e. patient merely subject to the activity of the agent). This type of construction may be exemplified by sentences like *John jogged Harry, John ran his son to school* or *John danced his son on his knees*. As can be seen, the verbs, here, do not denote self-agentive motion but categorially change their semantics; this shift in the verbal meaning is a prerequisite for the expression of the patienthood of the participant in the direct object position. These types of construction therefore admit verbs such as *stagger* (*John staggered Harry*), which cannot otherwise occur in SA constructions.[4]

As mentioned above, the focus of the paper is on SA constructions. The paper demonstrates that, with the exception of the verbs *gallop* and *pace* (encoding movements of horses), these constructions represent a later (and, in actual fact, a

---

[3] On total object inclusion see Anderson (1971).
[4] Needless to say, verbs of self-agentive locomotion also appear in transitive constructions with the direct object position taken up by an expression specifying space or distance traversed (*John walked the streets, John ran three miles*). From a diachronic point of view, the direct object status of specifications of space (distance) is justified by appealing to the occasional possibility of using these types of complement in the subject position in passive constructions (cf. Visser 1963: 135).

quite predictable) development, which attests, among other things, to the inherently intransitive status of verbs denoting self-agentive locomotion.

The later emergence of SA constructions is most probably underlain by two reasons. The first lies in the causal structuration of motion situation encoded in them. In contrast to canonical caused motion constructions (i.e. transitive causative constructions with the direct object position taken up by a fully-fledged patient), SA constructions involve a more complicated pattern. They represent a single clause (i.e. employ a single verb), yet they encode two self-contained causal situations (that is, they accommodate two actions). The later emergence of SA constructions may thus be explained by appealing to their more elaborate structure, which represents a fusion of two causal situations.

The second reason underlying the later emergence of these constructions lies, apparently, in the semantics of the verbs admitted into them. Self-agentive locomotion verbs encode movements underlain by an energy whose scope of operation is confined to the physical limits of the executor of the movement. This fact naturally predisposes these verbs to be used in intransitive constructions, which typically do not encode the transmission of energy from one entity to another.

Most probably, by analogy with canonical caused motion situations (which involve the transmission of physical energy from the agent onto the patient), verbs of self-agentive motion came to be used in caused motion situations including another entity apart from the mover themselves.

The verbs that appear in SA constructions are the following (they are enumerated in the order in which they will be treated in this paper): *run, walk, swim, dance, march, trot, leap, waltz, jump, prance, gallop, pace, canter* and *fly*. The analysis of SA constructions with these verbs is based on the examples provided in the online edition of the *Oxford English Dictionary (OED3)*. The discussion will first concentrate on the verbs *run* and *walk*, which designate the most natural (the most basic and frequent) types of self-agentive locomotion. These verbs also serve as good examples illustrating the emergence of SA constructions and the development of meanings that are superimposed on the skeletal causal frame.

2. The verb *run*

This verb is used to encode caused motion in a wide variety of situations but only some of these involve self-agentive causees, i.e. only some of the transitive causative constructions with the verb belong to the category of SA constructions.

As is well known, *run* is an intrinsically amphibious verb, illustrating the ease with which English verbs may fluctuate between transitive and intransitive uses.[5] In Old English the verb appeared in two forms: in the intransitive *i(e)rnan*,

---

[5] A lot of intransitives developed out of transitives and a lot of transitives developed out of intransitives, and it is sometimes uncertain which of the two uses is the original one (see, e.g., Jespersen 1949: 319-320).

i(o)rnan, e(o)rnan, (very rare) *rinnan,* and in the transitive *ærnan, earnan*; the Middle English successors were *rinnen, rennen.* The transitive form of the verb was "strictly causative" (Hall 1960: 10). In spite of its causative meaning (it usually meant "to ride, gallop"), it was used without an object - cf. example 1 with the metonymic use of the verb:

> (1) *c*893 þonne ærnað hy ealle toweard þæm feo; ðonne cymeð se man se þæt swiftoste hors hafað to þæm ærestan dæle and ...
>
> [Then they all run towards the treasure. Then comes the man that has the swiftest horse to the first part and ...]
>
> (Ælfred's *Orosius* I. i. 20)

The quotation evidence from the *OED3* shows that *run* was employed in SA constructions (in which the object position is taken up by a causee) in the Early Middle English period:

> (2) *c*1275 Somme gon hors earne, somme afote eorne.
>
> [Some began to run horses, some began to run on foot.]
>
> (Layamon's *Brut* 24696)

It was only later that the verb was used to encode caused motion situations with causees other than animals.[6] It is interesting to note, however, that the earliest constructions of this type occurred with inanimate entities which fulfilled the role of patientive causees (let us recall that, in contrast to fully-fledged causees, patientive causees participate in the execution of the motion because they are bearers of properties that make the movement possible: ships glide on water, carriages have wheels, etc.):

> (3) *a*1548 The Scottes ran their shippes on land, and the Englishmen folowed wyth boates and landed.
>
> [The Scots ran their ships on land and the Englishmen followed with boats and landed.]
>
> (E. Hall: *Chronicle (The union of the two noble and illustre famelies of Lancestre and Yorke),* 94, *a* 1548)

---

[6] Note that a more specialized, more idiomatic SA construction with horses as causees (encoding the meaning 'to enter a horse for a race') is recorded as late as the 18th century:
 1797 For this reason, no gre-hound of any value should be run at this course.
 (*Encyclopædia Britannica,* 3rd ed., vol. V, 499/2, 1797)

Caused motion situations with animates ('to drive an animate being somewhere'), involving coercive force on the part of the causer, represent a later development. SA constructions of this type are documented as late as the Modern English period:

(4) 1822 Arresting a free negro, with a view to run him out of the State.

   (J. Flint: *Letters from America*, 309, Edinburgh 1822)

3. The verb *walk*

It may come as a surprise to learn that the verb *walk*, a natural antonym of *run*, appears in a secondary agent type of construction much later. The earliest quotation provided in the *OED3* is from the Late Middle English period:

(5) **1485** And anon he was ware of a man armed walkynge his hors easyly by a wodes syde ...

[And anon he was aware of a man armed, walking his horse easily by the side of a wood ...]

   (T. Malory: *Le Morte d'Arthur* V. ix, 176)

From a purely synchronic point of view, this situation is even more surprising in view of the firmly established position of SA constructions with this verb. SA constructions with *walk* belong to the core of the present-day system of transitive causative constructions, for two reasons. First, the verb *walk* designates the most prototypical (in the sense 'most basic' and 'most frequent') manner of human locomotion. Second, SA constructions with this verb are typically endowed with a variety of pragmatic meanings, superimposed on the skeletal causal frame, some of them verging on idiomaticity.[7]

A closer look reveals that the reason for the relatively late emergence of SA constructions with *walk* should apparently be sought in the development of the senses of this verb. The Old English predecessors of the Middle English verb *walken* (*walkien*) (namely, the strong verb *wealcan*, used both intransitively and transitively, and the weak causative verb *wealcian*) did not designate a bipedal self-agentive locomotion but represented a motion from a different semantic class: 'to attack, assault; move, stir; roll; toss, throw, fling' (cf. Rot 1992: 549). It is only at the beginning of the Middle English period (around 1200) that the verb *walken* is

---

[7] The phrase *to walk somebody somewhere* may encode not only the skeletal causal frame 'to cause somebody to walk somewhere and act as a co-mover' but also 'to help somebody to walk', 'to cause somebody to walk in order to promote his recovery', etc. Symptomatically, a decrease in the specificity of the verb is accompanied by an increase in the idiomaticity of the phrase. For example, *to walk a dog* or *to walk somebody to the hotel* (meaning 'to send somebody to another hotel because of overbooking') need not express situations in which an actual walking is carried out.

documented in a sense which comes near to the bipedal locomotion sense, namely, in the global locomotion sense 'to move about, travel':

> (6) *a*1200 (? *a*1200) þat israelisshe folc was walkende toward ierusalem on swinche ...
> [The Jewish people were walking towards Jerusalem in toil ...]
> (Trinity College, Cambridge, MS, in R. Morris, *Old English Homilies,* 51, 1873)

The bipedal self-agentive locomotion sense of the verb in question (specified in the *OED3* as "to move or travel at a regular and fairly slow pace by lifting and setting down each foot in turn, so that one of the feet is always on the ground") is documented from a later period:

> (7) *a*1300 (*a*1250) Elpes arn in Inde riche... Hu he resteð him ðis der, ðanne he walkeð wide, herkne wu it telleð her ...
> [Elephants are abundant in India ...How this animal rests, when he walks far – hearken, how it tells here ...]
> (*Bestiary* 505)

The possibility of the verb's appearing in SA constructions (cf. example 5 above) may be taken as evidence of the fact that in the Late Middle English period the bipedal self-agentive locomotion meaning of *walken* was already firmly established in the network of the senses of this verb. Its stabilization may further be illustrated by the verb's potential to enter into a very specific type of transitive construction, namely, a construction with the object position taken up by a personal pronoun – cf. the first quotation from about the same period (the second half of the 15th century):

> (8) *a*1475 (? 1445) I wil now me walke from sege to sege ...
> [I will now walk myself from shrine to shrine ...]
> (J. Lydgate: *Minor Poems*, in H. N. MacCracken (ed.) *The Minor Poems of John Lydgate* I. 367, London 1911)

This type of transitive "quasi-causative" construction has certain features in common with SA constructions. As mentioned above, physical energy in movements designated by self-agentive locomotion verbs operates internally (i.e. is confined to the physical limits of the mover's body). In reflexive constructions with these verbs (in constructions with a personal pronoun fulfilling the function of a reflexive), the energy is conceptualized as transmitted from the mover's 'acting self' onto the mover's 'acted upon self'. Needless to say, an outcome of this very specific construal is a profiled exertion of one's will.

Coming back to the relatively late emergence of *walken* in the bipedal self-agentive locomotion sense, one might be tempted to evaluate this situation as pointing to a lexical gap in the Old English verbal lexicon. Quite expectedly, this is not the case. Owing to the prototypicality of 'walking', the function of representing this movement was fulfilled by the Old English verb *gān*: the *OED3* defines one of the verb's senses as "to walk; to move or travel one one's feet (opposed to *creep, fly, ride, swim*, etc.); to move on foot at an ordinary pace (opposed to *run*, etc.)". As can be seen, the sense in question is specified contrastively, against some other verbs which denote a manner of global self-agentive locomotion. This may, indeed, be taken as evidence of the verb's classification among the group of manner of motion verbs. However, the syntactic behaviour of *gān* (more specifically, the verb's impossibility of appearing in transitive causative constructions) serves as evidence against the manner of motion categorization of this verb. Let me offer an explanation.

First, let us recall that the formation of SA constructions is licensed by the transmission of energy from the causer onto the causee. There is, however, a further requirement that must be fulfilled, namely, that the energy must take on a concrete form, i.e. it must realize itself in a concrete physical modality of motion. Therefore, SA constructions are open to manner of motion verbs only. The verb *go* (and verbs of its kin, e.g. *come, arrive* or *appear*) belong to the category of the so called path verbs, which are much more restricted in their syntactic behaviour.[8]

The reason why path verbs cannot be used in transitive causative constructions apparently lies in the construal of motion encoded in them. These verbs present motion in its bare form, as a mere change of location, abstracted from concrete physical energy (see, e.g., Kudrnáčová 2008).[9] One result of this abstraction is the impossibility of the verb's causativization, i.e. the impossibility of positing a causal relation between the mover's 'going' somewhere and the mover's change of location (**John went Mary to the door*).

At this point in the discussion it may be interesting to mention that although neither the Old English *gān* (*gangan*) nor its successor, the Middle English *gōn*, are documented in transitive causative uses, the *OED3* adduces examples of constructions in which this verb is used in combination with a personal pronoun (fulfilling the function of the reflexive). As Mitchell (1985: 114) and Mustanoja (1960: 100) point out, in Old English and Middle English personal pronouns used reflexively were not infrequent with intransitive verbs, especially those denoting motion and rest (cf. also *Hu he resteð him ðis der* from example 7 above). The first quotation of this kind (labelled in the *OED3* as "quasi-transitive") with the verb *gōn* is from the Early Middle English period:

---

[8] On the distinction between path verbs and manner of motion verbs see, e.g., Levin (1993) or Rosen (1984); on the relation between verbs' lexical semantic representation and their syntactic behaviour see, e.g., Pinker (1989), Rappaport Hovav and Levin (1998), or Ritter and Rosen (1996).

[9] This argumentation is in line with Langacker's observation that verbs of the *come, go* or *arrive* type "impose an absolute construal on the movement they designate" (Langacker 1991: 390).

(9) c1175 þe unclene gast þe geð him of þan sunfulle mon and geð him of þan stude to stude

[The unclean spirit goes him [= himself] out of the sinful man and goes him [= himself] from place to place]

(*Lambeth Homilies*, 27)

In view of the fact that, for the reasons adduced above, transitive causative constructions are open to manner of motion verbs only, one might speculate that the capacity of this path verb to enter into what might be termed the transitive 'quasi-causative' construction was underlain (or, facilitated) by the verb's function to represent 'walking', i.e. to represent a concrete manner of self-agentive movement. In other words, one might evaluate the reflexive construction as an overt syntactic manifestation of the verb's specific lexical semantic position.[10]

There is another signal testifying to the verb's borderline categorization, namely, its capacity to appear in "a sort of periphrastic conjugation" (Hall 1960: 76) employing the path verb *cuman* and the infinitives of verbs of manner of motion (*cōm gangan* or *cōm swimman*). In this connnection, one might point out that the present discussion of the potential of verbs to form SA constructions attests to the need for a more detailed description of the development of syntactic patterning, which may provide a helpful insight into the development of verbal lexical semantic representation – see, e.g., Cortés Rodríguez and Mairal Usón (2002), who argue for the construction of a historical dictionary which would also contain information about syntactic configurations associated with a given lexical entry.

Coming back to SA constructions with the verb *walken*, a few remarks on the types of causees and on the development of the repertory of pragmatic meanings imposed on these constructions are in order. SA constructions with animal causees encode the meanings 'to lead, drive, or ride (a horse) at a walk; to exercise an animal (esp. a horse or dog) by causing it to walk'. SA constructions with human causees encode the meanings 'to force or help (a person) to walk by holding the arms or pushing from behind' or 'guide or accompany a person'. Given the significance of animals in the culture of the period, SA constructions with *walk* are, not surprisingly, documented with animal causees first (cf. example 5, from the year 1485) and only later with human causees (cf. example 10):

---

[10] 'Quasi-transitive' constructions with the verb *come* (a deictic counterpart of *go*), whose earliest evidence dates back as late as the Late Modern English period, did not encode caused motion situations and therefore cannot be taken as counterparts of transitive 'quasi-causative' constructions with *go*. Consider:

*c*1690 *Has he come it?*
(Has he lent it?)
(B.E.: *A New Dictionary of the Terms Ancient and Modern of the Canting Crew*, London *c* 1698)

(10) **1607** One of them ... was desired to lead the Bride a dance. He tooke her by the hand, and walked her a turne or two.

[One of them ... was desired to lead the bride a dance. He took her by the hand and walked her a turn or two.]

(E. Grimstone: *Admirable and Memorable Histories,* 332, London 1607, tr. by S. Goulart)

(11) **1809** The poor wretch, attended by part of the police, had been walked through the streets, in order to show him to the populace ...

(R. K. Porter: *Travelling Sketches in Russia and Sweden,* II. 21, London 1809)

As one might expect, the more specialized meanings superimposed on the basic skeletal frame 'to cause to walk' are documented from even later periods. Consider the first quotation evidencing the meaning 'to train and look after (a young hound)' in the following example:[11]

(12) **1845** Whelps walked, or taken care of, at butchers' houses ... are apt to be heavy-shouldered and throaty.

(W. Youatt: *The Dog* iii. 75, Philadelphia 1845)

SA constructions with inanimate patientive causees, i.e. participants that are (regardless of their inanimacy but owing to their properties) actively involved in the execution of a motion, represent a yet later development. Consider the first quotation expressing the meaning 'to wheel or push (a bicycle, motorcycle, etc.)':

(13) **1891** The officer went back and walked the bicycle over to the police station.

(*San Antonio Daily Light,* 4 Dec.)

The later emergence of this type of SA construction can be explained by appealing to its derived status. More specifically, one can evaluate this construction as being formed by analogy with SA constructions 'proper' (i.e. constructions with a fully-fledged, active causee). There seem to be two factors that underlie the formation of the SA construction in question. First, both the SA construction 'proper' and its variant with an inanimate causee include the transmission of energy from the causer onto the causee. What is of crucial importance is that in both these constructions the transmission of energy is not part of 'walking', i.e. is not part of

---

[11] It is worth noting that the more specialized meanings of SA constructions are accompanied by a decrease in the verb's reference to the basic, original locomotion (cf. example 11). In actual fact, the (partial) loss of the verb's reference to a concrete manner of motion is a prerequisite for the expression of meanings that abstract, to varying degrees, from the skeletal causal pattern.

the movement encoded in the verb. That is, when a causer walks an animate causee somewhere, the causer does not effect the causee's movement *by means of* walking. The same is valid for caused motion situations with inanimate causees. For example, when a person walks a bicycle somewhere, he effects the movement of the bicycle by means of exerting physical energy onto the causee (by means of pushing the bicycle) *while* walking. The second factor that makes it possible to form SA constructions with inanimate causees (with objects like bicycles or prams) is the active involvement of the causee in the execution of the motion (as mentioned above, inanimate causees possess properties that enable the causer to effect the movement), which is a feature that this type of causee has in common with a causee in SA constructions proper.

SA constructions with parts of the body as causees represent a yet later development. The formation of these types of construction is made possible by the unique (because organic) functional unity of the body and its parts. In this respect, these constructions are instantiations of the same causal structuration as SA constructions with animate causees. Consider the first quotation evidencing this construction in the *OED3*:

(14) **1949** She walked her fingers across the upholstery toward his knee.

(W. L. Gresham: *Limbo Tower*, 191, New York 1949)

SA constructions with *dolls* or *puppets* as causees (also documented from the 20th century) represent analogous formations with SA constructions proper (in which the causees represent fully-fledged agents, executing the motion in question) because the causees fulfil the role of agentive-like participants. Consider:

(15) **1991** Louisa, aged five and also adopted, was walking her doll.

(*New Internationalist* March 29/1)

Both SA constructions with body parts as causees and SA constructions with puppets or dolls as causees present the energy underlying the movement as operating internally (as is canonically the case in self-agentive movements). This special stylization of a caused motion situation also asserts itself in the capacity of these types of causee to enter into a subject position – cf. the sentences *Her fingers walked up his ribs* or *The puppet walked across the stage*, in which the causees are presented as volitional instigators and controllers of the movements.

4. The verb *swim*

Although the Old English *swimman* appears in *Beowulf* (the Middle English successor of this verb is *swimmen*), its use in SA constructions is attested as late as the 17th century. What is also of interest is the fact that SA constructions with patientive causees emerge almost simultaneously with SA constructions with fully-fledged, agentive causees – cf. examples (16) and (17), respectively:

> (16) **1613** I'le vndertake to swimme her Vnto the furthest strond, vpon my shoulders.
>
> [I'll undertake to swim her unto the furthest strand upon my shoulders.]
>
> (T. Heywood: *The Brazen Age* I. B4b, London 1613)

> (17) **1639** After swim him, and apply bathes.
>
> (T. De Grey: *The Compleat Horse-Man, and Expert Ferrier in Two Books*, 306, London 1639)

SA constructions with inanimate patientive causees whose motion is made possible by their properties (more specifically, by their position on the surface of a stretch of water) are recorded from the 18th century:

> (18) **1743** The People swam off three Casks of Water.
>
> (J. Bulkeley and J. Cummins: *A Voyage to the South-Seas in the Years 1740-1*, 160, London 1743)

5. The verb *dance*

This verb, a loan-word from French, is first recorded in the Middle English period (*dauncen, dancen, daunsen, dansen*). The first quotation of its use in a SA construction is from the Late Modern English period:

> (19) **1665** Having danced my people as long as I saw fit to sit up ...
>
> (S. Pepys: *Memoirs. Comprising his Diary from 1659 to 1669, and a Selection from his Private Correspondence*, 11 Oct., 1665)

6. The verb *march*

The verb is first documented from the Late Middle English period (*marchen*, from Middle French *marcher*) in a military sense. SA constructions appeared in the Early Modern English period – first in the verb's original (military) sense (cf. example 20) and only much later in an extended sense, serving as a basis for the expression of an evaluative, i.e. coercive caused motion situation (cf. example 21):

> (20) **1616** [...] Vn-sweare faith sworne, and on the marriage bed of smiling peace to march a bloody hoast?
>
> [(...) unswear faith sworn, and on the marriage-bed of smiling peace to march a bloody host?]

(W. Shakespeare: *The Life and Death of King John* (in the First Folio (1623), III. i. 172)

(21) **1847** Early the next morning the 'floaters' were marched ... with votes in hand, to the ballot box.

(*The Knickerbocker* 29, 329)

The later emergence of a coercive SA construction can be quite safely explained by the fact that in caused motion situations, including coercive force on the part of the causer, the verb, to a certain degree, has to deviate from its basic, military sense – only in this way can it signal coerciveness.

Much later, SA constructions with *march* took on more specialized meanings, e.g. 'to urge on (a team of dogs) through snow' (example 22) or, in American Football, 'to advance one's team, esp. rapidly, while playing offense' (example 23):

(22) **1959** The trappers ... gathered their supplies, hitched their dog teams, and 'marched them' out across the frozen river to their trap lines.

(W. A. Leising: *Arctic Wings,* 34, New York 1959)

(23) **1988** Throwing the ball on 18 consecutive plays, Walsh marched the Hurricanes, who were trailing 30-14, 80 yards for a score in just under two minutes.

(*Touchdown* Nov. 44/1)

7. The verb *trot*

The verb appears in Middle English (*trotten*), first in reference to horses ('to go at the gait between a walk and a run'), later in reference to humans (roughly, 'to go or to move quickly'). It was first used in SA constructions with horses as causees (in the Early Modern English period, cf. example 24) but only much later (towards the end of the 19th century) with humans as causees (SA constructions of this latter kind display an evaluative status, cf. example 25):

(24) **1592** Whether that he trots, or turnes, or bounds his barded Steede.

[Whether that he trots or turns or bounds his armoured steed.]

(W. Warner: *Albions England. The Third Time Corrected* VIII. xxxviii. 189)

(25) **1886** The public ... is being trotted up and down in front of Home Rule in the belief that, like a nervous horse, it can be familiarized with the alarming object.

(*The Saturday Review of Politics, Literature, Science and Art,* 6 March 315/1)

SA constructions carrying more idiomatic meanings ('to lead out and show off the paces of a horse' and 'to conduct or escort a person *to* or *round* a place'), superimposed on the skeletal kinetic frame, are also recorded as late as the 19th century – cf. the following two quotations:

> (26) **1841** A little cross-bred, vicious beast ... was 'trotted out' before a circle of ladies and gentlemen, to be admired.
>
> (G. Stephen: *Adventures of a Gentleman in Search of a Horse, by Caveat Emptor* xxiv, London 1841)

> (27) **1898** Perhaps you'll trot us round the works.
>
> (H. S. Merriman: *Roden's Corner* vi. 60, New York and London 1898)

8. The verb *leap*

Although this verb (Old English *hlēapan*; Middle English *lēpen*) is recorded in *Beowulf*, it appears in a SA construction as late as the Late Modern English period (at the end of the 17th century):

> (28) **1681-6** Those restless Furies ... will never cease stimulating and spurring us on ... till they have leapt us headlong into the everlasting Burnings.
>
> (J. Scott: *The Christian Life, from Its Beginning, to Its Consummation in Glory* III. 355, London 1747)

As is evident, this construction has a figurative, rather than a caused motion meaning and fulfills an evaluative function. A secondary agent construction expressing caused motion ('to cause a horse to take a leap') is documented as late as the 19th century:

> (29) **1860** [He] had leaped his horse across a deep nullah.
>
> (W. H. Russell: *My Diary in India, in the Year 1858-59* II. 287, London 1860)

9. The verb *waltz*

This verb (from German *walzen*) is first documented from 1794 and appears in a SA construction a century later:

> (30) **1881** How Edgar laughed as he waltzed me through the hall!
>
> (M. C. Hay: *Missing! and Other Tales* II. 237, London 1881)

As with the SA constructions employing the verbs *march, trot* and *leap*, SA constructions with *waltz* also have the potential to convey an evaluative presentation of the motion situation (cf. the example above).

10. The verb *jump*

This verb (apparently of onomatopoeic origin, as with *bump*) is of Early Modern English origin (it is first recorded in 1530). Interestingly, the first SA construction, evidenced as late as 1815, encoded a motion of a human, not an animal causee:

> (31) *c*1815 She ... ran up the steps to be jumped down again.
> (J. Austen: *Persuasion* I. xii. 310, London 1833)

Secondary agent constructions with animal causees appeared later, towards the end of the 19th century:

> (32) **1890** He nearly jumped his horse on to that last bullock's back.
> (R. Boldrewood: *A Colonial Reformer* 222, London 1891)

11. The verb *prance*

The verb appears in Middle English (*prancen, prauncen*); its self-agentive locomotion use (with both human and animal agents) is documented from the very end of the 14th century.
SA constructions, first recorded in the Early Modern English period (cf. example 33), only employed horses as causees ('to cause a horse to prance'):

> (33) **1530** I praunce an horse, I make hym fetche gamboldes and to flynge, *je pourbondys*.
> [I prance a horse, I make him fetch gambols and fling, *je pourbondys*.]
> (J. Palsgrave: *Lesclarcissement de la langue françoyse* 664/1)

12. The verb *gallop*

The Middle English *galopen* (apparently adopted from French *galoper*) is first recorded in the sense 'of a horseman: to ride at full speed' in 1523; the verb's use in the sense 'of a horse: to go at a gallop' is documented from the period before 1533:

> (34) *a* **1533** The horse wold nother trot nor gallop.
> [The horse would neither trot nor gallop.]

(J. B. Berners: *The Boke of Duke Huon of Burdeux* lv. 185)

Interestingly, a secondary agent construction ('to cause a horse to gallop') appears in the very same document:

(35) *a* **1533** I can ryght wel ... rynne & galop a hors.
   [I can right well ... run and gallop a horse.]
   (J. B. Berners: *The Boke of Duke Huon of Burdeux* liii.178)

13. The verb *pace*

This verb (originally a variant of *pass*) is first recorded in the sense 'of a horse: to move with a controlled, easy gait' in 1598:

(36) **1598** Hee mounted his Horse, and pacing easily towardes the Tents, which ...
   [He mounted his horse and pacing easily towards the tents, which ...]
   (H. Roberts, *Honovrs Conquest* sig.C2v)

Interestingly, the SA construction ('to cause a horse to move with a controlled, easy gait'), attested from 1595, represents a slightly earlier formation:

(37) **1595** Then these two champions turned about their neighing horses, and pacing them till they were a competent distance one from another, then ...
   (R. Parry: *Moderatvs* xiii. sig. R, London 1595)

14. The verb *canter*

This verb (a clipping from *Canterbury pace* or *Canterbury gallop*, designating the pace of mounted pilgrims heading for Canterbury, cf. Klein 1966: 233) is documented from 1706. Unlike the verbs *gallop* and *pace*, which occur in intransitive constructions and transitive causative constructions in the same period, the verb *canter* enters into a SA construction more than a century later:

(38) **1845** The knight gracefully cantering an elegant cream-coloured Arabian.
   M. A. Titmarsh: *A Legend of the Rhine* xii., in G. Cruikshank's *Table-Book* 243, London 1845)

15. The verb *fly*

This verb is recorded in *Beowulf* (*flēogan*). Its Middle English successors are *flēogen, flīen*. It occurs in a variety of constructions which express the causation of the movement of participants that are mere receivers of the energy exerted by the agent (i.e. that are fully-fledged patients). Naturally, *fly* can only occur in SA constructions with birds as self-agentive causees. The caused motion situation 'to set (birds) flying one against the other' is documented from the Early Modern English period:

> (39) **1607** Meet me to morrow At Cheuy-chase, Ile flie my Hawke with yours.
> [Meet me tomorrow at Chevychase, I'll fly my hawk with yours.]
> > (T. Heywood: *A woman kilde with kindnesse* 1607 II., in *Works* II. 96, London 1874)

The verb *fly* may also be used in a SA construction encoding the caused motion of an inanimate patientive causee ('to cause a kite to rise and maintain its position in the air') – let us recall that, owing to its properties, this type of causee is actively involved in the execution of the motion. As mentioned above, this type of SA construction represents a subsequent development, cf. the earliest quotation from the Late Modern English period:

> (40) **1739** If you were to fly your kite.
> > (P. D. S. Chesterfield: *Letters* I. xxxi. 108, London 1792)

16. Conclusion

Building on the quotation evidence provided in the online edition of the *Oxford English Dictionary (OED3)*, the paper traces the emergence of secondary agent constructions (SA constructions) in the historical development of English and looks into the factors that determine their relatively late formation.

SA constructions are a sub-type of transitive causative constructions which express the external causation of self-agentive locomotion: the causer acts upon the causee, in this way inducing him to carry out a self-generated movement (*John walked Mary to the station* or *John jumped the horse over the fence*). The causee is thus an animate being, i.e. a participant endowed with the capacity to carry out a self-generated movement. The causee may, however, be an inanimate entity as well (*John walked the bicycle*). In spite of the fact that this participant does not execute the movement independently of the causer, it also represents a second energy source because it is, on account of its properties (bicycles have wheels, e.g.), actively involved in the execution of the movement.

The verbs that appear in SA constructions are the following: *run, walk, swim, dance, march, trot, leap, waltz, jump, prance, gallop, pace, canter* and *fly*. This largely restricted repertory of verbs is the outcome of two basic factors. The first is a pragmatic one: there is a strong tendency to reserve SA constructions for the expression of more or less prototypical motion situations (this fact is related to the semantics of these verbs, which designate the basic, most neutral types of self-agentive locomotion). The second factor is a semantico-syntactic one: the causee can occupy a direct object position (reserved for participants totally included in the event) only if the movement is intentional, i.e. only if it falls under the scope of the operation of both the causer and the causee in its entirety (this stipulation rules out verbs like *stagger,* etc.).

The paper demonstrates that, with the exception of the verbs *gallop* and *pace* (encoding movements of horses), verbs of self-agentive locomotion were first used intransitively and only later did they come to be used in SA constructions. The verbs *gallop* and *pace* are the only two verbs that are attested in both intransitive and transitive causative use in the same period.

The later emergence of SA constructions is most probably underlain by two reasons. The first reason lies in the causal structuration of motion situations encoded in these constructions. In contrast to prototypical caused motion constructions (transitive causative constructions with the direct object position taken up by a fully-fledged patient), SA constructions involve a more complicated causal pattern. In spite of employing a single verb they effect a fusion of two self-contained yet causally related situations.

The second reason underlying the later emergence of SA constructions lies in the semantics of the verbs admitted into them. Self-agentive locomotion verbs encode movements underlain by an energy whose scope of operation is confined to the physical limits of the executor of the movement. This fact naturally predisposes these verbs to be used in intransitive constructions. Verbs of self-agentive motion came to be used in SA constructions most probably by analogy with canonical caused motion situations, in which the patient functions as a receiver of the energy transmitted to him by an external agent.

SA constructions involving coercive force on the part of the causer (e.g., *John ran /marched) Harry to the bathroom* used in the sense 'John forced Harry to walk (probably quickly) to the bathroom') represent a further development. The later emergence of coercive SA constructions can be quite safely explained by the fact that in these types of situation the verb has to gain in the generality of its reference because only in this way can the SA construction express additional meanings like 'coercion'.

SA constructions endowed with very specialized meanings (sometimes verging on idiomaticity), which are superimposed on the basic kinetic frame, represent a yet later development (e.g., *to trot a person* may mean 'to conduct or escort a person to or around a place', *to march the dogs* may mean 'to urge on a team of dogs through snow' or *to walk a young hound* may mean 'to train and look after it', etc.).

At this point of the discussion a short summary of the history of the formation of SA constructions with the verbs under analysis will now be offered.

As discussed in the paper, the formation of SA constructions with all the verbs under analysis (apart from the verbs *gallop* and *pace*) represents a later development. The verbs *march, trot* and *prance,* first documented in the Middle

English period, appear in SA constructions in the Early Modern English period. The verb *dance,* also documented in the Middle English period, appears in SA constructions even later, namely, in the Late Modern English period. Interestingly, the verb *jump,* documented in the Early Modern English period, is documented in SA constructions as late as the 19th century. The verbs *canter* and *waltz,* first recorded in the 18th century, enter into SA constructions a century later.

In spite of the aforementioned reasons underlying the later emergence of SA constructions, it still comes as a surprise to learn that the verbs *swim, leap* and *fly,* as used in *Beowulf,* are attested in these types of construction as late as the 17th century.

As for the verb *run,* in Old English it appeared in the intransitive and the transitive forms (the latter one was used to encode caused movements). The use of this verb in SA constructions is first recorded in the Early Middle English period.

The verb *walk* represents a special case. Given the fact that this verb designates the most prototypical type of locomotion and, as such, represents a natural antonym of *run,* one might expect that the verb will appear in SA constructions relatively early. *Walk* is, however, attested in SA constructions at the end of the 15th century, most probably because this verb came to be used in a self-agentive locomotion sense as late as the 13th century.

As mentioned above, the verbs *gallop* and *pace* are the only two verbs that were used intransitively and transitively (in caused motion situations) in the same period. As for the verb *run,* in Old English it appeared in the intransitive and the transitive forms and it was the latter one that was used to encode caused movements. As for the verbs *gallop* and *pace,* their practically simultaneous intransitive use and transitive causative use may be attributed to the fact that these verbs appear in the Early Modern English period, in which SA constructions already represented a relatively well-established syntactical pattern – let us recall that in this period SA constructions were used with the verbs *run, walk, march, trot* and *prance.*

Dictionaries

Hall, J. R. Clark
    1960   *A concise Anglo-Saxon dictionary.* 4th edition with a supplement by H. D. Meritt. Cambridge: Cambridge University Press [many reprints].

Klein, Ernst
    1966   *A comprehensive etymological dictionary of the English language.* Vol. I. Amsterdam, New York, London: Elsevier.

Liberman, Anatoly
    2008   *An analytic dictionary of English etymology: An introduction.* Minneapolis: University of Minnesota Press.

OED3   *The Oxford English Dictionary*, 3rd edition, also known as the *OED online*. In progress 2000- <http://www.oed.com> or <http://dictionary.oed.com>

References

Anderson, John M.
1971 *The grammar of case: Towards a localistic theory.* Cambridge: Cambridge University Press.

Cortés Rodríguez, Francisco J. -- Ricardo Mairal Usón
2002 "A preliminary design for a syntactic dictionary of Old English on semantic principles", in: *A changing world of words: Studies in English historical lexicography, lexicology and semantics,* ed. J. E. Díaz Vera. Amsterdam and New York: Rodopi, 3-46.

Davidse, Kristin -- Sara Geyskens
1998 "Have you walked the dog yet? The ergative causativization of intransitives", *Word* 49: 155-180.

Huddleston, Rodney D. -- Geoffrey K. Pullum
2002 *The Cambridge grammar of the English language.* Cambridge: Cambridge University Press.

Jespersen, Otto
1909-1949 *A modern English grammar on historical principles,* 7 vols. London: George Allen & Unwin; Copenhagen: Ejnar Munksgaard [repr. 1954].

Kudrnáčová, Naděžda
2008 *Directed motion at the syntax-semantics interface.* Brno: Masaryk University.

Langacker, Ronald W.
1991 *Foundations of cognitive grammar.* Vol. 2: *Descriptive application.* Stanford: Stanford University Press.

Levin, Beth
1993 *English verb classes and alternations: A preliminary investigation.* Chicago: University of Chicago Press.

Mitchell, Bruce
1985 *Old English Syntax,* vol. 1 (*Concord, the Parts of Speech, and the Sentence*). Oxford: Clarendon Press.

Mustanoja, Tauno F.
1960 *A Middle English Syntax,* part 1 (*Parts of Speech*). Helsinki: Société Néophilologique.

Pinker, Steven
1989 *Learnability and cognition: The acquisition of argument structure.* Cambridge, Mass.: MIT Press.

Quirk, Randolph -- Sidney Greenbaum -- Geoffrey Leech -- Jan Svartvik
1985 *A comprehensive grammar of the English language.* London: Longman.

Rappaport Hovav, Malka -- Beth Levin
1998 "Building verb meanings", in: *The projection of arguments: Lexical and compositional factors,* ed. Miriam Butt & Wilhelm Geuder. Stanford: CSLI Publications, 97-134.

Ritter, Elizabeth -- Sara Thomas Rosen
1996 "Strong and weak predicates: Reducing the lexical burden", *Linguistic Analysis* 26: 29-62.

Rosen, Carol
    1984   "The interface between semantic roles and initial grammatical relations", in: *Studies in relational grammar 2*, ed. David M. Perlmutter & Carol Rosen. Chicago: University of Chicago Press, 38-77.
Rot, Sándor
    1992   *Old English.* Budapest: Tankönyvkiadó - Magyar Macmillan.
Shibatani, Masayoshi -- Prashant Pardeshi
    2002   "The causative continuum", in: *The grammar of causation and interpersonal manipulation*, ed. Masayoshi Shibatani. Amsterdam: John Benjamins, 85-126.
Sweet, Henry
    1898   *A new English grammar. Part 2: Syntax.* Oxford: Clarendon Press.
Visser, Fredericus Th.
    1963-1973   *An historical syntax of the English language.* 4 vols. Leiden: Brill.

Part III. Conjunctions, clauses, and sentences

Connectives before Chaucer: conjunctive *for* and its competition in early Middle English

Mary Blockley (Austin, Texas, USA)

Abstract

Middle English conjunctive *for* has both tensed and untensed verbal complements, but unlike Present-Day English these clauses are frequently expressions of neither purpose nor reason. Attention to dialectical effects on semantic change in the use of *for* with infinitivals has not accounted for the greater frequency of *for* heading tensed clauses. The more numerous finite clauses before *for* could have led the way to the decoupling of *for* and the expression of purpose, producing a short-lived conjunction with the semantic range of *that*.

This paper will consider some aspects of the complements of conjunctive *for* from its emergence in late Old English through the thirteenth century, with a view to identifying the factors that contributed to its subsequent narrowing of function and consequent status as a "common hard word" in student editions of Middle English texts.[1] Hard words have soft semantics, and in this case, while the word's syntax and semantics overlap with those of the preposition *for* that is their source, it has ambiguous syntax as well, heightened by the near-equal likelihood of tensed and tenseless complements.

Since the Renaissance there have been three kinds of constitutents governed by *for*: *for* as a conjunction, a complementizer with an infinitival phrase, and as a simple preposition, though *Coriolanus* is unusual in employing all three within a single sentence.

> (1) We have power in ourselves to do it, but it is a power that we have no power to do; *for* if he show us his wounds and tell us his deeds, we are to put our tongues into those wounds and speak *for* them; so, if he tell us his noble deeds, we must also tell him our noble acceptance of them. Ingratitude is monstrous, and *for* the multitude to be ingrateful were to make a monster of the multitude; of the which we being members should bring ourselves to be monstrous members.
>
> *Coriolanus* (1608) 2.3.4-10, ed. Bevington
>
> *OED for*, B.2.a (1.), A.5, III.7.a (2.)// B.18.a first 1508 *for...to* (3.)

For flourished as a conjunction in the early Middle English period, though our evidence for this state of the language exists mostly in poetic texts, including both apparently original compositions and those which are known to be translations from or versions of poems in Anglo-Norman or French. It should be noted that Lenker (2007: 199) claims that *for* as a Causal/Resultative adverbial connector does not appear at all in Middle English, following Bernd Kortmann's semantic analysis (1997: 342) and rejecting the *OED*'s evidence from early (pre-thirteenth century) Middle English that *for* alone begins to serve as a conjunction equivalent to

---

[1] E.g. Treharne 2004.

because and *since* in introducing both "the cause of a fact" or "the ground or reason for something previously said" (s. v. for, conj. B. 1, 3, and 4. 2nd 1989, June 2011). However its connective status in Middle English may be determined, *for* becomes a conjunction in Early Modern English. This *for* was later replaced in many of its functions: not only by *because* in clauses of cause, result and purpose, but by (to follow the lexicographers) *since, as, that, so that,* and other subordinating headwords; comparatives and relativizers as well as adverbials. What could provide the model for a preposition becoming this sort of a conjunction? Middle English inherits from Old English the form of complex predicates that take two non-parallel objects, [NP IQ/S], called CLAN-constructions (Warner 1982, López-Couso 2007) or earlier, in Anthony Kroch's terminology, the double object construction. Warner 1982: 91 defines this construction as a noun phrase [NP] followed by a finite [S[entence]] or nonfinite [IQ is an abbreviation for Indirect Question, which may of course be finite or nonfinite] clause. CLAN itself is an abbreviation for "clause and nominal".

(2) (a) besceawiað æcyres lilian hu hig weaxað, ne swincað hig ne hig ne spinnað.

(Matt 6:28)

[Consider the lilies of the field, how they grow; they neither work nor spin]

(b) sceawiaþ þa lilian hu hi wexað, hi ne swincað ne ne spinnað

(Luke 12:27)

[Consider the lilies, how they grow; they neither work nor spin]

(c) sceawiað ðæt land, hwæðer hit wæstmbære sy & mid wudum gemencged
(Numbers 13:19)

[Examine the land, [see] if it is fruitful and mixed with woods][2]

In a parallel crucial for Middle English developments, one of the objects may precede part of the verb, with the clausal second object not only following it, but separated from it by other material:

(3) ac ic wille nu, swa ic ær gehet, þara þreora landrica gemære gereccan, hu hie mid hiera wætrum tolicgeað. (*Orosius* 1.9.18)

[But now I intend, as I promised before, to describe the three great landmasses, how they extend amid the waters [of the ocean]]

It is nevertheless a question whether CLAN-constructions can incorporate true conjunctions like *gif,* and compound conjunctions like *for ðam ðe* as well as ditransitive verbs like *gereccan* and *sceawian*. Examples are ambiguous, as it is

---

[2] Old English examples are cited from the *DOEWC* (diPaolo Healey et al. 2009): <http://www.doe.utoronto.ca/pages/pub/web-corpus.html>. Translations are my own.

impossible to eliminate the possibility of taking the clausal second 'object' as an adverbial clause, as in the Luke 24:39 example, with Latin *quia* translated with conjunctive *for* in the King James version as "see, a spirit hath not flesh and bone."

(4) (a) He cwæð, Ic secge eow, sceawiað þas eardas, ðam ðe hi synd gearwe to geripe nu

(Ælfric *Homily* 5)

[He said, I tell you, behold the fields, those which are now ready for harvest [Aelfric here is paraphrasing John 4:35]]

(b) Palpiate et videte quia spiritus carnem et ossa non habet sicut me videntis habere

Grapiað & sceawiað gif ic gast were þonne næfde ic flæsc & ban

(Luke 24:39)

[Touch [me] and see; if I were a spirit, then I would not have flesh and bones]

The loss of this two-part predicate overlaps with the sudden appearance of the new preposition-derived conjunctions in the early twelfth century.

Prepositionally-derived conjunctions take the pressure off the verb to manage complex predicates all by itself by transferring parts of that predicate to adverbial-like derivatives of the preposition. The diminution of the role of the double-object construction may even have provided an analogical model for an enclitic reduction of prepositional object + relativizing particle conjunctions like Old English *for ðam ðe* > to Middle English *for*.[3] By contrast, ModE proclitically reduces the prepositional element of *because* > '*cos*.

Many examples of twelfth-century simplex *for* as a conjunction are apparently identical with the modern English conjunction, a situation that would soon change. The twelfth-century prose examples in (5.) are conjunctive, but they are not part of a two-part predicate. They are rather clauses of the variety many grammarians would call 'ground' or 'reason'. Syntactically they belong not to the objects of the main clause, but are adverbials that are extraposed or attached in other ways to shorter subordinate clauses.

(5) (a)... þet wæs here elces riht hand & heora stanen beneðan; þet wæs *for* se man ðe hafde an pund he ne mihte cysten ænne peni at anne market.

(*Peterborough Chronicle* 1125)

[that was that each of them [the false moneyers] lose his right hand and his testicles below; that was because the man that had a pound [from these men] could not exchange it at market for a single penny]

---

[3] The literature on *for ðam ðe* 'because' is voluminous; the most recent addition at the time this article was going to press is Chapters 4 and 5 (pp 85-201) of Molencki 2012. The author thanks Professor Sauer for the reference.

(b) ... men hit wiðcwæðen fulle twa dagas, ac hit naht ne beheld, *for* se biscop of Særesbyrig wæs strang & wealde eall Engleland & wæs þær togeanes eall þet he mihte & cuðe.

(*Peterborough Chronicle* 1123)

[men withstood it two whole days, but it did not signify, because the bishop of Salisbury was powerful and controlled all of England and there opposed [them] to the best of his ability and knowledge]

(c) Þone frigdom hæfde mann on neorxenewange, ac nu is se fridom geðeowtod, *for* se mann ne cann nan god, bute God þurh his geofe him tæce.

(*Elucidarium*, Vespasian D XIV, 12th century)

[man had that freedom in paradise, but now such freedom is enslaved, because man knows no good, unless God, through his gift, should teach him]

(d) ... *for* he is min hlaford and min help and min werigend and min fultum wið þe and wið eallum þinum leasum gewitum.

(*LS* 14 (Margaret) CCCC 303, 12th century)

[because he is my lord and my help and my guardian and my support against you, and against all your evil counselors]

Such uses are in accord with Present-Day English. Here, the presence of nominative inflection in *se man, se bisceop* reinforcing SVO or Complement order rules out the least trace of any prepositional parsing of the *for* that immediately precedes each subject.

However, a century later, with the loss of case in the demonstrative pronoun, many thirteenth-century texts follow *for* with noun phrase material that is more difficult to parse. The examples in (6) show that *for* can be followed by nouns, which though they are the objects of the fronted preposition phrase (*O&N* 792, 793; *Horn* 1510), risk confusion with the fronted object of a subordinated clause (*Havelok* 2751). In the other direction, a pronoun in the objective case is not the object of a preposition (*Havelok* 455), but is the patient of an impersonal verb in a clause subordinated by a conjunction, which E.V. Smithers translates here as "because" rather than as "for". In *Havelok* 602, the noun *man* is the subject of *shal* rather than the object of a preposition.

(6) (a) Bet þan þu alle yer longe:

Vor myne crafte men me luuyeþ,

Vor þine strengþe men þe schunyeþ. (*Owl and Nightingale* 790-92)

[(I, with my one song, do) better than you the whole year long; men love me for my power; men shun you for your strength]

(b) Horn makede Arnoldin thare

King after King Aylmare
Of al Westernesse
For his meoknesse.
The king and his homage
Yeven Arnoldin trewage.   (*King Horn* 1507-11)

[After King Aylmare (died), Horn made Arnoldin king of all Westerness for the sake of his meekness. The king and his vassals paid tribute to Arnoldin.]

(c) For his swerd he hof up heye,
And the hand he dide of fleye
That he smot him with so sore –   (*Havelok* 2751-3)

[[Havelok disgraces Godrich in retaliation for his blow:] For he [Havelok] raised high his sword and struck off the hand with which he [Godrich] had so painfully struck him.]

(d) "For us hungreth swithe sore" -
Seyden he, "we wolden more:"   (*Havelok* 455-56)

[["Why do you cry?"] "Because we greatly hunger," he said, "we would like more"]

(e) He stirten bothe up to the knave
For man shal god wille have,
Unkeveleden him and swithe unbounden (*Havelok* 601-03)

[Both of them, because a human desires to do the right thing, rose up to the boy, removed his gag and quickly freed him.]

Of course, the old personal pronouns like *he* 'he; they; she' were joined in Middle English by new distinctively nominative pronouns like *thei* and eventually *she*, and these pronouns lighten the parsing load in many other cases.

The appearance of *for* together with the infinitival marker *to* has occasioned the most linguistic interest in the development of *for* as a clausal marker. Debate on whether *for* was a complementizer before the early modern period has focused on the diachronic development of the infinitival construction. For example, a recent paper summarily notes:

Notably, the majority of *for*-marked infinitives in ME have null subjects. The standard ModE system, in which infinitival *for* occurs only if it is followed by an overt subject, does not develop until the early modern period, long after subjectless *for to* infinitives have proliferated across dialects. (Pak 2005: 3)

Table 1 summarizes the homonym environment of the infinitival constructions. It shows that throughout the early Middle English period the *for to* construction competed with one of its homonyms, the conjunction *for*, which introduced tensed clauses, as well as with the prepositional *for* that was the source of both the conjunction and the infinitival marker. The proportion of infinitival to tensed, finite clauses headed by *for* is higher in all three texts, while the preposition is much less frequent than either; there are only a few instances of the past tense singular of the intransitive strong verb *faran, for* from the OE strong verb class VI.

Table 1: Infinitival for to *clauses and* for/vor *as either conjunction introducing tensed clauses or as preposition in three early Middle English verse texts*

Owl and Nightingale, 1250-1300, Southern: Kent (Stanley 1964), or more generally (Cartlidge 2001) "the Home Counties" of London and the SE, Wessex, SW Midlands

For to 2x

Tensed *for*	61x	prepositional *for*	34x
Tensed *vor*	73x	prepositional *vor*	20x
Total clausal	136/1800 lines	total prepositional	54/1800 lines
1/13 lines	7.5%	1/33 lines	3%

King Horn, circa 1250, Southern and Midland, CUL Gg 4.27.2, Harley 2253, Bodl. Laud Misc 108; Possibly SW: Iyieri says W Berkshire (J. Hall, 1901, Herzman, Drake and Salisbury 1999)

***For to** 26x

Tensed *for*	30x	prepositional for	15x
Tensed *vor*	1x	prepositional *vor*	1x
Total clausal	57/1542 lines	total prepositional	16/1542 lines
1/27 lines	3.7%	1/100 lines	1%

*variants in infinitivals in lines 558 (no *for* in H and L) and 1519 (no *for* in H)

Havelok (circa 1300 Bodl Laud Misc 108) NE Midlands with Northern (2nd sing pres. -es, sometimes -t) and Southern (-inde) dialect features (Sands 1966: 57, Smithers 1987, Herzman, Drake and Salisbury 1999)

For to 51x

Tensed *for*	57x		
Total clausal	138/3000 lines	prepositional	50x/3000 lines
1/20 lines	4.6%	1/70 lines	1.7%

Note that in ME the conjunction is not equivalent to, but higher in frequency than is the preposition. *For* is an Old English preposition of moderately high frequency, occurring more than twelve thousand times in the Old English corpus of 6 million words, and so, about twice in every thousand words. About half of those OE *for*s are in composition, forming the conjunction with the relative complement marker *þæm þe*, while the remainder are simple prepositions. In Modern English the loss of inflection has only raised the prominence of *for*, which, though only the fifth most frequent preposition, is thirteenth in frequency among all words.

The Middle English poetic texts are well-known for showing signs of dialect mixture, as for example in rhymes that are no longer true, or that are not consistent with the pronoun system of the poem. As well as in phonology and morphology, the syntax of these texts may represent a compromise between new syntactic structures developing in one dialect area and taken, in written form, to another area where they have to undergo some semantic reanalysis. In the introduction to the *Linguistic Atlas of Late Medieval English (LALME* 1986: I, 4-5, 13-16, and 29-32) Angus McIntosh notes that most scribes are enthusiastic revisers; orthographically influenced by their source text, they nonetheless change spellings when their own dialect prefers another form. For Early Middle English, Marjorie Pak (2005) finds evidence both structural and semantic for a difference between the East and West Midlands in the use of *for* with *to*.

In the early Southern Middle English *Owl and Nightingale (O&N)*, the *for to* construction barely puts in an appearance. The only two examples of *for to* both have the voiceless fricative. This voiceless (and non-Southern) form, at least in the spelling of the manuscripts, also predominates for the preposition, but the voiced form predominates in the even more frequent occurrence of the conjunction. It would be pleasant to find that this mixture of voiceless and voiced forms is affected by the syntax-phonology interface – that is, that the voiceless form, as more effortful than the voiced, signals a larger constitutent than does its Southern equivalent, or even, to turn from phonotactics to orthography alone as a marker, that the voiced *vor* form reflects a scribal "constrained selection" (in the McIntosh sense of the phrase: 1986: 19), a form retained by a copyist who may have been more Southern than his predecessor. But the shift from phonological dialect criteria alone seen in the *Linguistic Atlas*'s dot maps does not draw primarily upon the very highest frequency words like the major prepositions and conjunctions' evidence of distinctive spelling, but instead on the tier just below them, words like WHICH, SUCH, and THOUGH. At any rate, the voicing of initial fricatives was a road not taken in differentiating the preposition from the rapidly emerging Middle English conjunction.

The Southwest, and the West in general are important for other reasons. In a paper drawing on the Penn-Helsinki parsed corpus, Marjorie Pak (2005) draws a syntactic and semantic distinction between the form and function of infinitival phrases with *for* in texts in western Early Middle English dialects (*Ancrene Riwle* (1200), the Katherine Group, and the Lambeth Homilies) and texts that can be located in the eastern regions.

The western texts allow univerbation of *forte*, and even where the *to* remains separate and unreduced, it allows the objects or other complements to precede the *for*. Residual Object Verb order in tensed subordinate clauses (particularly with object pronouns) occurs more in the east than in the west, and Pak finds that fronted noun objects of the infinitive occasionally precede the *for* in western infinitivals (the "Susannah for to see" pattern), but such preposed objects follow the *for* in the east; her example is "mankenn to aliesen" 'to redeem mankind' *Vices and Virtues* 1, p. 117, line 1445. Only 50 of her total of 778 infinitivals have this pattern. Perhaps most significantly, given critical response, she finds that the eastern texts have a stronger association of the *for to* infinitival with the expression of purpose, though Pak stops short of taking this difference as an eastern innovation towards the standard language.

The most remarked-upon evidence offered by Pak is semantic: the rise between 1250 and 1350 in *to* infinitives that do *not* express purpose, and the link of the weakening of its semantics with the forms characteristic of the West. Her binary distinction between purpose and non-purpose infinitives reflects her goal of arguing for dialectal influence in the standard vs nonstandard varieties of Present-Day English (as for example Belfast English), finding that the survival of the *for to* infinitive, though later also narrowed in meaning to the expression of purpose, had a different source.

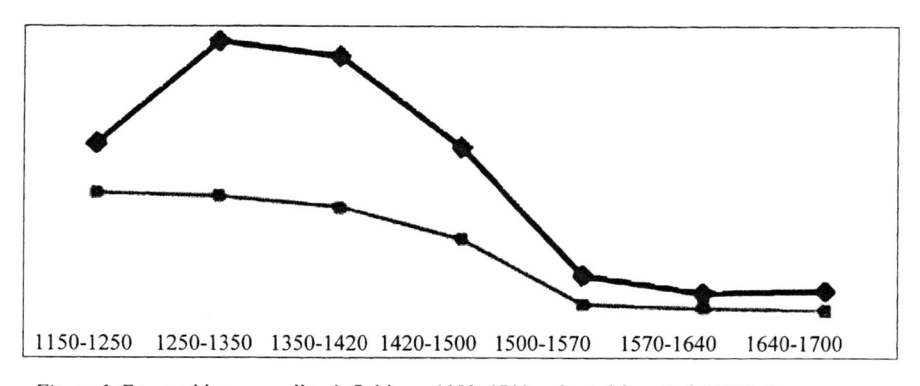

Figure 1: For-marking *over all* to-infinitives, *1150–1710; adapted from Pak (2006: 3)*

Pak's intriguing analysis is also consistent with the idea that the motivation for the non-purpose meaning lay in the use of *for* as a full conjunction, with tensed clauses. Her tables show that while in the other two texts the *to* infinitivals make a larger contribution to the total of clausal constructions with *for* as the proportion of the prepositional uses goes down, the conjunction remains more common than is the infinitival. And the difference, if any, between West and East is slight, to the extent that *King Horn* represents the one and *Havelok* the other. The significant variable across these texts seems rather to be the conjunction as the hidden half of the infinitival iceberg.

The preposition *for* has a close relationship with purpose and even with purpose clauses. In their resolutely synchronic semantic study of the Modern English preposition *for* the cognitive linguists Tyler and Evans (2003: 153) indirectly draw attention to the clausal quality of the expression of "motives, intents, and purposes", which require a motivator, intender, or purporter, and conclude:

> In contrast to the semantics of *to* – where a number of senses were related to direction, attaining a particular target or goal, and contact – the preponderance of senses associated with *for* are primarily concerned with motives, intentions, and purposes, reflecting the more intentional character of the functional element associated with the proto-scene.

Yet the conjunction in its Middle English meaning receives short shrift from editors and lexicographers alike. It is noteworthy that in the glossary to his scholarly edition of *Havelok*, E. V. Smithers gives no fewer than 8 meanings for the 50 instances of the preposition *for*. A ninth meaning, oddly included among the prepositions, designates the *for* of the *for to* construction as a "hypercharacterized *for*" and this *for* occurs fifty times by itself. Yet Smithers refers the Middle English student to *OED*'s *for* definition, one that emphasizes "ground or reason for something previously said" for the Middle English conjunction, which occurs 57 times, even though Smithers himself glosses only two of these 57 clausal instances as meaning "because".

Unlike prepositions, which particularly in the absence of case distinctions create relationships between a noun and another constituent, clausal connectives can only reinforce an interpretation that is already possible if not actually implied by the relationship between contiguous clauses. The motivation for the change in semantics, broadening away from purpose alone, may be the difference between the greater variety of relations that may hold between the clauses, particularly for a listener not fully possessed of the speaker's intended expression. It is a relationship enhanced, perhaps, but not created by the conjunction, and enabled only by the weakening of the conjunction's contribution to the meaning as it takes upon itself some of the functions served by the *that* clause in OE, a parallel intriguingly consistent with the derivation of conjunctive *for* from the OE relativizing phrasal conjunction *for ðam ðe*.

The semantic relation between a *for* headed clause and the clause adjacent to it – whether preceding it – or following it, is determined primarily by the relations holding between the two clauses themselves in that order, as perceived, and not necessarily as intended. In these early texts, the infrequency of expanded verb phrase forms tolerates a wider range of presumed semantic relationships than is possible now. Of the previous *Havelok* examples, only one of the three, that in line 455, can be linked by cause. *Havelok*'s mix of dialects may have something to do with this, and *Havelok*'s predilection for phrasal verbs might be thought to play a role, though *for* does not form phrasal verbs in this text.

Quantifying degrees of clausal purposiveness seems to me not an exact science, and so I have not calculated the purpose/non-purpose proportions for these poetic texts. That the broader, non-purpose meanings exist at all for *for* as well as they did, and do, for the relativizing *that* is indisputable, if diachronically doomed to get only the most passing reference in the *OED*'s treatment.

The *MED*'s categories allow for conjunctive *for* to function almost as a relative clause, collectively terming examples variously as a clause of amplification or expansion, as you can see from its second definition:

> In a clause which amplifies or explains another clause by giving an example, citing an authority, making a comparison, restating in different terms, etc.: inasmuch as, since, so that, seeing that, as, that.

Unfortunately, the *MED* citations may give the (false) impression that conjunctive *for* follows its main clause in early Middle English until the time of Chaucer, from whom they cite some fronted examples. Neil Cartlidge's (2001) edition and translation of *The Owl and Nightingale* reflects this newer notion of ME *for* as frequently equivalent to the Modern English non-restrictive relative clause, as when he translates the *for* clause beginning in line 233 with "which", i. e., the clause is adjectival in function. I suggest that the displacement of the clausal *for* of *The Owl and Nightingale* by infinitivals in later texts is a response to, rather than a consequence of, the weakening of the sense of purpose begun in the conjunctive use of *for*.

What Olga Fischer (2000: 19 [section 3.4.4]) has described as the Middle English infinitive's "loss of semantic integrity" – that it can do the work of a present participle or a tensed adverbial clause – might also have something to do with the prevalence of the tensed clauses with conjunctive *for* and with the *MED*'s definition 2 for conjunctive *for*. This loss of semantic integrity may be the work of the *for* itself temporarily re-purposing, or altering its prepositionally-based assignment of internal (grammatical subject) intention, and instead becoming grammaticalized to express, sometimes almost parenthetically, the narrator's intentions of association through narrative and description, no longer limited to the expression of purpose, cause, result, and end.

Is the shift from preposition to conjunction facilitated by features of tense and aspect in the controlled clause, by those of the principal clause, or neither? The three texts examined here offer grounds for only a preliminary consideration of the issues. What does appear is that the proportions seen in these three Middle English poems go in the other direction from the hypothesis that Rohdenburg has developed (e.g. 1996, 2002), about the length of complements in EModE playing a crucial role in the diachronic shift from infinitival to tensed clausal complements, and also, to some extent, in the other direction from Wasow's (1997) proposal in his article on "grammatical weight" in Modern English; the idea that endweight, in favoring writer over reader, is a product of a particular kind of literacy. In these Middle English poems a majority of clausal complements in the earliest texts quickly changes to a situation in which the clausal load is divided by and with infinitivals, and the consequent and consequential lack of necessity to specify the subject.

For can in Modern English now serve only as internal explanation – in Modern English, *for* is the conjunction of internal reason and speaker's explanation of causality – because such a clause in Modern English must follow the clause it qualifies, and it also must have an intonational pause before the *for*, showing that the clause is a deduction rather than a consequence, more of a parenthetical comment:

> (7) The neighbors left, for their mail from yesterday is still in the box
> Blockley 2001:182-3, following Traugott 1992: 252-55

Moreover, and significantly for the Middle English development, the relationship of the speaker's explanation of causality holds even without the *for*, when the clauses are in asyndetic parataxis:

> (8) The neighbors left. Their mail from yesterday is still in the box.

The presence of the *for* helps only to establish that the second statement applies to the first, to make a link through a division.

The brief strange flowering of Middle English *for* as a non-purposive, out-of-the-blue clause-opening particle has, I think, left at least one relic in Present-Day English. Conjunctive *for* survives to the present day in the nineteenth century congratulatory popular song, "For he's a jolly good fellow":

> (9) "For he's a jolly good Fellow,
> For he's a jolly good Fellow,
> For he's a jolly good Fellow,
> Which nobody can deny."
> (James Payn (1830-1898), published in *Household Words* 1857: 142)

I have not been able to trace this text beyond 1857, when it opens "Crumpled Rose-Leaves at St. Boniface", one of many short tales of contemporary life published in Charles Dickens' magazine *Household Words* and composed by the then-young old Etonian James Payn. In "For he's a jolly good Fellow, [...] which nobody can deny" the initial *for* does no necessary syntactic work, as it is followed by a broad-reference *which* that applies to the clause as a whole. Substituting an introductory and interjectionary "oh" for the conjunction would keep the meter without materially changing the meaning. If the *for* does anything, it is to suggest an otherwise unexpressed matrix clause, such as "we sing" or "our reason for singing must be".

However, it may be observed in passing that the recent and abrupt loss of the acceptability of *for* as a causal conjunction in the United States outside this fixed collocation can be pin-pointed from variation in the two most successful world releases of the American song "(What a) Wonderful World". Sam Cooke (born 1931), who shared writing credits with Lou Adler (born 1933) and Herb Alpert (born 1935), recorded the original version, which was released in 1960. When Art Garfunkel (born 1941) covered the song in 1977, he changed the third line of the lyrics in the song's bridge, which in the 1960 version as sung and in published music are:

(10) "Now I don't claim to be an "A" student,
But I'm trying to be.
For maybe by being an "A" student, baby,
I can win your love for me."

to

(11) "*I think that* maybe by being an "A" student, baby".

Other cover versions and parody versions appearing since 1977 have substituted for the mid-century conjunctive *for* any of a number of other connectors, such as *'cos, but, so,* or even simply begin the second part of the verse with "Maybe."

In conclusion, the intermediate stage of complementizing *for* heading predominately finite clauses seen in *The Owl and the Nightingale* did not simply precede the heavy use of *for* with infinitive clauses seen in texts of the next generation in the South and Midlands. The two constructions appeared in nearly equal numbers, and in contexts that as often as not supported either the finite or the non-finite verb. The constructions appeared in texts that spanned the usually conservative West, which tended to merge the *for* in the head of the predicate with the infinitive marker *to* and the innovative East, where the infinitival *for* was less frequent, more free in allowing predicate constituent material after rather than before it, and much more separable from the *to*, the sign of the infinitive.

The semantic bleaching of the early Middle English conjunction *for*, as recorded both in the dictionary definition of the clause of explanation, and the semanticist's category of the commenting clause of speaker's reason, parallels later developments more commonly seen in conjunctions that develop from adverbs, like that of conjunctive *now*, and even the adverbialization of the declarative *you know* into a particle. It appears that conjunctive *for* was a victim of its own success, undergoing a radical and ultimately fatal re-purposing. By the time of the composition of *Havelok*, *for* could appear almost anywhere in the clause, mean almost anything, and so was well on its way to meaning nothing and appearing nowhere.

Postscript:
Subsequent to the presentation of this paper Ursula Lenker has written of the "recursive" *for* equivalent to Latin *nan/enim* that "from the beginning of the thirteenth century… marks the second connect as having an illocutionary weight of its own and, more importantly, explicitly marking the voice of the speaker who comments on his view of the relation of textual portions", and further that this "*for* highlighting the line of argument is the predominant one from the middle of the fourteenth century" (Lenker 2010: 162-163). See also Blockley (2001: 74)

Sources

Bevington, David (ed.)
    1997   *The complete works of Shakespeare*, updated 4th edition, New York: Longman p. 1365.
Cartlidge, Neil
    2001   *The owl and the nightingale*. Exeter: University of Exeter Press.
Hall, Joseph
    1901   *King Horn: A Middle-English romance*. Oxford: Clarendon Press.
Herzman, Ronald B. -- Graham Drake -- Eve Salisbury (eds.)
    1999   *Four romances of England*. Kalamazoo, Michigan: Western Michigan University.
Sands, Donald B.
    1966   *Middle English verse romances* Exeter: University of Exeter Press [reprinted 1997].
Shakespeare, William
    [1608]   *Coriolanus* in, *The complete works of Shakespeare*. Updated 4th edition (1997), ed. David Bevington, New York: Longman.
Smithers, E. V. (ed.)
    1987   *Havelok*. Oxford: Clarendon Press.
Stanley, E. G. (ed.)
    1960   *The Owl and the Nightingale*. Manchester: Manchester University Press.
Treharne, Elaine (ed.)
    2004   *Old and Middle English c. 890-c.1400: An anthology*. 2nd ed. Oxford: Blackwell.

Dictionaries

DOEWC   *Dictionary of Old English Web Corpus*, eds. Antonette diPaolo Healey, John Price Wilkin & Xin Xiang. Toronto, 2009. <http://www.doe.utoronto.ca/pages/pub/web-corpus.html>
LALME   *A linguistic atlas of Late Mediaeval English*, ed. Angus McIntosh, M. K. Samuels & M. Benskin. Aberdeen: Aberdeen University Press. 1986.
MED   *Middle English Dictionary* ed. Hans Kurath, Sherman M. Kuhn, John Reidy, Robert E. Lewis. Ann Arbor: University of Michigan Press, 1952-2001. online: <http://ets.umdl.umichedu/m/med> or <http://quod.lib.umich.edu/m/med/>

OED1	*A New English Dictionary on Historical Principles*, ed. Sir James A. H. Murray, Henry Bradley, Sir William A. Craigie, Charles T. Onions. Oxford: Oxford University Press, 1884-1928. Reprinted 1933 in 10 vols. with supplement and bibliography under the title *The Oxford English Dictionary*.
OED2	*The Oxford English Dictionary*, 2nd edition in 20 volumes, ed. John A. Simpson and Edmund S. C. Weiner. Oxford: Oxford University Press, 1989 [incorporates the *Supplement* in 4 vols. ed. Robert W. Burchfield, 1972-1986].
OED3	*The Oxford English Dictionary*, 3rd edition, also known as the *OED online*. In progress 2000- <http://www.oed.com> or <http://dictionary.oed.com>

References

Birner, Betty J. -- Gregory Ward
    1998   *Information status and noncanonical word order in English.* Amsterdam: John Benjamins.

Blockley, Mary
    2001   *Aspects of Old English poetic syntax: Where clauses begin.* Urbana and Chicago: University of Illinois Press.

Brinton, Laurel -- Elizabeth Traugott
    2005   *Lexicalization and language change.* New York: Cambridge University Press.

Fischer, Olga
    1992   "Syntax", in: *CHEL* II, 207-408.

Fischer, Olga -- Annette Rosenbach -- Dieter Stein (eds.)
    2000   *Pathways of change: Grammaticalization in English.* Amsterdam and Philadelphia: John Benjamins.

Iyieri, Yoko
    2001   *Negative constructions in Middle English.* Fukoaka: Kyushu University Press.

Ingham, Richard
    2006   "On two negative concord dialects in early English",*Language Variation and Change* 18: 241-266.

Kortmann, Bernd
    2007   *Adverbial subordination: A typology and history of adverbial subordinators based on European languages.* Empirical Approaches to Language Typology. Berlin/New York: Mouton de Gruyter.

Laing, Margaret
    2000   "Never the twain shall meet: Early Middle English: the East – West divide", in: *Placing Middle English in context,* ed. Irma Taavitsainen. Berlin and New York: Mouton de Gruyter: 97-124.

Lenker, Ursula -- Anneli Meurman-Solin (eds.)
    2007   *Connectives in the history of English.* Current Issues in Linguistic Theory 283. Amsterdam and Philadelphia: John Benjamins.

Lenker, Ursula
    2010 *Argument and rhetoric: Adverbial connectors in the history of English* (Topics in English Linguistics 64). Berlin and New York: Mouton de Gruyter.

López-Couso, Marie José
    2007 "Adverbial connectives within and beyond adverbial subordination: The history of *lest*", in: Lenker and Meurman-Solin 2007: 11-30.

Mazzon, Gabriella
    2004 *A history of English negation*. New York: Longman.

Milroy, James
    2003 "On the discourse of historical linguistics: Language-internal explanation and language ideologies", *Forum for Modern Languages Studies* 39: 357-370.

Molencki, Rafał
    2012 *Causal conjunctions in mediaeval English: A corpus-based study of grammaticalization*. Katowice: Uniwersytet Slaski: Oficyna Wydawnicza.

Pak, Marjorie
    2006 "Infinitive marking with *for*: a diachronic account", in: *U.Penn Working Papers in Linguistics* 10: 1-14.
                      <http://marjoriepak.com/pak-for-to.pdf>

Payn, James
    1857 "Crumpled rose-leaves at St. Boniface", in: *Household words*, ed. Charles Dickens, vol. XV: 142-44. London: Office 16, Wellington Street North.

Rohdenburg, Günter -- Britta Mondorf (eds.)
    2003 *Determinants of grammatical variation in English*. Topics in English Linguistics 43. New York: Mouton de Gruyter.

Traugott, Elizabeth
    1992 "Syntax", in *CHEL* I, 168-289.

Tyler, Andrea -- Vyvyan Evans
    2003 *The semantics of English prepositions*. New York: Cambridge University Press.

Visser, Fredericus Th.
    1963-1973 *An historical syntax of the English language*. 4 vols. Leiden: Brill.

Warner, Anthony
    1982 *Complementation and the methodology of historical syntax*. London: Croon Helm.

Wasow, Thomas
    1997 "Remarks on grammatical weight", *Language Variation and Change* 9: 81-105.

A history of *because*-clauses and the coordination–subordination dichotomy

Yuko Higashiizumi (Tokyo, Japan)

Abstract

This paper reconsiders the traditional dichotomy between coordination and subordination using the diachronic and synchronic data of *because*-clauses in the written record of spoken English. *Because*-clauses are generally characterized as causal subordinate clauses in Present-Day English (PDE). There are, however, cases where they do not fit this characterization, especially in spoken language. Moreover, some modern studies have pointed out that the traditional dichotomy calls for further consideration. In the literature on grammaticalization, Hopper & Traugott (2003) propose a subordination–hypotaxis–parataxis continuum of complex clause constructions in grammaticalization. This study illustrates that *because*-clauses have been developing from less into more paratactic clause-combining constructions in structure and meaning, based on the correlation between the degree of clause integration and the interpretation of *because*-clauses. It shows that the continuum is more relevant to representing the diachronic process and the synchronic diversity of *because*-clauses than the dichotomy.

1. Introduction

The purpose of this paper is to reexamine the traditional two-way distinction between coordination and subordination. As other recent studies have argued, the traditional dichotomy and definitions of subordination call for further consideration.[1] This study will explore clause combination and the interpretation of combined clauses from a historical perspective.

Because-clauses are usually called causal subordinate clauses in Present-Day English (PDE henceforth). However, it has been argued that some of them cannot be considered subordinate nor do they express causal meaning, especially in spoken PDE.[2] This paper will use "written records of spoken language" (Jacobs & Jucker 1995: 7) to examine the diachronic process and synchronic diversity of *because*-clauses. Section 2 observes PDE *because*-clauses from the viewpoint of the correlation between their interpretation and clause-combining structure. Section 3 briefly introduces a background to this study. Section 4 reports, based on Higashiizumi (2006), how the usage of *because*-clauses has been developing. Section 5 gives some concluding remarks.

---

[1] E.g., Haiman & Thompson 1984; Lehmann 1988; Matthiessen & Thompson 1988; Cristfaro 2003; Van Valin 2005.
[2] E.g., Quirk et al. 1985; Schleppegrell 1991; Ford 1993; Couper-Kuhlen 1996; Stenström & Andersen 1996; Stenström 1998.

2. *Because*-clauses in Present-Day English

This section presents examples of PDE *because*-clauses based on the correlation between their interpretation and the degree of clause integration.[3] According to Sweetser (1990), a *because*-clause can be interpreted as being connected to its main clause in the content domain (i.e., connection in the real world), in the epistemic domain (i.e., connection in the epistemic domain), and in the speech-act domain (i.e., connection in the conversational domain).

The *because*-clause in (1) exemplifies a subordinate or hypotactic clause with causal meaning in PDE. The connection is in the content domain.

(1) We base ourselves mainly in LA *because* at least over there you can get products done.

(1993 Liverpool Echo & Daily Post [BNC K97 2665])

As has been pointed out in the literature, there are examples of *because*-clauses that can be counted neither as subordinate nor as expressing a real-world causality. For example, the *because*-clauses in (2) and (3) are paratactic to the preceding clause as indicated by the tone unit boundary (#) (most of the symbols in LLC are omitted for ease of reading here). The connection is in the epistemic domain in (2) and in the speech-act domain in (3) respectively.

(2) B: I know it is Innocent the Fourth# I'm sure# *because* I ((you know#)) I've seen the portrait in lectures on Velasques# ((4 sylls illustrate#))

(1963 [LLC 1 4 40 6040–6080])

(3) A: do you want somewhere to warm to work# at the weekends#;*- .; *because* there's my place you can [@]*

B: I go to AC# - - fine# thanks#*   (1970 [LLC 2 4a 42 4380–4470])

Furthermore, a *because*-clause sometimes appears independently in the utterance-initial position as in (4). It can be regarded as an independent clause with a clause-initial pragmatic marker in the sense of Brinton (1996).

(4) a: *how* soon do you want **these ((back))**

A: ((don't know# doesn't really *2 sylls))*

a: *[@m]* [@m] *because* it may take us a month or so to/ sort of sort through them and and decide [@m] you know whether we wish to approach you to ask if we /could make use of them

A: yeah#   (1969 [LLC 2 2a 36 2090–37 2130])

---

[3] See e.g., Schiffrin 1987; Sweetser 1990; Traugott 1992.

Table 1 summarizes the classification of PDE *because*-clauses based on the correlation between their interpretation and clause-combining structure. Building upon this classification, I will investigate the diachronic process they have been undergoing.

Table 1. Because-*clauses in PDE*[4]

Example	(1)	(2), (3)	(4)
Clause Combination	[CL1 [*because* CL2]]	[[CL1] [*because* CL2]]	[*because* CL]
because-clause	subordinate or hypotactic	non-subordinate or paratactic	independent
Interpretation in Sweetser's (1990) term	content conjunction	(2) epistemic conjunction (3) speech-act conjunction	N/A

3. Background

3.1 Data

As it turned out that paratactic and independent *because*-clauses often appear in spoken PDE, I analyzed some written records of spoken language from 1590 to 2000 in Southern British English for comparison purposes.[5]

In order to observe the correlation between the interpretation of *because*-clauses and clause-combining structure, I counted the number of expressions that overtly led to epistemic conjunction interpretation such as a so-called epistemic modality and an epistemic verb, e.g., 'I know' and 'I'm sure' in (2). For those examples that overtly led to speech-act conjunction interpretation, the speech-act verbs, imperatives and interrogatives, e.g., the interrogative in (3), were included.

3.2 Cline of clause-combining constructions in grammaticalization

As seen in Section 2, PDE *because*-clauses include subordination, parataxis and independence. In order to trace the pathway to such synchronic diversity of clause combination, I adopted the cline of clause-combining constructions in grammaticalization (Hopper & Traugott 2003: 176–184) instead of the traditional coordination–subordination dichotomy. The summary of properties relevant to the cline of clause-combining constructions is given in Figure 1.

---

[4] CL = clause; CL1 = first clause in the sentence; CL2 = second clause in the sentence.
[5] See Higashiizumi 2006: 40–41 for the details of the data; see also Suzuki 1999; Onodera 2004.

Figure 1: Properties relevant to the cline of clause-combining constructions (Hopper & Traugott 2003:179)

parataxis ——————— hypotaxis ——————— subordination
(relative independence)   (interdependence)   (dependence)
nucleus ————————————————————— margin
minimal integration ————————————— maximal integration
maximal overt linking ————————————— minimal overt linking

3.3 Subjectification and intersubjectification

We saw in Section 2 that a *because*-clause is used not only as a means of expressing a real-world causality but also as a means of expressing the speaker's epistemic stance or their motive for the speech-act being performed. As it will become evident in Section 4 that *because*-clauses are starting to be used for epistemic and speech-act conjunction interpretation in PDE, the diachronic process they have been undergoing serves as an instance of 'subjectification' and 'intersubjectification'.[6]

In what follows, I will explore *because*-clauses based on the correlation between their interpretation and clause-combining structure from a diachronic perspective.

4. History of *because*-clauses

4.1 Previous studies on the history of *because*-clauses

Because derives from the phrasal construction *by (the) cause (that)* in Late Middle English (Late ME), which is said to be a borrowing from Old French *par cause de*. It became popular in the fourteenth century and was used originally in various forms. The subordinator *that* gradually fell into disuse, leaving only *because*. *Because* spread rapidly in the Early Modern English (EModE) period. It gained popularity in the sixteenth century, beginning to gain on *for* in frequency during the seventeenth century, and became one of the typical causal clause markers in PDE.[7]

4.2 From less to more paratactic clause-combining construction

This section examines how the clause-combining constructions of *because*-clauses have been changing. Table 2 shows a transition of the distribution of *because*-clauses by position. Note that (i) in Table 2 includes examples such as (1) to (3) above. What is worth mentioning here is that (iii), i.e., independent *because*-clauses

---

[6] See Traugott & Dasher 2002; Hopper & Traugott 2003; Traugott 2003.
[7] See, e.g., Kortmann 1997; Rissanen 1999, 2006; Lenker 2007 for further details.

such as (4) above, increase in proportion from around 1950 onwards, whereas the use of (i), i.e., canonical clause-combining constructions, is more or less proportionately constant from around 1650 onwards. Roughly speaking, we can see that *because*-clauses are becoming more paratactic towards the present.

Table 2. The transition of the distribution of because-*clauses by position*

	−1650	−1750	−1850	−1950	−2000 (written) (BNC)	−2000 (spoken) (BNC)	−2000 (spoken) (LLC)
(i) CL1 *because* CL2	30 (63.8%)	22 (66.7%)	61 (69.3%)	86 (59.3%)	46 (75.4%)	44 (69.8%)	115 (79.9%)
(ii) *Because* CL1,CL2	2 (4.3%)	4 (12.1%)	3 (3.4%)	5 (3.5%)	2 (3.3%)	7 (11.1%)	5 (3.5%)
(iii) *Because* CL	1 (2.1%)	0 (0%)	3 (3.4%)	7 (4.8%)	10 (16.4%)	6 (9.5%)	18 (12.5%)
(iv) Others	14 (29.8%)	7 (21.2%)	21 (23.9%)	47 (32.6%)	3 (4.9%)	6 (9.5%)	6 (4.2%)
TOTAL	47	33	88	145	61	63	144
TOTAL				313			268

4.3 From less to more subjective meaning

This section observes the uses of *because*-clauses diacronically. As seen in the preceding subsection, the canonical clause-combining construction "CL1 *because* CL2", i.e., (i) in Table 2 above, is relatively constant in proportion from around 1650. However, the distribution of expressions that overtly lead to epistemic or speech-act conjunction interpretation has been changing. Table 3 gives the distribution of such expressions in "CL1 *because* CL2". Note that such expressions increase in frequency both in CL1 and in CL2 in PDE.

Table 4, on the other hand, shows the distribution of such overt expressions in independent *because*-clauses, i.e., (iii) in Table 2 above. No such expressions appear before 1950 in my data.

Table 3. The distribution of overt expressions of epistemic or speech-act conjunction interpretation in "CL1 because CL2"

	CL1		CL2 (*Because*-clause)	
	Diachronic (1590–1949)	PDE (1950–2000)	Diachronic (1590–1949)	PDE (1950–2000)
(i) Epistemic	35 (17.6%)	50 (24.4%)	29 (14.6%)	38 (18.5%)
(ii) Speech-act	31 (15.6%)	43 (21.0%)	5 (2.5%)	15 (7.3%)
(iii) Others	133 (66.8%)	112 (54.6%)	165 (82.9%)	152 (74.1%)
TOTAL	199	205	199	205

Table 4. The distribution of overt expressions of epistemic or speech-act conjunction interpretation in "Because CL"

	CL (*Because*-clause)	
	Diachronic (1590–1949)	PDE (1950–2000)
(i) Epistemic	0 (0%)	10 (29.4%)
(ii) Speech-act	0 (0%)	5 (14.7%)
(iii) Others	11 (100%)	19 (55.96%)
TOTAL	11	34

We have recognized so far that some types of expressions of epistemic or speech-act conjunction interpretation began to appear overtly both in CL1 and *because*-clauses from around 1950 to the present. In other words, *because*-clauses have started to be used for expressing the speaker's epistemic stance or motive for speech-act being performed, i.e., for more (inter)subjective meaning, in PDE.

4.4 What does the history of *because*-clauses tell us about clause-combining structure?

As illustrated in Section 2, there are examples of *because*-clauses that can neither be counted as subordinate nor expressing a real-world causality in PDE. Some of them are paratactic in structure and meaning and do not fit into the traditional coordination–subordination dichotomy (see also Aarts 2007 for a synchronic gradience). Moreover, we saw in Sections 4.2 and 4.3 that they have been becoming more and more paratactic to their surrounding clauses over the course of time. In conclusion, the diachronic process is better represented than the dichotomy in the cline of clause-combining constructions in grammaticalization (see also Verstraete 2007 for an alternative both to the continuum and to the dichotomy).

5. Concluding remarks

Because-clauses are becoming more paratactic to the surrounding clauses and are beginning to be used to express more (inter)subjective meaning. In other words, they have been developing from less to more paratactic clause-combining constructions in structure and meaning. Furthermore, I recognized that their diachronic process and synchronic diversity are better represented in the subordination-hypotaxis-parataxis cline of clause-combining constructions in grammaticalization than in the traditional coordination-subordination dichotomy. Further cross-linguistic study on the diachronic process and synchronic diversity of causal clauses would be a valuable future task to test the usefulness of the continuum over the dichotomy.[8]

Sources

BNC	British National Corpus
	1991-1994 <http://www.natcorp.ox.ac.uk/>
HC	The Helsinki Corpus of English Text: Diachronic Part, ICAME Collection of English Corpora, 2nd ed.
LLC	The London-Lund Corpus of Spoken English, in the ICAME Collection of English Corpora, 2nd ed.

References

Aarts, Bas
    2007   *Syntactic gradience: The nature of grammatical indeterminacy.* Oxford: Oxford University Press.

Brinton, Laurel J.
    1996   *Pragmatic markers in English: Grammaticalization and discourse functions.* Berlin: Mouton de Gruyter.

---

[8] This paper is a revision of the one given at the 15th ICEHL. I would like to thank Ursula Lenker, Matti Risannen, Reijiro Shibasaki and the participants for discussion and helpful comments. I also thank Jane Boughton for correcting my English. An earlier version of the paper originates in part from Higashiizumi (2006). Any remaining errors are my own responsibility.

Couper-Kuhlen, Elizabeth
    1996 "Intonation and clause combining in discourse: The case of *because*", *Pragmatics* 6: 389-426.

Cristfaro, Sonia
    2003 *Subordination*. Oxford: Oxford University Press.

Ford, Cecilia E.
    1993 *Grammar in interaction: Adverbial clauses in American English conversations*. Cambridge: Cambridge University Press.

Haiman, John -- Sandra A. Thompson
    1984 "'Subordination' in universal grammar", *Berkeley Linguistics Society* 10: 510-523.

Haiman, John -- Sandra A. Thompson (eds.)
    1988 *Clause combining in grammar and discourse*. Amsterdam: John Benjamins.

Higashiizumi, Yuko
    2006 *From a subordinate clause to an independent clause: A history of English because-clause and Japanese kara-clause*. Tokyo: Hituzi Syobo.

Hopper, Paul J. -- Elizabeth C. Traugott
    2003 *Grammaticalization*. Cambridge: Cambridge University Press.

Jacobs, Andreas -- Andreas H. Jucker
    1995 "The historical perspective in pragmatics", in: *Historical pragmatics: Pragmatic developments in the history of English*, ed. Andreas H. Jucker. Amsterdam: John Benjamins, 3-33.

Kortmann, Bernd
    1997 *Adverbial subordination: A typology and history of adverbial subordinators based on European languages*. Berlin: Mouton de Gruyter.

Lehmann, Christian
    1988 "Towards a typology of clause linkage", in: Haiman & Thompson 1988: 181-225.

Lenker, Ursula
    2007 "*Frowhi* 'because': Shifting deictics in the history of English causal connection", in: Lenker & Meurman-Solin 2007: 193-227.

Lenker, Ursula -- Meurman-Solin (eds.)
    2007 *Connectives in the history of English*. Amsterdam & Philadelphia: John Benjamins.

Matthiessen, Christian -- Sandra A. Thompson
    1988 "The structure of discourse and 'subordination'", in: Haiman & Thompson 1988: 275-329.

Onodera, Noriko O.
    2004 *Japanese discourse markers: Synchronic and diachronic discourse analysis*. Amsterdam & Philadelphia: John Benjamins.

Quirk, Randolph -- Sidney Greenbaum -- Geoffrey Leech -- Jan Svartvik
    1985 *A comprehensive grammar of the English language*. London: Longman.

Rissanen, Matti
    1999 "Syntax", in: *CHEL III*, 187-331.
    2006 "On the development of borrowed connectives in fourteenth-century English: Evidence from corpora", in: *The beginnings of standardization*, ed. Ursula Schaefer. Frankfurt am Main: Peter Lang, 133-146.

Schiffrin, Deborah
1987 *Discourse markers.* Cambridge: Cambridge University Press.
Schleppegrell, Mary J.
1991 "Paratactic because", *Journal of Pragmatics* 16: 323-337.
Stenström, Anna-Brita
1998 "From sentence to discourse: *Cos (because)* in teenage talk", in: *Discourse markers: Descriptions and theory,* ed. Andreas H. Jucker & Yael Ziv. Amsterdam & Philadelphia: John Benjamins, 127-146.
Stenström, Anna-Brita -- Gisle Andersen
1996 "More trends in teenage talk: A corpus-based investigation of the discourse items cos and innit", in: *Synchronic corpus linguistics: Papers from the Sixteenth International Conference on English Language Research on Computerized Corpora (ICAME 16),* ed. Carol E. Percy, Charles F. Meyer & Ian Lancashire. Amsterdam & Atlanta: Rodopi, 189-203.
Suzuki, Ryoko
1999 *Grammaticalization in Japanese: A study of pragmatic particle-ization.* Ph.D. dissertation, University of California, Santa Barbara.
Sweetser, Eve
1990 *From etymology to pragmatics: Metaphorical and cultural aspects of semantic structure.* Cambridge: Cambridge University Press.
Traugott, Elizabeth Closs
1992 "Syntax", in: *CHEL* I, 168-289.
2003 "From subjectification to intersubjectification", in: *Motives for language change,* ed. Raymond Hickey. Cambridge: Cambridge University Press, 124-139.
Traugott, Elizabeth Closs -- Richard B. Dasher
2002 *Regularity in semantic change.* Cambridge: Cambridge University Press.
Van Valin, Robert D., Jr.
2005 *Exploring the syntax–semantics interface.* Cambridge: Cambridge University Press.
Verstraete, Jean-Christophe
2007 *Rethinking the coordination–subordination dichotomy: Interpersonal grammar and the analysis of adverbial clauses in English.* Berlin: Mouton de Gruyter.

The replacement of *þe* by *þat* in the history of English

Cristina Suárez-Gómez (Palma, Spain)

Abstract

In Old English *þe* was the invariable particle used to introduce relative clauses. In early Middle English, this function was fulfilled not only by *þe* but also by *þat*; from this period onwards, *þat* would become more and more common as *þe* fell gradually out of use. The aim of this paper is to shed some more light on the replacement of *þe* by *þat* and to identify the factors that instigated the change. For this purpose, I intend to analyze the distribution of invariable relativizers in the relevant periods of the English language (from Old English to late Middle English), as represented in *The Helsinki Corpus of English Texts: Diachronic and Dialectal*. The corpus data will demonstrate that the loss of *þe* cannot be attributed solely to phonological factors but that other aspects of a more syntactic nature also played a part in its decreasing frequency and final disappearance in favour of *þat*.[1]

1. Introduction

Different relativization strategies have coexisted throughout the history of the English language:

(a) the pronominal or deictic relativization strategy, represented in Present-Day English by the *wh*-relativizers (e.g. *who, which*, etc.) and by demonstrative elements in earlier English (e.g. *se/seo/þat* or the complex form *se þe/seo þe/þæt þe*), as in the following examples;

    (1) I like the island [in which I've taken the decision to live].

    (2) Eower Fæder [se on heofenum is], wat hwæs eow þearf biþ
        Your Father REL in heaven is knows what for you necessary is
    [Your Father who is in heaven knows what is needful for you.]
                                          [Q O2/3 IR HOM BLICK2: 103]

    (3) Ælce dæg we syngiað and ælce dæg we sceolon urne Hælend gladian mid
        every day we sin   and every day we must   our Saviour gratify with
    sumre godnysse, [se ðe æfre wile us mannum mildsian].
    certain goodness REL ever wants us to men show mercy
    [We sin every day and every day we must gratify our Saviour with certain goodness, who always wants us to show mercy to men.]
                                        [Q O3 IR HOM AELFR15:47]

(b) the gap relativization strategy, represented by relativizer *zero*:

    (4) I like the island [I've taken the decision to live in].

---

[1] I am grateful to the Autonomous Government of Galicia (grants INCITE08PXIB204016PR) and the Spanish Ministry of Science and Innovation and the European Regional Development Fund (grant HUM2007–60706 and FFI2011-26693-C02-02) for generous financial support.

(c) and, finally, the invariable relativization strategy – the focus of this paper – represented in Present-Day English by *that* (5), and in earlier English by *þe* (in Old and early Middle English), see example (6), and *þat/þæt* (from Middle English onwards), see example (7).

(5) I like the island [that I've taken the decision to live in].

(6) Scel beon se læsta   dæl   nyhst   þæm tune [ðe se deada man on lið].
    Shall be the smallest part closest to the town REL the dead man in lies.
    [The smallest part must be closest to the town in which the dead man lies.]
                                                    [Q O2/3 NN HIST OHTHR3 1.20.30]

(7) We agen to understonden hwer boð þe wepne [þet adam wes mide forwunded].
    We ought to understand what are the weapons REL adam was with wounded.
    [We ought to understand what the weapons are that Adam has been wounded with.]
                                                    [Q M1 IR OM LAMB8: 83]

These relativization strategies exhibit a complementary pattern of distribution, as numerous earlier synchronic and diachronic studies have previously shown.[2] My intention in this paper, however, is not to analyze the distribution of relativization strategies in earlier English, but to examine the elements used in the invariable relativization strategy and to reconstruct the conditions under which *þe* came to be replaced by *þat/that*. I will analyze the distribution of the invariable relativizers during different periods of the English language (Old and Middle English), taking into account a number of internal factors which may have influenced the change: namely, the syntactic function of the relativizer; the type of relative clause (restrictive or non-restrictive); and, finally, the animacy of the NP antecedent. From my analysis I will attempt to provide an answer to the questions of why and how *þat/that* replaced *þe* as an invariable relativizer in the history of English.

2. Description of the corpus

To begin that analysis, I selected a sample of data from the *Helsinki Corpus of English Texts: Diachronic and Dialectal*. As Table 1 shows, the sample is taken from texts from Old English (950-1150) (O3, O4) and Middle English (1150-1420) (M1, M2 and M3).

---

[2] See Quirk 1957, Romaine 1982, Dekeyser 1986, Yamashita 1994, Ball 1996, Stein 1998 and Suárez-Gómez 2004, among many others.

Table 2: Description of the corpus[3]

Period	Sub-periods	No of words	No of tokens
OE	O3 (950-1050)	36,630	539
	O4 (1050-1150)	47,445	576
ME	M1 (1150-1250)	75,800	1,184
	M2 (1250-1350)	4,489	81
	M3 (1350-1420)	57,774	741
TOTAL		222,238	3,121

The corpus comprises approximately 222,000 words and has rendered 3,121 examples of relative clauses introduced by an invariable relativizer. The last period included in the analysis is late Middle English (M3), since by then (1350-1420) the relativizer *þat/that* was the only remaining invariable relativizer in use, thus removing the need to examine texts dating from any later than this time. In order to keep the corpus as homogeneous as possible, only original prose texts have been selected. Translations (as so classified in the *Helsinki Corpus*) were discarded with the aim of avoiding potential influences from language contact. The same selection criterion, however, had the additional effect of upsetting the balance between sub-samples, a problem which I have corrected by normalizing the frequencies (per one thousand words).

3. Invariable relativizers in the history of English

Invariable relativizers have always been present in the English language and, by and large, they have been used more frequently than any other relativization strategy, as Figure 1 below illustrates. The presence of this relativization strategy throughout the history of the English language is not an idiosyncratic feature of English, but one which is well-attested cross-linguistically.

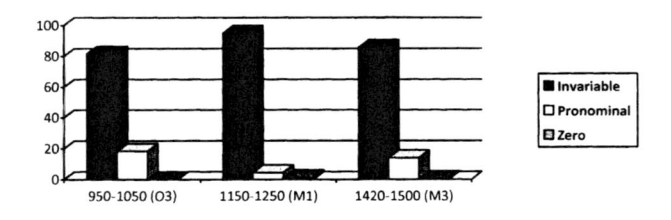

Figure 1: Distribution of relativizers (adapted from Suárez-Gómez 2004: 216)

---

[3] The low number of words in M2 (1250-1350) is linked to the unavailability of original material in the *Helsinki Corpus*. Only 3 texts (*Select English Historical Documents of the Ninth and Tenth Centuries, The Bee and the Stork* and the *Kentish Sermons*) from this period are classified as non-translations. Nevertheless, one of these texts (the *Kentish Sermons*), although not classified as a translation in the *Helsinki Corpus*, is considered in the literature to be a translation from French.

The items used to represent the invariable relativization strategy down through the history of the English language are þe and þat/that, as examples (5), (6) and (7) above show. Table 2 presents the distribution of invariable relativizers in the corpus under analysis: it includes raw numbers and their normalized frequencies per one thousand words.

Table 2: Chronological distribution of pronominal relativizers

	O3 (950-1050)	O4 (1050-1150)	M1 (1150-1250)	M2 (1250-1350)	M3 (1350-1420)	TOTAL
þe	526 (14.3)	551 (11.6)	846 (11.2)	1 (0.2)[4]	-	1924
þat	13 (0.3)	25 (0.5)	338 (4.5)	80 (17.8)	741 (12.8)	1197
TOTAL	539	576	1184	81	741	3,121

Þe-relative clauses are by far the most numerous group of relative clauses in late Old English (O3, O4) and early Middle English (M1). Nevertheless, by early Middle English, there were already signs of a decrease in the frequency of þe relative clauses in favour of relative clauses introduced by þat, an element which had already been found sporadically in the earlier periods:

(8) Se þridda sinoð wæs eft, [þæt wæs twa hund   bisceopa, under þam gingram

the third sinod was again REL was two hundred bishops   under the younger

þeodosige]

Theodosius

[The third synod, which had two hundred bishops, was celebrated again under the younger Theodosius.]

[Q O3 IR RELT LWSTAN1: 60]

Here in example (8), the relativizer þæt is clearly being used as an invariant relativizer, as demonstrated by the lack of agreement in gender with the NP antecedent it refers back, the masculine NP *se þridda sinoð*.[5]

By early Middle English, the frequency with which þat was used as an invariant relativizer had increased considerably (Kivimaa 1966: 133-136), an increase that was to become dramatic in late Middle English (M2, 1250-1350), when þat was by far the most important relativizer.[6] This sudden increase is depicted in Figure 2 (also in Table 2), which demonstrates graphically the progress of þat to become the most important relativizer from the second half of the thirteenth century on; and, similarly, how þe, in recession from the twelfth century

---

[4] An analysis of all the texts dating from this period in *The Helsinki Corpus* produced a total of 8 examples introduced by þe as the invariable relativizer (sometimes spelled as þo).
[5] In Old English, in addition to its function as an invariable relativizer, þat could also be part of the paradigm of the pronominal relativizers *se/seo/þæt* and, as such, it was used to resume neuter antecedents when the case required was the nominative or accusative singular.
[6] McIntosh 1947-1948: 73; Kivimaa 1966: 134; Fischer 1992: 196; Fischer et al. 2000: 93.

onwards, became almost invisible. By the fifteenth century, þat was the only invariable relativizer.

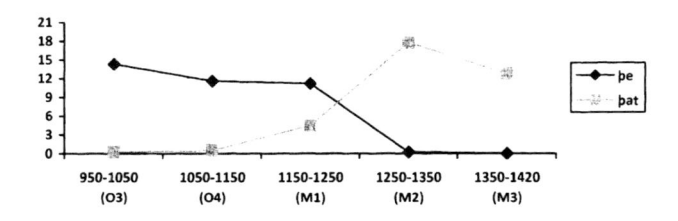

Figure 2: Chronological distribution of invariable relativizers[7]

This substitution of one element for another in the invariable relativizer strategy is a good example of Maxwell's diachronic generalisation V, which holds that "two strategies in a given language tend to complement each other, as one advances, the other recedes" (Maxwell 1982: 150). Here, for instance, the use of a new invariable relativizer in the English language grew in frequency in order to fill the gap left by the progressive loss of þe. As happened in the case of wh-relative pronouns, the use of which rose as that of the demonstrative relative pronouns receded (Suárez-Gómez 2008), here the gap left by the declining invariable relativizer þe started to be clearly occupied by þat in early Middle English, until it eventually became the only invariant relativizer by late Middle English. This led ultimately to the complete disappearance of þe as a relativizer to produce the current state-of-affairs prevailing in Modern Standard English. Around the thirteenth century, invariant þat was the norm everywhere, potentially occuring with any kind of antecedent and in any context, in most dialectal areas, with both restrictive and non-restrictive relative clauses, and with both animate and inanimate antecedents. The specialization of invariant *that* in restrictive relative clauses did not take place until around the fourteenth century, when wh-relative pronouns began to occur in the English language with some frequency.[8] It was also in the thirteenth century that þe's role as the invariable definite article in the English language became consolidated (Fischer 1992: 218), following the progressive weakening and final loss of declensions, a linguistic change which may have fostered, and even accelerated, the replacement of invariable relativizers. Not only does the substitution of þe by þat coincide with the consolidation of þe as the definite article, it was also the period during which þat gained ground as a

---

[7] This refers to normalized frequencies per one thousand words.
[8] Mustanoja 1960: 197; Fischer 1992: 297; Fischer et al. 2000: 93.

subordinator,[9] something which may have had an additional bearing upon the loss of *þe* as a relativizer.[10]

4. Analysis

4.1 Invariable relativizers and syntactic function

The syntactic function of the relativizer has generally been considered one of the main factors governing the choice of relativizer. As such, I have judged it appropriate to analyze it in detail in the present study. Syntactic function, in fact, is the variable most frequently mentioned in the literature on the expansion of *wh-*relativizers to occupy the space left by pronominal relativizers in earlier English (Suárez-Gómez 2008: 345-346). For my analysis I have adopted (and adapted) Keenan and Comrie's Accessibility Hierarchy (Keenan & Comrie 1977) so that three different categories are distinguished: subject (S), as in example (8) above, object (O), comprising both direct and indirect objects, as in example (9) (as direct object) and oblique (Obl), which refers to relativizers that function as prepositional phrases (all of which are stranded, as it must be with invariable relativizers at the periods under analysis), as in examples (6) and (7) above. The categories GEN and OCOMP were not included since no examples were found of invariable relativizers being used in either of these types of positions.[11]

(9) þis is þe miracle [þet þet godspel of te dai us telþ]
    this is the miracle REL the gospel of today us tell
    [This is the Miracle that today's gospel tells us.]

[Q M2 IR HOM KSERM: 218]

The question of which positions in a language may be subjected to relativization is closely linked to the degree of explicitness of the relativization strategy. Relative clauses which are introduced by invariable relativizers allow a narrower range of positions to be relativized in comparison with those introduced by pronominal relativizers. With that in mind, we would expect invariable relativizers to be able to

---

[9] Kivimaa 1966: 248; Fischer 1992, 293; Rissanen 1997: 375.

[10] One major issue regarding invariable relativizers which I have omitted from the present paper relates to their status. The general view, especially from a generativist perspective, treats these relativizers as subordinating particles functionally very similar to the prototypical complementizer used to introduce complement clauses (Jespersen 1909-1949: III §8.71; Allen 1980: 166; Radford 1988: 482; Dekeyser 1988: 173). According to Seppänen 1997 and Seppänen & Kjellmer 1995, these relativizers are clearly pronominal in nature. Seppänen 2004 suggests that the invariable relativizer *þe* may have started out as a subordinating particle, but ended up as a relative pronoun.

[11] Contrary to the claims of Seppänen & Kjellmer 1995 who have identified (albeit rare) examples in PDE of *that's* as the genitive form of the relativizer *that*, as in the example which gives their paper its title: "The dog that's leg was run over".

relativize only the most accessible positions in the hierarchy. Table 3 shows the distribution of invariable relativizers in the periods under analysis.

The results show that, with respect to late Old English, the indeclinable relativizer *þe* is most frequently used when it appears as the subject or the object of the relative clause, as Kivimaa (1966: 28) and Traugott (1992: 226) have previously shown. In other words, the most frequently relativized positions are those which correspond to the roles highest up on the 'Accessibility Hierarchy', as the behaviour of *þe* demonstrates. The same situation is observed in the distribution of *þat* (subjects and objects being the most commonly relativized positions), although the number of examples in this case is extremely low. The most notable aspect of *þat*'s behaviour, however, is that the expected hierarchy is not respected: objects are as frequently relativized as subjects. In relation to early Middle English, Kivimaa (1966: 135) and Jack (1975: 104; 1988: 49)[12] have observed that the invariable relativizer *þe* is used almost exclusively in the subject slot; such exclusivity was not observed in the case of *þat*. The correlation between the syntactic function of the relativizer and the choice of relativizer has also produced interesting results in relation to my corpus of early Middle English (see Table 3). All syntactic roles are more frequently performed by the invariable relativizer *þe*, in particular, though not exclusively, that of the subject (just as Kivimaa and Jack had found previously). The most notable development in this period (M1) involves *þat* whose importance as an invariable relativizer rises and which, although more commonly used as subject, achieves an extremely high frequency also as an object (in comparison with the other periods).

Table 3: Invariable relativizers and syntactic function

		S	O	Obl	TOTAL
O3	*þe*	369 (10.1)	133 (3.6)	24 (0.7)	526
(950-1050)	*þat*	8 (0.2)	1 (0.02)	4 (0.1)	13
O4	*þe*	352 (7.4)	138 (2.9)	61 (1.3)	551
(1050-1150)	*þat*	11 (0.2)	11 (0.2)	3 (0.02)	25
M1	*þe*	593 (7.8)	183 (2.4)	71 (0.9)	846
(1150-1250)	*þat*	173 (2.4)	135 (1.8)	30 (0.4)	338
M2	*þe*	1 (0.2)	-	-	1
(1250-1350)	*þat*	58 (12.9)	19 (4.2)	3 (0.7)	80
M3 (1350-1420)	*þat*	487 (8.4)	191 (3.3)	63 (1.1)	741
TOTAL		2,051 (9.2)	811 (3.6)	259 (1.2)	3,121

S=subject; O=object; Obl=oblique.

This change in the element used to represent the invariable relativization strategy may be viewed as an example of Maxwell's diachronic generalisation V mentioned above in section 2. A similar process to that observed in the substitution

---

[12] The conclusions of Jack 1975 and 1988 are based on an analysis of only one text in each case: Jack 1975 is based on *Ancrene Wisse*, Jack 1988 is based on Laʒamon's *Brut*.

of *se* pronominal relativizers by *wh-* words could be at work here: in its expansion *þat* is stronger as object, a position in which *þe* is proportionally less frequent, as illustrated in O4 and M1. The already mentioned unavailability of relevant data from M2 does not allow us to confirm this tentative hypothesis.

4.2 Invariable relativizers and type of relative clause

Another important variable affecting the distribution of relativizers is that of the restrictiveness of the relative clause, according to which relative clauses are divided into restrictive and non-restrictive types. The hypothesis being examined here is whether the distribution of invariable relativizers correlates significantly with the distinction between restrictive and non-restrictive relative clauses. The distribution of relativizers in Present-Day English changes depending on this variable: restrictive relative clauses can be introduced by any of the available items, namely *zero*, *that* and *wh*-pronouns and non-restrictive relative clauses favour (indeed almost require) a *wh*-word; only very rarely are they introduced by the relativizer *that* (Jacobsson 1994; Huddleston & Pullum 2002: 1059), and never by the relativizer *zero*. Throughout the history of the English language, invariable relativizers (as well as other relativization strategies) have been used to introduce both restrictive and non-restrictive relative clauses, though more commonly in relation to restrictive relative clauses (Andrew 1940). Scholars such as McIntosh (1947-1948: 79 fn. 19), Mitchell (1985: §2283) and Traugott (1992: 223) are not as categorical on this point but, broadly speaking, are of much the same opinion. Jack (1975: 106-107, 1988: 52-53), on the other hand, denies that the choice between the two major relativizers *þe* and *þat* is a function of the type of relative clause; nonetheless, his analysis still indicates a higher proportion of invariable *þe* in non-restrictive relative clauses, and the prevalence of *þat* in restrictive relative clauses (Jack 1988: 53).

Table 4: Invariable relativizers and type of relative clause

		RRC	NRRC	TOTAL
O3 (950-1050)	*þe*	422 (11.5)	5 (0.1)	427
	þat	104 (2.8)	8 (0.2)	112
O4 (1050-1150)	*þe*	360 (7.6)	191 (4.0)	551
	þat	23 (0.5)	2 (0.04)	25
M1 (1150-1250)	*þe*	694 (9.1)	279 (3.7)	973
	þat	152 (2.0)	59 (0.8)	211
M2 (1250-1350)	*þe*	1 (0.2)	-	1
	þat	66 (14.7)	14 (3.1)	80
M3 (1350-1420)	*þat*	587 (10.2)	154 (2.7)	741
TOTAL		2,409 (10.8)	712 (3.2)	3,121

Table 4 shows that the choice of *þe* does not relate to any type of relative clause in particular, but is simply a reflection of the general distribution of higher frequency in restrictive than in non-restrictive relative clauses across all the periods, and especially in late Old and early Middle English. During these periods of coexistence, *þat* exhibits a higher tendency to introduce restrictive relative clauses. However, from M2 onwards, when *þat* becomes the only invariable relativizer, it inherits the behaviour of *þe* in O4 and M1, so that the number of non-restrictive relative clauses introduced by *þat* also increases. This new distribution leads us tentatively to conclude that, when *þat* substituted *þe*, it adopted *þe*'s distribution in relation to the type of relative clause, thereby, reinforcing the substitution process already observed in terms of syntactic function and confirming Maxwell's Diachronic Generalization V.

4.3 Invariable relativizers and animacy of the antecedent

The NP antecedent is one of the most complex variables that have been hypothesized to affect the distribution of relativizers. According to Jack, the preference for a relativizer (in particular *þe* and *þat* in early Middle English) should be interpreted with regard to the type of antecedent involved "for it is the connection of *þe* and *þat* with certain types of antecedent that is the source of their apparent association with non-restrictive and restrictive clauses respectively" (Jack 1988: 53). In this study, I intend to focus on the degree of animacy of the antecedent; in other words, whether an antecedent is animate or inanimate. There is no complete agreement in the literature as to the influence of the animacy of the NP antecedent on the choice of relativizer. From the results of her analysis of relativizers in Middle Scots (c. 1530-1550), Romaine concludes that "the effect of different types of antecedent (grouped according to certain characteristics or features of the modification which precedes the head noun) is in most cases negligible" (1982: 143), and, more categorically, that "the animacy of the antecedent has virtually no effect in determining which form of the relative will occur" (1982: 142).

Table 5: Invariable relativizers and animacy of the antecedent

		Animate	Inanimate	TOTAL
O3	*þe*	321 (8.8)	205 (6.0)	526
(950-1050)	*þat*	1 (0.03)	12 (0.3)	13
O4	*þe*	323 (6.8)	228 (4.8)	551
(1050-1150)	*þat*	4 (0.8)	21 (0.4)	25
M1	*þe*	429 (5.6)	417 (5.5)	846
(1150-1250)	*þat*	117 (1.5)	221 (2.9)	338
M2	*þe*	1 (0.2)	-	1
(1250-1350)	*þat*	42 (9.3)	38 (8.5)	80
M3	*þat*	329 (5.7)	412 (7.1)	741
(1350-1420)				
TOTAL		1,567 (7.1)	1,554 (7.0)	3,121

By contrast, the results in Table 5 demonstrate that at least some relativizers are indeed sensitive to the animacy of the antecedent. The figures show that *þat* is preferred where inanimate antecedents are involved (in O3 and especially in M1); however, it is also used to refer back to animate antecedents in O4 and M2. Its even distribution in the latter period in fact mirrors closely the relative frequency of animate and inanimate antecedents overall. In contrast, no preference regarding the animacy of the antecedent is observed with invariable *þe*. It is as frequently used with animate as with inanimate antecedents (M1), contrary to the findings of McIntosh (1947-1948: 74), Kivimaa (1966: 135) and Jack (1975: 101; 1988: 58), who suggested a preference for *þe* to occur with animate antecedents. Later on, as relativizer *þat* emerged as the main relativizer, its use with animate antecedents increased: moving into the gap left by *þe* (Fischer 1992: 295), it becomes the only invariable relativizer used with both animate and inanimate antecedents.

To summarize, then, the data from Table 5 above show that, in some cases, the choice of *þe* and *þat* is in some cases sensitive to the animacy of the antecedent. However, once *þat* becomes the only invariable relativizer, it begins to be used very frequently with both animate and inanimate antecedents. Once again the environments abandoned by *þe* are taken over by *þat*, in yet another display of the substitution process observed above in sections 4.1 and 4.2.

5. Conclusion

The invariable relativizer *þe* was the predominant relativizer in late Old and early Middle English, but was replaced by *þat* in late Middle English. Early Middle English marks the turning point in the status of *þat*, as its use expanded into a growing number of contexts, irrespective of its agreement with the antecedent. Emergent in late Old English, its frequency then rose slightly in early Middle English, before increasing still further until, by classical Middle English, it had become the only remaining invariable relativizer. In the periods of coexistence (especially in early Middle English), there is a (weak) tendency for *þat* to be used more frequently as an object or related to inanimate antecedents; in other words, the environments in which *þe* is less prevalent. In my opinion, however, the notion of a complementary distribution is unsustainable; instead the gradual and progressive introduction of a new item into the paradigm, *þat*'s emergence is one of almost immediate substitution (from M1, where *þe* was favoured, to M2, where *þat* was almost the only choice). By the end, it had become possible for *þat* to be used with any kind of antecedent and in any kind of context. The weakening and disappearance of inflectional markers which took place in the English language from late Old English onwards and the progressive levelling of declensions which was completed by Middle English, at which point *þe* had also become the invariable article, may well account for the sudden nature of the substitution. The overuse of *þe* probably favoured the introduction of or, rather, the preference for an already existing, if yet infrequent, element in the paradigm. Though initially occupying the less favoured environments of *þe* (the object position and referring back to inanimate ancedents), *þat* rapidly became the only choice in all environments: animate/inanimate, subject/object, restrictive/non-restrictive. The replacement of *þe*, likewise, coincides to some extent with the period during which *that* was gaining ground as the general subordinator. These hypotheses are purely tentative, though. The critical period of analysis in this regard is probably M2, however the lack of available texts for this preliminary study means that any definitive conclusions will have to wait.

Sources

Rissanen, Matti -- Ossi Ihalainen -- Merja Kytö
    1991   *The Helsinki Corpus of English Texts: Diachronic and Dialectal.*
                Helsinki: Department of English, University of Helsinki.

References

Allen, Cynthia
    1980   "Movement and deletion in Old English", *Linguistic Inquiry* 11: 261-323.

Andrew, Samuel O.
    1940   *Syntax and style in Old English.* New York: Russell and Russell.

Ball, Catherine N.
    1996   "A diachronic study of relative markers in spoken and written English", *Language Variation and Change* 8: 227-258.

Dekeyser, Xavier
    1986   "Relative markers in the Peterborough Chronicle: 1070-1154 or linguistic change exemplified", *Folia Linguistica Historica* 7: 93-105.
    1988   "Preposition stranding and relative complementizer deletion: Implicational tendencies in English and the other Germanic languages", in: *Leuvense Bijdragen* 77: 161-181.

Fischer, Olga
    1992   "Syntax", in: *CHEL II,* 207-408.

Fischer, Olga -- Ans van Kemenade -- Willem Koopman -- Wim van der Wurff
    2000   *The syntax of Early English.* Cambridge: Cambridge University Press.

Huddleston, Rodney -- Geoffrey K. Pullum
    2002   *The Cambridge grammar of the English language.* Cambridge: Cambridge University Press.

Jacobsson, Bengt
    1994   "Nonrestrictive relative that-clauses revisited", *Studia Neophilologica* 66: 181-195.

Jack, George
    1975   "Relative pronouns in language AB", in: *English Studies* 56: 100-107.
    1988   "Relative pronouns in Layamon's Brut", *Leeds Studies in English* 19: 31-66.

Jespersen, Otto
  1909-1949 *A modern English grammar on historical principles*, 7 vols. London: George Allen & Unwin; Copenhagen: Ejnar Munksgaard [repr. 1954].

Keenan, Edward -- Bernard Comrie
  1977 "NP accessibility and universal grammar", *Linguistic Inquiry* 8: 63-99.

Kivimaa, Kirsti
  1966 "*Þe* and *þat* as clause connectives in early Middle English with special consideration of the emergence of the pleonastic *þat*", *Commentationes Humanarum Litterarum* 39: 1-271.

Maxwell, Dan
  1982 "Implications of NP accessibility for diachronic syntax", *Folia Linguistica Historica* 3:135-52.

McIntosh, Angus
  1947-1948 "The relative pronouns *þe* and *þat* in early Middle English", *English and Germanic Studies* 1: 73-87.

Mitchell, Bruce
  1985 *Old English Syntax*. 2 vols. Oxford: Clarendon Press.

Mustanoja, Tauno F.
  1960 *A Middle English Syntax*. Memóires de la SocietéNéophilologique de Helsinki 23. Helsinki: Societé Neophilologique.

Quirk, Randolf
  1957 "Relative clauses in educated spoken English", *English Studies* 38: 97-109.

Radford, Andrew
  1988 *Transformational grammar*. Cambridge: Cambridge University Press.

Rissanen, Matti
  1997 "Optional THAT with subordinators in Middle English", in: *Language History and Language Modelling: A Festschrift for Jacek Fisiak on this 60th Birthday*, ed. Raymond Hickey & Stanislaw Puppel. Berlin: Mouton de Gruyter, 373-383.

Romaine, Suzanne
  1982 *Socio-historical linguistics: Its status and methodology*. Cambridge: Cambridge University Press.

Seppänen, Aimo
  1997 "Relative *that* and prepositional complementation", *English Language and Linguistics* 1: 111-133.
  2004 "The Old English relative *þe*", *English Language and Linguistics* 8: 71-102.

Seppänen, Aimo -- Göran Kjellmer
  1995 "*The dog that's leg was run over*: On the genitive of the relative pronoun", *English Studies* 76: 389-400.

Stein, Dieter
  1998 "Relative sentences in Late Middle English: The Paston and Cely Letters", in: *The Virtues of Language: History in Language, Linguistics and Texts. Papers in Memory of Thomas Frank*, ed. Dieter Stein and Rosanna Sornicola. Amsterdam: John Benjamins, 67-80.

Suárez-Gómez, Cristina
  2004 *Relativization in Early English (with special reference to the distribution of relativizers and the position of relative clauses)*. Universidade de Santiago de Compostela: Servizo de Publicacións [CD-ROM].

2008	"Strategies in competition: pronominal relativizers in the history of English", in: *English Studies* 89: 339-350.
Traugott, Elizabeth Closs	
1992	"Syntax", in: *CHEL I,* 168-229.
Yamashita, Junko	
1994	"An analysis of relative clauses in the Lancaster/IBM Spoken English Corpus", *English Studies* 75: 73-84.

Impersonal and passive constructions from a viewpoint of functional category emergence

Fuyo Osawa (Tokyo, Japan)

Abstract

The purpose of this paper is to give an answer to the question of why impersonal and passive sentences are said to have a functional similarity. My answer is that both types of sentences are completely similarly constructed. Earlier languages[1] are lexical-thematic, which means that a given language deploys only lexical categories without functional categories and only arguments which are required by the meaning of the predicate verb have to be syntactically realised. If an argument which should carry the agentive theta role is not required, the subject which should appear in the nominative case need not be realised. Both types of sentences are an instantiation of this situation. They are agentless constructions since the essential function of these constructions is to describe the situation without referring to an agent. The function of both constructions is neither subject demotion/agent defocusing nor object promotion. Both constructions involve no agent argument in the clause structure from the beginning.

1. Introduction

In this paper, I try to give an answer to the question of why impersonal and passive constructions are said to have a functional similarity. I claim that, using earlier English data, it is because syntactically they are completely similarly constructed in a lexical-thematic language.[2] 'Lexical-thematicity' is a key notion in understanding the nature of these constructions and what happened in the history of English. Furthermore, I argue that both constructions are formalized normally, based on the meaning of the predicate only. They do not deviate from the norm at all.

It has long been recognized that in a variety of languages impersonal and passive constructions are intimately connected, and are said by many linguists to have functional similarity.[3] This similarity has been given a slightly different analysis by Relational Grammar, proposed by Perlmutter & Postal (1977) and Perlmutter (1978). However, this correlation is almost obliterated by generative grammar, although passive constructions have long been analyzed within the Government and Binding framework. Both approaches, i.e. non-generative approaches and generative approaches, assume functional or grammatical changes involved in the derivation of passives/impersonals, even if there is no direct derivational relation involved.

---

[1] I focus on English examples in this paper and then earlier languages roughly refer to Old English. However, the Old English texts available to us are mostly from late Old English, and this stage shows often incipient movement from the pure situation of lexical-thematicity. Nevertheless, the data and the discussion provided in this paper are basically sufficient to support this hypothesis.
[2] Cf. Abney 1987, Radford 1990, Osawa 2003.
[3] Including functionalists or cognitive linguists such as Lyons 1971, Langacker and Munro 1975, Comrie 1977, Givón 1979, 1981, Siewierska 1984 and Shibatani 1985.

My claim is different from the previous ones in which passives are supposed to be formed on the basis of transitive verbs; the previous claims assume syntactic relations such as subject and object and argue that a universal characterization of passives can be best captured in terms of a change in such syntactic relations. I claim that there is no such syntactic change in grammatical relations in the derivation of impersonals and passives and that a correct analysis of the correlation between the passive and the impersonal constructions requires a totally different view from the previous studies mentioned above.

In what follows, in chapter 2 I briefly summarise the two approaches, i.e. non-generative approaches and generative approaches to the relevant constructions and point out that both approaches cannot grasp the true nature of these constructions. In chapter 3, I will next examine what the things are in the history of English and then in chapter 4 I will propose my analysis and try to give an answer to the question of why impersonal and passive constructions are said to have functional similarity. Finally, in section 5, I will conclude my discussion.

2. Previous studies

2.1 Introduction

This chapter is divided into two; the first part deals with non-generative approaches and the second with generative approaches. Among the non-generative approaches, Relational Grammar proposed by Perlmutter and Postal (1977) will be first mentioned, which tries to account for the derivation of passives and impersonals in terms of a change in grammatical relations.

Next, functional approaches are introduced. As an alternative to Relational Grammar's 'structural' approach, partly depending on Relational Grammar, and partly criticizing Relational Grammar, many of these approaches place the emphasis on more functional aspects. As for the generative approaches, I will introduce a traditional analysis and a minimalist one.

2.2 Non-generative approaches

2.2.1 Relational Grammar

Perlmutter and Postal (1977) argue that a universal characterization of passives can be best arrived at not in terms of word order, case, or morphology, but rather in terms of a change in grammatical relations. Within the theory of Relational Grammar, the derivation of a passive sentence like *John was kissed by Mary* involves two changes of syntactic relation to the underlying structure, similar to the corresponding active *Mary kissed John*. The two changes are:
   (i) an object (in this case, the direct object) is changed into a subject;
   (ii) the subject is changed into a syntactic relation which is neither subject, direct object, nor indirect object.

Hence, it is claimed that the two operations, i.e. object promotion and subject deletion/demotion are taking place in the derivation of passives. The passive is a 'promotional' phenomenon, whereby a direct object nominal at one level is a subject nominal at a later level. In this approach, there is no need for an independent mechanism of deleting/demoting the original (i.e. active) subject, since this is said to be achieved by a general principle, effected by a newly created subject. Like this, within Relational Grammar, passives and impersonal passives are the same phenomenon, involving the advancement of the direct object to the subject.

2.2.2 Functional approach

Examining Mojave and Uto-Aztecan, Langacker and Munro (1975) argue that passive sentences are basically impersonal, and that passive sentences involve a subject complement embedded in the predicate BE. The underlying subject of the complement clause, i.e. N1, is unspecified (unspecified semantic subject). Normally, N2, the direct object of the complement clause, will be substituted for the unspecified subject N1, and appear as the surface subject of the lower V. If it does, we will refer to the sentence as being 'passive'; if it does not (and the surface subject remains unspecified), we will refer to the sentence as impersonal.

Comrie (1977), criticizing Perlmutter and Postal's (1977) analyzes, points out that so-called impersonal passives do not involve promotion of a direct object, despite the fact that subject demotion occurs. Comrie (1977) argues that a mechanism of spontaneous subject demotion is necessary. The admissibility of rules of spontaneous demotion is, however, controversial in Relational Grammar.

Givón (1979: 186) states: "Passivization is the process by which a non-agent is promoted into the role of 'main topic' of the sentence", whether or not *man*, *on* or *uno* are indefinite human subjects or empty grammatical markers is irrelevant. Since they are indefinite and non-referential, they cannot be regarded as topics. The clauses must, therefore, be viewed as possessing non-agent topics which, according to Givón (1979), is the defining characteristic of passive clauses.

According to Siewierska (1984: 2), passive constructions have the following characteristics:
    (a) the subject of the passive clause is a direct object in the corresponding active
    (b) the subject of the active clause is expressed in the passive in the form of an agentive adjunct or is left unexpressed
    (c) the verb is marked passive.

For example:
(1)   "They gave a book to the king." (Active clause)
(2)   a. "A book was given to the king by them." (Passive clause with agentive adjunct)
        b. "A book was given to the king." (Passive clause without agentive adjunct)
        c. "The king was given a book." (Indirect passive, see below (9) & (15))

It is argued that what all the sentences which are called 'impersonal passives' in many languages have in common is the lack of a specified subject. Since impersonal passives are typically viewed as lacking a subject, they are seen as primary evidence for the demotional definition of the passive.

Shibatani (1985: 831, 837) states that the formal approach advocated by Relational Grammar is too restricted to account for the patterns of distribution which a passive morphology exhibits. Most importantly, passives center around agents, and their fundamental pragmatic function is agent defocusing.

2.2.3 Summary of this section

Although details are different, non-generative approaches are almost similar in that passives and impersonals are basically the same, and two operations, object promotion and subject demotion/deletion are involved. Concerning this, they are divided into two groups; either imposing more emphasis on the object promotion, or imposing more emphasis on the agent defocusing/deletion/demotion.

2.3 Generative approach

2.3.1 Introduction

Within the generative framework, passivization is today assumed to be a syntactic operation whatever operation it is; either NP-movement, merge or extension for case reasons (Chomsky 1995, 2005). Syntactic passives are dependent on the presence of the functional category TP.[4] There is no derived relation between active sentences and passive sentences. They are generated independently of each other by the operation move/merge.

2.3.2 Government and Binding theory

In the generative framework, as mentioned above, the analysis that the passive construction is derived directly from the active is abandoned. Rather, the passive is derived to meet the morphological requirements of a passive verb.

Under this analysis, the base-generated internal argument NP of a passive verb (i.e. *the dog* in sentence (3) below) must move to the subject position, which is empty, in order to be case-marked, since the position after the passive verb (i.e. *beaten*) is a theta-position, but not a case-marked position. Like this, the following features are required for syntactic passive operation to take place, although they are inter-related:

---

[4] TP means a tense (T) projection or tense phrase. As a noun is built into a noun phrase, tense into a tense phrase. Assuming that a tense constitutes an independent head, a clause is analyzed to be built around a tense head, i.e. a clause is a projection of a T head, TP. In generative grammar, a tense specification such as [+past] is given in this T head.

(I) the presence of non-thematic subject position, i.e., the presence of an underlying empty subject position;

(II) the presence of verbs which cannot assign case to their complements, although they can theta-mark them;

(III) EPP[5], i.e. the subject requirement is established. The subject position is always guaranteed in the clause.

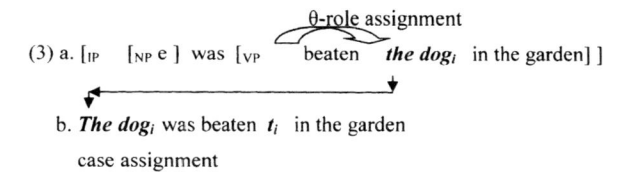

(3) a. [$_{IP}$ [$_{NP}$ e] was [$_{VP}$ beaten *the dog$_i$* in the garden]]

    θ-role assignment

    case assignment

b. *The dog$_i$* was beaten t_i in the garden

The passive verb, i.e. the past participle has an internal argument only and somehow loses the ability to assign/check the accusative case. Therefore the internal argument NP must move to the case-marked/case-checked position, which must be a theta-bar position, i.e. a position to which no theta role is assigned. Otherwise, the NP is doubly theta-marked. This causes the theta criterion violation.

2.3.3 Minimalist approach

Under the Minimalist Program (MP), the reasoning is somewhat different, although essentially similar; a nominal placed after the passive verb must move into the subject position. Under the MP, this NP-movement is triggered in order to satisfy morphological requirements of moved elements. The (pro)nominal arguments have case properties which have to be checked in the appropriate position in the course of merge. Case is not assigned any more to a nominal or DP[6] in the course of derivation, but, the DP is taken from the lexicon, already specified with case, and the case properties are checked subsequently.

---

[5] EPP means the Extended Projection Principle. The Projection Principle states that lexical information is syntactically represented. The lexical information is the thematic structure of the predicate, i.e. the number and types of arguments which the predicate takes. However, independently of the argument structure of the predicate, it is assumed that clauses must have subjects, which is called the Extended Projection Principle. In other words, this principle posits that every T must be extended into a TP projection which has a specifier. This is why this principle is called the Extended Projection Principle.

[6] DP means Determiner Phrase/Determiner Projection like *the king of England,* which comprises a determiner *the*, and a Noun Phrase (NP) complement *king of England*. A structure like *the king of England* was analyzed as a noun Phrase (NP), comprising the head noun *king*, its complement *of England* and its specifier *the*. Under the DP analysis, the status of this phrase is DP and its head is a determiner *the*. This difference between NP and DP is irrelevant to our current discussion. See Abney (1987).

(4) a. John killed her
   b. *was killed her
   c. *It was killed she
   d. She was killed

Since the passive verb loses the ability to assign/check the accusative case in (4b), the case features carried by an internal argument, in this case *her,* cannot be checked in the complement position of a passive verb and then the derivation crashes. If we put the nominative *she* instead as in (4c), the derivation still crashes, since a nominative pronoun cannot check its nominative case in this passive-verb complement position. Then, *her* must move into a nominative case checked position. The pronoun moves first to the [Spec[7], VP] position, and next to the [Spec, TP] position, where its nominative case can be checked by the finite T/I.[8] See (6) below. Like this, it is assumed that morphological requirements force passivization.

2.3.4 [EPP]-feature

In a more recent minimalist framework, the role of TP is much more emphasized. A finite T has an [EPP] feature requiring it (= T) to have a specifier with person/number properties. To satisfy this [EPP] feature, the thematic object of the verb is raised into the subject position. That is, the specifier position of TP must be filled by some element with person/number properties.

(5) The team was beaten.

---

[7] Spec means specifier. The specifier of XP is the sister of the intermediate projection of X, i.e. X', and the daughter of the maximal projection of X, i.e. XP.

[8] I means INFL, i.e. Inflection. IP means Inflection Phrase/ Inflectional projection, i.e. a projection of inflectional features such as person, number and tense. TP is used in place of IP.

(6)

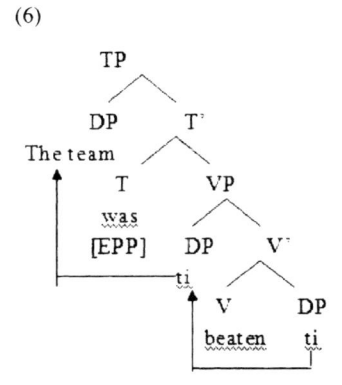

```
          TP
         /  \
        DP   T'
     The team / \
            T    VP
           was  /  \
          [EPP] DP   V'
                ti  / \
                   V   DP
                 beaten ti
```

2.4 Summary of section 2

In this section, I have introduced two approaches. Concerning non-generative approaches, probably, as Lyons (1971) mentions, there is some idea among those researchers in which active sentences are more 'basic' than passives. There are some functional or grammatical changes involved in the derivation of passive/impersonals. Passive constructions have been defined *vis-à-vis* active constructions and thus regarded as a deviation from the syntactic norm.

But there remains a fundamental question of why we should construct the 'basic' active sentence first and derive the less-basic 'passive' version from the active. Such a derivation is very uneconomical.

Meanwhile, according to the generative analysis, there is no derived relation between active and passive sentences. They are generated independently of each other. In this point, the generative approach is supposed to be better than the traditional functional approach. However, the generative approaches cannot account for the historical facts, as we will see in the next section.

3. From Old English to Present-Day English

3.1 Introduction

In this section, I will go into the historical data and examine what the situation was in the early stages of English. I want to show that, although I assume the generative approach for Present-Day English, it cannot account for what happened in the history of English. Non-generative approaches mentioned above cannot grasp the nature of earlier languages correctly either. I propose a new view on passives/impersonals and on the historical development of languages.

3.2 Old English

There are striking differences between Old English 'passives' and Present-Day English passives. First, in Present-Day English prepositional passives like (7) are widely used:

>(7) He was spoken to.

This type of passive did not exist in Old English, however. The earliest examples of prepositional passives are from Middle English, as shown below:

>(8) þer   wes   sorhe te   seon hire leoflich lich faren so
>   there   was   sorrow to   see   her   dear body   dealt so
>   reowliche wið
>   cruelly   with
>   (C1225 Juliana (Roy)22.195, from Denison 1993: 125)

Second, indirect passives like *He was given a book* were not attested in Old English; instead, so-called impersonal passives were used:

>(9) ac   him   næs   getiðod ðære lytlan lisse
>   but   him (DAT.) not-was   granted that small   favour (GEN.)
>   [But he was not granted that small favour]
>   (ÆCHom. I.23.330.29, Denison 1993: 108)

Indirect passives appeared in Middle English and the impersonal passives went out of use.

Similarly, in Old English impersonal constructions were widely used, too. An impersonal construction is one whose verb takes the third person singular inflection, no matter what NP arguments are present, and which lacks a nominative NP. In addition to the example (9), above, I give a few more examples, (10) to (12):

>(10) norþan sniwde
>   [it snowed from the north]
>   (*Seafarer* 31)
>(11) Siððan him hingrode
>   [he was hungry afterwards]
>   (ÆCHom. I .11.166.12)

(12) hu   us   bið   æt   Gode   gedemed
     how   us (DAT.)   is (3SG.)   at   God (DAT./INST.)   judged
     [how we shall be judged by God]
     (ÆCHom I. 3.52.31, from Denison 1993: 104)

In (10) there is no NP, and in (11) there is only a dative-marked NP, no nominative NP. All those impersonal constructions lack nominative-marked NPs, and they are thus called subject-less sentences by many researchers. The important thing is that Old English clause structure had the potential for subject-less constructions, whereas Present-Day English has no such potential any more. The transition from impersonal to personal constructions was at least partly due to the loss of inflexional endings and the fixing of word-order (SVO), e. g.:

(13) a. "þæm cyninge þohte.": Old English (OV)
     b. "The king thought.":   Modern English (SV)

3.3 Present-Day English

In Present-Day English, both prepositional passives and indirect passives are allowed, while impersonal constructions, including impersonal passives, are not allowed any more, and only expletive impersonals using expletive *it* are possible.

(14) "He was spoken to.":   prepositional passive
(15) "He was given the car.":   indirect passive
(16) a. * "Last night snowed.":   impersonal sentence
     b. * "Him thirsts.":   impersonal sentence
     c. *"Him was given a book.":   impersonal passive
(17) "It seems to me that he is mistaken.": expletive impersonal

It follows that there were drastic changes between Old and Present-Day English. My aim in the next chapter is to give an answer to the question of what caused these changes and why impersonal and passives are said to be similar.

4. My approach
4.1 Puzzling facts

The facts to be explained are:
a. non-presence of prepositional passives in Old English
b. non-presence of indirect passives in Old English
c. presence of impersonals (passives) in Old English
d. apparent agent/subject lacking phenomenon in Old English impersonals

e. prepositional passives are allowed in Present-Day English
f. indirect passives are allowed in Present-Day English
g. no more impersonal passives are allowed in Present-Day English; only expletive impersonals are allowed

4.2 Lexical-thematicity

As touched upon above, 'lexical-thematicity' is a key notion in understanding the nature of these constructions and what happened in the history of English. Radford (1990) defines lexical-thematic structures as below:

> [...] the earliest structures produced by young children are *lexical-thematic* structures (i.e. structures in which all constituents belong to lexical categories, and in which all sister constituents are thematically inter-related). [...] every constituent theta-marks or is theta-marked by any sister constituent [...] (Radford 1990: 46).

Abney (1987) also argues that thematic constituents typically belong to lexical categories, i.e. Nouns, Verbs, Adjectives, Prepositions and their projections (NP, VP, AP, PP), whereas non-thematic constituents belong to functional categories, i.e. Determiners, Auxiliaries, Complementizers, and their projections.

Although Radford refers to early child English at the two-word stage, I propose that this lexical-thematicity is applied to earlier English. Based on their arguments, I define lexical-thematicity like this:

> Lexical-thematicity: This means that the syntactic structure is (completely) lexically and thematically constructed. Then, this means that lexical-thematic languages have no functional categories such as DP, or TP, but only lexical categories (N, V, A, P) (or only content words) and their phrasal projections (NP, VP, AP, PP).

Note that in lexical-thematic languages, every constituent must be thematically related. This means that only arguments which are required by the meaning of a predicate must be syntactically realized (cf. Osawa 2003). All constituents in the clause structure are thematically related. There are no thematically unrelated constituents like expletives.

I argue that Old English is one instantiation of lexical-thematicity. It deploys the lexical categories and their phrasal projections (NP, VP, AP) and no functional categories, which are non-thematic, as Abney (1987) suggests.

As has often been discussed,[9] functional categories developed very limitedly in Old English. I propose the following syntactic structure for earlier Old English. Look at (18) and compare this structure with (6) above:

---

[9] Cf. van Gelderen 1993, 2000, 2004; Osawa 2000, 2003.

(18) Old English clause structure

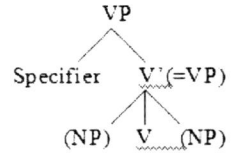

```
          VP
         /  \
   Specifier  V'(=VP)
             /  \
          (NP)  V  (NP)
```

That is, the clause is the projection of V, VP. It has no functional categories. In (18) the two NPs are not ordered with respect to each other. The parentheses show that NPs are optional. Then, this structure can deal with impersonal constructions in which there is no NP argument or in which there is only one NP argument mentioned above such as (10) or (11). There is no TP, and then, no EPP-feature, and hence, there is no subject requirement. If a predicate verb needs an argument, which has an agentive thematic role, this nominal should have the nominative case. If a predicate needs no agent, there is no subject. I will talk about this in more detail below.

Furthermore, I propose that languages typically start as lexical-thematic without any functional categories (i.e. typically DP, TP/IP, CP[10] or whatever), this means that a given language deploys the lexical categories or content words in traditional terms, and their phrasal projections (NP, VP, AP). Then, over a period of time, a new functional category is introduced in a given language. The emergence of a new functional category brings about many syntactic changes and hence new constructions (cf. Osawa 2003). The history of English is an instantiation of this shift from a lexical-thematic to a functional stage. Present-Day English has a full-fledged set of functional categories. Their presence determines how the clause structure of Present-Day English is constructed. Against this background, the changes which happened to 'passives' in the history of English can be better understood.

4.3 Impersonal constructions

Let us consider the semantics of impersonal constructions. Some examples of verbs which can occur in impersonal constructions are given below:[11]

> 1. non-intentional sensory and mental expressions: *þyncan* 'seem', *mætan* 'dream';
> 2. emotional experiences: *eglian* 'be in trouble', *hreowan* 'feel sorrow';
> 3. physical and biological experiences: *hyngrian* 'hunger', *þyrstan* 'thirst';
> 4. happenstance: *gebyran* 'happen'.

---

[10] CP means complementiser phrase/ complementiser projection, which is a clause headed by a complementiser.
[11] Cf. Gaaf 1904; McCawley 1976: 194; Elmer 1981.

The impersonal construction expressed a situation in which a human being is unvolitionally/unself-controllably involved (cf. McCawley 1976). There is no agent in the situation. The most typical example is provided by a weather verb like *snow* or *rain*, etc. or physical and biological experiences such as *hyngrian* 'hunger'. Then, in a lexical-thematic language, if the meaning of the predicate does not require an agent, which should be realized as a nominative NP, then as a subject, the clause structure of a given verb lacks the nominative argument NP and hence, lacks a subject. Since there is no functional category to require a subject, the clause can do without a subject. The essential of impersonal constructions is to describe the event or situation without referring to an agent. The argument position for an agent is not projected from the beginning.

4.4 Passive constructions

Similarly, passive constructions are typically agentless constructions. In passives the speaker wants to describe the situation from a viewpoint of a patient, not a viewpoint of an agent. If he wants to describe the situation from a viewpoint of an agent, he would use a different sentence form.

As has been pointed out by many researchers, even in Present-Day English the agent *by*-phrase is optional and not used frequently. Approximately four out of five English passive sentences have no expressed agent (Quirk et al. 1985: 164-165). According to Svartvik (1966), 80% of the passives in his written corpus were agentless. That is to say, the function of English passive sentences is not for expressing an agent of the action/event.

The Old English 'passives' are constructed lexically, based on the meaning of a predicate verb. If the speaker wants to express agent, he/she should use active constructions, not passive ones. The passive sentence is a construction which is intended to express Patient, Theme, or Recipient, etc., but not agent. The passive verb (i.e. past participle) is used for such a purpose, i.e. to express Patient, Theme, etc. The function of passive voices is to describe the action/situation from a viewpoint of Theme or Patient, not from the Agent's viewpoint. This is the same situation as is observed in impersonals.

Hence, the passive verb does not require an argument which should have an agentive theta role. The argument position for the agent is not projected in the clause structure from the beginning. Like impersonals, the passives are a construction in which there is no argument position for the agent, hence, no position for a subject. There is no empty subject position for an NP to move into for case checking. There is no syntactic operation involved there. A subject-less construction is the norm for passives/impersonals.

In short, the passives and impersonals are a construction in which there is no argument position for the agent, hence, subject. Then, a subject-less construction is the norm for passives/impersonals. This will follow automatically if a given language is lexical-thematic. Rather, a subject is not required automatically in such a lexical-thematic language. My proposal is different from the generative approach in that the subject[12] is not universally required.

My proposal is definitely different from functional approaches, too. The function of passives/impersonals is neither the subject demotion/agent-defocusing nor object-promotion, but passive/impersonals are constructions which involve no agent argument from the beginning, which is the nature of these constructions. In Present-Day English, due to the presence of a functional category TP, the subject position must be filled somehow. Then, the expletive subject fills the subject position, or, NP should move to the subject position.

However, since earlier languages are lexical-thematic, there are no functional categories, then, no subject requirement. Impersonal/passive constructions are constituted only by arguments which are required by the meaning of the predicate. The speaker can choose a syntactic structure which is the most appropriate form to express what he/she wants to convey. If he/she wants to describe the situation from a viewpoint of Patient, he/she selects the passives which have no argument position for agents. Both impersonals and passives are normally constructed in structure (18) without any syntactic operations; they are not deviant at all.

4.5 Morpho-semantic case system

This lexical-thematicity is based on a semantic-motivated case system. I assume that in Old English, the morphological case such as nominative, dative, and accusative was assigned to thematically related NP. The morphological case was closely related to the thematic roles of nouns (cf. Plank 1981, 1983).

In Old English, there were systematic correlations between the morphological case, the semantic role and the syntactic function; look at the following hypothetical pairings in Old English as given in Table 1:

---

[12] I will explain my concept of the subject here. The subject is considered to be a linguistic universal, even though it is very difficult to give a universal definition of subject. The term 'subject' is often used differently across researchers. Subject is a nominative-marked noun to someone, while subject is defined to be the agent of the predicate by others. However, there are many counterexamples to these associations. Keenan (1976) gives more than 30 properties of basic subjects, demonstrating that it is almost impossible to give necessary and sufficient conditions of subjecthood. The subjecthood seems to be a matter of degree in any one language.

The only solution is the syntactic approach I take in this paper. A subject in Present-Day English is a purely syntactic element which is not always associated with the particular theta-role. A specifier position of TP must be filled by some element with person/number properties. This element is called subject. See (6) and the discussion there. However, this syntactic definition is valid against the established functional T projection. Before the emergence of TP, then, the subject is not a linguistic universal.

Table 1: The correlations between morphological case, semantic role and syntactic function

Agent	Nominative	subject
Patient (adversative)	Accusative	(direct) object
Recipient, Experiencer Patient (cooperative)	Dative	(indirect) object
Cause of the action or state	Genitive	Object

If then the meaning of the predicate does not require an agent, or if the speaker does not want to describe the event/situation from a viewpoint of an agent, which should be realized as a nominative NP, the clause structure of a given verb lacks the nominative argument NP. This is called subject-less constructions. A subject is not necessary a priori. The requirement that all sentences should have a subject is a later development, due to the emergent TP, or due to the EPP-feature, as I have argued above.

We can summarise what we have discussed as follows. Lexical-thematic languages have no functional categories. They have only lexical categories like N, V, or A. There is no subject requirement since there is no TP, and hence no EPP-feature. In languages which have no relevant functional categories, the speaker can construct his sentence without the subject, if the meaning of the predicate does not require an agentive argument. The subject is a structurally required element by a functional category, TP/IP.

4.6 The emergence of TP: the emergence of new constructions

The Middle English period saw the appearance of new constructions such as prepositional passives and indirect passives. What made these constructions possible was a newly emergent functional T-system in English (cf. Osawa 2003). Present-Day English may have non-thematic constituents due to the presence of functional categories. The emergent TP requires the presence of a subject, irrespective of a thematic role. There is an empty position available for a case-less NP to move into (NP-movement). Raising constructions and passive constructions are an instantiation of this NP-movement. There is no need to say that prepositional and indirect passives are an instantiation of NP-movement.

Due to the demise of case morphology, thematically motivated (morpho-semantic) case system deteriorated. A new case system, i.e. a structure-based case system, appeared instead and brought about the separation of case from theta role. Thanks to this separation, a non-thematic subject position is made available. A new functional T has acquired a one-case assigning/checking ability, while a verb has lost one-case assigning ability. Syntactic passives are made possible against such a background.

In Present-Day English, the subject position, i.e. the Specifier of TP Position in (6), must always be filled due to EPP-features, or due to the functional category

T. Nominal elements with person/number properties are then inserted, by whatever operation it is, either NP-movement, merge. The nominal which occupies the [Spec, TP] positions is the subject, i.e., external argument. The insertion of expletive *it* is required if there is nothing to occupy the position. Impersonals without nominative NPs, including impersonal passives, are not allowed any more.

5. Concluding remarks

In this paper, I have proposed a new view of the changes which happened in English. The presence in Old English of apparently subject-less constructions, the absence of prepositional passives and indirect passives, their later appearance and the disappearance of subject-less constructions are all closely connected. Impersonals are not a deviation from the syntactic norm. Both impersonals and passives the essential of which is agentless structure are constructed normally, i.e. lexically. The key issue behind this is the shift of English from a lexical-thematic to a functional stage over the course of time.

Sources

Gordon, Ida (ed.)
    1960   *The Seafarer.* London: Methuen.
Thorpe, Benjamin (ed.)
    1844   *The Sermones Catholici or Homilies of Ælfric I.* London: Ælfric Society.

References

Abney, Steven P.
    1987   *The English noun phrase in its sentential aspect.* Ph.D. dissertation, MIT.
Chomsky, Noam
    1995   *The minimalist program.* Cambridge, Mass.: MIT Press.
    2005   "Three factors in language design", *Linguistic Inquiry* 36: 1-22.
Comrie, Bernard
    1977   "In defense of spontaneous demotion: The impersonal passive", in: *Syntax and Semantics* 8: *Grammatical Relations*, ed. Peter Cole & Jerrold Sadock. New York: Academic Press, 47-58.
Denison, David
    1993   *English historical syntax.* London: Longman.
Elmer, Willy
    1981   *Diachronic grammar: The history of Old and Middle English subjectless constructions.* Tübingen: Niemeyer.
Gaaf, Willem van der
    1904   *The transition from the impersonal to personal construction in Middle English.* Heidelberg: Carl Winter.

Gelderen, Elly van
  1993 — *The rise of functional categories*. Amsterdam & Philadelphia: John Benjamins.
  2000 — *A history of English reflexives pronouns*. Amsterdam & Philadelphia: John Benjamins.
  2004 — *Grammaticalization as economy*. Amsterdam & Philadelphia: John Benjamins.

Givón, Talmy
  1979 — *On understanding grammar*. New York: Academic Press.
  1981 — "Typology and functional domains", *Studies in Language* 5: 163-193.

Keenan, Edward L.
  1976 — 'Towards a universal definition of "subject"', in: *Subject and Topic*, ed. Charles N. Li. New York: Academic Press.

Langacker, Ronald -- Pamela Munro
  1975 — "Passives and their meaning", *Language* 51: 789-830.

Lyons, John
  1969 — *Introduction to theoretical linguistics*. Cambridge: Cambridge University Press [many reprints].

McCawley, Noriko A.
  1976 — "From OE/ME "impersonal" to "personal" constructions: What is a "subject-less" S?", in: *Papers from the Parasession on Diachronic Syntax*, ed. Sanford B., Steever et al., 192-204.

Ogura, Michiko
  1996 — *Verbs in medieval English: Differences in verb choice in verse and prose*. Berlin: Mouton de Gruyter.

Osawa, Fuyo
  2000 — *The rise of functional categories: Syntactic parallels between first language acquisition and historical change*. Ph.D. dissertation, University College London.
  2003 — "Syntactic parallels between ontogeny and phylogeny", *Lingua* 113: 3-47.

Perlmutter, David
  1978 — "Impersonal passives and the unaccusative hypothesis", *Berkeley Linguistics Society* 4: 157-189.

Perlmutter, David (ed.)
  1983 — *Studies in relational grammar, I*. Chicago: University of Chicago Press.

Perlmutter, David -- Paul Postal
  1977 — "Toward a universal characterization of passivization", *Berkeley Linguistics Society* 3: 394-417. [revised version in Perlmutter 1983, 3-29.]

Plank, Frans
  1981 — "Object cases in Old English: What do they encode?": A contribution to a general theory of case and grammatical relations. Ms., Englisches Seminar, Universität Hannover, 1-67.
  1983 — "Coming into being among the Anglo-Saxons", in: *Current topics in English historical linguistics*, ed. M. Davenport et al. Odense: Odense University Press, 239-278.

Quirk Randolph et al.
  1985 — *A comprehensive grammar of the English language*. London: Longman.

Radford, Andrew
  1990 — *Syntactic theory and the acquisition of English syntax*. Oxford: Blackwell.

Shibatani, Masayoshi
1985 "Passives and related constructions: A prototype analysis", *Language* 61: 821-848.

Siewierska, Anna
1984 *The passive: A comparative linguistic analysis.* London: Croom Helm.

Svartvik, Jan
1966 *On voice in the English verb.* The Hague: Mouton.

Part IV. Dialects and their representation

The southern dialect in Thomas Churchyard's *The Contention bettwixte Churchyearde and Camell* (1552)

María F. García-Bermejo Giner (Salamanca, Spain)

Abstract

The purpose of this paper is a description of the southern dialect features in a mid-sixteenth century non-dramatic text: Thomas Churchyard's *The Contention bettwixte Churchyearde and Camell* (1552). It is one of the earliest instances of the representation of the southern (eastern or Kentish rather than western) dialect. Also of interest are the Northern English traits present in sections of the text where no attempt at dialect representation was made.[1]

1. Introduction

In the century following the Master of Wakefield's linguistically disguising Mak,[2] the thief, as a southerner, writers such as John Lydgate (c1370-c1451) or John Skelton (c1460-1529) began to mark their characters linguistically. Initially only colloquial or archaic forms were used. A literary standard was gradually established. People became more aware of regional varieties, and comments on accents and dialects little by little became more frequent. As is well known, by 1589 George Puttenham, in *The Art of English Poesie,* considered that the "best" English was the one spoken in: "the Court, and ... London and the shires lying about London within lx. myles, and not much aboue". As the awareness of "better" forms of speech developed,[3] so did the use of dialect traits for characterization purposes: Kentish, South-Western, Northern, Scottish, Welsh, Irish, etc.[4] The characters whose speech was thus marked belonged to the lower social strata and the scenes in which they appeared were usually comic. As a result, when the use of dialect traits became more frequent, they came to be associated with rustic, humorous characters. In the sixteenth and seventeenth centuries the Kentish dialect and South Western English were the varieties preferred by playwrights, poets and prose writers.[5] Gradually a tradition for the representation of regional speech was

---

[1] The research for this paper was funded by a Grant from the Spanish Ministry of Education, reference BFF 2003-09376.
[2] About the use of dialect in this play see Cawley 1958, Blake 1981: 65-66, Gómez Soliño 1985, Irace 1990 and Wales 2006: 69-80.
[3] About the contemporary sociolinguistic panorama and its effect on the use of literary dialects see especially Blank 1996, Barber 1997: 10-20, Görlach 1999 and Nevalainen 2006: 29-44, 134-48.
[4] On the use of dialect traits in drama see Eckhardt 1910-11, Hughes 1929, Bartley 1954, Truninger 1976 and Bliss 1979. García-Bermejo Giner 1999: 250-52 gathers detailed information about the relevant literature on the topic. Ruano García 2010b analyzes and describes the lexical aspects of the literary representation of the northern dialects, especially Lancashire, in the Early Modern English period.
[5] Wakelin 1986: 51-56, 84-86, 115-18, 178-180 studies early lyrical and dramatic texts from Cornwall, Devon, Somerset and Wiltshire.

established and the result was often a mixture of traits of different geographical origins and diachrony. But before this happened it seems possible that authors were more faithful in their representation of dialect features. They may thus provide us with valuable information from a time period about which we do not yet know enough.

The scientific interest for language variation had a parallel development to its literary representation but we have to wait until the 17th century to find the first descriptions of specific features from specific areas. I am referring, of course, to Alexander Gill and his *Logonomia Anglica* (1619, 1621) or a *Collection of English Words not generally used* (1674, 1691) by John Ray, as well as to the incidental material which can be gleaned from contemporary dictionaries and grammars devoted to the standard variety.

The purpose of this paper is a description of a selection of dialect features in a mid-sixteenth century non-dramatic text: Thomas Churchyard's *The Contention bettwixte Churchyearde and Camell, vpon Dauid Dycers Dreame sett out in suche order, that it is bothe wittye and profitable for all degryes. Rede this little communication between Churchyarde: Camell and others mo: Newlye Imprinted and sett further for thy profit gentill Reader* (1552).

2. Contemporary uses of the Kentish or southern dialect for literary purposes

As shown by Blake 1981: 47-48, due to political and social reasons the Kentish and south eastern area had been regarded "with a mixture of trepidation and contempt" since the late 14th ct. Derogatory comments during the 15th ct. may explain why its dialect came to be considered as provincial and lacking in status. Four verses in Stephen Hawes' (?-1523?) *Pastime of Pleasure* (1509) (Blake 1981: 48) are the first known instance of Kentish literary representation. They introduce a foolish dwarf:

    3510   Sotheych quod he whan I **cham** in kent
    3511   At home I **cham** though I be hyther sent
    3512   I **cham** a gentylman of moche noble kynne
    3513   Though **Iche** be cladde in a knaues skynne

Twenty years later, St. Thomas More (1478-1535) used *cha* (I have), *chave*, *ych*, *chote* (I wot) in the speech of an old man from Sandwich, in Kent, who believed the local haven had decayed because of a tall steeple:

> **cha** marked this mater as wel as sūm other.& by god I **chote** how it waxed nought well ynoughe for I knew yt good and have marked so **chave** whĕ it bygan to wax wors. And what hath hurt it, good father, quod thes gentylmen. By may fayth, maysters, quod he, yonder same Tenterden stepel & nothyng ellys that by ye masse **cholde** t'were a fayre

fyshepole. Why hath ye steple hurt ye hauen, good father, quod they, Nay byr lady, maystersm quod he **ych** can not tell you wel why but **chote** well yt hath for, by god, I knew yt a good haven tyll ye steple was bylded, And by ye Mary masse **cha** marked it well, yt neuer throue synnys. (*A dyaloge of syr Thomas More knyghte* (1529): Bk iv. fo. cxx).

He added the comment, "And thus wisely spake these holy Lutherans".

In the next decades, morality authors such as John Redford (c 1500-1547) or John Bale (1495-1563) included these traits in the speeches of characters such as Ignorance (*chwas, ich, choold, cham, chyll*) in *The Play of Wit and Science* (c 1530-1547) or Idolatry (*Ych, cha*) in *Thre Lawes* (1548). *Respublica* (1553), the morality attributed to Nicholas Udall (1505-1556), is the work traditionally considered as the first one in which "we find a character using the south-western dialect consistently" (Blake 1981: 71). Wakelin (1988: 135) calls it "the crude representation of supposed Devonshire dialect"). People, a sort of clown, represents the suffering peasant community. Beside *ich*-forms, we find instances of the voicing of initial fricatives characteristic, at the time, not only of south-western English, but common to southern dialects in general and heard as far north as Buckinghamshire and as far east as Kent and Essex.[6] *Isfearde* and *Isshoulde* could be representing 'Us feared' and 'Us should' rather than *Ich feared* or *Ich should* (see Wakelin 1986: 86). Similar features occur in a couple of instances in the comedy by the same author, *Ralph Roister Doister* (first performed 1552-54, first published 1567?).

Jestbooks, so popular at the time, are a clear indicator that London and the adjacent towns and counties were becoming very well known at the time. Most of those jestbooks are very precisely located from a geographical point of view. In a previous study on the use of dialect markers in this genre in the 16th ct.,[7] I found the southern dialect represented only in two tales: In *Merie Tales Newly Imprinted and Made by Master Skelton Poet Laureat* (1567) a cobbler of the parish of Dis, Suffolk, uses *ich* three times, and the standard *I*, fifteen. The second tale is included in *Mery Tales, Wittie Questions and Quicke Answeres, very pleasant to be Readde* (1567). Proclitic *ich*, in *chadde*, appears in a sentence used by a "homely", "blunt" fellow, whose geographical origin is not stated. The southern counties, eastern and western are the scenario of many of the tales, as can be seen in Table 1. However, the characters' speeches are only indicative of colloquial English.

Table 1: *HMT, −CC, &MMG, $WE, #MTWQ, @MS, %TN (Garcia-Bermejo Giner 2001: 216-17) (For an explanation of the initials and symbols see fn 7.)

---

[6] Cf. the information provided by Alexander Gill (1619). See also Voitl 1988, Wakelin 1988, etc.
[7] See García-Bermejo Giner 2001. The study was based on the following corpus of extant 16th ct. collections: *The Wydow Edyth* (1525) $ [WE], *A C. Mery Talys* (1526) * [HMT], *Merie Tales of the mad men of Gotam.* (c 1565) & [MMG], *Mery Tales, Wittie Questions and Quicke Answeres, very pleasant to be Readde* (1567) # [MTWQ], *Merie Tales Newly Imprinted and Made by Master Skelton Poet Laureat* (1567) @ [MS], *A verie merie Historie, of the Milner of Abington* (1575), *The Cobler of Caunterburie* (1590) + [CC], *Tarltons Newes Ovt of Pvrgatorie* (1590) % [TN].

London Sites	Other English Towns	Other Counties or Regions
*White Friars	*Stony Stratford, Bucks	*Middlessex
*Lombard's Street	$Windsor, Brks	*Essex
*Cornhill	*@Oxford	$Surrey
*@Charing Cross	*Botley, Bck, Hmp, Ox?	*Northamptonshire
*Gray Friars	+Romney, Knt	&Nottingham
*$Holborn Bridge	+Gravesend, Knt	&Leicester
*Fleet Street	+$Canterbury, Knt	*Warwickshire
*Knightsbridge	$Sevenoaks, Knt	#Cheshire
*Saint John's	$Rochester, Knt	*The North Country
*St. Paul's	$Otford, Knt	*Wales
*St. Lawrence's	+Cambridge	
$Chelsea x2	@Abington, Cam.	
*$@Westminster	+Cherryhington, Cam.	
+Billingsgate	+Trumpington, Cam.	
*Brentford	*$Colebrook, Dev	
*$Barnett	$Exeter, Dev.	
$Wandsworth	$Bury St. Edmunds, Sf.	
$Kew	$Horringer, Sf.	
$Stratford	$Brandon, Sf.	
$Barking	$Bradfield, Sf.	
$Fullham	$Theford, Nf	
$Southwark	# Walsingham, Nf.	
$St. Mary Cray	@Norwich, Nf.	
$Foots Cray	@Dis, Nf.	
$Croydon	$St. Albans, Hert.	
$Eltham	+Wickham, Hamp.?	
$Whetstone	$Tooting, Sr	
@Uxbridge	$Battersea, Sr	
%Hoxton	$Colne, Ess.	
*$St. Thomas of Akres	$Hatfield, Ess.	
%Bridewell	&Loughborough, Lei.	

*&$Kingston-upon-Thames *Stratford-Upon-Avon, Wa
*St. Nicholas Fleshambles *Shottery, Wa.
%Doncaster, Yks.
%York

Andrew Boorde (ca. 1490-1549), a native of Sussex, attempted in 1547 a representation of the English spoken in Cornwall in *The Fyrst Boke of the Introduction of Knowledge*. These twenty-six lines are the first recorded example of Cornish English dialect literature. We find the *ich*-forms, the voicing of initial fricatives and also the use of the voiceless alveolar plosive /t/ instead of the voiceless interdental fricative /θ/ in *thick, thin*, etc. Wakelin (1975: 206-10) shows that Boorde was representing an east Cornwall variety but also included a few northern English forms (*gos(se)* 'gossip, friend', *fleg* 'fit to fly', *soole* 'flavouring, meat') as well as more widespread dialectalisms. Some of the vocabulary selected by Boorde remains unexplained (*taale, watysh, starre*).

Thomas Howell (fl 1560-1581) was a native of Dunster in Somerset. In "Iacke showes his qualities and great good will to Ione" (1568), included in his collection *The arbor of amitie* (1568), he seems to have attempted to represent a southern dialect, maybe Kentish, as the county is mentioned by name.

As regards dialect literature, the Kentish dialect was used in a song as early as 1611 ("A Wooing Song of A Yeoman of Kents Sonne"), and in William Strode's Poem "The Wonders of Plymouth" (ca. 1620),[8] thus antedating the first instances we have of Northern English dialect literature (*A Yorkshire Dialogue between an Awd Wife, a Lass, and a Butcher* (1673),[9] 'I'll tell o how Gilbert Scott sowd is mere Berry'[10] or the well known *In Praise of Yorkshire Ale* (1683) attributed to George Meriton.[11] William Strode was born at Shaygh Prior, near Plymouth, Devon, and received his early education there.

3. *The Contention bettwixte Churchyearde and Camell*

The Contention bettwixte Churchyearde and Camell, vpon Dauid Dycers Dreame is a collection of verse pamphlets and broadsides composed during a sort of *flyting* or abusive contest provoked by the publication of Thomas Churchyard's *Dauid Dycers Dreame* (1551). They were printed together in 1560 but their composition dates back to a few years earlier. Only some of the authors are identified by name beside Churchyard: Thomas Camell, Thomas Hedley, W. Waterman, Geoffrey Chapel and Steven Steeple. These last two may have been alter egos of Churchyard

---

[8] About the dialect in this poem see Wakelin 1988: 138.
[9] For a detailed linguistic analysis of this poem see Ruano 2008.
[10] Ruano 2010a offered a thorough linguistic analysis of this hitherto unstudied piece.
[11] About the dialect in this dialogue see Dean 1962 and also Cawley's 1959 *Introduction* to his edition.

(notice that their surnames correspond to parts of a church, just as Churchyard does).[12] Thomas Churchyard (1523?-1604) was a prolific Elizabethan poet, translator and prose writer. He was born in Shrewsbury, Shropshire (Churchiard I am, In Shreiwsbury townne, thei say where I was borne 58 [6]).[13] His father was also a Salopian and his mother was of Welsh origin. He was an ensign bearer or lieutenant, serving in France, Germany, the Low Countries, Scotland and Ireland, participating in every war England was involved in between 1543 and 1575, a soldier-poet.[14] It seems likely that in this way he would get to know men from all regions of the country.

Because of *Davy Dycars Dreame* Churchyard was questioned by the Privy Council of King Edward VI as they suspected it might contain a veiled attack against some Privy Councilors ruling the country during the king's minority. This was also the reason for the flyting. Thomas Camell' poems attacked Churchyard and all the others' supported him from different perspectives. Of special interest to us in this paper are those by W. Waterman, Geoffrey Chappel and Thomas Steeple because familiar language, colloquialisms and southern traits appear in them. A reason for this may have been an attempt to defuse the seriousness of Camell's accusations against Churchyard. However, also of interest is the language of the text in general as it also contains traits that would eventually be considered regional or were already regional at the time but well known to the general public.

4. The characters and the places mentioned

The mariners in "Western Wyll" (text [9]) come from Maldon Mead. This must refer to some place in or near the also mentioned town of Maldon, in the Blackwater estuary in East Essex. The action takes place in London where they have travelled to sell their fish, probably at Billingsgate Market[15]. Because of unfavourable winds they have had to postpone their departure and have decided to explore the city. They go to the St. Paul's area, where the all the printers' shops were. Their names are Wilkin, Watt[16] and Herman and they are offered "Davy Dicar's Dream" and Churchyard and Camell's exchanges about it. Their speech is not dialectally marked, although they do use some colloquial expressions and

---

[12] See Lucas 2002 for an explanation of the controversy and its relation to Spencer's "September" eclogue.
[13] The numbers in square brackets refer to the numbers given in the Sources (p. 260 below) under Churchyard 1560.
[14] About his life and works see especially Adnitt 1880, Geimer 1965, King 1982, Schutte 1984, Kyne 2004.
[15] It has been associated exclusively with the fish trade since the 16th ct. The reading of the word in the text is difficult as it stands at the beginning of a line and is rather blurred, it could be something like Billin/geigate. There are several printers' errors in the same page.
[16] Watt is also called Watkin 45 [9]. The *-kin* suffix, diminutive of Dutch origin, had already fallen out of use in personal names by the 16th ct., traces of it remaining only in surnames. Curiously enough Watkin appears in the C-texts of *Piers Plowman* thought to be the source of *Davy Dicars' Dreame*. Wilkin appears in Chaucer. See *OED*.

familiar language. An explanation for this may be found at the end in the words of the teller of the story:

> And for to pen it out the bed did to myself resorte
> And drew it there into a somme, as I had harde it tolde.
> Not with suche wordes as they it spake, but in suche wordes as I,
> Had partly learned of my dame, and lyst to fantasy,
> Suche happe may happe, to giue a second fytte. 132-136 [9].

This is one of the techniques which would later be most frequently used by writers to remind us of the linguistic origin of their characters without tiring their readers with deviant spellings or grammar.

Geoffrey Chappel (Text [11]) says he is a town crier in the, then, small town of Whitstable on the north-east coast of Kent. At the time it consisted of a very small fishing settlement.[17] His purported letter to Thomas Camell is intended to suggest a dialect speaker and it contains dialect traits as well as colloquialisms, familiar language and malapropisms. In "To goodman Chappels Supplication", Thomas Camell apparently answers to him in kind, using the same sort of language and with an increased number of dialectalisms. However, although the letter is signed by him, Camell is referred to in the letter by name and in the third person. The dialect thickens in the last letter, the one sent by Stephen Steeple to Master Camell. He seems to know Geoffrey Chappel and to be a Kentish man as well. The density of non-standard features is such that it resembles dialect literature.

5. Linguistic Analysis

Both the original edition of ca. 1552 and the compilation of 1560 have come down to us. They are available through *EEBO* (*Early English Books Online*); the London Society of Antiquaries owns copies of the ca. 1552 printing. In the *EEBO* transcription all tildes indicating nasals in the original text are omitted. Transcription errors are frequent.[18]

The fact that the original edition of ca. 1552 and the compilation of 1560 have survived allow us to remedy obvious printers' errors that may have been misleading when analizing the text linguistically, and, on occasion, would have meant the loss of important data. For instance, in the 1560 edition we find the word *nourt*, rhyming with *coutier* and preceded by the rhymes *sort/short*:

---
[17] For a detailed account of the contemporary history of the town see: <http://www.simplywhitstable.com/town_history/worigins.htm> [Accessed 19th Aug. 2008].
[18] For instance: *Danye Dikers dreme* [9] for *Dauye Dikers dreme*; "When faith in **fre? Esl** ere fruit and folysh fracyes fade"1 [2] for "When faith in frēdes bere fruit and folysh frāncies fade"; I mean mad **taungers**, that so raunge at large 45 [5] **for** "I mean mad raungers, that so raunge at large"; And such men I bad, as then I **had** you 47 [5] **for** "And such men I bad, as then I bad you", etc.

But twas vnleudly dooe, and after an homly sort,
So faire a beast as you ben, to tiyen/tyen vp so short,
I pray you holden scused twas but, for lacke of **nourt**
For cham sure, hannot ben, past. vii. or viii. yer a coutier 13-16 [11]

We might have thought that *nourt* was a variant of *nought*. In the *OED* we read that from the 17th ct. on *nort* was found in the south and south-west and from the 19th ct. *nurt* in Somerset. The *English Dialect Dictionary* (*EDD*) records the spelling *nort* in War. Suf. w. Som^1, Dev.^{2} Cor.^{2}. There are no citations in *OED* to support this information. In the text it could be interpreted as a malapropism meaning "for lack of any good reason". However, in the 1552 edition, the verses read: "I pray you holden scused, twas, but, for lacke of nourter (=nurture =education), /For cham sure, hannot bē, past. vii or viii. yer a courter". So, an apparent southernism turns out to be an error on the part of the printers. The reverse is also true. Sometimes the 1560 version ommits obvious southernisms. When comparison has been possible I have included both readings in the examples.

5.1 Northernisms, malapropisms, colloquialisms and archaisms

Apart from the obvious southernisms in the sections where Kentish English appears, the seventeen pieces that comprise the text are rich in other features that can improve our understanding of Early Modern English. We find instances of *h*-dropping and hypercorrect-*h*, as seen in examples (1) – (5). As shown in Milroy (1983) *h*-dropping was wide-spread in this period and it would not become stigmatized until the late eighteenth century.[19]

(1) By which all y^t know you, will thinke you well **hable** 107 [5]

(2) He had is helpe his parysshe prest I venture durst my **hăde** 60 [9]

(3) And nowe a man (ye saye he **his**) against a Dreame to spurne 110 [9]

(4) But twas vnleudly dooe, and after **an homly** (=homely) sord 11 [11]

(5) Nor nere solde his landes: ofr ych herd **an hasard** (= herald) of armes 18 [11]

We read in *OED* that "In the northern dialect, ME. and mod., the s marker, is used for all persons of the sing., and also for the plur., when not immediately joined to the nom. pron., *e.g.* when the subject is a noun or relative." (the Northern Subject Rule; see further Klemola 2000; Pietsch 2005). As seen in examples (6) – (18), we find thirteen instances of this feature in three pieces written by Thomas Churchyard ([1], [6] and [16]) and in one written by W. Waterman ([15]) where no attempt is being made at representing a different dialect. Two questions arise: Was this rule

---

[19] See García-Bermejo Giner & Montgomery (1997: 172-175) for a full discussion of story of this feature in the nineteenth century.

also operational at the time in the West Midland dialect of Shropshire, where Churchyard came from? Why didn't the London printers "silently" emendate this usage?

(6) Then answeringe sleapinge he momblethe this out,
And cawllethe thē fomblers **that stondes** him aboute. 21-22 [1]

(7) But those **that knowes**, suche fishing hokes, shal sone perceyue the bayt. 10 [6]

(8) Unto the good, it is not yll, nor hurtfull vnto none.
Nor vnto those, **that loues** ye light lyght, it is no stūblyng stone.
But thos **that stāds**, to watch a time, the innocent to spyll,
May wrest the truth, cleane out of frame and turne good thyngs to yll. 33-36 [6]

(9) What thinkes this man he hath more witte, & learning in his head.
Than **hathe** fyue thousand other men, **that** Dicarres dreame **hath** read. 12-16 [16]

(10) But tyll suche spyders bee wede out, and all theyr cob webes to,
That sekes to trappe the sellye flies, as you begyn to do. 177-78 [16]

(11) And let them lyue in peace and rest, **that thinkes** no harme to the. 210 [16]

(12) The wiked sort, whose vice is knowne, by those **which writes** their liues,
Can not abyde, to heare their fauts, but styll against theym **striues**. 25-26 [6]

(13) And soe saithe that sleaping nedes no Dremes at all
Whiche yet neuer **hathe** ben, nor to come neuer shall. 9-10 [1]

(14) The wiked sort, whose vice is knowne, by those **which writes** their lyues.
Can not abyde, to heare their fauts, but styll against theym **striues**. 25-26 [6]

(15) But yet suche dreadfulle whans and thens, **which doth** the matter marre
were bette quight, pulled out of syght, then shewed as they are. 145-146 [15]

(16) Y^e vprighte men **whiche loues** thee light, whose heartes be voyd of gyle:
Condene no cause till trueth be tryed, giue eare and lyst a whyle. 1-2 [16]

(17) But comenly these sclaunder tonges, **whiche** still **delyts** in lyes:
Who maketh war, **who soweth** strife, **who brīgeth** Realms to ruine 100-101 [6]

(18) The roote and branche and chefeest groūd, of mischeefs all and some,
Is euyll tongues, whose sugred words, **hath** wyse mē ouercome 103-4 [6]

Northern dialect lexis is also present in sections where the writer does not attempt to represent a regional variety. There are five instances of *barnes* 'children', as can be seen in examples (6) – (18), but *child* and *boyes* are also present in the text. As shown in *OED* and *EDD* this, now, traditional northern form, had a wider distribution in mediaeval times. In the mid-sixteenth century it was, apparently, already considered a northernism.[20] In examples (19) – (22) it could be argued that the writer decided to use this word for alliterative reasons, but the implication remains that readers and writer were familiar with it.

(19) Then baelful **barnes** be blyth that here in England wonne, 27 [1]

(20) then balefull **barnes** be blyth, that her in Englande wonne 26 [15]

(21) Than balefull **barnes** bee blithe you say, that here in England wonne: 123 [14]

(22) An assurance her you make that baleful **barnes** we be, 124 [14]

(23) The **barnes** I say that here do wonne, with in this brittaine lande, 179 [14]

(24) The dogge, the cat, and syb the mayde, eche couchen them about.

Into their **hernes** where they warre wont, and al was huist and styll 84-85 [9]

(25) Then Wylkyn gan at once vp brayed, and sware by godes dyne harte

A rushe for bookes, me leuer warre that I could tel this tale

Then of your **scablings** for to haue, a loade by wayne or carte 87-89 [9]

(26) But I was bent another waye, methought it very yl

All day to **rucken** on my taile, and poren on a booke 96-97 [9]

Example (24) shows the word *hernes*, 'a corner, nook, hiding-place' which, according to *OED*, was "Chiefly Sc. (in form *hirn, hyrn*) or *dial.* after 1500". This is also the distribution indicated later by *EDD*, which records it also in Yks. Lin. and E. An. However, contemporary sources do not associate it with northern or Scottish English. Its presence is noted by *Lexicons of Early Modern English* (hereinafter *LEME*) in Nowell's 1567 *Vocabularium Saxonicum* (*Herne, id est Hyrn, A Corner*), in Thomas Speght's 1598 edition of *Geoffrey Chaucer's Works* (*halke or herne (angulus) a corner*) and in François de Chassepol's 1677 *The History of the Grand Visiers* (*halke, (angulus) b. corner, valley. Herne*).

In example (25) we find the word *scabblins* which, according to *OED* means 'chips of stone' and is attested as a northern word in Grose's *A provincial glossary with a collection of local proverbs and popular superstitions* (1790) and in later Leicestershire and Northumberland glossaries. Nevertheless, *EDD* records the word in s. Cheshire, pronounced [skjablinz], and with the sense "The remnant of hay left on the ground after the cocks have been loaded." Given the context in which it appears, this could very well be the meaning intended. The proximity of s. Cheshire to Churchyard's hometown makes it likely that the word had a more widespread distribution at the time.

---

[20] About the history of *barn* see Ruano García forthcoming.

Example (26) shows the verb *rucken*, 'To squat, crouch, cower, huddle together', recorded by *OED* as a northern word in John Ray's *North Country Words* (1691). However, *LEME* states its presence in Elisha Cole's 1676 *An English Dictionary* meaning "Cowre, kneel, fall down for fear, also ruck down (ut mulier ad mingend.)" and it is not regionally marked. It is not clear, therefore, what its regional distribution in the 16th ct. was. From the 1820s on it is attested (*OED, EDD*) in glossaries of the n. Cy, Cheshire, Lin., East Anglia and Northamptonshire as well as in Som. Dev. and Cor.

The texts are also rich in malapropisms. As was to be expected, they are more frequent in Chappel's letter than in Camell's or Steeple's, see examples (27)- (28).

(27)   But twas **vnleudly** dooe, and after an homly sort/sord 11 [11]
(28)   To **spout** with such a gemān, of so hie a **petidegree** 16 [11]

Example (27) is not recorded by *OED* but under *Lewdly* we find the obsolete meanings "†1. In unlearned fashion; ignorantly; foolishly" (Last citation 1477), and also "†3. Badly, poorly, ill. *to think lewdly of*, to have a poor opinion of. *Obs.*" The citation provided for this meaning dates from 1596 (Spencer, *State Irel.* Wks. [Globe] 621/1 Those sayd gentellmens children, being thus in the ward of those Lordes, are therby brought up lewdly, and Irish~like.)

As regards example (28), *spout* seems to be an unlearned corruption for *spute* or *dispute*, first attested by *OED* in a text dating four years later than ours. *Petidegree* is a humorous variation of *pedigree*.

In examples (29)-(36) we find colloquialisms, vulgarisms and familiar language common in the sixteenth century.

(29)   **For God swete bones** quod watkyn tho, for bokyshe be we not 45 [9]
(30)   Uor zure charde hym swear **by goges dygne dayntie bones** 7 [12]
(31)   **Te** heare a poore man his tale for to tell 2 [11]
(32)   To spout with such a **gemā**, of so hie a petidegree 16 [11]
(33)   **Yer** of a strudy [1552 sturdy] stock, for your fader nere raised his farmes 17 [11]
(34)   **Bum** fay chil treate no more, do withen what ye can 26 [11]
(35)   A dynkte ye wyll be mad, all out, beuore dat May be done 10 [12]
(36)   Churcharde wers a bell at **staill** to make his frendes sport 14 [12]

The corrupt form *gog* for 'God'[21] is recorded by *OED* since the fourteenth century and attested in the sixteenth century in Nicholas Udall's *Ralph Royster Doister* (a

---

[21] Probably used as an euphemism.

1553). The vulgar pronunciation of *gentleman* in example (32), *gemã*, is only attested once in *OED*, in a ca. 1550 text, *Dr. Doubble Ale*. The variant *gentman* is recorded twice in Udall's play. *Bum*, the vulgar contraction of 'by my', is attested by *OED* only after 1571. Contractions and weak forms such as those in examples (31, (33), (35) and (36) were indicative of colloquial speech.

Since Skelton's days, archaisms had been frequently used when attempting to suggest the colloquial or non-standard nature of a character's speech. In examples (37)-(38) we find two instances of their presence in one of our texts. According to *OED*, *ythewed*, 'well mannered', was already obsolete in the mid-sixteenth century. There is only one quotation dating from the fourteenth century. *LEME* records it in the anonymous *Medulla Grammatice* (ca. 1480), Morigeratus: Well thewed. *Huist*, 'husht', is only attested in the early fifteenth century by *OED*.

(37)　For Dikers feawe in my contrey, so well **ythewed** bene 64 [9]

(38)　The dogge, the cat, and syb the mayde, eche couchen them about.

　　　Into their hernes where they warre wont, and al was **huist** and styll 84-85 [9]

5.2 Southernisms

In attempting to suggest a Kentish or southern dialect, the authors of these texts opted for selecting grammatical traits and the two better known phonological ones. Many of these features were included by Alexander Gill in *Logonomia Anglica* (1619) as characteristic of the speech of people from the south, east and west of the country.

The examples (39)-(43) attest the trait considered by Gill as characteristic of Western English, especially of Somerset: "Before past participles beginning with a consonant they put an i, as ifrör or ivrör for frözen, <gelu concretus>, hav yi idü for dün <perfecisti>" (Danielsson et al. 1972 II: 103). This use was already common in ME in the South and West-Midlands. According to *OED*, s.v. Y- Prefix 4:

> In the 16th century it was adopted as an archaistic feature from Chaucer and Lydgate by many poetical writers…In modern dialects its use in the form *a* (ə) extends over a triangular area of which the angles lie in Worcestershire, Surrey, and Cornwall; it is found also in Pembrokeshire and Wexford.

It is first attested as a dialect trait in Thomas Howell's 1568 "Iacke showes his qualities and great good will to Ione", where, as we saw, a Kentish dialect was intended.

(39)　Thou shoodes be newe **yshod**, to träp these olde stones/stons 8 [12]

(40)　And al their fraught **y brought** a borde; to wende to Maldon towne 10 [9]

(41)　For Diker feawe in my contrey, so well **ythewed** (= mannered) bene 64 [9]

(42) Harry who bal harke, maste Camell hathe **yzeene** 1 [12]
(43) Twas but blockshly **y do**, of one so vnbase as he 15 [11]

There are also instances of unmarked past participles and of *bee* for 'been', as seen in examples (44)-(46). This form of the past participle was the common literary form in the fourteenth and fifteenth centuries according to *OED* which considers it as representative of south western dialects since the sixteenth. It is first attested in *Gammer Gurton's Needle* (1575).

(44) But twas vnleudly dooe 11 [11]
(45) Er twaie daies bee agoe 17 [12]
(46) For yche ha bee brought vp 6 [11]

Southern [ən] for *him* appears once ((47) Bum fay chil treate no more, do **withen** what ye can 26 [11]). As shown by *OED*, s.v. HIM:

> In 10th c. (as in the parallel *her, hem*), the dative appears to have begun to be used for the accus. *hine* in north-midl. dialect; by 1150 *him* had supplanted *hine* in north and midl., and before 1400 had become the general literary form, though some south-western writers of the 15th c. retained *hin, hen*, which, in the form *en, un, 'n*, is still current in southern dialect speech.

EDD records this variant in Lei. Hrf. Pem. Glo. Brks. Hrt. Sur. Sus. Hmp. I.W. Wil. Dor. Som. Dev. Cor. (Cf. EDG § 407).

There is one instance of plural *-en*: (48) Which com from olde **housen**, of moch inpossibilitie 20 [11]. Gill (1619) also considers plural *-en* as characteristic of the south western dialect:

> Also they have this peculiarity, that they alter certain irregular nouns of either number ending in z in order to distinguish the number, e.g. hooz **hose** (singular and plural) <caliga> or <caligae> with them remains as höz in the singular, but is hözn in the plural..." (Danielsson et al. 1972.II: 103)

As seen in Table 2, frequent in the texts are variant forms of the first person singular pronoun *ich* which would become the archetypical way of indicating the rusticity of a character. According to *OED*, they could still be

> Found in remains of s.e. (Kentish) dial. in 16th and early 17th c., in s.w. dialect 16-18th c., and often introduced in specimens of dialect speech in the dramatists.

Gill (1611) considered it characteristic of the speech of Southerners "they say Ich for J <ego>, cham for I am <sum>, chil for J wil <volo>, chi vör yi for I warant you <certum do>" (Danielsson et al. 1972. II: 103).

Table 2: Ich *forms*

Cha 19 [13], Cham 14 [11], Charde 7 [12], Chil 24 [11], Chote 5 [12], Chud 26 [13], Chyll 8 [11], Ich 16 [13], Ich 19 [13], Ich 21 [13], Ich 6 [12], Ichã 2 [12], Ych 10 [11], Ych 18 [11], Ych 18 [13], Ych 25 [13], Yche 6 [11]

As regards phonological characteristics, the two most frequent ones, shown in Tables 3 and 4, are the voicing of initial fricatives (See further Voitl 1988, Wakelyn 1988b, etc.) and the substitution of the interdental fricatives for the voiced dental plosive.

Table 3: Voicing of initial fricatives

Bevore 10 [13], Dervore 23 [13], Uor 7 [12], Varre 18 [12], Vart 24 [13], Vast [12], Vayle 9 [13], vayre 1 [13], Vende 20 [13], vor 4 [13], Vor 10 [12], Vor 16 [12], Vor 16 [13], Vor 20 [13], Vor 4 [12], vor 4[12], vor 6 [13], vor 6 [13], Vor 7 [12], Vor 8 [13], Vorbod 20 [13], Vorde 11 [12], Vorrayle 12 [12], Vorstande 17 [13], Vorth 20 [13], Vortune 5 [12], vortune5 [12], vrom 2 [13], Zad 3 [12], zad 3 [12], Zauacion 16 [13], Zay 17 [13], Zedge 20 [13], Zee 21 [13], Yzeene 1 [12], yzeene 1 [12], Zeete 8 [13], Zelf 22 [13], Zent 12 [13], zent 2, 3 [13], zent 5 [13], Zereuerence 18 [13], Zet 8 [13], Zit 20 [12], Zit 9 [12], Zo 3 [12], Zo 3 [12], Zo 9 [13], Zo 11 [13], Zo 28 [13], Zone 9 [13], zoote 7 [13], Zore 10 [12], Zore 9 [13], Zorry 2 [12], Zory 2 [12], Zounded 12 [13], zuch 5 [13], zum 5 [13], Zupplication 15 [13], zure 7 [12], Zure 7 [12], Zwap 14 [13], Zwear 16 [13], zyckish 7 [12], Zyde 22 [13], zyerd 6 [13], zyr 1 [13], Zyr 13 [13], Zyr 15 [13]

Table 4: Voiced alveolar plosive for interdental fricatives

Dan [than] 24 [13], Dan [then] 23 [13], Dat 10 [13], Dat 11 [13], Dat 12 [13], Dat 12 [13], Dat 24 [13], Dat 4 [13], De 15 [13], De 4 [13], Der 6 [13], Deron 6 [13], Dervore 23 [13], Dicke 21 [13], Dyng 24 [13], dyng 4 [13], Dynkte 10 [13], Noding 12 [13], Wort 24 [13]

As can be seen in the section dealing with the previous use of Kentish, southern and southwestern features in literature, they were associated with the rural speech of these areas. Gill (1619) mentioned the voicing of initial fricatives as a common feature of Southerners, Easterners, and Westerners (cf. Danielsson et al. 1972.2: 103).

6. Conclusions

The linguistic analysis of *The Contention bettwixte Churchyearde and Camell* (1552) has allowed us to gather interesting information not only about 16th century southern dialects but also about the colloquial and vulgar language of the time. Numerous ante-datings to *OED* quotations have been obtained. Also of importance are the instances of northern traits present in sections of the text where no attempt was being made at suggesting a different language variety. Literary dialects in the Early Modern period have traditionally been considered as an archetypical representation of regional speech and therefore not a valid linguistic data source. However, in its initial stages, writers seem to have been rather accurate in their selection of features, thus providing us with very relevant information about a time period that still remains pretty much in the dark. A thorough study of sixteenth century texts in which an attempt is made to suggest dialect lexis, morphology or phonology can help us fill the vast emptiness of Early Modern English dialectology.

Sources

Anonymous
    1611   "A wooing song of a yeoman of Kents Sonne", in: *Melismata. musicall phansies. Fitting the covrt, citie, and covntrie hvmovrs. To 3, 4 and 5. Voyces.* London: Printed by William Stansby for Thomas Adams.

Bale, John
    1538   *A comedye concernynge thre lawes, of nature, Moses, & Christ, corrupted by the Sodomytes, Pharysees and Papystes.* Imprinted per Nicolaum Bamburgensem.

Bevington, David (ed.)
    1975   *The play of wit and science* in: *Medieval Drama*: Boston: Houghton Mifflin: 1029-60.

Brown, Arthur (ed.)
    1951   *Wit and science.* London: Malone Society.

Churchyard, Thomas
    1552?   *Dauy dycars dreame quod. T. Churcharde* or *When faith in frendes beare fruit.* London: Imprinted at London in Aldersgate strete by Rycharde Lant.

    1552?   *To dauid dicars when.* London: Imprinted by Hary Sutton, dwellyng in Poules Churchyarde, at the signe of the blacke boye.

    1552?   *A playn and fynall confutacion: Of cammells corlyke oblatracion.* London: Imprinted in Fletstrit by Wyllyam Gryffyth, a lyttle aboue the condit at the syne of the Gryffyn.

    1552?   *A replicacion to Camels obiection.* London: Imprinted by Rychard Lant.

    1552?   *The surreioindre vnto Camels reioindre.* London: In Aldersgate strete by Rycharde Lant.

    1552?   *A decree betwene Churchyarde and Camell quod W. Ilderton.* London: Imprinted by Rychard Haruy, dwellyng in Foste [?]

    1552?   *Westerne wyll upon the debate betweene Churchyarde and Camell.* London: Imprinted at London in Fletestrete at the signe of the George next to saynt Dunstones Church by Wyllyam Powell.

    1552?   *A supplicacion unto mast Camell.* London: Imprinted by Richard Lant.

    1552?   *To goodman Chappels supplication.* London: Imprinted by Richard Sutton.

    1552?   *Steuen Steple to mast Camell.* London: Imprinted by Rychard Lant.

    1560   *The contention betwyxte Churchyeard and Camell, vpon Dauid Dycers dreame sette out in suche order, that it is bothe wyttye and profytable for all degryes. Rede this littell comunication*

EEBO

Furnivall, F. J. (ed.)
1870

Grossart, Alexander Balloch
1879

Halliwell, James Orchard (ed.)
1848

Happé, Peter (ed.)
1985

Howell, Thomas
1568

More, Thomas
1529

Redford, John
1908 [c 1530]

betwene Churchyarde: Camell: and others mo newlye imprinted and sett furthe for thy profyt gentill reader: Preface [1], Dauy Dycars Dreame [2], To Dauy Dicars when [3], The Debate between A Replicacion to Camels objection [4]. Camels rejoindre, to Churchyarde [5]. Surrejoindre unto Camels rejoinder [6]. Decree betwene Churchyarde and Camell [7]. The iudgement of the Authour [8]. Westerne wyll, upon the debate betwyxte Churchyarde and Camell [9]. Of such as on fantesye decree & discuss: on other mens workes, lo Ovides tale thus. Thomas Hedley [10]. Supplicacion unto mast Camell. Geoffray Chapell [11]. To goodman Chappels supplication [12]. Steven Steple to mast Camell [13]. Camelles conclusion [14]. Westerne will to Camell and for hym selfe alone. W. Waterman [15]. Playn and fynall confutacion: of cammells corlyke oblatracion [16]. Camelles Crosse Rowe [17]. Imprinted at London: By Owen Rogers, for Mychell Loblee dwelyng in Paulls churchyeard, anno. M.D.LX.
Early English Books Online: <http://eebo.chadwyck.com/home>

The fyrst boke of the introduction to knowdledge by Andrew Borde. Early English Text Society. Extra Series 10. London: Published for the Early English Text Society by Kegan Paul, Trench, Trübner and Co.

The poems of Thomas Howell (1568-1581). Blackburn: Printed for the subscribers by C. E. Simms.

The moral play of wit and science and early poetical miscellanies from an unpublished manuscript. London: Printed for the Shakespeare Society: 1-54.

The complete plays of John Bale. Bury St. Edmunds: St. Edmundsbury Press.

The Arbor of Amitie, wherein is comprised pleasant Poëms and pretie Poesies, set foorth by Thomas Howell, Gentleman. Imprinted at London by Henry Denham, dwelling in Pater Noster Rowe, at the Signe of the Starre.

A dyaloge of syr Thomas More knyghte: one of the counsayll of our souerauyne lorde the kyng and chaunceloure of hys duchy of Lancaster Wheryn be treatry dyuers maters, as of the veneracyon [and] worshyp of ymagys [and] relyques, prayng to sayntis, [and] goynge on pylgrymage....[Enprynted at London: [By J. Rastell] at the sygne of the meremayd at Powlys gate next to chepe side in the moneth of June, the yere of our lord. M. [and] C.xxix.

The play of wit and science. Tudor Facsimile Texts. London: Malone Society. Rpt. 1970 New York: AMS.

Dictionaries

EDD *The English Dialect Dictionary*, ed. Joseph Wright. 6 vols. London: Henry Frowde, 1898-1905.

OED2 *The Oxford English Dictionary*, 2nd edition in 20 volumes, ed. John A. Simpson and Edmund S. C. Weiner. Oxford: Oxford University Press, 1989 [incorporates the *Supplement* in 4 vols. ed. Robert W. Burchfield, 1972-1986]. Also as CD-ROM Version 3.1.

References

Adnitt, Henry W.
1880 "Thomas Churchyard", in: *Transactions of the Shropshire Archaeological and Natural History Society* 3: 1-68.

Barber, Charles
1997 *Early Modern English*. Edinburgh: Edinburgh University Press.

Bartley, J.O.
1954 *Teague. Shenkin and Sawney. Being an historical study of the earliest Irish, Welsh and Scottish characters in English plays*. Cork: University Press.

Blake, Norman
1981 *Non-standard language in English literature*. London: André Deutsch.

Blank, Paula
1996 *Broken English: Dialect and the politics of language in renaissance writings*. London. Routledge.

Cawley, A.C.
1958 "Mak's imitation of Southern English", in: *The Wakefield Pageants in the Towneley Cycle*, ed. A. C. Cawley. Appendix IV. Manchester: University Press, 131.

Danielsson, Bror -- Arvid Gabrielson (eds.) -- Robin C. Alston (trans.)
1972 *Alexander Gill's Logonomia Anglica*. 2 vols. Stockholm: Almqvist and Wiksell.

Eckhardt, Eduard
1910-11 *Die Dialekt- und Ausländertypen des älteren Englischen Dramas*. Materialien zur Kunde des älteren englischen Dramas, nos 27 & 32. Louvain: A Uystpruist.

García-Bermejo Giner, María F.
1999 "Methods for the linguistic analysis of Early Modern English literary dialects", in: Pilar Alonso et al. (eds.) *Teaching and research in English language and linguistics*. León: Celarayn, 249-266.

2001 "Regional dialects in Sixteenth century Jest Books", in: *SEDERI (Yearbook of the Spanish Society for English Renaissance Studies)* 12: 209-28.

García-Bermejo Giner, María F. -- Michael Montgomery
1997 "British regional English in the nineteenth century: The evidence from emigrant letters", in: *Issues and methods in*

Geimer, R. A.
1965

Görlach, Manfred
1999

Irace, Kathleen
1990

King, John N.
1982

Klemola, Juhani
2000

Lucas, Scott
2002

Lyne, Raphael
2004

Milroy, James
1983

Nevalainen, Terttu
2006

Pietsch, Lukas
2005

Ruano García, Francisco Javier
2008

2010a

2010b

Forthcoming

dialectology, ed. Alan R. Thomas. Bangor: University of Wales Bangor, 167-83.
"The life and works of Thomas Churchyard". Ph. D. dissertation, Northwestern University.

"Regional and social variation", in: *CHEL III,* 459-538.

"Mak's Sothren Tothe: A philological and critical study of the dialect joke in the Second Shepherd's Play", in: *Comitatus: A Journal of Medieval and Renaissance Studies. University of California, Los Angeles*: 38-51.

English reformation literature. Princeton: University Press.

"The origins of the Northern Subject Rule: a case of early contact?", in: *Celtic Englishes II,* ed. Hildegard Tristram. Heidelberg: Winter, 329-346.

"Diggon Davie and Davy Dicar: Edmund Spenser, Thomas Churchyard, and the Poetics of Public Protest", *Spenser Studies* 16: 151-166.

"Churchyard, Thomas (1523?-1604)", in: *Oxford Dictionary of National Biography.* Oxford: University Press. Online edn, May 2006. <http://www.oxforddnb.com/view/article/5407>, [accessed 13 Aug 2008].

"On the sociolinguistic history of /h/-dropping", in: *Current Topics in English Historical Linguistics. Proceedings of the Second International Conference on English Historical Linguistics held at Odense University 1981,* ed. M. Davenport et. al. Odense: University Press, 37-55.

An introduction to Early Modern English. Edinburgh: Edinburgh University Press.

Variable grammars: Verbal agreement in northern dialects of English. Tübingen: Niemeyer.

"North-East Yorkshire speech in the late seventeenth century: a phonological and orthographical evaluation of an anonymous printed broadside", in: *SEDERI (Yearbook of the Spanish Society for English Renaissance Studies)* 18: 97-119.
"'I'll tell o how Gilbert Scott sowd is mere Berry': 'A Lancashire tale' as a source for Lancashire speech in the late seventeenth and early eighteenth century". *Papers from methods* XIII. Barry Heselwood & Clive Upton (eds.). Bamberger Beiträge zur Englischen Sprachwissenschaft. Frankfurt am Main: Peter Lang, 53-66.
Early modern northern English lexis: A literary corpus-based study. Linguistic insights 105. Bern: Peter Lang.
"On the distribution of *barne* in Early Modern England".

Schutte, William
   1984   "Thomas Churchyard's *Dollfull Discourse* and the death of
                 Lady Katherine Grey", *The Sixteenth Century Journal* 14: 471-87.
Voitl, Herbert
   1988   "The history of voicing of initial fricatives in Southern England:
                 A case of conflict between regional and social dialect", in:
                 Historical Dialectology, ed. Jacek Fisiak. Berlin: Mouton
                 de Gruyter, 565-600.
Wakelyn, Martyn F.
   1986   *The Southwest of England*. Amsterdam: John Benjamins.
   1988a   *The archaeology of English*. London: B. T. Batsford.
   1988b   "The phonology of South-Western English 1500-1700", in:
                 Historical Dialectology, ed. Jacek Fisiak. Berlin: Mouton de
                 Gruyter, 609-44.

Scoto-Cumbrian? The representation of dialect in the works of Josiah Relph and Susanna Blamire

Julia Fernández Cuesta & Christopher Langmuir (Sevilla, Spain)

Abstract

This paper is part of a project on the history of northern English. So far we have been mainly working on the continuity between the Old and Middle English periods as regards some phonetic and morphosyntactic features, and on the resilience of these northern features in Modern English; see Fernández Cuesta & Rodríguez Ledesma (2004, 2007, 2008), Fernández Cuesta (2011 and forthcoming). The second part of this project addresses the representation of northern dialect in literary works from the 16th century onwards. The aim of this article is to compare the representation of the Cumberland dialect in the work of two lesser known poets from the first and the second half of the 18th century: Josiah Relph (1712-1743) and Susanna Blamire (1747-1794). Our purpose is twofold: on one hand, we shall analyze what dialectal features are represented in their poems and what this selection of features tells us about their attitude to dialect. On the other hand, since the influence of Scottish poets such as Allan Ramsay is clear in the case of both Relph and Blamire (some of the poems of Blamire are published in anthologies of Scottish poetry), our second aim is to establish to what extent the representation of dialect is different in the Scottish and the English traditions.[1]

1. Introduction

Dialect literature has traditionally been regarded with suspicion as a legitimate source of linguistic information. Wright (1892: 168) was dismissive of the literature available in his own dialect of Windhill, describing it as "practically worthless" for the purposes of his grammar and judging the transcription "neither accurate nor consistent". In the same way, Brillioth, author of one of the first monographs on a Cumberland dialect, affirms that '[Lorton] dialect works ... are – from a purely linguistic point of view – of small value, owing to the imperfectness of spelling and the constant mixing up of true dialect forms with those of the literary language and standard English.' (1913: 168). More recently, Shorrocks (1988: 91-92) also sounds a note of caution:

> There are many considerations which can prevent too close a connection between dialect orthographies and dialects themselves: 1. the technical limitations of dialect orthographies; 2. the limitations of the dialect authors themselves, who were writing before Alexander Ellis and Joseph Wright and who had no knowledge of modern phonological theory; 3. the influence of other dialects on the dialect writers; 4. the desire of authors to reach a wider readership (...); 6. The possible influence of publishers. Whether or not the publishers influenced dialect orthographies, or even normalised them, is a matter about which we appear to know all too little. An investigation of this question is urgently required.

---

[1] We are grateful to Manfred Görlach and Katie Wales for comments on a draft version of this article. The errors that remain are of course our own. This research has been funded by the Spanish Ministry of Education under grant (HUM2007-62926).

These caveats, particularly the third, are especially applicable to the case of Cumberland (historically a wrestling ground between England and its northern neighbour), where two related dialect traditions overlapped. One mid-19th century Cumberland writer, Craig Gibson (1889: v) dismisses his predecessors as writing in a kind of Scoto-Cumbrian hotch-potch:

> The Cumberland speech as written herein is pure Cumbrian, as the speech of the Scottish pieces, introduced for variety's sake, is pure Scotch. Miss Blamire, Stagg, Anderson, Rayson and others, have all written their dialect pieces, more or less, in the Scoto-Cumbrian, which prevails along the southern side of the West border.

Two of the writers under discussion had a close connection with Scotland. Josiah Relph studied at Glasgow University and Susanna Blamire lived in Scotland for a number of years and was in her lifetime better known for her poetry in Scots than that in her native dialect. Hugh MacDiarmid regarded her first poetry as "so good that they can be set beside the best that have ever been produced by Scotsmen writing in their own tongue." (BBC Scotland broadcast in 1947 to celebrate the bicentenary, quoted in Maycock (2003: 48))

The aim of this article is twofold. Firstly, we propose to examine the alleged hybrid nature of Cumberland poetry in order to establish to what extent the spelling conventions used for the representation of dialect are derived from the Scottish tradition. Secondly, we will identify salient northern features represented in the poems and determine how accurately they reflect what is known of the Cumberland dialect from other sources.[2]

Josiah Relph (1712-1743) is generally acknowledged to have been the first writer in the Cumberland dialect to be published.[3] After a brief stay in Glasgow, where poverty forced him to cut short his studies, Relph led a retiring life as a schoolmaster in his native village of Sebergham (seven miles south of Carlisle). His single volume of poetry (*A Miscellany of poems, consisting of original poems, translations, pastorals in the Cumberland dialect, familiar epistles, etc.*...(henceforth *A Miscellany*)) was printed in Glasgow in 1747, four years after his death, by one his pupils, Thomas Denton. Relph's dialect pastorals were to influence the work of two later 18th century Cumberland poets, Ewan Clark and Charles Graham, but not – so far at least as dialect writing is concerned – their more illustrious contemporary, William Wordsworth.

Susanna Blamire (1747-1794) was born near Dalston in the year in which Relph's poems were published. Known as the 'muse of Cumberland' and the 'poet of friendship', she was partly educated by some of Relph's Sebergham pupils. Some of her poetry was written in collaboration with her friend and fellow poet

---

[2] Eighteenth century grammars such as Kirkby (1746), Ellis's *EEP*, Wright's *EDD* and modern surveys and monographs (Hirst 1906, Brilliolth 1913, Reaney 1927, Orton 1933, and the *SED*).
[3] Cf. Stafford (2005: 358 fn. 49)

Catherine Gilpin. Like Relph, Blamire also died young. Her poetry was collected and published in Edinburgh fifty years after her death.

Only a small portion of the poetic output of Relph and Blamire is in dialect.[4] The reason is possibly connected with the still dubious respectability of dialect writing in the period, lacking as it seemed to many the dignity and formality of the standard.[5] In the period dialect was mostly used for comic purposes, to give a local setting and celebrate native wit. It also shows the interest that these writers had in dialect speakers and their culture, although irony and condescension are evident in much of their work.

In Relph there is also a strong antiquarian strain, as evidenced by his reliance for a high proportion of his dialect vocabulary on John Ray's *A Collection of English Words Not Generally Used*, 1674). The glossary appended to *A Miscellany* also contains numerous Anglo-Saxon etymologies and references to Chaucer and Spenser. In this sense, dialect, and northern dialect in particular, was considered a repository of ancestral English.

The genres chosen by Relph to illustrate the Cumberland dialect are pastoral and classical translations – a Theocritus idyll, and three translations of Horace odes, in one of which he transposes the landscapes of Italy to the becks and fells of Cumbria, in a way reminiscent of Ramsay's relocation of Soracte in the Pentlands (in *To Phiz an Ode*):

> The snow has left the fells and fled,
> Their tops i' green the trees hev' cled;
> The grund wi' sindry flowers is sown,
> And to their stint the becks are fawn;
> Nor fear the nymphs and graces mair
> To dance it in the meadows bare,
> The year, 'at slips sae fast away,
> Whispers we mun not think to stay:
> The spring suin thows the winter frost,
> To meet the spring does simmer post
> Frae simmer autumn cleeks the hauld,

---

[4] Görlach (2001: 51) states that the 18th century continued the tradition of Spenser and Meriton, since texts were written with the aim of documenting particular dialects: 'the demands of literary etiquette meant that dialect works should be pastoral, satiric and of an ephemeral kind ('fugitive' pieces); many of them were probably not meant for print, or failed to be printed because nobody was interested in them'.

[5] The sole precursor in the genre of dialect pastoral is Ramsay's *Gentle Shepherd* (1721). Cf. Unwin (1954: 150): 'Apart from the Scottish writers, who, under Allan Ramsay, then as always were pursuing an independent course, Relph was the first to use an English dialect as a poetic form since the days before the language had become unified'.

> And back at yence is winter cauld.
> Yit muins off-hand meake up their loss:
> But suin as we the watter cross,
> To Tullus great, Aeneas guid,
> We're dust and shadows wuthout bluid.
> And whae, Torquatus, can be sworn
> 'At thame abuin 'ill grant To-mworn?
> Leeve than; what's war't I'murry chear
> Frae thankless heirs is gitten clear
> When Death, my friend, yence liggs you fast,
> And Minus just your duim has past,
> Your reace, and wit and worth 'ill mak
> But a peer shift to bring you back.
> Diana (she's a Goddess tee)
> Gets not Hyppolytus set free;
> And, Theseus aw' that strength o'thine
> Can never brek Pirithous' chyne.
>
> (*Horace, book II (sic), Ode VII in the Cumberland dialect*)[6]

The case of Blamire, however, is slightly different. As regards subject matter, she uses dialect not only for comic purposes or to represent the speech of local people, but also as a means to criticize aspects of contemporary society: the condition of small landowners, as in *Wey, Ned, man!*, the situation of women in marriage (*Barley broth, The Cumberland scold, O Donald! Ye are just the man*)[7] and topics such as love, longing and the transience of life (*Auld Robin Forbes*), which were not really dealt with in dialect in the 18th century (or even later for that matter),[8] as the following extracts from two of her poems illustrate:[9]

> Thus treyfles vex, and treyfles please,
> And treyfles mek the sum o' leyfe;
> And treyfles mek a bonny lass
> A wretched or a happy weyfe! (*Barley Broth*)
>
> Of aw hours it telt *eight* was dearest to me,
> But now when it streykes there's a tear i' my ee.

---

[6] Two more of Relph's dialect translations are included in Poole & Maude (1995).
[7] In this she belongs to the same tradition as other 18th female writers such as Anne Finch, Mary Astell and Lady Mary Wortley Montagu, who were unwilling to accept the social stereotypes imposed on them, had faith in reason and education, and defended freedom of choice.
[8] See also Anne Wheeler (Westmorland).
[9] See also Anne Wheeler's *The Westmorland dialect in four familiar dialogues* (1802).

> O Willy! dear Willy! it never can be
> That age, time, or death, can divide thee and me!
> For that spot on earth that's aye dearest to me,
> Is the turf that has cover'd my Willy frae me! (*Auld Robin Forbes*)

The fact that Blamire wrote verse in both Scots and the Cumberland dialect makes her especially interesting for our purposes: to see to what extent there is an affinity (and/or a difference) between both traditions of dialect writing.

We will now proceed to examine the dialect features represented by these early writers. As a preliminary study, we will concentrate mainly on the work of Relph and Blamire. We have also analyzed the work of two other Cumberland poets, Ewan Clark's *Miscellany of Poems* (Wigton, 1779), and Charles Graham's pastoral dialogue *Gwordy and Will* (1778), together with another idiosyncratic example of 18th century Cumberland dialect literature, *The Borrowdale Letter*, attributed to Isaac Ritson (1761-1789), which appeared in James Clark's *A Guide to the Lakes* (1768).

2. Spelling and pronunciation[10]

2.1 <ang> for the reflex of Germanic */a/ when followed by /mb, nd, ng/

One of the diagnostic features used to characterise the traditional North is the reflex of Germanic */a/ when followed by /mb, nd, ng/. Relph and Blamire consistently use <ang> to represent the reflex of Gmc */a/ when followed by /ng/ in words such as AMONG, LONG, WRONG, SONG.[11] At first sight this looks as a Scotticism, but is actually a common feature in the modern Cumberland dialect, well documented in scholarly literature,[12] and is in fact the only form attested in the *SED* for AMONG and WRONG.[13]

---

[10] The poems analyzed are: Relph's *Harvest; or the bashful Shepherd: A Pastoral. In the Cumberland Dialect, Hay-time; or the Constant Lovers. A Pastoral, St Agnes Fast or the amorous Maiden. A Pastoral, Horace, book II (sic), ode VII, The 19th Idyllium of Theocritus attempted in the Cumberland Dialect* and Blamire's *The Toiling Day His Day his Task Has Duin, Wey, Ned Man!, The Cumberland Scold, Barley Broth, The Meeting, We've Hed Sec a Durdum*, and *Auld Robin Forbes*.

[11] Relph (13x) and Blamire (15x). There is only a single instance of <ong> in Relph: 'longer'.

[12] According to Brillioth (1913: 20) 'a (o) followed by nasal and nasal combinations has remained unchanged (/əlaŋ/'along', /əmaŋ/ 'among', /laŋ/ 'long', etc.), except in the case of /mb/, where lengthening has taken place in Early Middle English'. See also Wright's *EDG* (1905: 7-8) and Reaney (1927: 25).

[13] [aŋ] is the only form attested in the *SED* for AMONG (IX.2.12) and WRONG (IX. 7.1).

2.2 <ea>, <ya>, <ai>, <aCe> for the reflex of Old English /a:/

The spelling <ea> is consistently used by Relph and Blamire to represent the breaking of the reflex of northern ME /a:/ (from Old English /a:/), represented by Reaney (1927: 29) as:

[a:] > [æ:] > [æ:ə] > [ɛ:ə] > [e:ə] > [iá] (já).[14]

In *The Borrowdale Letter* (1768), <ya> predominates in MOST (*myast*), BROAD (*bryad*), ROPE (*ryaps*), etc., which would indicate more clearly than <ea> a diphthongal pronunciation. In Relph and Blamire the digraph <ai> is used only for *baith, mair, maist* and *sair*, which might be thought to mark a phonetic distinction. However, the coexistence in *Gwordy and Will* of the same word with spellings <ea> and <ai> (*baith* and *beath*) suggests that this may not be the case.[15] It is more plausible that Relph and Blamire were drawing on a Scottish tradition, which was familiar to them from the Border Ballads and earlier Scottish literature.

Nineteenth century Cumberland dialect writers continue to use <ai> in MORE (*mair*), except when Scots and Cumberland speech are contrasted, as is the case in Joseph Burroughs's *Willie Wattles's mother* (1950: 142-143). In this tale a Scots character is represented using <ai> in BOTH, MORE and MOST (*baith, mair* and *maist*), whereas the form used to represent the Cumberland speaker is <ea> e.g. *an' wad hev nea **mear** drink*. This shows that the writer associated the <ai> spelling with Scots.

The spelling <aCe> is also used sporadically in Blamire (*ane* 'one' (1x), *hale* 'whole' (1x)), and Relph (*sare* (2x) 'sore', *ane* (1x)).[16] In Blamire's *The toiling day his task has duin* the spelling *ane* co-occurs with *ilk: ilkane*, suggesting that, as in the previous case (<ai>), it could also be a Scotticism.

Another spelling used for the reflex of OE /a:/ is <ae> in words such as *frae, nae, sae*.[17] Of the 15 occurrences of *nae*, five appear in the collocation *nae mair*, which again may indicate influence from the Scottish spelling tradition.[18]

In an initial position we usually find the spelling <y>, indicating a /j/ glide. In fact, the most frequent spelling for ONE is *yen, yan, yeane* (Blamire: *yen* (8x)) and Relph (*yen, yence* (6x)). The *SED* records /jin, jɛn, jan/ for ONE (V.7.11) and ONCE (VII.2.7).

---

[14] This spelling is also used by Meriton in *A Yorkshire Dialogue* (*beath* 'both', *mead* 'made' and *nean(e)* 'none').
[15] Ewan Clark uses <aa> in such words, e.g. *maar*.
[16] Blamire: *ane* (1x), *hale* (1x) and Relph: *sare* (2x), *ane* (1x).
[17] *frae*: Blamire (9x), Relph (5x); *nae*: Blamire (7x), Relph (8x); *sae*: Blamire (11x), Relph (14x).
[18] Meriton also has the spelling <ea> for GO *geay* and NO *neay*.

2.3 <ea> for the reflex of ME /a:/

The spelling <ea> is also used to represent the reflex of ME /a:/ in words such as FACE (*feace*), NAKED (*neaked*), NAME (*neame*), SAME (*seame*), TASTE (*teaste*), etc. The dialectal spelling co-occurs with the standard form, but the latter is far less frequent.[19] This spelling is widespread in Cumberland writers up to the present day. According to Wakelin (1988: 137), this digraph, which is first found in *A Yorkshire Dialogue*[20], may represent /æə/ /ɛə/, described as an 'intermediate sound between ME /a:/ and ModE /iə/'.[21] In 20th century monographs on Cumberland and other northern English dialects the diphthong is described as '/iá/' (Brillioth 1913: 25, Reaney 1927: 30 and Orton 1933: 50). The *SED* records: /ea, ɪa, ɪə/.[22]

2.4 <ey> for the reflex of ME /i:/

Here Blamire and Relph diverge. In words such as FINE, LIKE and TIME, Relph retains standard spelling, whereas Blamire consistently uses <ey> (47x as against 5x).[23] The development of ME /i:/ into /ɛi/ in the north would account for these spellings (cf. Lass 1999: 76). Twentieth-century monographs on northern English record this northern diphthong as well as standard /ai/ (Reaney 1927: 51).

We find no <ey> spellings in FIND and KIND.[24] The short /ʊ/, which the SED (IX.3.2) records as universal in Cumberland and throughout the North, is evidence that lengthening failed to occur in northern English (Reaney 1927: 36).[25]

2.5 <ee> for *breet, neet, leet* and *reet*

The forms *breet, neet, leet* and *reet*, consistently found in Blamire, represent the long vowel /i:/, which is the result of the loss of /x/ and compensatory lengthening (BRIGHT, NIGHT, LIGHT, RIGHT).[26] Relph, however, uses only the standard spelling in these words. This long monophthong is widely recorded in the *SED*: NIGHT (VII.3.9, VII.3.11, and VII), SIGHT: (VIII.3.9) and RIGHT-HANDED (VI.7.13), and can be still heard today throughout the North.[27]

---

[19] Blamire has 14x <ea> as against 8x <aCe>. In Relph we find 18x <ea> as against 1x <aCe>.
[20] e.g. *beath* 'both', *mead* 'made' *nean(e)* 'none'.
[21] For the northern development of the vowel see Reaney (1927: 29) and Anderson (1987: 56).
[22] GAPES (VI.3.7) and TASTED (V.4.20).
[23] The data are: *beyble* (1x), *feyne* (2x), *leyfe* (3x), *leyke* (12x), *meynded, neyce* (2x), *preyce* (1x), *reyce* (4x), *treyfles* (4x), *weyfe* (3x), *wreyte* (2x). This spelling is also found in Clark.
[24] *Meynd* appears once in Blamire.
[25] In 18th century Yorkshire poetry we find spellings with <nn> to indicate a short vowel. See *finnd* and *blinnd* in Carey's *An Honest Yorkshireman* in Moorman (1916).
[26] The data are: *breet* (1x), *neet* (1x), *leet* (1x) and *reet* (4x). There is only one instance of *night* in Blamire.
[27] The diphthongal pronunciation is recorded for RIGHT-HANDED.

2.6 <ui> for the reflex of ME /o:/

Relph, Blamire, and Clark consistently use <ui> to represent the reflex of the northern fronting of ME /o:/.[28] In the case of Relph, Wales (2006: 111) interprets this digraph as /ø:/. Graham employs <ue> in addition to <ui> and in *The Borrowdale Letter* the spelling is <yu>. It is generally accepted that /y:/ diphthongised in northern English sometime in the early Modern English period (Reaney 1927: 53; Jordan 1974: 86; Lass 1999: 76).[29] Reaney (1927: 54) remarks on the lack of correlation between the dialect spellings and the pronunciation: 'There was evidently some difficulty to represent the diphthong and we have both <ui>, <eu> and <yu>'. The adoption of the familiar Scots convention <ui>[30] might be motivated less by a desire for accuracy of representation than by alignment with an underlying common tradition. The *SED* records both the northern and standard influenced pronunciation /ʉ/, /ʊ/: LOOK (III.13.18, VIII.1.23); TOOK (IX.3.7.); TOOTH (VI.5.6).

2.7 <wo> for the reflex of ME /ɔ:/

The spelling <wo> in words such as CLOSE (*clwose*), COAT (*cwoat*), MORNING (*mworn*), NOTICE (*nwotisihn*) and ROAR (*rwoar*) is frequent in Relph and Blamire and also in later Cumberland writers.[31] This spelling represents the Cumberland development to /wǫ/ of ME /ɔ:/ or /o/+/rC/ (Brillioth 1913: 35, Reaney 1927: 39 and Orton 1933: 73, 228-29).[32] The *SED* records this pronunciation only sporadically.[33] Wright (1979: 33) comments on the continued representation of this salient feature by modern Lakeland writers in spite of its having all but disappeared: 'Here again, and rather like the old literary convention of Victorian Cockney before George Bernard Shaw and others came to the scene, the old dialect seems to have changed faster than writers seem to admit.' Similarly, Beal (2000: 348-9) refers to the retention of the form *toon* 'town' as a dialect marker serving to reinforce regional identity in Tyneside English.

---

[28] The data are: Blamire (21x), Relph (37x), Graham (6x), Clark (31x). In Graham we also find <ue> (5x).

[29] The change of ME /o:/ in the northern dialects has been traditionally described as a fronting of the vowel to /ø:/ and then a later raising to /y:/. These processes, confined to the three northernmost counties, are assumed to have taken place in the late 13th or early 14th century on the basis of spellings with <u> and rhymes with French words containing /y:/ (Jordan 1974: 86; Lass 1999: 76).

[30] <ui> is originally found in the works of 16th century Scottish writers such as Gavin Douglas to represent the fronted vowel /y:/.

[31] Among the forms found are: *cwoat, clwose, cworn, fwok, Gworge, Jwohn, lword, mworning, mwort, nwotishin, rwoar, spworts*.

[32] According to Reaney (1927: 39) the lengthening of OE /o/ (ME /ɔ:/) has regularly become /wo/ in the Lorton dialect: *kworn* 'corn', *mwornin* 'morning'.

[33] COAL (IV.4.5), CORN: [kwǫən] (I.7.4), but not for FOAL (III.4.1) and MORNING (VII.3.11).

2.8 <ou, ow> for the reflex of ME /u:/

Although the northern reflex of ME /u:/ remains a long monophthong in words such as COW, DOWN, FOUND, HOUSE, NOW, OUT, etc., Relph and Blamire do not depart from the standard forms <ou, ow>.[34] The spelling <oo> is the predominant form in *The Borrowdale Letter*. It would be rash to assume, however, that standard spellings always imply standard pronunciation. In *The Collier's Wedding* by Relph's Newcastle contemporary, Edward Chicken (*bap.* 1698, *d.* 1745/6), the rhyme requires a monophthongal pronunciation of <ow>:

> She ply'd all the after<u>noon</u>
> And kept her warm to melt her <u>down</u>
>
> You hug, you kiss, and squeeze me <u>now</u>
> But what will Wedding make you <u>do?</u>

2.9 <u> in words such as COME, BROTHER and ANOTHER

ME /u/ was not lowered and centralised in the north. Since the standard spelling accurately represents the northern sound /ʊ/, it is kept as such, except in cases where the spelling is <o> as in *come, brother, another*. In these words the spelling <u> is frequently found to signal avoidance of /ʌ/: *anudder, brudder, cum, mudder*.

2.10 <k> spelling in EACH and MUCH and SUCH

EACH, MUCH and SUCH appear as *ilk, mickle* and *sec(k)*.[35] We also find examples of standard forms. The <k> forms are recorded in the Cumberland monographs and in the *EDD*. Brillioth's glossary gives /mikl/ and /sek/ (187, 191) and Reaney records /mutʃ, mitʃ, mukl/ and /sɛk/ (129). The *EDD* records /sik, sek, sitʃ/ and /mutʃ, mukl/ in North Cu. It is striking that the *SED* (VIII.9.7) records the form /sek/, /sɛk/ in five of its six Cumberland localities (/sɪk/ is recorded only in the northernmost locality).

The implied long vowel in Relph's spelling *seek* is attested in the *OED* as a variant of *sic*. Orton (1933: 138) speculates that [saɪk] may have arisen under the influence of *slike* (from ON *slīkr*). *A Yorkshire Dialogue* also has the form *sike*, a northern form widely attested in the *EDD*.

---

[34] The *SED* confirms that the long monophthong must have been widespread in this area: HOUSE (V.1.1), MOUSE (IV.5.1), etc. *LAE* map Ph 149 shows the long monophthong throughout Cumberland.

[35] *ilkane, sec* (Blamire); *mickle, seek* (Relph); *mickle, sec, sic* (Graham); *mickle, seck* (Clark).

2.11 <s> spelling for SHALL and SHOULD

The spelling <s> for SHALL and SHOULD appears in Relph, Blamire and Clark.[36] There are also sporadic instances of the contracted form *I's* (*I sall*):

> I dreamt – the pleasant dream I's ne'er forgit ...
>
> (Relph, *St Agnes Fast*)

> And I'se set down just how I find myself
> When I'se with Nell, my heart keeps such a rout,
> It lowps --- and lowps, as if it wad lowp out
>
> (Clark, *Costard's Complaint*)

The *EDG* states that *sal* is reduced to 's' in combination with personal pronouns, citing an example from Cumbria: *We's be wet a top a Nan* (Bield' Briggs *Remains* 1825). This reduced form is also found in Middle Scots: *Iis, ʒeis* (Aitken 1971: 196).

2.12 <dd> in FATHER, MOTHER, GATHER

This spelling reflects the northern form with the dental plosive in words such as FATHER, MOTHER, GATHER. There is variation between <d> and <th> in 15th century legal texts from Yorkshire (Fernández Cuesta & Rodríguez Ledesma 2004: 294). Their analysis revealed considerable variation in the percentage of each spelling, which is still predominantly conditioned by the original Old English consonants: <d> is dominant for words which had etymological /d/ in Old English.[37] In the *SED* we find the northern variant recorded not only in words that had an original plosive in Old English, but in those which had a fricative ('brother','either').[38]

3. Morpho-syntax
3.1 Plural demonstratives

We find the form *thur* for THESE and possibly THOSE in Relph (4x) and Clark (7x).

---

[36] Relph: *sal* (1x), *sud* (4x); Blamire: *sud* (1x); Clark: *sud* (1x).
[37] However, for the spelling variation, which may or may not be indicative of phonological change, see Lass & Laing (2009: 99) and Fernández Cuesta & Rodríguez Ledesma (2004: 294).
[38] For the development of /d/ > /ð/ ('with an intermediate sound') see Reaney (1927: 120).

Farewell my flute then yet or Carlile fair;
When to the stationers I'll stright repair,
And bauldly for **thur** compliments enquear;
Care I a fardin, let the prentice jeer.

(Relph, *Harvest* II. 86-89)

Wright (1905: 77) includes *thir* as a a proximal and distal demonstrative in Scots and Yorkshire, North Country and Lancashire. Hirst (1906: 131) also gives [ðɔr] as the plural of THAT. According to the *EDD*, this is an exclusively northern form. Brillioth (1913: 108) gives the form *ður* and *ðurənz* as obsolescent in Lorton: 'Still often heard from the older generation of true dialect-speakers'. Reaney reports the survival of the form in *ðə* as practically extinct.[39] No traces of these *r*-forms are recorded in the *SED* for Cumberland, which records only *them* as the plural of THIS and *those* as the plural of THAT, forms also recorded in contemporary corpora (*NECTE* and *Corpus of Sheffield Usage*).

3.2 Personal pronouns

The second person pronoun singular *thou, thee, tou, ta, te* is widely attested in the work of these Cumberland writers. Blamire uses the dialect forms with <t> (*tou, te*), whereas these forms are not recorded in Relph.[40] *Thou* forms predominate for the singular in all texts. Forms with <t> are not exclusively used in unstressed position; the forms *tou* and *ta* are also used as a subject by Blamire and Graham respectively. The *EDD* records a stressed form *tā* and a weak form *ta*.

Brillioth (1913: 104-5) and Reaney (1927: 145-47) attribute these forms to assimilation of the fricative with the verbal inflexion in interrogatives. Forms with the plosive in interrogative structures are recorded by the *SED* when the pronoun is cliticised to the verb (VI.5.8, VIII.2.8, VIII.3.7, IX.7.2/3, IX.7.5/6).

As regards the third person plural pronoun, in Blamire we find both *tem* (4x) and *them* (2x) for the object. There is a single attestation in the *EDD* from the 19th century. The *SED* records forms with the fricative only.

---

[39] For discussion on the origin of *thir* see Brillioth (1913: 108) and the *OED* under *thir*.
[40] The data are: Blamire: *thou*: (2x), *thee* (8x), *tou* (26x), *te* (2x); Relph: *thou* (4x), *thee* (7x). There are no examples of *t*-forms in Relph; Graham: *thou* (14x), *thee* (2x), *the'* (4x), *tu* (only as subject) (3x), *ta* (4x) (corresponding to either subject or object):

Thou dud I know it was but I tother wee
what said t'tull her? Did **ta** never speak (*Gwordy and Will*, p. 68)
What mead **ta** luik sea skar, and seem sea bleate; (*Gwordy and Will*, p. 69)

3.3 Verbal inflexions

3.3.1 Present indicative

There is only one example of the -*s* inflexion with a lexical verb in the first person singular present indicative: 'says I' (Relph)[41], but I's is found for the 1sg. indicative of BE (I's = I am).[42] For the second person singular we find the -*s* inflexion throughout. This form is characteristic of north-west dialects (Reaney 1927: 164). The *SED* records -*s* for the second person present indicative as the general form in Cumberland (IX. 7.3). For the third person plural present indicative we find two examples of verbal -*s* in conjoined NPs. It would be tempting to regard these as examples of the resilience of the Northern Subject Rule in this variety. However, since the nouns are in the singular in both cases, they could be considered as cases of attraction:

> Thy Jean and the**'s** parted (Blamire, *The toiling day his task has duin*).
>
> And now the sang an' tale **gaes** roun / An' the pint smiles wi' heartsome ale.
>
> (Blamire, *The toiling day his task has duin*)

3.3.2 Present participle

Participial endings in <en> (e.g. 'But when I saw him *scrawlen* on the plain...' in Relph's *Hay-Time*), could conceivably be a remnant of the old northern inflexion for the present participle -*and*. All the texts analyzed have -*ing* and -*en* forms, which might indicate that the writers were aware that -*en* was the specific northern variant and a vestige of northern -*and*. Wright (1905: 81) states that in the dialects of England, the present participle ends in [in] except in parts of north Northumberland and north Cumberland, where the ending is [ən]. In the dialects of south Scotland, the present participle ends in [ən], from Northern ME -*and*, and the verbal noun ends in [ɪn], from ME -*ing*. In the *SED* (IX.2.14) only /-ən/ is recorded for Cumberland, but in Lancashire and Yorkshire both forms (/-ən/ and /-in/) are found, although /-ɪn/ predominates. These forms could be respectively reflexes of northern -*and* and standard -*ing*, but since the weakening of both would yield the same result, the findings are inconclusive.[43]

---

[41] "The first person singular is now frequently the same as the infinitive except when the pronoun follows the verb." (Reaney 1927: 164).

[42] Graham uses *I'se* with what could be a sort of scribal 'e' to indicate that the consonant is voiced.

[43] Murray (1873: 211, quoted in Beal 1997: 356) states that 'it is as absurd to a southern Scot to hear *eating* used for both his *eating* and *eatand*, as it is to an Englishman to hear *will* used for both his *will* and *shall*. When he is told that 'John was eating', he is strongly tempted to ask what kind of *eating* he proved to be?'

4. Editorial license

Neither Relph nor Blamire lived to oversee publication of their work (Blamire in any case jealously guarded her anonymity when alive), which has been subject to occasionally heavy-handed editorial interference.[44]

Nineteenth-century editors of Relph and Clark, in particular, or at least those prior to the burgeoning of philological interest in dialectal writing (Skeat and Wright), took liberties at the levels of spelling, morphology and lexis. The most egregious of these editors was Sidney Gilpin, pseudonym of a Carlisle bookseller, George Coward, the author of *The Songs and Ballads of Cumberland* (1867). The following illustrates some of the Gilpin's alterations:

Table 1: Use of punctuation devices – apostrophe and hyphenation

Relph (1747) [JR] Ewan Clark (1779) [EC]	Gilpin (1866)	
way	'way (=away)	JR
lwonin	lwonin' = lane	JR
lavrock	lav'rock	EC
off hand	off-hand	EC
pit, pat	pit-pat	EC
ailsta	ails-ta	EC
harmin't	harm in't	JR
bustling	bustlin'	JR

These examples show the addition of the apostrophe, helpful in some instances (e.g. the aphetic form of 'away'), less so in others such as *lwonin'* and *lav'rock*, which are readily intelligible in their original forms. The use of the hyphen and word separation (*ailsta, harm in't*) is another instance of light editorial intervention for the purposes of clarification.

The alterations illustrated in the following tables (2, 3, 4) curtail the dialectal texture of the writing by standardising the spelling:

Table 2: Substitution of non-standard spellings

keam	comb	JR
cuil	cool	JR
duim	doom	JR
muins	moons	JR
chyne	chain	JR
santer	saunter	JR
dum	dumb	EC
breest	breast	EC

---

[44] One literary curiosity is *A Choice Collection of Poems in Cumberland Dialect* published in Sunderland in 1780(?) and purporting to have been written by a Cumberland clergyman, Robert Nelson, "about one hundred years since" (p. 2). They are in fact Relph's three pastorals lightly paraphrased in parts and with the spelling extensively altered.

| strwoak'd | strok'd | EC |
| furst | first | EC |

Table 3: Substitution of non-standard morphology

Is I ...?	Am I ...?	JR
cruep	crept	EC
the ... dream **I's** ne'er forgit	the ... dream **I'll** ne'er forgit	JR

Table 4: Substitution of dialect lexis

scrawlen ('crawl, creep', *EDD*)	sprawling	JR
clout ('patch' *EDD*)	scratch	EC
arr [a. ON. *örr, ör*; cf. Da. *ar.*]	scar	EC
the bluimen pezz green **ment** with reed and blue	the blooming pezz green **mix'd** with reed and blue	JR

Arr and *scar* happen to be two etymologically unrelated words of identical meaning, but whereas *arr* has a specifically northern provenance *scar* does not. The rare past participle *ment* ('obs. N.Cy Cum. Mixed, mingled' according to the *EDD*, Relph being the principal citation) gives way to semi-standard *mix'd*. In some instances, for example in Relph's *Harvest, or the bashful Shepherd*, the editor arbitrarily replaces an obscure dialectal word, *eith* ('easy', according to the glossary of the 1747 edition), with *eye* – phonetically similar – but entirely unrelated.

The principal motivation for Gilpin's alterations seems to have been to make the text more intelligible by reducing the density of dialect representation, presumably to appeal to a wider, non-local readership and obviate the need for a glossary. This is a perennial problem in the publication of dialect writing.[45]

5. Conclusions

Differentiating varieties that are closely related geographically and linguistically is often fraught with problems. Scots itself was a development of northern Middle English (Aitken 1971: 181) and some of the first attestations of what later were to be seen as Scottish spellings actually derive from the north of England (Kniesza 1997: 33).[46]

Though rooted in Ramsay's poetic use of the Scots vernacular, 18th century Cumberland dialect writing can best be seen as a semi-independent offshoot, in which certain spelling practices were imported (from Meriton's *Yorkshire Dialogue*, for instance) and others were innovative.

(1) The following spellings are most probably derived from Scots:

---

[45] See Wales (2006: 131-132).
[46] Contemporary York and Durham texts also provide many examples of <i> as a diacritic to indicate vowel length, some of them earlier than the Scots types (Vikar 1922; in Kniesza 1997: 33).

<ae> in words such as *frae, gae, nae* and *sae*.
<ui> in words such as *buik, fuil, guid, luik, schuil, tuik, tuith*, etc.
<ai> in *mair, maist*
<aCe> in *ane, hale*
(2) Those common to Northern English dialect literature and Scots are:
<ang>in *wrang, amang*, etc.
<k> in *se(e)k* 'such' and *mickle* 'much'. The *SED* records the form /sek/ /sɛk, which is precisely the one found in Cumberland.
<s> in *sall* 'shall' and *sud* 'should'.
(3) The following spellings are characteristic of northern English dialect literature in general:
<ea> in *heam(e), gean(e), lean, whea, nea*, etc.[47]
<ee> in *breet, neet, leet* and *reet*.
<u> in *cum, brudder, anudder*
(4) The following are typical of Cumberland:
<ey> *feyne, leyfe, leyke* etc.[48]
<wo> in *clwose, cwoat, mworn* etc.[49]

Our analysis broadly supports Wales' contention (2006: 111) that Cumberland dialect poetry represents a hybrid tradition: although some spelling conventions are partly derived from the Scottish tradition, there are nevertheless some features that are innovative and may have been adopted to characterise the Cumberland dialect as a distinct variety.

With regard to differences in the spelling practice between Relph and Blamire, Blamire by and large conforms to Relph's practices, although she also introduced her own spellings: <ey> to represent the diphthong in *teyme, leyke, leyfe*. She also uses *tou, tee* for the second singular person pronoun and *neet, reet* ('night', 'right') instead of the standard forms found in Relph.

We have also shown that further research is called for into how 18th century dialect texts were edited in the following century. As an example of editorial practice, we have drawn attention to a number of alterations made by one not particularly conscientious editor.

Sources

Cawley, A. C. (ed.)
    1959   *George Meriton's A Yorkshire Dialogue 1683*. York: Yorkshire Dialect Society Reprint II.

---

[47] First found in Meriton: *beath* 'both', *mead* 'made' *nean(e)* 'none'.
[48] See *EDD: leyke* (Cum. N.Yks. NEYks.), *meynd* (Cum.), *neyce* (Cum.).
[49] See *EDD*: *cwoat* (Cum. And NYks), *mworn* (Cum.), *rwoar* (Cum and Wm.).

Clark, Ewan
    1779   *Miscellaneous Poems*, by Mr. Ewan Clark. Whitehaven: Ware & son.

Denton, Thomas (ed.)
    1747   *A Miscellany of Poems, consisting of original Poems, etc. by The Late Reverend Josiah Relph of Sebergham, Cumberland. With a Preface and a Glossary.* Glasgow: Robert Foulis for Mr. Thomlinson in Wigton.

Denwood, M. -- T. W. Thompson
    1950   *A Lafter o' Farleys in t' Dialects o' Lakeland (1760-1945).* Carlisle: Charles Thurnam & Sons.

Gilpin, Sidney (ed.)
    1867   *The Songs and Ballads of Cumberland, to which are added Dialect and Other Poems; with Biographical Sketches, Notes and a Glossary.* London: Routledge / Edinburgh: John Menzies / Carlisle: Geo. Coward.

Graham, Charles
    1778   *Miscellaneous Pieces in Prose and Verse by Charles Graham of Penrith in Cumberland.* Kendal: Pennington.

Lonsdale, Henry (ed.)
    1842   *The poetical works of Miss Susanna Blamire "The muse of Cumberland." Now for the first time collected by Henry Lonsdale, M.D. with a preface, memoir, and notes by Patrick Maxwell.* Edinburgh: John Menzies. Electronic edition: <http://libdev2.ucdavis.edu/English/BWRP/Works/BlamSPoeti.sgm>

Nelson, Robert (ed.)
    1780   *A Choice Collection of Poems in Cumberland Dialect. I. The Harvest or Bashful Shepherd, A Pastoral by the Rev. Mr. Robert Nelson, late of Greatfalkeld near Penrith in Cumberland. II. Hay-Time or the Constant Lovers. A Pastoral. III St Agnes Fast or the Amorous Maiden. A Pastoral. And other Subjects no less entertaining.* Sunderland: R. Wetherald.

Poole, Adrian -- Jeremy Maude
    1995   *The Oxford Book of Classical Verse in Translation.* Cambridge: Cambridge University Press.

Relph, Josiah
    1747   *A miscellany of poems, consisting of original poems, translations, pastorals in the Cumberland dialect, familiar epistles, ... By the late Reverend Josiah Relph ...* Glasgow.
    1797   *Poems by the Reverend Josiah Relph, of Sebergham. With the life of the author, and a pastoral elegy on his death. By Thomas Sanderson.* Carlisle.
    1798   *Poems by the Rev. Josiah Relph, of Sebergham. With the life of the author. Embellished with picturesque engravings on wood, by Mr. T. Bewick, of Newcastle.* Carlisle.
    1799   *Poems by the Rev. Josiah Relph, of Sebergham. With the life of the author. Third edition, with improvements. Embellished with picturesque engravings on wood, by Mr. T. Bewick, ...* Newcastle on Tyne.
    1805   *Poems, Humorous and Sentimental. Consisting of Cumberland Pastorals: Translations and Imitations from the Classics, Epistles, Fables, Songs, and Epigrams. By the Rev. Josiah Relph. With Memoirs of the Author.* Third ed. London: Vernor and Hood, & Champante, & Whiteow.

Smith, John Russell
1839 (1747) *Dialogues, Poems, Songs and Ballads by various writers in the Westmoreland and Cumberland Dialects, now first collected with a copious Glossary of words peculiar to those counties.* London: John Russell Smith.

The Caledonian Miscellany
1762 *Consisting of Select and much approv'd Pastorals, Choice Fables and Tales, with other occasional poems, By A. Ramsey and other eminent northern bards. Newcastle upon Tyne.* Printed for Thomas Slack (including *Harvest of the Bashful Shepherd. A Pastoral. In the Cumberland Dialect. By J. Ralph*).

Wheeler, Ann
1902 *The Westmorland dialect in four familiar dialogues.* London: W. J. Richardson and J. Richardson by M. Branthwaite.

Dictionaries

DOST   *A dictionary of the older Scottish tongue*, ed. Sir William Craigie et al., 12 vols., London: Oxford University Press, 1937-2002.

EDD   *The English dialect dictionary*, ed. Joseph Wright. 6 vols. London: Henry Frowde, 1898-1905.

References

Aitken, A. J.
1971 "Variation and variety in written Middle Scots", in *Edinburgh Studies in English and Scots*, eds. A. J. Aitken, Angus McIntosh & Hermann Pálsson. London: Longman, 177-210.

Anderson, S. et al.
1987 *Structural atlas of English dialects.* London: Croom Helm.

Beal, Joan
1997 "Syntax and morphology", in: *The Edinburgh History of the Scots language*, ed. Charles Jones. Edinburgh: Edinburgh University Press, 335-377.

2000 "From Geordie to Vizz: Popular literature in Tyneside English", *Language and Literature* 9: 343-349.

2004a "English dialects in the North of England: Phonology", in: Kortmann et al. 113-143.

2004b "English dialects in the North of England: Morphology and syntax", in: Kortmann et al. 114-141.

Benskin, Michael
1989 "Some aspects of Cumbrian English, mainly mediaeval", in: *Essays on English Language in Honour of Bertil Sundby*, eds. Leiv Egil Breivik, Arnoldus Hille & Stig Johanneson. Oslo: Novus, 13-45.

Bergström, Folke
1955 "John Kirkby (1746) on English pronunciation", *Studia Neophilologica* 27: 65-104.

Brillioth, Börje
1913 *A grammar of the dialect of Lorton (Cumberland).* London: Oxford University Press.

Denwood, M. -- T. W. Thompson
  1950   *A Lafter o' Farleys in t' Dialects o' Lakeland (1760-1945).* Carlisle: Charles Thurnam & Sons.
Dobson, E. J.
  1968   *English pronunciation 1500-1700.* 2 vols. 2nd ed. Oxford: Oxford University Press.
Fernández Cuesta, Julia -- Maria Nieves Rodríguez Ledesma
  2004   "Northern features in 15th-16th-Century legal documents from Yorkshire", in: *Methods and data in English historical dialectology*, eds. Marina Dossena & Roger Lass. Bern: Peter Lang, 287-308.
  2007   "From Old Northumbrian to Northern ME: Bridging the divide", in: *Studies in Middle English Forms and Meanings*, ed. Gabriella Mazzon. Frankfurt am Main: Peter Lang, 117-132.
  2008   "Northern Middle English: towards telling the full story", in: *English Historical Linguistics 2006. Volume III: Geo-historical Variation in English*, eds. Marina Dossena, Richard Dury & Maurizio Gotti. Amsterdam: John Benjamins, 91-109.
  2009   "The Northern echo: Continuities in contemporary Northern English", in *Studies in English and European historical dialectology*, eds. Marina Dossena & Roger Lass. Bern: Peter Lang. 157-191.
Fernández Cuesta, Julia
  2011   "The Northern subject rule in first-person-singular contexts in early Modern English", *Folia Linguistica Historica* 32: 89-114.
  Forthcoming   "The voice of the dead: Analyzing sociolinguistic variation in early Modern English wills and testaments".
García-Bermejo Giner, Maria Fuencisla
  1998   "The Northern/Scottish dialect in Nataniel Woodes' *A Conflict of Conscience*", *Sederi* 9: 9-21.
Gibson, Alexander
  1869   *The folk speech of Cumberland.* London: John Russell Smith; Carlisle: Geo. Coward.
Görlach, Manfred
  2001   *Eighteenth-century English.* Heidelberg: Winter.
  2002   *A Textual history of Scots.* Heidelberg: Winter.
Hirst, T. O.
  1906   *A grammar of the dialect of Kendal.* Heidelberg: Winter.
Jordan, Richard
  1974   *Handbook of Middle English grammar: Phonology.* Translated by Eugene J. Crook. The Hague: Mouton.
Kniesza, Veronika
  1997   "The origins of Scots orthography", in: *The Edinburgh history of the Scots language,* ed. Charles Jones. Edinburgh: Edinburgh University Press, 24-47.
Kolb, Eduard
  1966   *Phonological atlas of the Northern region: The six Northern Counties, North Lincolnshire and the Isle of Man.* Bern: Franke.
Kortmann, Bernd et al. (eds.)
  2004   *A handbook of varieties of English.* Berlin: Mouton.

LALME	*A linguistic atlas of Late Mediaeval English*, ed. Angus McIntosh, M. K. Samuels & M. Benskin. Aberdeen: Aberdeen University Press. 1986.
Lass, Roger	
1992	"Phonology and morphology", in: *CEHL II*, 23-155.
1999	"Phonology and morphology", in *CEHL III*, 56-186.
Lass, Roger -- Margaret Laing	
2009	"Databases, dictionaries and dialectology: Dental instability in Early Middle English. A case study", in: *Studies in English and European Historical Dialectology*, eds. Marina Dossena & Roger Lass. Bern: Peter Lang, 91-135.
Macafee, Caroline	
2001	*A history of Scots to 1700: Introduction to the history of the older Scottish tongue*. Oxford: Oxford University Press, xxix-clvii.
Maycock, C. H.	
2003	*A passionate poet: Susanna Blamire, 1747-94: A biography*. Penzance: Hypatia.
Moorman, F. W.	
1916	*Yorkshire dialogue poems: 1673-1915*. London: Sidwick & Jackson.
Murray, James A. H.	
1873	*The dialect of the Southern counties of Scotland: Its pronunciation, grammar, and historical relations*. London: The Philological Society.
Nicholson, Norman	
1977	*The Lake District: An anthology*. Harmondsworth: Penguin.
Orton, Harold	
1933	*The phonology of a South Durham Dialect*. London: Kegan Paul.
Reaney, Percy H.	
1927	*A grammar of the Penrith (Cumberland)*. Manchester: Manchester University Press.
Stafford, Fionna	
2005	"Scottish poetry and regional literary expression", in: *Cambridge history of the English literature 1660-1780*, ed. John Richetti. Cambridge: Cambridge University Press, 340-363.
SED 1 = Harold Orton & W.J. Halliday (eds.)	
1962	*Survey of English dialects: The basic material*. Vol.1, Parts 1, 2 & 3. Leeds: E. J. Arnold & Son Ltd.
SED 2 = Harold Orton	
1962	*Survey of English dialects: An introduction*. Leeds: E. J. Arnold & Son Ltd.
SED 3 = Clive Upton et al.	
1994	*Survey of English dialects: The dictionary and grammar*. London: Routledge.
Shorrocks, Graham	
1988	"A phonemic and phonetic key to the orthography of the Lancashire dialect Author James Taylor Staton (1817-1875)", in: *Lore and Language*, 91-108.
1999a	"Working class literature in working class language: The North of England", in: A. J. Hoenselaars & Marius Buning (eds.) *English literature and other languages* DQR Studies in Literature 24. Amsterdam: Rodopi.
1999b	*A grammar of the dialect of the Bolton area*. Frankfurt: Peter Lang.

Smith, Jeremy
1994 "The Great Vowel Shift in the North of England, and some forms in Chaucer's *Reeve's Tale*", in: *Neuphilologische Mitteilungen* 95: 433-437.

Tidholm, Hans
1979 *The dialect of the parish of Egton in North Yorkshire.* Goteburg: Bokmaskinen.

Unwin, Rayner
1954 *The rural muse.* London: Allen & Unwin.

Wakelin, Martyn
1988 *The archaeology of English.* London: Batsford.

Wales, Katie
2006 *Northern English: A cultural and social history.* Cambridge: Cambridge University Press.

Wright, Joseph
1905 *The English dialect grammar.* Oxford: Oxford University Press.
1892 *A grammar of the dialect of Windhill in the West Riding of Yorkshire.* London: Kegan Paul.

Wright, Peter
1979 *Cumbrian dialect.* Clapham, North Yorkshire: Dalesman.

Wyld, Henry Cecil
1920 *A history of modern colloquial English.* London: Fisher Unwin.

(# Part V. Scholars, authors and their use of the past)

J.R.R. Tolkien and the historical study of English

John Insley (Heidelberg, Germany)

Abstract

Although Tolkien is best known for his works of fiction, most notably *The Hobbit* and *The Lord of the Rings*, he was a philologist of no mean distinction. Starting with the review articles he wrote for *The Year's Work in English Studies* in the nineteen-twenties, the present paper examines Tolkien's philological works. Some attention is given to his interest in the early Middle English texts of the *Ancrene Wisse*/Katherine Group and his famous articles on dialect in Chaucer's *Reeve's Tale* (1934) and on *Beowulf* (1936) are examined in some detail. The paper is concluded by a demonstration of the ways in which linguistic material, especially Old English lexical and onomastic material, is an essential element in Tolkien's fiction, in particular in *The Lord of the Rings*.

The basic facts of J.R.R. Tolkien's (1892-1973) intellectual biography are well known – Oxford undergraduate before the First World War, research assistant on the *Oxford English Dictionary* and professor in Leeds and Oxford – and need no repetition here. They are sketched with admirable clarity in Humphrey Carpenter's biography (1977). Much has been written about Tolkien and much of it is one-dimensional and beside the point. The best commentators like Tom Shippey have made it clear that Tolkien's philological training was fundamental for his fictional work – in other words, only a philologist could have written much that was in *The Hobbit* and *The Lord of the Rings*. In the present short paper, I intend to indicate some of the directions of Tolkien's intellectual development, but it is perhaps best to begin with his own words taken from his valedictory address of 1959:

"I cannot help recalling some of the salient moments in my academic past. The vastness of Joe Wright's dining room table (when I sat alone at one end learning the elements of Greek philology from glinting glasses in the further gloom). The kindness of William Craigie to a jobless soldier in 1918. The privilege of knowing even the sunset of the days of Henry Bradley. My first glimpse of the unique and dominant figure of Charles Talbut Onions, darkly surveying me, a fledgling prentice in the Dictionary Room (fiddling with the slips for WAG and WALRUS and WAMPUM). Serving under the generous captaincy of George Gordon in Leeds. Seeing Henry Cecil Wyld wreck a table in the Cadena Café with the vigour of his representation of Finnish minstrels chanting the Kalevala" (Tolkien 1983: 238).

Here we have some of the scholars who formed Tolkien. There is the Icelandic scholar Craigie and there are the great lexicographers Bradley and Onions. There is also George Gordon with whom Tolkien produced a famous edition of *Sir Gawain and the Green Knight* in 1925. Tolkien's glossary to this edition is an early example of that exacting lexicological and etymological work which was to be an abiding characteristic of his scholarship. Particularly noteworthy is Tolkien's link to Joseph Wright, who was not only famous for his dialect dictionary and grammar, but also for a series of grammars of Old and

Middle English, Early Modern English, Gothic and Middle High German which were noted for the faithful rigidity with which they adhered to the Neogrammarian principles evolved in Leipzig by Brugmann, Leskien, Osthoff and Paul a generation earlier. By the early twenties, Tolkien had begun to express careful scepticism about Neogrammarian tenets and we find some indication of his views in the bibliographical surveys he made under the heading "Philology: General Works" in volumes 4 (for 1923), 5 (for 1924) and 6 (for 1925) of *The Year's Work in English Studies* between 1924 and 1927. At the same time, he was aware of the need for systematic analysis of word-fields. This is quite clear from his examination of an early classic of historical lexicology, J. K. Wallenberg's *The Vocabulary of Dan Michel's Ayenbite of Inwyt*, a book which is in effect a dictionary of Middle Kentish. Tolkien analyzed the Middle Kentish form *rearde* 'voice, language', which, as Wallenberg recognized (1923: 200 and n. 3), unlike the normal OE form *reord* f., corresponds exactly to Gothic *razda*, OHG *rarta* and ON *rǫdd* and stands for an Old Kentish **reard-*. Like them it reflects a Germanic **razdō* with *o*-ablaut in contrast to OE *reord* < **rezdō* with *e*-ablaut. Tolkien (1924: 24–25) unravelled Wallenberg's somewhat involved discussion with admirable clarity and also drew attention to the fact that the usual Old English form *reord* is not without phonological difficulties. Whilst appreciating Wallenberg's elaborate discussion of individual lexical items, Tolkien was critical of his somewhat inadequate appreciation of the importance of spelling variation in the analysis of Middle English texts. Here again, Tolkien's insistence on the primacy of the transmitted text comes through.

Tolkien was deeply interested in the use of onomastic material for historical linguistics, and we can observe this in his treatment of an article by Max Förster in which the loss of the plosive [g] in the Middle English personal name *Edith* < Old English *Ēadgȳð* is compared with the development of *if* < OE *ġif*, *itch* < OE *ġiċċ(e)an* and *icicle* < OE **īsġicel* (Förster 1923: 94). Tolkien (1924: 23) saw what Förster had failed to see, namely, that we are concerned with a secondary palatalization of the plosive [g] in conjunction with Middle English unrounding of OE /y:/. Tolkien examined the initial volume of the English Place-Name Society's survey (Mawer & Stenton 1924) as part of his work for the *Year's Work* in some detail (Tolkien 1926: 55-65). Here again he was aware of fundamental problems, such as those posed by monothematic personal names of the type *Æffa* and *Dudda*. He recognized the ways in which such names were formed and pointed out the morphological parallels to such Middle English forms as *Robin*, *Dobbin*, *Hob* and *Bob* for *Robert* (Tolkien 1926: 59; cf. also Tolkien 1927: 39). Tolkien (1926: 59) regarded dithematic names like OE *Dēorlāf* as being of higher antiquity than the monothematic type, pointing out that there are close parallels outside Germanic in Celtic, Greek and Sanskrit. We can extend this to Slavonic and Baltic and cite such names as Polabo-Pomeranian (Elbe-Baltic Slavonic) **Dobro-slav* (Schlimpert 1978: 42) or Old Prussian *Taute-narwe* (Krahe 1954: 66). The truth is of course more complex than Tolkien thought. Modern research has revealed chronological and typological strata within the Indo-European naming system. In Germanic we must distinguish between 'primary' compounds with semantic content and links to the poetic language, such as OE *Heaðuwulf* 'battle-wolf', and arbitrary 'secondary' compounds, which are semantically empty, such as OE *Wulfstān*, a compound of OE *wulf* m. 'wolf' and OE *stān* m. 'stone' (see Greule 1986: 1183-1184). In the early twenties, and indeed for a long time afterwards, English place-name studies were dominated by the towering figure of Eilert Ekwall. One of the most significant early works of Ekwall was his monograph of 1923 on the group-names in **-ingas** and **-ingahām**, e.g., HASTINGS in Sussex 'Hǣsta's people' and BIRMINGHAM in Warwickshire 'village or homestead of Beorma's people'. Names in **-ingas** and its genitive plural **-inga** belong to an early level of English nomenclature and have Continental parallels. So, for example, the specific of HASTINGS, the unrecorded Old English personal name **Hǣsta*, has an etymological parallel in the first element of the name of an eighth-century Langobardic king, *(H)aistulf* (cf. Gothic *haifsts* f. 'argument, dispute, quarrel'). Similarly, the first element of the Suffolk place-name REDLINGFIELD, an unrecorded diminutive personal name formation **Rǣdel/*Rǣdla*, has a direct etymological parallel in OHG *Râtilo* (see Ekwall 1960: 383). Tolkien (1924: 30-32) examined Ekwall's book in some detail, but in some respects his remarks require revision. It is true that in the early days of place-name study too much emphasis was given to explaining obscure first elements of place-names as unrecorded personal names, but Tolkien is unduly sceptical here. For example (1924: 32), he remarks:

> In dealing with *Walsingham*, indeed, it seems purely misleading to give simply 'OE. *Wæls*, pers. n.' when the sole authority for this *Wæls* is the Sigemund-episode in *Beowulf*.

In fact, a direct Continental cognate to OE *Wæls* occurs as the first element of the Flemish place-name WALZEGEM, while a suffix derivative in independent use is attested in the form of OHG *Welisung* (Insley 1996: 77-78), and there is no reason to doubt that WALSINGHAM is, as Ekwall indicated, 'the homestead of the followers of Wæls'. With remarkable foresight, Tolkien (1924: 32) drew attention to the importance of the *-ington* and *-ingham* names in north-west France for the elucidation of the English names of this type. It is only recently that progress has begun to be made here.

Tolkien's abiding interest in Old English anthroponymy is at its most apparent in his edition and commentary on *The Fight at Finnsburg* and the Finn Episode in *Beowulf*, which was published posthumously by Alan Bliss and based on Tolkien's Oxford lectures on these texts held from 1928 onwards (Tolkien 1982). An important part of this work is a glossary of names with an exhaustive philological and historical commentary (Tolkien 1982: 27-79), which seems to have been put together in the early war years (see the comments of Alan Bliss, Tolkien 1982: vi). Tolkien's awareness of the importance of place-name material is evident in a long note discussing the appearance of the names *Hengest* and *Horsa* as the first elements of place-names (Tolkien 1982: 66-67 n. 65). In this note,

Tolkien also cites Sir Frank Stenton's evidence (Stenton 1924: 187) on the survival of the 'heroic' names *Swanhild, Widi(g)a* and *Hengest* into the early Middle English period.

There are occasions on which Tolkien's explanations are in need of substantial alteration. For example, he quite rightly takes the Bedan *Oisc*, the name of the eponymous ancestor of the Kentish royal dynasty, the *Oiscingas*, to correspond to an OE **Ēsc*, but incorrectly gives the ultimate base as **Ōski, *Anski*, citing as evidence the statement in the Ravenna Cosmography that the 'Saxon' invaders of Britain were led by a prince called *Anschis (Ansehis)* (Tolkien 1982: 69 n. 69). In fact, as Max Förster demonstrated in 1938, we are concerned with a diminutive of a name in *Ōs-* formed with the *-k-* suffix, Primitive OE **Ōs-ik-* (< West Germanic **Ans-ik-*) (see Förster 1938: 60 n. 1).

Tolkien ended the first of these articles for the *Year's Work* with a plea for comparative historical linguistics, a discipline which had been regarded in England as something quintessentially German which had to be combated at all costs (Tolkien 1924: 36-37). Tolkien examined German scholarship more closely in the second of his surveys. In particular, several articles from the Streitberg and Behagel *Festschriften* came in for close scrutiny, and on several occasions Tolkien was unable to suppress a mild irritation with the opacity of some of these papers. Characteristic are his remarks on Sievers' "Ziele und Wege der Schallanalyse" ['Aims and Methods in the Analysis of Sounds']:

> The relations of the *Bechingkurven, Taktfüllkurven,* and *Signalkurven* are very difficult to follow on paper. This Part II is not made easier to understand by the use of formulae such as 6 w^e (*nm-me*) which require familiarity with [Sievers'] *Metrische Studien*, since one is referred thither for their elucidation. For Part I also familiarity is assumed in the audience with the words and airs of German songs (Tolkien 1926: 42).

Tolkien's three general surveys show that he was aware of the current trends in the German scholarship of the early twenties. He was also fully cognizant of the importance of the discovery of Hittite and Tocharian for Indo-European studies (cf. Tolkien 1926: 27, 38-39). Importantly, he knew the work of Meillet, Sapir and Saussure, and this is symptomatic of the fact that, in contrast to his mentor Wright, he had begun to free himself of the intellectual constraints of the Neogrammarian tradition.

Tolkien never forgot his place of birth in the West Midlands. This appears occasionally in his literary works, but one must be careful here. For example, I tend to think that the Swedish dialectologist Johannesson is far too precise in his localization of the speech of the Hobbits to the Warwickshire/Oxfordshire region (Johannesson 1994: 54-58). One can rather see their vocabulary at least as being generally West Midland, but no more than that. Old English traditions survived the Norman Conquest better than elsewhere in the West Midlands, possibly due to the long episcopate of Bishop Wulfstan II in Worcester (1062-1095), and the survival of such traditions is evident in the language of the Corpus manuscript of *Ancrene*

Wisse (Cambridge, Corpus Christi College 402) and the Bodleian manuscript of the Katherine-Group (Oxford, Bodleian Library, Bodley 34). In his famous article of 1929, "*Ancrene Wisse* and *Hali Meiðhad*", Tolkien demonstrated that we are concerned with a regional literary language, which he placed in Herefordshire. In 1976, E. J. Dobson localized *Ancrene Wisse* to the Abbey of Wigmore in northern Herefordshire (Dobson 1976: 114-173). Tolkien's "AB-language" is closely related to the language of the more conservative of the two manuscripts of Laȝamon's *Brut* (London, British Library, Cotton Caligula A. ix) and is a linear descendant of the dialect of the twelfth-century homily on the life of St Chad in Oxford, Bodleian Library, Hatton 116 (5136) and in turn of the West Mercian language of the ninth-century interlinear glossary of the Vespasian Psalter (London, British Library, Cotton Vespasian A. i). Tolkien's article of 1929 is not only important for its delineation of the "AB-language" itself, but also for the fact that it pointed the way forward in the elucidation of regional literary languages in Middle English. More recent research has pointed to a large group of manuscripts of texts like *Prick of Conscience, Speculum Vitae* or *Cursor Mundi* from Yorkshire around 1300 and we also have the south Midland group of Wycliffite manuscripts from the later part of the fourteenth century (Samuels Type I) (see Beadle 1994). Tolkien continued to work on the AB-group for many years. In 1962, he edited the Corpus manuscript of *Ancrene Wisse* for the Early English Text Society and his pupil Simone d'Ardenne edited the Legend of St Juliana from Bodley 34.

In the nineteen-thirties, Tolkien published two articles which still have the character of philological classics. The first of these articles appeared in 1934 and deals with the use of dialect in the well-known passage in Chaucer's *Reeve's Tale* in which a miller from East Anglia meets two Cambridge students from the North. Tolkien did not regard this passage as a dialect text as such, but as perceived dialect, and adds that the scribes of the copies must also be considered. For this reason, he underlines the necessity of using all the manuscripts of the text, and shows that the scribes had a tendency to adapt the passage to the language of the South-East. The important question for Tolkien was that which asked how the language of the North would have been perceived by Chaucer's audience and he emphasizes the position of the language of East Anglia as a mediator between North and South. Tolkien shows that Chaucer's students did not use extreme dialect forms, but used forms which would have been readily understood as northernisms in London, such as /ɑ:/ in *ham* 'home' and *banes* 'bones' (instead of Southumbrian /ɔ:/) or the Northern forms of the third person plural *they, their, theim*. Tolkien's article is not only a study on the literary use of dialect, but is also an important investigation of the word geography of the fourteenth century. Unfortunately, works on the word geography of Middle English are still relatively thin on the ground, although now that the *Middle English Dictionary* is complete, the material basis for such studies is incomparably better than it was in Tolkien's day.

The second article from the thirties that I wish to examine is far more famous and has often been reprinted. This is his British Academy lecture, "Beowulf: The Monsters and the Critics", which appeared in 1936. This is of course not a linguistic study, but a philological study in the true sense of the term. Tolkien recognized that *Beowulf* research in the nineteenth and early twentieth century had treated the poem primarily as evidence for the early history of Scandinavia or as a source for the study of Germanic antiquity. As a result, the literary qualities of the poem had been sadly neglected. The eminent critic and literary historian of the Dark Ages W. P. Ker took the view that "the great beauty, the real value, of *Beowulf* is in its dignity of style", but regarded the construction of the poem as weak and curiously askew with "the irrelevances in the centre and the serious things on the outer edges" (Ker 1955 [1904]: 253). Ker was dismissive of the theme of the battle with the dragon, but Tolkien restored it to its proper place as the central element of the poem, a fiend from hell against whom kings and heroes battle in vain and suffer inevitable defeat. Tolkien implicitly accepted the traditional dating of *Beowulf* to the eighth century and, like the majority of modern commentators, accepted that the poet had antiquarian interests, but he regarded these antiquarian elements as merely incidental and not central to the theme of the poem. The *Beowulf*-poet was naturally a Christian, but he was not free of inherited heathen ideas of futile struggle against the forces of darkness. Tolkien described this inner contradiction between Christian piety on the one side and Germanic ideas of heroism and struggle on the other in masterly fashion, and we can do no better than quote his own words:

> Beowulf's byrne was made by Weland, and the iron shield he bore against the serpent by his own smiths: it was not yet the breastplate of righteousness, nor the shield of faith for the quenching of all the fiery darts of the wicked (Tolkien 1936: 266).

Tolkien returned to *Beowulf* in 1940 with a set of preliminary remarks to Wrenn's revision of Clark Hall's *Beowulf*-translation. He made no secret of his reservations about the translation of literary works and his "Prefatory Remarks" form a short sketch of the Old English poetic language and the difficulties resulting from its use of archaic vocabulary and *kenningar*. Again, he employed his etymological knowledge to good purpose, as, for example, when he indicates the etymological connection between OE *hōs* f. 'retinue, following' and Gothic, OHG *hansa* f. 'troop' (Tolkien 1940: xii). Although he held a cultivated language to be appropriate for *Beowulf*-translations, Tolkien was against archaism and emphasized that the translator should always take semantic change into account. As Tolkien points out, we cannot, for example, translate OE *wann* with Modern English *wan* 'pale', but should rather link it semantically to Modern English *dark* (Tolkien 1940: xx).

The last academic paper of Tolkien which I wish to examine is his O'Donnell lecture of 21 October 1955, "English and Welsh" (Tolkien 1963). Here again, we see the breadth of Tolkien's philological range. He starts with the Tudor period and works back to the early Middle Ages. For Tolkien, language rather than descent was the defining factor in the delineation of ethnic identity in early medieval Britain (Tolkien 1963: 5-6). Although the number of British loanwords in Old English is minimal, Tolkien indicates other lines of inquiry for the ascertaining of linguistic contact, notably in the English verb system (Tolkien 1963: 30-32). This is an area which has attracted renewed attention in recent years, most notably in the work of Hildegard L. C. Tristram and Markku Filppula. Tolkien (1963: 32-33) makes a typological comparison between Old English *i*-mutation and the *i*-epenthesis of late British which moves in the direction of Sprachbund theories. Unfortunately, he never developed this further. The controversy about the relations between the Anglo-Saxons and the British is still open, and the adherents of the clean sweep theory, that is, that the English invaders swept away the British inhabitants of eastern England, have returned to the debate with a vigour that would have been unthinkable ten years ago.

On the day before Tolkien held his O'Donnell Lecture, the third and last volume of *The Lord of the Rings* was published and it is this work and *The Hobbit* which have impregnated Tolkien's name in the consciousness of audiences far beyond academic circles. It is also here that Tolkien's literary application of Old English and Germanic philology is most apparent.

We can start with the name of the dragon of *The Hobbit, Smaug*. In a letter of 11 February 1938 to Stanley Unwin, Tolkien wrote: "The dragon bears as name – a pseudonym – the past tense of the primitive Germanic verb *Smugan*, to squeeze through a hole: a low philological jest" (Tolkien 1981: 31). The Germanic verb is in fact **smeug-a-* [OE *smūgan* 'to creep'] (Seebold 1970: 439), a strong verb of class II. Derivatives of the preterite singular form include OE *smēah* 'sagacious, acute, subtle' < **smaug-a-* and OE *ġesmēah* n. 'intrigue' < *smaug-a-m (Seebold 1970: 440). Perhaps we can take Tolkien's *Smaug* to be a Primitive Germanic *Smaugaz, an original byname with the sense 'the cunning creeper'. Interestingly, the figure Gollum of *The Lord of the Rings* originally bore the name *Sméagol* (Tolkien 1966: I, 62–63). This is an Old English diminutive of *Sméag < **Smaug (-az)* formed with the *-l-*suffix. *Sméagol* would then be an original byname with the sense 'the cunning little creeper'.

Sometimes the borrowings are quite obvious. One of the most subtle and dangerous adherents of the forces of darkness in *The Lord of the Rings* bore the name *Saruman*. This is a compound of OE *searu* n. 'art, skill, cunning; device, deceit, trick, treachery' and *man(n)* 'man' and we can cite such Old English compounds as *searonīð* m. 'treachery, deceitful enmity'. Shippey (1982: 128-129) points out that OE *searo*, when used as the first element of compounds, often denotes metal (e.g. in the Beowulfian *searo-net* n. 'coat of chain-mail, corslet'), and goes on to interpret Saruman's name as having the implication of 'cunning man' or 'machine man' or 'technological man', though I would prefer to interpret it merely as 'cunning schemer'. Shippey (1982: 128) is somewhat confused about the dialectology of the name in that he interprets the word-form *searu* as West Saxon and *saru as Mercian. OE *searu* belongs to the Germanic *wa*-declension and generally shows breaking of Primitive OE /æ/ > /æə/, apart from in Northumbrian, where the stem vowel is retracted to /ɑ/ to give the form *sarwo* (= *saru*) (see

Campbell 1959: 56 [§ 144 and n. 1]). Saruman's stronghold was called *Isengard*, a straightforward hybrid formed from OE *īsen* n. 'iron' and ON *garðr* m. 'enclosure'.

There are also less obvious and more subtle cases of invention and the use of Old English material. A minor figure in *The Lord of the Rings* was called *Derufin* (Tolkien 1966: III, 43, 125). The source here is doubtless OE *Merefin*, a name which was borne by a seventh-century prince of the *Magonsætan* (see Stenton 1971: 47). The territory of the *Magonsætan* lay in Tolkien's home region in the West Midlands, or, more precisely, in Shropshire and Herefordshire, that is, in the area where *Ancrene Wisse* originated. Tolkien's poetic licence allowed him to alter the name *Merefin* by adapting the first element to partly conform to the common Old English name element *Dēor-*.

The use of Old English onomastic and lexical material in *The Lord of the Rings* is most pronounced in the case of the *Riders of Rohan* or the *(Ridder)mark*. These are a martial people of horse-breeders, and characteristic for their onomastic usage is the name element *Eo-*, as in *Eomer* and *Eowynn*. *Eo-* is of course a derivative of the Old English word *eoh* m. 'horse', an old word with IE cognates outside Germanic, such as Latin *equus* and Sanskrit *áśvaḥ* (see Shippey 1982: 94). The cavalry unit of the *Riders of Rohan* is designated *éored* (Tolkien 1966: II, 39) which is a straight borrowing from Old English. OE *ēored* n. is used to gloss Latin *equitatus* in the ninth-century Mercian Vespasian Psalter glossary (Kuhn 1965: 151), another text whose linguistic links are with Tolkien's West Midland homeland. We can also cite comparable compounds from the Old English Riddles, such as *ēoredmæcg* m. 'horseman' and *ēoredðrēat* m. 'mounted troop' (see Tupper 1910: 250).

The king of the riders bore the name *Théoden*, son of *Thengel*. Both *þēoden* and *þengel* are words for 'prince' in the Old English poetic language and both have cognates elsewhere in Germanic, such as Gothic *þiudans* and ON *þengill*. In Old Norse, *þengill* is attested in independent use as a personal name (Lind 1905-1915: 1122-1123). Earlier kings of the Mark bore names belonging to the same semantic field – *Eorl*, *Brego*, *Aldor*, *Fréa*, *Brytta* and *Walda*, for example (Tolkien 1966: III, 349-350). King *Théoden*'s hall was called *Meduseld*, a straight borrowing of OE *meduseld* 'hall where mead was consumed', a pure piece of Beowulfian terminology (Shippey 1982: 94-95). Tolkien uses Old English for the typical place-names of the territory of the Riders. We find a river named *Entwash* (Tolkien 1966: I, 389: II, 23, 26, 39, etc.) and a ford named *Entwade* (Tolkien 1966: II, 37). In both cases, the first element of these names is OE *ent* m. 'giant'. In the first the second element is OE *gewæsć* n. 'surge of water', while the second contains OE *gewæd* n. 'ford'.

But this is not all. There are other Germanic elements in use among the riders, an example being the name of *Erkenbrand of Westfold*. The source of *Westfold* is quite clearly the Norwegian province name *Vestfold*, but *Erkenbrand* is an interesting name. The first element, Germanic **erkna-* 'pure', is primarily Frankish and we might compare, for example, the name of the Neustrian *maiordomus* of the period between 641 and 658, *Erchinoald* (Ebling 1974: 137-

139). In England, this name-element was used by the Kentish royal house of the *Oiscingas* in the seventh century (cf. King *Eorcenberht* of Kent [640-664] and his daughter *Eorcengota*, who became abbess of Faremoûtier-en-Brie in the kingdom of the Franks [see Ström 1939: 166]), where its appearance is doubtless the result of Merovingian influence. The second element *-brand* was early and typical among the Langobards in Italy, cf. Langobardic *Ansprand, Hildiprand, Liutprand* and *Teutprand*, and only later occurred in the North, cf. ON *þorbrandr*, though it never spread to Old English.

Then there is the name *Rohan* itself, a peculiarly un-Germanic name whose prototype must be the Breton place-name *Rohan*. Here Tolkien's inspiration is clearly the use of British names such *Deira* and *Bernicia* as the names of Anglo-Saxon kingdoms.

The name of the central figure of *The Lord of the Rings*, *Frodo Baggins* also displays Continental influence. Tom Shippey quite properly links the name to that of Froda, father of Ingeld, who is mentioned in *Beowulf*, and to the *Frothi/Fróði* of Saxo Grammaticus and Snorri Sturluson (Shippey 1982: 155-156). However, the name of *Frodo Baggins* is a reflex of Continental Germanic (Frankish) *Frôdo*, final *-o* being the normal nominative singular inflectional ending for nouns of the Germanic *n*-declension in the Continental dialects (Old High German, Old Saxon). It is perhaps significant that Frodo's father also bore a Continental Germanic name, *Drogo* (Tolkien 1966: I, 30-31: II, 266), a Frankish name introduced into England by the Normans.

One can perhaps notice elements from other Indo-European languages in Tolkien's nomenclature. In *The Lord of the Rings*, we find mention of a wizard named Radagast the Brown (Tolkien 1966: I, 269-271). *Radagast* is not Germanic, but Slavonic. It corresponds to the Old Sorbish personal name **Radogost*, Elbe-Baltic Slavonic *Radegast* (see Eichler 1993: 136).

The court of Hrothgar in *Beowulf* seems to have been Tolkien's inspiration for the court of the kings of Rohan. Tolkien treats the heathenism of the riders with discretion. Like the *Beowulf*-poet he ignores the more concrete details of Germanic heathenism, such as sacral kingship, human sacrifice and the cult of the "terrible sovereign" Wōden/Óðinn (see the perceptive remarks of Shippey 1982: 152-153). His riders are a creation of fiction. If their names are largely, but not entirely, Old English, their mode of battle is not. They are not forest and marsh barbarians of the North Sea coastal regions, like the ancestors of the English, but are barbarians of the steppe who fight on horseback with the lance and, as Tom Shippey remarked (1982: 97, 225), they are more akin to the Goths and Langobards than to the Anglo-Saxons. A short sketch of this kind can do no more than to indicate directions for possible future investigations, but perhaps it is time to restore some balance to the study of Tolkien's work and to view it more in the context of the author's philological background. We should always remember that Tolkien was a philologist of rare distinction and that this permeated his entire œuvre.

Dictionaries

Ekwall, Eilert
1960 — *The concise Oxford dictionary of English place-names.* 4th edition. Oxford: Clarendon Press.

References

Beadle, Richard
1994 — „Middle English texts and their transmission 1350-1500: Some geographical criteria", in: *Speaking in our tongues. Medieval dialectology and related disciplines*, ed. Margaret Laing and Keith Williamson. Cambridge: D.S. Brewer, 69-91.

Campbell, Alistair
1959 — *Old English grammar.* Oxford: Clarendon Press [many reprints].

Carpenter, Humphrey
1977 — *J.R.R. Tolkien: A biography.* London: George Allen & Unwin.

Dobson, Eric J.
1976 — *The origins of 'Ancrene Wisse'.* Oxford: Clarendon Press.

Ebling, Horst
1974 — *Prosopographie der Amtsträger des Merowingerreiches von Chlothar II. (613) bis Karl Martell (741).* Beihefte der Francia 2. Munich: Wilhelm Fink Verlag.

Eichler, Ernst
1993 — *Slawische Ortsnamen zwischen Saale und Neiße. Ein Kompendium.* Bd. III: *N-S*. Bautzen: Domowina-Verlag.

Ekwall, Eilert
1923 — *English place names in -ING.* Skrifter utgivna av Kungl. Humanistiska Vetenskapssamfundet i Lund/Acta reg. societatis humaniorum litterarum Lundensis 6. 1923. Lund: C. W. K. Gleerup.

Förster, Max
1923 — "Proben eines englischen Eigennamen-Wörterbuches", in: *Germanisch-romanische Monatsschrift* 11: 86-110.
1938 — "Die heilige Sativola oder Sidwell. Eine Namenstudie", *Anglia* 62: 33-80.

Greule, Albrecht
1986 — "Morphologie und Wortbildung der Vornamen: Germanisch", in: *Namenforschung/Name Studies/Les noms propres. Ein internationales Handbuch zur Onomastik/An international handbook of onomastics/manuel international d'onomastique*, ed. Ernst Eichler, Gerold Hilty, Heinrich Löffler, Hugo Steger and Ladislav Zgusta. HSK 11.1-2. Berlin/New York: Walter de Gruyter, 1182-1187.

Insley, John
1996 — Review of L. van Durme, *Toponymie van Velzeke-Ruddershove en Bochoute* (Ghent: Koninklijke Academie voor Nederlandse Taal- en Letterkunde1986-1991). *The English Place-Name Society Journal* 28 (1995-1996): 77-78.

Johannesson, Nils-Lennart
1994 — "Subcreating a stratified community — On J.R.R. Tolkien's use of non-standard forms in *The Lord of the Rings*", in: *Nonstandard varieties of English: Papers from the Stockholm symposium 11-13*

Ker, William Paton
    1904

Krahe, Hans
    1954

Kuhn, Sherman M. (ed.)
    1965

Lind, Erik Henrik
    1905–1915

Mawer, Allen -- Frank Merry Stenton (ed.)
    1924

Schlimpert, Gerhard
    1978

Seebold, Elmar
    1970

Shippey, T. A.
    1982

Sievers, Eduard
    1924

Stenton, Frank Merry
    1924

    1971

Ström, Hilmer
    1939

Tolkien, John Ronald Reuel
    1924

    1926

    1927

    1929

    1934

    1936

April 1991, ed. Gunnel Melchers and Nils-Lennart Johannesson. Acta Universitatis Stockholmiensis /Stockholm Studies in English 84. Stockholm: Almqvist & Wiksell International, 53-63.

The dark ages. London: William Blackwood & Sons [repr. Thomas Nelson, 1955].

Sprache und Vorzeit: Europäische Vorgeschichte nach dem Zeugnis der Sprache. Heidelberg: Quelle & Meyer.

The Vespasian Psalter. Ann Arbor: University of Michigan Press.

Norsk-isländska dopnamn ock fingerade namn från medeltiden. Uppsala: A.-B. Lundequistska Bokhandeln/Leipzig: Otto Harrassowitz.

Introduction to the survey of English place-names. English Place-Name Society I. Cambridge: Cambridge University Press.

Slawische Personennamen in mittelalterlichen Quellen zur deutschen Geschichte. Deutsch-slawische Forschungen zur Namenkunde und Siedlungsgeschichte 32. Berlin: Akademie Verlag.

Vergleichendes und etymologisches Wörterbuch der germanischen starken Verben. The Hague-Paris: Mouton.

The road to Middle Earth. London: George Allen & Unwin.

"Ziele und Wege der Schallanalyse". *Stand und Aufgaben der Sprachwissenschaft: Festschrift für Wilhelm Streitberg*. Heidelberg: Carl Winter's Universitätsbuchhandlung, 65-125.

"Personal names in place-names", in: Mawer & Stenton 1924: 165-189.

Anglo-Saxon England, 3rd ed. Oxford: Clarendon Press.

Old English personal names in Bede's history: An etymological-phonological investigation. Lund Studies in English 8. Lund: C.W.K. Gleerup/London: Williams & Norgate. Ltd/Copenhagen: Levin & Munksgaard [Ejnar Munksgaard].

"Philology: General works", *The Year's Work in English studies* 4: 20-37.

"Philology: General works", *The Year's Work in English studies* 5: 26-65.

"Philology: General works", *The Year's Work in English studies* 6: 32-66.

"*Ancrene Wisse* and *Hali Meiðhad*", *Essays and Studies by Members of the English Association* 14: 104-126.

"Chaucer as a philologist: The Reeve's Tale", *Transactions of the Philological Society*: 1-70.

"Beowulf: The monsters and the critics", *Proceedings of the British Academy* 22: 245-295 [many reprints].

	1940	"Prefatory remarks on prose translations of 'Beowulf'". *Beowulf and the Finnsburg Fragment*: A translation into Modern English prose by John R. Clark Hall. New Edition. Completely revised with Notes and an Introduction by C. L. Wrenn. With Prefatory Remarks by J. R. R. Tolkien. London: George Allen & Unwin Ltd. ix-xliii.
	1962	*The English text of the Ancrene Riwle: Ancrene Wisse CCCC MS 402*, ed. J.R.R. Tolkien & N.R. Ker. EETS OS 249. Oxford: Oxford University Press.
	1963	"English and Welsh", *Angles and Britons. O'Donnell lectures*. Cardiff: University of Wales Press, 1-41.
	1966	*The Lord of the Rings*, 2nd ed. London: George Allen & Unwin Ltd. [1st ed. 1954-1955].
	1981	*Letters of J.R.R. Tolkien*. A selection edited by Humphrey Carpenter with the assistance of Christopher Tolkien. London: George Allen & Unwin.
	1982	*Finn and Hengest: The fragment and the episode*. Ed. Alan Bliss. London: George Allen & Unwin.
	1983	"Valedictory address to the University of Oxford". J. R. R. Tolkien. *The Monsters and the critics and other essays*, ed. Christopher Tolkien. London: George Allen & Unwin, 224-240.
Tupper, Frederick (ed.)		
	1910	*The riddles of the Exeter book*. Boston: Ginn and Company.
Wallenberg, J. K.		
	1923	*The vocabulary of Dan Michel's Ayenbite of inwyt: A phonological, morphological, etymological, semasiological and textual study*. Uppsala: Appelbergs Boktryckeri Aktiebolag.

Chinese translations of *Beowulf*:
International Anglo-Saxon studies and modernity
Stella Wang (Rochester, USA)

Oferēode þā æþelinga bearn / stēap stānhliðo....
[Then the descendant of noble lineage passed over the steep rocky slopes....]
Beowulf 1408-09a

Abstract

From 1926-27 through 2006, *Beowulf* was introduced and rendered into Chinese in China, Hong Kong, and Taiwan in precarious, yet transformative political and cultural contexts. Coinciding with the global spread of modernization and Romantic nationalism, the production of the earliest Chinese translations was also predicated by the contentious language revolution that, over the first decades of the twentieth century, saw the replacement of classical Chinese by modern vernacular Chinese to become the dominant literary and translating language. In addition, all existing Chinese translations of *Beowulf* were conditioned by the uneven circumstances of medieval studies across the Sinophone regions, where specific Anglo-Saxon studies did not exist until very recently. Built on prior scholarship and extensive further bibliographical research, this paper offers the first historical account of the little studied translations of *Beowulf* in Chinese. From brief plot summaries to criticism interspersed with a substantial amount of translated verses, from partial to full-length and indirect to direct translations, these renditions of *Beowulf* in the still-transforming modern vernacular Chinese display an uncanny mirroring of the fierce linguistic contention inherent in the Old English poem.[1]

1. Introduction

Nine Chinese translations of *Beowulf* have so far been published in China, Hong Kong, and Taiwan, ranging from the earliest and most unusual examples of 1926 and 1927 through two important recent efforts of 1992 and 2006.[2] These creative and at times controversial renderings, including synoptical summaries, paraphrase, partial and complete translations, have appeared in prose, verse, as well as mixed forms. Among them the earlier works are intended primarily for general audiences, while the later ones aim increasingly for academic readership, often provided with copious notes and translator's commentaries (see the chronological checklist at the end). It is the underlying goal of this paper to give the first historical account of these Chinese renditions of *Beowulf* by placing them in a broad international context, exploring in particular the extent to which their production intersects with the state of contemporary Anglo-Saxon scholarship as well as western and Japanese translations of the poem. In this way, the paper investigates a previously unexplored area in the study of *Beowulf*-translation that has been admirably

---

[1] All quotations from *Beowulf* refer to Klaeber 2008. English literal translations are my own, so are the back translations of the cited examples from the Chinese translations of *Beowulf*.
[2] Xidi (Zheng Zhenduo) 1926 & 1927; [Liang] Zhipan 1934; Chen Guohua 1959; Yan Yuanshu 1983/74; Liang Shiqiu 1985; Feng Xiang 1992; Chen Caiyu 1999; Li Funing 2005/6.

launched by Chauncey Brewster Tinker (1903), sharply expanded by Marijane Osborn (1997, 2003), and meticulously brought up to date most recently by Hans Sauer (2011). Global connections aside, this paper also seeks to consider the local significance of the Chinese translations of *Beowulf*. Above all, they point to the tumultuous socio-political conditions that drive the continuous attempts to translate *Beowulf* in Chinese, connecting it with not only the transnational but also regional and local ideas of modernity throughout the twentieth century. To scholars of Chinese culture bent on imagining a modern Chinese nation state, the Anglo-Saxon poem offers an important model of a western cultural heritage. The symbolic and ideological currency that makes it desirable to introduce the poem by way of translation varies nonetheless from one endeavor to the next. These variations are also specific to geo-historical settings. The settings include colonial and national ones during the Republican era (1911-1949), the succeeding cold war era rivalry between mainland China and Taiwan following 1949, and the post-cold war, post-socialist era of contemporary China. These settings all have staged deliberate strategies for translating significant foreign texts, including *Beowulf*, based on their perceived relevance to the modernity projects in the region. Translation of *Beowulf* in all these contexts, moreover, is complicated by the circumstances of local western medieval studies, where specific Anglo-Saxon studies have remained virtually nonexistent until very recently.

Under the circumstances outlined above, three results follow diachronically over a period of eighty years. First, despite invested efforts, during the first two historical periods, until the end of the cold war, all literary translations and critical discussions of the Old English poem produced in the Chinese-speaking regions had to rely on sources in a third, more accessible modern language such as English and possibly, in the first decades of the twentieth century, Japanese. The initial translations of *Beowulf* (of 1927/1926; 1934) reflect in particular the serendipitous character of such twice-removed literary transmission. The double linguistic mediation makes it difficult, in practice, for the translators to deal with the prosodic requirements and stylistic characteristics of *Beowulf* not only at lexical and syntactical levels but also in rhetorical manipulation. Regardless, the multiple translations of *Beowulf* during the second, cold-war era (of 1959; 1983/1974; 1985) reveal a remarkable range of indigenous literary resources and cultural-political positions that the translators were able to employ to justify their Chinese renderings. Second, during these early attempts, the concurrent, competing nationalist modernization movements coupled with an unfortunate lack of a more sophisticated understanding of Anglo-Saxon culture has also made for an exceptionally hit-or-miss translation in both the diegetic and mimetic spaces of the rendered poem. The problems, however, with textual and cultural translations mediated by the discourse of modernity, especially that of Romantic nationalism, are certainly not reserved for these Chinese works only. Synchronically they reflect much of the modern transmission history of *Beowulf* in the West — if with some time lag. The particular challenges of language and related ideological discourses on cultural and national identity, nonetheless, cannot have been more adequately dealt with in the Sinophone regions until the third period when translators trained in Anglo-Saxon and related medieval European literature and cultures began to take up the poem. Lastly, this third period has since delivered the first complete Chinese verse translation of *Beowulf* derived directly from the Old English text. As such, Feng Xiang's translation (1992) marks the long-awaited act of independence from a third language mediation in the history of *Beowulf*-translation in Chinese. After this performative publication, two additional, and very dissimilar, Chinese translations follow. Each of them appears to have relied on a separate modern English translation for source text, while an OE edition is also cited as reference. These latest translations raise intriguing linguistic and discursive issues for the now specialized field of translating *Beowulf* (as well as other Anglo-Saxon literary texts) into Chinese. In particular, Li Funing's partial prose translation (2006) runs more closely to the grain of the OE text in contrast to Feng Xiang's poetic but notably liberal rendition, thus unexpectedly challenging the latter's Old English-Chinese direct translation vis-à-vis not only these more recent but also all previous indirect translations. Their multi-directional proximity to the Old English poem shows that the differences in all existing Chinese translations of *Beowulf* must not be considered merely as separate cases of uneven linguistic faithfulness to the Old English text. Far more useful is to understand them as part of a continuous translingual project in which the renderings of *Beowulf* share with other modern translated literature in Chinese the modernist impetus for linguistic experimentation and creative control.

The following discussion revisits the nine Chinese translations of *Beowulf* by eight translators grouped under three historical periods. A few words concerning the first group should be added now for two reasons. First, the production of these translations in the late 1920s and early 1930s is most directly tied to the revolutionary process for vernacular Chinese to replace classical Chinese and establish itself as the modern Chinese language — a key issue of the Chinese negotiation with modernity. Second, the problems and controversies that arose during their production point to the long-standing challenges of such translation projects in the given context of the region's nationalistic struggle as well as western medieval studies. In many ways, they anticipate the areas of breakthrough and continuous efforts made by the later groups.

2. Zheng Zhenduo (Xidi, 1927, also 1926) and [Liang] Zhipan (1934)

In May 1927 Zheng Zhenduo, using one of his pennames Xidi, published a translation of Hélène Adeline Guerber's paraphrase of *Beowulf* from her popular *Legends of the Middle Ages* (London, 1896). Since Xidi's work was not indicated as a translation, its source has remained unknown until now. Guerber's text, however, deserves due attention. Throughout her prose synopsis, for instance, she had arranged to include several short passages of verse translations of *Beowulf* by noted nineteenth-century translators ranging from John Josias Conybeare to Henry Wadsworth Longfellow. For some reason, Zheng Zhenduo chose or was obliged to omit all of these verse insertions. A comparison of the two texts, however, makes it clear that much of his work is a near verbatim representation of Guerber's text. As such, it inherits all of her dramatic rearrangements of the Anglo-Saxon poem. Among the most significant features of Guerber's adaptation is the inclusion of the character of a minstrel who, hiding in the dark, was said to have not only witnessed and survived Grendel's initial raid at Heorot but also fled to Geatland, recited the carnage in front of Hygelac and Beowulf, and to have been earnestly questioned afterward by the young hero for greater details of the monstrous attack. Other significant rewritings include elaboration on the swimming contest between Beowulf and Breca and, after Hygelac's death, Beowulf's refusal to take the Geatish throne from Heardred. Zheng Zhenduo was probably unaware of the changes and expansion Guerber had made. In fact, he added a couple of brisk, but no less imaginative lines himself, such as the description of the dumfounded Danes gathering around the mysterious smiling infant (Scyld) just brought ashore in his well-furnished boat, or the part about Hrothgar's grateful court chanting "Beowulf, Beowulf" after the purge of Heorot. Passages like these might have been penned by Zheng Zhenduo, but they could also have been incorporated from or mediated by other sources.

While fascinating, this silent, joint creative rewriting of *Beowulf* across international borders is probably not unique. Guerber's adaptation turns out to have its own international connections as well. All of the three inventive elements cited above regarding the minstrel, the swimming contest, and Geatish power transmission can be traced back or compared to the Wägner-MacDowall paraphrase (Philadelphia, 1883), first discussed by Tinker in the Appendix to his pioneering bibliographical study of *Beowulf*-translation (1903: 130-32). This German-to-English rendition was based on Wilhelm Wägner's substantial rewriting, included in an anthology of Teutonic heroic tales titled *Deutsche Heldensagen für Schule und Haus* (Leipzig, 1881). The English adaptation by W. M. MacDowall, over Tinker's protest, enjoyed enduring popularity, with the eighth edition appearing in 1896, the same year in which Guerber's *Legends of the Middle Ages* came out across the Atlantic. Tinker did not cite Guerber's work in his study. He probably did not expect, either, just how widely the Wägner-MacDowall bent of *Beowulf*-rewriting could travel and inspire. Via Guerber it zigzagged its way to China and apparently continued to grow in the popular imagination and local reception of the Anglo-Saxon poem through Zheng Zhenduo.

Beowulf offered a vision of ethnic community, led by heroes, united by language and cultural achievements. These were all elements that attracted Chinese intellectuals in a year, 1927, when Zheng Zhenduo's translation appeared, that saw severe challenges to this vision in Chinese society. Chinese writers and scholars were divided within and between competing political movements whose bloody rivalries in 1927 would deeply affect the history of even the translations discussed here up to the present. As nationalistically engaged as the translators were, some of the most important cultural centers for the work of translators were colonial territories, such as Shanghai, where Zheng Zhenduo worked, and Hong Kong, where the next translation appeared. Hence, the admiration of the translators for the heritage of England and the literary inspiration it offered was never free of anti-imperialist sentiment. Moreover, this ambivalence extended to the very language and style that a modern Chinese literature, including translated literature, should use.

In 1927 Zheng Zhenduo was one of the active players in all of these political and cultural arenas, and translation was important for understanding the extended histories of the evolving new Chinese literature in its negotiation with modernity. At issue was an iconoclastic review of the Chinese language begun ten years earlier. In 1917, the Columbia University-educated philosopher Hu Shih published his much-celebrated essay "Wenxue gailiang chuyi" ('A preliminary discussion of literary reform'). In this essay, he proposed eight guidelines for modern Chinese literary writing and advocated the adoption of, not *wenyan wen*, classical Chinese, but *baihua*, vernacular speech, as the means for creative experimentation as well as practical communication. This vernacular writing does not, however, mean a mere, or even unprecedented, aesthetic paradigm shift endorsed by a closed circle of the cultural elite. As Edward Gunn notes, the vernacular movement "was in its origins, and in a major portion of its appeal to intellectuals, a political act," aiming at the public for a broad response (1991: 38). Championing the use of the cognitively powerful regional and local languages, experimental literature and scholarly research were produced throughout the ensuing May Fourth new literature movement to show that vernacular writing had not only historical literary presence but also contemporary relevance to the causes of resisting imperialist aggression and building a modern democratic China (Gunn 1991: 38-42). Later, with the highly symbolic publication of *Zhongguo xin wenxue daxi* ('Compendium of new, i.e., modern, Chinese literature'), the year 1927 was deliberately taken up by its editors, Hu Shi and Zheng Zhenduo included, as the watershed moment of their transformative project.

But the nature and impact of the May Fourth new literature movement remained heavily contested then as now. Earlier in 1925, in the postscript to *Chule xiangya zhi ta* ('Out of the ivory tower') — a translation of Kuriyagawa Hakuson's collected essays, Lu Xun, the sophisticated stylist and often uncooperative voice among the Chinese modernists, criticized the returning students from Europe, the United States, and Japan for only using their foreign education and language skills to secure employment as arms-deal mediators and government officials' interpreters, and thereby to enjoy lavish meals, cushioned motorcycles, and the perfect excuse to remain politically nonchalant. They did not need to bother, either, with translating Dickens, Irving, and Tokutomi Roka, since Lin Shu had translated them all. This last comment is particularly bitter, as Lin Shu's translation was not only extensive, popular, but also in *wenyan* classical Chinese and extremely well paid. In contrast, the protagonist in Lu Xun's own short story "Sangshi" ('Regret for the past') also of 1925, could neither get employed nor make a living on translation, presumably translation in vernacular Chinese. So, if China's modernization was to hinge on the vernacular revolution, both undertakings also required the intervention of a host of political, economic, and cultural forces at the publishing houses that were in control of the circulation of crucial translated, as well as creative, texts. In this way, translation was highlighted as an extended site to gauge the all-important language base of China's modernization movement. It did not seem a secure or congenial base for vernacular Chinese. In "Wusheng de zhongguo" ('Silent China'), one of his two important speeches delivered in colonial Hong Kong in 1927, Lu Xun, frustrated by the prolonged language tug of war, found himself once again accentuating vernacular *baihua*'s bearing on not only the Chinese cultural and political consciousness but also China's self-image in the world. If, as the argument goes, China was to have a voice, a modern and global voice at that, it had to be a voice of the people and that would be a *baihua* vernacular voice.

This voice of the people and its manifestation in vernacular writing are as germane to the early Chinese translations of *Beowulf* as they are crucial to the artistic and political grounds of the new literature movement. It is no coincidence that whatever prompted Zheng Zhenduo to elaborate on Guerber's text, the additions foreground the common people alongside Beowulf as a folk hero. The juxtaposition reflects the Romantic nationalism that, as several scholars have observed, also underscores the nineteenth-century readings and translations of *Beowulf* in Denmark and across Scandinavia, Germany, England, and the United States.[3] The texts of both Wägner-MacDowall and Guerber evidently continue to popularize one strand of this romantic nationalistic tradition by eliminating all biblical references from the poem and recasting the related details in a Teutonic folkloric light. Thus, in their version, Scyld was sent by Odin, the scop's "creation song" is replaced by the minstrel's tale of Grendel, and Grendel, not related to Cain or God's wrath, was exiled by a magician. Zheng Zhenduo, via the already de-Christianized rendition by Guerber, could not have had knowledge of the controversy over the "problem of Christian interpolation" in *Beowulf*. But the poem described as an exemplary vernacular work of a national literature suited the cause of the May Fourth intellectuals and Zheng Zhenduo responded.

In 1934, Liang Zhipan would pick up where Zheng Zhenduo had left off and use the Anglo-Saxon poem for a discussion of national character and epic as the quintessential genre of national literature. He was editing and contributing to a special anniversary issue for *Hongdou man kan* ('Red bean magazine'), a journal based in Hong Kong that provided important publishing space for the local writers as well as visual artists in the 1930s. World epics are the theme of this special issue, which contains Liang Zhipan's own commentary on *Beowulf*, in addition to other articles on eight more epics from around the world, including the *Iliad*, *Ramayana*, and *Kalevala*. The *Beowulf* essay comprises three sections of approximately equal length: introduction, plot summary, and closing comments.

---

[3] Bjork 1997: 115-23; Osborn 1997: 347-49; Stanley 2000: 6-14 and passim; Hall 2001: 434-54.

Interspersed in it are four short translated passages from the poem, including fights with Grendel and Grendel's mother, Beowulf's death speech, and the evocative sketch of the mere. Liang Zhipan's sources appear to be highly mixed, yet ideologically consistent with his world epic project. A vague reference leads to George Saintsbury, possibly his *Short History of English Literature* (London 1898, with later editions). Consultation of this volume, if positive, includes a prominent rendition of Saintsbury's famed patriotic comment that amongst *Chanson de Roland*, *Poema del Cid*, and *Nibelungenlied* "it is thanks mainly to *Beowulf* that our poetry can claim the oldest lineage, and poetical coat-armor from the very first" (Saintsbury 1898: 7). Another quote, appearing in the conclusion of Liang Zhipan's essay, refers to Stopford A. Brooke. Traceable to his *English Literature from the Beginning to the Norman Conquest* (London 1898), the quote contains Brooke's description of *Beowulf* as England's "Genesis, a book of our origins" (Brooke 1898: 83). Unlike these passing, yet acknowledged quotes of English authors, one Chinese source is used substantially, yet without reference. It is an essay by Zheng Zhenduo, published in 1926, which, concerning mostly *Poema del Cid*, allows nonetheless a lone paragraph of sweeping plot summary and one closing remark on *Beowulf*. If short, this plot summary does not contain the same dramatic adaptation as occurs in Zheng Zhenduo's 1927 translation of Guerber's work. Liang Zhipan lifted the text of this brief plot summary, making minor sporadic changes of wording and providing new paragraphing to accommodate the inserted *Beowulf*-quotations in Chinese. These quotations represent the earliest instances of Chinese rendering of the poem itself. Whatever the source text is, the quotations, well cast in vernacular Chinese prose, give a glimpse of the unfamiliar language and literary tropes of the Old English poem. Without, for instance, specifically discussing the Anglo-Saxon poetic conventions, Liang Zhipan includes a parenthetical note to explain the Chinese rendering of the kenning from the fight with Grendel's mother: 戰光zhanguang (指劍zhi jian), 'battle-light (meaning sword).'

Liang Zhipan and his *Beowulf*-essay-translation from Hong Kong provide a telling signpost of the May Fourth proponents' precarious negotiation with language, literature, and politics in the 1930s, a period marked by looming imperialist menace and atrocious civil and international wars in China. At this historical moment, the search for a national identity by way of the search for a national literature became urgent. "Juan tou yu" ('opening remarks') of the *Hongdou* special issue sums up its running proposition: as literature contains elements of national character, ancient epics that inscribe historical national struggles can be particularly revealing as sources of national identity. Given the overriding discourses on cultural heritage and national origins, the ensuing ideological reading and translation of *Beowulf* among other selected world epics is not surprising. This political use of Anglo-Saxonism also echoes the nineteenth-century western scholarship and translations of *Beowulf*. It is true, as T. A. Shippey points out, that by the late 1890s and over the first decades of the twentieth century, a new consensus of *Beowulf* scholarship has appeared, specifically shifting "from the German hegemony to the English language hegemony (midwifed ... by critical contribution from Denmark)" (1998: 62). These changes, based on the newly emergent research model, are nonetheless ideologically not discriminating or far-reaching enough to release *Beowulf* from the nationalist grip, especially in the face of the gathering storm of global imperialism and world wars. Considered in this context, the Chinese modernist translations of *Beowulf*, especially their oblique use of Anglo-Saxonism in search for a national literature, are typical, but also significantly atypical as well. In line with the expansive modernity and associated political rhetoric, the translated texts were deliberately produced to perpetuate pre-determined nationalistic literary claims. A comparable case in the West is the nineteenth-century German elitist theorization and promotion of translation. Led by Friedrich Schleiermacher, this movement advocates foreignizing over domesticating translation with a view to rendering the German language plastic enough to contain world literature in accordance to the literary taste and political agenda of that elite cultural group (cf. Venuti 1998: 76-78; García 2004: 8-9). What has differentiated, however, the massive translation by the early Chinese modernists is its fundamental clash with the domestic cultural norms on the issue of the translating language. By rejecting *wenyan* classical Chinese for its association with homogenizing traditional values and by bringing the historically marginalized vernacular *baihua* to task, the resultant translation is doubly scandalous, exposing the alterity of not only the foreign text but also the fledging indigenous writing in modern vernacular Chinese. Lu Xun's complaints against Lin Shu's widely accepted translations in classical Chinese come to mind, and they are political as well as aesthetic complaints.

It was therefore up to its practitioners to define vernacular Chinese as a viable vehicle for China's modernization and for command of the discourse on knowledge, democracy, and nation building. Translation, as a site where the most rebellious, and innovative, use of vernacular Chinese was put to test, provided ample and amply challenging opportunities to import new concepts and to reinvent vernacular *baihua* through linguistic and stylistic experiments. The goal was to shape vernacular Chinese for modern use. Following the trajectory of this politically inflected translingual project, Edward Gunn observes that the late 1920s are critical to the cultural production of a Chinese vernacular modernity. By this time, modern Chinese vernacular writing had shown signs of reaching the limits of its experimentation and had begun to stabilize by absorbing into common practices foreign constructions such as Euro-Japanese syntax, special rhetorical tropes, as well as imported diction. The crux, however, of this vibrant vernacularism via foreignization is how it remained well within the range of the historically available indigenous language paradigms and, perhaps more often overlooked, how it was also aided by the resourcefulness of regional and local languages (Gunn 1991: 63-64; Chapters 2 and 4; Appendix). Wang Jiankai's (2003) bibliographical research on the Chinese translations of English and American literature in the Republican era (1919-1949) also suggests that the Chinese cultural field finally opened up wide for foreign literary works rendered in the maturing vernacular *baihua* in the late

1920s and early 1930s. Drawing on contemporary publication data, he highlights the catalytic role of the periodicals in accommodating and supporting the increasing output of literary translation after 1928 (Wang, Jiankai 2003: 64-71; 135-37; Chapter 4). When Liang Zhipan was working on the *Hongdou* special issue, the year 1934 saw the count of popular and specialized literary journals in China shoot to 2,086, compared to 877 just two years before. The year was thus dubbed by the publishing industry as "Zazhi nian" ('year of the journals'), followed by talk about "Fanyi nian" ('year of translation') for 1935 (Wang, Jiankai 2003: 107-08; 135; Chapter 4).

Beowulf, however, did not return to the translation scene for another twenty-five years in China and, in Taiwan, not until about forty years later. A comparison with the concurrent western learning, modernization, and translation in Japan may be illuminating. Specifically with regard to English language and literature studies at the turn of the twentieth century, Lafcadio Hearn (1850-1904), among a succession of western writers and philologists teaching at the Tokyo Imperial University (later Tokyo University), was inspiring to many (Fukuhara 1974: 28-30) — and was well-known to the Chinese literary public during the new literature movement. His lectures, arranged and published posthumously by his students (1938), including those on Anglo-Saxon poetry, are unusual in two respects. They are often tinted with a special strand of nineteenth-century gothic medievalism that Hearn's own journalistic and creative writing is known for. There is also a variety of fleeting references to Japanese literary works for the purpose of explanation and comparison, showing a unique sensitivity to the indigenous culture. But as William Schipper, Tadao Kubouchi, and Shigeru Ono have commented, it was left to John Lawrence (1850-1916), who succeeded Hearn in 1906, to ground Anglo-Saxon and medieval studies in a solid linguistic base in Japan (Schipper and Kubouchi 1986: 24, 28; Ono 2005: 129, 142). Generations of Japanese medievalists have since established themselves. Among them are Sanki Ichikawa (1886-1970), Lawrence's student and later chair of the English Department during the 1930s, who was the first Japanese professor of English Language and Literature at Tokyo University (Fukuhara 1974: 21; Ono 2005: 129), and Junzaburo Nichiwaki (1894-1982) who established Keio University as another powerhouse in medieval studies in Japan since the early twentieth century, and whose student and distinguished medievalist Fumio Kuriyagawa (1907-78) was to produce in 1941 the first complete translation of *Beowulf* in classical Japanese prose (Schipper and Kubouchi 1986: 27). As many as ten more translations rendered in classical or modern Japanese, in verse or prose, by individuals or via collaboration, would follow in the decades to come, including a remarkable surge of output in the 1990s by five translators, among them Kinshiro Oshitari's classical Japanese translation, and the most recent publication of a 2007 dual-language edition by Tsunenori Karibe and Ryoichi Koyama (Imai 2008).

If linguistically and materially not quite accessible as it was to the first Japanese translators, neither did *Beowulf* remain a mere expedient pastiche of shadowy sources to its first Chinese translators. The poem, together with other perceived canons of foreign literatures, was deeply integrated in the searching and diversifying national projects in modern Asia as it was in the West. But imagining and negotiating with it in Chinese was a singular hermeneutic experience. Both Zheng Zhenduo and Liang Zhipan inevitably asked why there was no epic in the Chinese literary tradition. Zheng Zhenduo, perhaps predictably, sought to find an equivalent in historical Chinese folk literature. He claimed to have found it in *tanci* (plucking rhymes), a form of music-accompanied story telling in the local language of the Yangtze River Delta ("Yanjiu Zhongguo wenxue de xin tujing" 'New course for the study of Chinese literature', 1927: 290-91). He then went on to compile an unprecedented history of Chinese popular literature (*Zhongguo suwenxue shi* 1938) as well as an illustrated history of Chinese literature (*Chatuben Zhongguo wenxue shi* 1932). Incorporated in both were liberal discussions of *tanci* and other vernacular performing literature that challenged the Chinese and even western standards of legitimate literary studies. The overzealous search for China's foundational literature betrays the modernist-nationalist-essentialist subject. But the epic-question is an authentic one, anticipating more discordant and stimulating reflections on the relation between literature, identity, and cultural modeling (Wang, C. H. 1975: 25-26; Mair 1995: 251-52; Owen 2007: 1390-91).

It is in this context of international Anglo-Saxon scholarship that the early Chinese modernist translations of *Beowulf* take on additional political and cultural meanings. Both Zheng Zhenduo and Liang Zhipan had to work with limited and mostly recycled materials on *Beowulf*. But their restricted and chance access to resources was only one of several factors that shaped the initial translation and reception of *Beowulf* in China. The global spread of modernity and Eurocentric learning, the nationalistic motives of *Beowulf* scholarship at the time, and not least the indigenous translators' own politics and appropriation of Anglo-Saxonism all had profound impacts on the outcome. From here, where would the next Chinese transitions of *Beowulf* go? While, for instance, the language barriers did not let up, how would *Beowulf* continue to test the strategies of foreignizing vs. domesticating translation — an issue at the core of a major literary debate during the late 1920s and early 1930s that had put not only the integrity but also the subjectivity of the translated text at stake? With regard to *Beowulf*, one might ask, what strategies were available to render such defining elements of the Anglo-Saxon poem as compounds, kennings, litotes, paratactic syntax, and interlaced structure? In what way might the resulting foreignizing or domesticating translations serve their audience, and who were the people they claimed to serve? Eva Hung (2001) also highlights the significant role the government has played throughout the Chinese history of translation. When the choice of texts and the translator's strategies are examined against the institutionalized policy, the nature of the translated works can indeed become ambiguous.

3. Chen Guohua (1959), Yan Yuanshu (1983/1974), and Liang Shiqiu (1985)

The three *Beowulf*-translations of the second period represent some of the historical responses to the issues raised above. At this stage, plot summary or paraphrase was no longer enough as an end product of translation; all three translators were also much more forthright about the source texts for their works. In addition, as increased attention was paid to the poem itself, the translators had become more specific about their intended readers as well. This concern for the local audience's needs has its political and cultural ramifications and deeply influences the use of Chinese as a translating language. In 1959, Chen Guohua published the first complete Chinese translation of *Beowulf* in Beijing. Based on David Wright's *Beowulf: a Prose Translation*, his is also rendered in a plain, denotative language intended for young and general readers. The next two translations by Yan Yuanshu and Liang Shiqiu were published in Taiwan in 1983 and 1985 respectively (Yan Yuanshu's is a substantial expansion of an earlier essay that first came out in 1974). Both of these works are partial verse translations intended for academic as well as general use. Yan Yuanshu's rendering of selected passages from *Beowulf* follows Charles W. Kennedy's translation, *Beowulf, the Oldest English Epic*. These passages are interspersed in an extended critical analysis of *Beowulf* and presented in a unique dual-language form with the Chinese translation following the corresponding verses from Kennedy's text. Liang Shiqiu's translation is based on John Duncan Spaeth's verse rendition of 2,807 out of the total 3,182 lines of *Beowulf*. The translation follows Spaeth's formal arrangement in all details from the numbered fitts, their supplied subtitles, to the brief summaries of the omitted lines.

While these translations are necessarily conditioned by their modern English sources, far more choices are made on the end of the translating language that suggest the translators' own pressing concerns regarding their respective projects. Chen Guohua's translation is a case in point. Bypassing Wright's "Introduction", Chen supplies his own "Foreword," in which he explains the reason for his choice of the base text. In particular, it was hoped that the translation in straightforward prose would better serve his intended young and general audience (Chen, Guohua 1959: 17). On the other hand, Chen's previous experience with translating dramatic texts such as *The Trojan Women* (1938) and *Field Marshal Suvorov* (1946) by I. Bakhterev and A. Razumovsky also appears conducive to the rendition of important speeches in *Beowulf*. Dramatic dialogues, for instance, come alive in his mannered but evocative colloquial rendering of the flyting between Unferth and Beowulf. The coastguard, who has initiated this series of verbal challenges, holds his own ground as another memorable character. The positive effect is achieved in part through the strategic use of regional speech in Chinese. Take the translation of "spear" for example. Chen Guohua adopts an unusual Chinese compound to render Wright's "spear" as *touqiang* 投槍, literally 'thrusting spear' (javelin). Otherwise obscure, the term is a favorite of Lu Xun and is used in conjunction with another term, *bishou* 匕首 ('dagger') in a 1933 article. In "Xiaopinwen de weiji" ('The crisis of familiar essays'), Lu Xun criticizes the light essays cultivated by some of his contemporary writers for being petty, morally complacent, and irrelevant to the immediate modernity project in China. He argues that essay writing, which has played a vital role in modern Chinese literary and political revolutions, must and can only thrive in its assumed social functions, like *bishou* and *touqiang* ('dagger' and 'javelin'), relentlessly sharp and critically piercing. Chen Guohua's resort to the highly descriptive Chinese compound suggests shrewd perception of the literary and political currency of Lu Xun's famed construct, thereby projecting his translation of *Beowulf* as a relevant literary undertaking for modern China. This and other examples of taking a calculated chance on local lexicon (prominent also in his vivid rendering of Beowulf's homecoming voyage) stand out especially in light of the debatable underplaying principles of Wright's translation that, as a rule, suppresses compounds, kennings, and otherwise unfamiliar poetic phraseology of the Old English poem (Wright 1957: 21-25).

In Chen's own "Foreword", the conspicuous disavowal of the fantastic, heavy emphasis on social realism, and constant references to Soviet communist ideas about "Renmin de wenxue" ('people's literature') also lend special historicity to his construal of *Beowulf*. Quoting Nikolai Chernyshevsky, Chen Guohua concludes that *Beowulf* comes through centuries as "a living textbook" relevant to the modern people in modern China (1959: 17). Read in this context, the translation appears to have come out under tremendous ideological pressures and possibly government-backed constraints. Eva Hung's observation (2001) on the state control on translation cannot be more relevant here. Similarly, in a separate review, Li Yao-chung (2003) calls attention to the problem of overt ideological dogmatism in the Chinese translations of European medieval literature throughout most of the twentieth century. It is, however, also worth noting that Chen Guohua's translation engages Wright's text imaginatively and, at its best, is able to build on it, catching a rhetorical anastrophe here, subtle litotes there, and, in between, plenty of dignified colloquial drama and fantastic landscape, almost despite the "Foreword". Prior to the onset of the Cultural Revolution, the latter part of the 1950s is identified by Sun Zhili as a particularly productive period for Chinese translation of English and American literatures. Among others, he highlights the achievements of Fang Zhong who revised and re-published in 1955 his prose translations of *The Canterbury Tales* and *Troilus and Criseyde*, an immense task initiated and carried out from the 1930s through 1940s (Sun 1996: 5; 75-76; 94-97). Given only a bibliographical mention in Sun Zhili's study (1996: 37) and not even making it to Li Yao-chung's checklist, Chen Guohua's rendition of *Beowulf* nonetheless fits well alongside that spurt of Chinese literary translation in the late 1950s.

Different translation strategies and cultural-political positions are employed in Yan Yuanshu's and Liang Shiqiu's verse renditions of *Beowulf* published in Taiwan in the 1980s. Each of these works belongs to a much larger translation and editorial project that aimed to produce a multi-volume anthology of English literature in Chinese. For their respective projects, Yan Yuanshu and Liang Shiqiu selected, compiled, and translated all of the English literary works in the anthologies. But their similarities end here. Of the earlier generation of the May Fourth new literature movement, Liang Shiqiu first distinguished himself as a rising literary critic by rebuffing what he saw as the subjective (affective) and objective (empirical) fallacies in the literary views of his more politically driven contemporary. Literary criticism, as he wrote in a 1927 essay, should instead be reason-based and concern the common and essential matter of humanity ("Wenxue piping bian" 'On literary criticism', 1927: 4). This narrative of universal humanism in turn governs his literary reading, his selections from the English literature for translation, and, most importantly, his view on the art of translation itself. To him, sense is the paramount task of the translator, and its delivery demands both denotative and domesticating translation strategies.

Of a younger generation of the émigré intellectuals, Yan Yuanshu was first and foremost instrumental in revolutionizing the studies of English language and literature in Taiwan after he became, in 1969, chair of the Department of Foreign Languages and Literatures at the National Taiwan University. Two unusual items of his curricular reform, which were modeled in full or in part outside the NTU campus, have had an especially enduring impact on later scholars in Taiwan across a wide range of language and literary fields. First, the credit hours of the course on the English literary history were doubled, making it a two-year 12-credit-hour study for English majors. Second, besides American Literature, European Literature, Shakespeare, and genre studies, Chinese Literature became a required two-year 12-credit-hour subject as well. Chinese-western comparative literature was also to be established in the early 1970s as a most electrifying new field of studies in his department. It is in this context that, in post-1949 Taiwan during those self-asserting decades of the 1960s and 1970s, English Language and Literature Studies was rigorously expanding itself as a discipline, curiously de-centered and intellectually border-crossing. It is also in this context that Yan Yuanshu began to publish a series of critical essays in Chinese introducing major English literary works. Among them, the inaugural 1974 essay on *Beowulf* contains the first extended verse rendition of the Anglo-Saxon poem in Chinese based on a modern English translation. Taken together, this series of articles became the foundation of Yan Yuanshu's anthologizing project.

As stated in the preface, Yan Yuanshu's main purpose was to render a history of English literature that is written from a local perspective and answers the specific needs of readers of the Chinese language (Yan 1983; 1987: ii-v). These objectives, driven by a dialectic of the local and global, influence the selection, discussion, and physical layout of his anthology of English medieval literature. Take the chapter on *Beowulf* for example. On account of the projected needs of the audience, the Modern English-Chinese dual-language form is employed for textual accessibility. This deliberate formal arrangement has practical and hermeneutic significance. It not only facilitates but also complicates the reception of the foreign poem in the intertextual space where the authority of the translations in both

English and Chinese are put on hold, allowing significance to play out through the delay of signification. The ensuing close reading of the translated passages also shows the attempt to engage the poem critically via a New Critical approach. The results may be mixed, but it is in this and other important ways that Yan Yuanshu and Liang Shiqiu have produced markedly different verse translations of *Beowulf*, despite both appearing around the same time and targeting the same academic and general readership in Taiwan.

The disparity, it should be noted, is brought about not so much by the different choices of modern English source texts as by the translators' own specific ways of using them. In principle, Yan Yuanshu, in part bound by the dual-language format, follows Kennedy's syntax more deliberately than Liang Shiqiu does Spaeth's. As a result, his translation, although twice removed, retains more pronouncedly than Liang Shiqiu's — or any other available Chinese translations — the salient appositive and paratactic characteristics of the Anglo-Saxon poem. This engagement with the source text goes deep to the lexical level. Kennedy's attention to diction is surely a factor. But a comparison of the translations by Kennedy and Spaeth shows that Kennedy is in fact more willing to be expedient and creative than Spaeth. Consider *middangeard* of 751b, for instance. While Kennedy renders it as "all the earth," Spaeth has "midearth." In turn, Yan Yuanshu, following Kennedy, has it as "zhengge diqiu" ('the whole earth', 1983; 1987: 188; 189) and Liang Shiqiu, glossing over Spaeth, has it as "shijian" ('the world', "Bei ao wu fu" Beowulf 1985: 48). Yan Yuanshu had no choice but to pass up the conceptual implication of "a land in the middle (of encircling ocean)" in *middangeard*, but Liang Shiqiu might have caught it. The compound and kenning *beadoleoma* in 1523a from the fight with Grendel's mother offers another example. Both Kennedy and Spaeth have it as "battle-flasher" for sword. One recalls that in 1934 Liang Zhipan, who must have followed his unidentified source text closely, had it as "zhanguang" ('battle-light'). Yan Yuanshu, also generally staying close to his source, renders the compound as "hanguang jian" (literally 'chill-light sword', 1983; 1987: 198; 199). It is true that, in the metaphorical context of the Old English kenning, the light is conceived as quite warm, such as that of a torch, which might be put out when the battle turns bleak for the user of the flashing sword. But "hanguang jian", a sword of icy gleam, is cognitively more congenial to the Chinese imagination of such a weapon wielded in a battle of injured pride and hushed pain. It at least tactfully plays with the idea of light. This light goes out completely when Liang Shiqiu translates "battle-flasher" as mere "wuqi" ('weapon', "Bei ao wu fu" Beowulf, 1985: 84). The point is not which translation is more faithful: They both are. But they are so in significantly different styles.

Back in 1929-1930, Liang Shiqiu and Lu Xun were engaged in a series of debates propelled by ideological as well as aesthetical concerns over the latter's partiality for foreignizing literal translation. Lu Xun's "hard translation", Liang Shiqiu criticized, often stretches the syntax of the Chinese sentences to such a point that they cease to make sense ("Lun Lu Xun xiansheng de 'yingyi'" 'On Mr. Lu Xun's "hard translation"', 1929: 67-68). The question about syntax and sense is an acute one. But Lu Xun quickly connects it to the social and ethical issues in translation, retorting that the sort of smooth sensible translation Liang expounds only perpetuates the kind of literature enjoyed by a privileged bourgeois class incapable of discerning the bias of power structure in their claims of propriety and pleasure ("'Yingyi' yu 'wenxue de jieji xing'" "'Hard translation" and the class of literature', 1930: 87-88). By contrast, his own hard translation is meant to be annoying, with the hope of shocking the readers into cultural and political consciousness of difference. Unfamiliar borrowed syntax, he maintains, is integral to this hermeneutic experience. It also forces the Chinese language to explore uncharted territories of sentence structures and lexical construct, and thereby to frustrate routine thought habits and remain message-oriented ("'Yingyi' yu 'wenxue de jieji xing'" "'Hard translation" and the class of literature', 1930: 80; 82-83).

By foregrounding the discursive effect of language, this series of debates intensely complicates the issue of syntax and sense in translation. It shows that while translation entails at every turn an arduous search for semantic and linguistic equivalents, the translingual struggle neither begins nor ends there. Negotiating between languages, translation makes palpable what is cognitively and politically no longer or not yet present in the target culture. It involves ambivalent exchanges that come to define a complex subject position for the translation. For this reason, Lu Xun insists on reflecting on the communities the work of translation serves as well as those it ignores. He attacks Liang Shiqiu and his literary circle for their bourgeois aesthetics and apathy to the socially disadvantaged. But the controversy runs deep. Differences in ideologies and literary taste may have compelled Liang Shiqiu to question whom Lu Xun's hard translation hopes to serve, considering its eccentric use of Chinese syntax compounded by excessively foreignized diction. On the flip side, his essay also interrogates aptly whom Lu Xun's translation might in fact alienate. Consider, for instance, the domestic sub-audiences, or mainly Lu Xun's own intended audience among the urban working class. Far from homogenous, this social group is overwhelmingly diversified by local languages with markings of regionalism as well as trades. It thus becomes clear that even Lu Xun stands to lose his case for the political and epistemological edge of, not just his foreignizing translation, but also the resultant modern vernacular Chinese as a literary, translating, and ultimately national language. What the debates between Liang Shiqiu and Lu Xun come to show are the complex sub-language groups that vernacular Chinese either overlooks or is yet to serve.

This lapse has also been linked to the central premise of the May Fourth new literature movement in which vernacular Chinese was categorically pitched against classical Chinese. Each was assumed to be monolithic and independent of the other, each unproblematically claimed to represent the mass/newly enlightened/modern vis-à-vis the elite/intellectually unprogressive/past, hence one to uphold, the other to erase. These assumptions could come back and haunt the May Fourth advocates of Chinese modernity. Ironic and particularly troubling, for instance, are Lu Xun's famed speeches discussed earlier, that he delivered in Hong

Kong in 1927. Again in "Wusheng de zhongguo" ('Silent China'), modern vernacular Chinese, while not receptive to the rich traditions of the local language and literature of Hong Kong and indifferent to the colonial experience of the local community, was assumed to represent the voice of its people and championed as such. By no means, however, is the haunting described above unique to modern vernacular Chinese as a national language. The problem resides in the very postulation of a standard national language, whose need and capacity to suppress both non-mainstream native voices and alien noises have made modernity projects alarmingly traumatic worldwide. The case proves to be especially aggravating throughout the Sinophone regions as within either a particularly multilingual location such as Hong Kong and Taiwan or a given dialect area such as Beijing, Shanghai, Chongqing and Chengdu, numerous local languages and prolific subcultures of long histories co-exist (Gunn 2006: 3-5, Conclusion, and passim). To confront this linguistic complexity at both the macro and micro levels with knowledge in hindsight of the twentieth-first century is to acknowledge the inner inconsistency of the ideology of anti-imperialist nationalism and its violent regressive politics on language. The struggles of modern vernacular Chinese continue. Particularly useful is to recognize its past and evidently continuous interpenetrations with classical Chinese on the one hand and local languages on the other hand, while translation serves as a vital third site for the production of this heterogeneous vernacular.

4. Feng Xiang (1992), Chen Caiyu (1999), and Li Funing (2005/06)

The three Chinese translations of *Beowulf* of the third group present the continuous transformative drive of modern vernacular Chinese against the backdrop of political and economic changes in the post-cold war, post-socialist China and concurrent international Anglo-Saxon studies. The significance of Feng Xiang's translation (1992) goes beyond the distinction that his is the first, and remains the only direct Chinese translation of the Old English poem. To make the Anglo-Saxon poem accessible in translation to a national audience, the educational opportunities, institutional supports, market economy, popular interest, and not least a mass language must be in place. These complex prerequisites have challenged the Chinese modernization movement since it began in the late nineteenth century. The publication of Feng Xiang's direct translation of *Beowulf* thus represents an extraordinary breakthrough of this process. The translation is based on the 3rd edition of Klaeber's *Beowulf* and the revised edition of Charles L. Wrenn and W. F. Bolton. It displays, and often surpasses many successful aspects of the previous translations, thanks to Feng Xiang's deliberate negotiation for key Old English poetic tropes. Knowledge of the original OE text, for example, adds precision and sophistication to his rendering of compounds and kennings. It is true that, like many of the past examples, these are often represented through verbose explanatory paraphrases, such as 佩帶金環的丹麥人 *peidai jinhuan de danmairen* 'Danes who wore gold rings' for *Hring-Dene* 'Ring-Danes' of 116b, and by direct naming, such as 身軀 *shenqu* 'body-trunk' for *bāncofan* 'bone-house' of 1445a and 戰劍 *zhanjian* 'battle-sword' for *beadoleoma* 'battle-light' of 1523a. There are nonetheless abundant examples that strike up intelligent, succinct metaphorical equivalents, such as 利劍交鋒 *lijian jiaofeng* 'crossing of the sharp edges of swords' for *sweorda gelāc* 'sword-play' of 1040a and *ecga gelācum* 'edge-play' of 1168a.

On the prosodic front, Feng Xiang, joining all other Chinese translators, decided from the outset to attempt at neither a systematic representation of the four-beat alliterative measures of the OE poem nor its elevated classic diction (1992: 2-3). The decision is regrettable, but it is a choice on the whole coherent with Feng Xiang's other translating strategies, and ultimately points to his interpretation of *Beowulf*. The most immediate impact of this decision is on the accelerated cadence and familiar tone of the rendered poem. This effect is further reinforced when the paratactic, appositive, and interlaced structures of the original text are substantially reduced to either accentuate other literary effects or allow control over the length of a given line and total line count of a given passage. The rendition of Grendel's approach to Heorot in lines 720-27 is a good example:

```
720  Cōm þā tō recede       rinc sīðian
     drēamum bedǣled.       Duru sōna onarn
     fȳrbendum fæst,        syþðan hē hire folmum (æt)hrān;
     onbrǣd þā bealohȳdiġ,  ðā (hē ġe)bolgen wæs,
     recedes mūþan.         Raþe æfter þon
725  on fāgne flōr          fēond treddode,
     ēode yrremōd;          him of ēagum stōd
     liġġe ġelīcost         lēoht unfæġer.
```

[To the hall came journeying the warrior [Grendel],
bereft of joys. The door quickly gave way,
bound fast by the fire-forged bands, after he, with his hands, touched it, [and]
hostile, swung open — as he was enraged —
the hall's mouth. Immediately after that
on the fair shining floor the fiend treaded [and]
went angrily; from his eyes issued,
most like fire, a light not fair.]

720   這被剝奪了歡樂的罪犯
       大步逼近鹿廳。那由鐵環扣緊的

大門，一碰上他的魔爪便倒了。

他殺氣騰騰，野性發作

一下衝進大殿，踏上彩磚地板。

725 這怪物惡狠狠四下掃視，

眼睛裏閃爍出陰森森的光芒，

活像兩團火焰。

[This joy-deprived criminal

with giant strides closed in on Heorot. That iron-ringed fast-locked

door, upon the touch of his devilish claws, collapsed.

He, with a boiling intent to kill and his wild nature unleashed,

instantly barged into the great hall, [and] stomped on the color-stoned floor.

This monster viciously scanned the four corners [of the hall];

his eyes flared with frigid eerie lights,

Verily two shafts of flames.]

The focus of the translated passage is clearly on the bursting energy of Grendel's entry into Heorot, one that is violent, unstoppable, and only presently checked by the description of the intruder's gaze of terror. To achieve the effect, the interlaced structure of the original lines, which works to disrupt this entry several times before Grendel is finally inside Heorot, has to be streamlined. Most prominent is the loss of the further description of Grendel's swinging the door open, possibly a second door to the great hall, and with it the reference to this second or interior entrance as Heorot's mouth. On the other hand, the enjambment in lines 721-22 is so conspicuous that it not only carries the reading rapidly onward, but also calls attention to the juxtaposition between the invisible force of the touch of Grendel's hands and the visible giving way of the door. Furthermore, there is no "vicious scanning" of Heorot in the Old English text. This added detail and all other changes made throughout this passage are used to highlight Grendel's unapologetic assault. One could argue, however, if as rendered, Grendel has been revealed too swiftly and too vividly. The original passage, as Michael Lapidge suggests, might aim for horror of a different kind, of a formless phantasmic monster, of unnamed unhappy emotions lurking half-intelligibly beneath the frustrating compound-complex sentences, and manifest in nothing specific except for the uncanny light in the monster's eyes (1993: 391-94). But Feng Xiang's forte is in rendering a spirited heroic narrative, and using concerted, if reworked, poetic images to anchor crucial passages. Where he takes considerable liberty to rearrange syntax, taking off or adding details, he also makes random but strategic use of essential Old English poetic features. The enjambment discussed above is a case in point; so are the re-created two half-lines in lines 723 and 724 and paratactic structure of lines 725 and 726. All of these techniques are available and prominent in the Chinese language and literary traditions as well.

More problematic is the next translation by Chen Caiyu (1999). The translation cites John Porter's 1991 edition and word-for-word translation of *Beowulf* as its main reference. However, Chen Caiyu tends to ignore the significance of the former and peculiarity of the latter so much so that the translation eventually bears no distinct relationship to Porter's edition and literal translation. Even Grendel is overwhelmed by the confusing translating tactics. The mighty one's entry into Heorot in lines 720-27 reads:

720 被剝奪了歡樂的怪物爬行著
     來到大廳。鐵環緊扣的大門
     被他用手一碰就搖晃起來，
     他於是殺氣騰騰地把門拉開，
     然後就怒氣沖沖地踏上
725 閃閃發光的地板。他的眼睛
     像一團燃燒的火焰，發出
     惡濁的光芒。

> [The joy-deprived monster came crawling
> to the great hall. The iron-ringed fast-locked door,
> upon the touch of his hand, began to shake.
> He then, with a boiling intent to kill, pulled the door open,
> [and] after that, with fuming rage, stomped on
> the shiny gleaming floor. His eyes,
> resembling a shaft of burning flames, gave off
> evil hazy light.]

From the beginning the translation appears to stumble over Porter's "creeping" for *sīðian* of 720b, and thus Grendel is seen 爬行 *paxing* 'crawling' toward the great hall. It is also unclear how Porter's "gave way" for *onarn* of 721b ends up as 搖晃 *yaohuang* 'shake' in Chen's line 722, or how "light unlovely" for *lēoht unfæger* of 727b becomes 惡濁的光芒 *ezhuo de guangmang* 'evil hazy light' in Grendel's eyes. But most disconcerting is how nearly every line of this passage appears to have built around Feng Xiang's translation, adopting its key lexical and phrasal constructs as well as the rearranged syntax. And such examples of imitation abound. On the other hand, the translation might have aimed to restore many of the local details missing in Feng Xiang's translation. But the project is crippled by its own unwarranted alteration and expansion of the poem, showing a lack of adequate grasp of the source and reference texts in both English and Chinese.

While Porter's edition is also cited as a reference source for Li Funing's partial prose rendition of *Beowulf* (2005/2006), his meticulous work is evidently largely based on E. T. Donaldson's prose translation (1966) in *The Norton Anthology of English Literature*, of which a 1993 edition is also listed as a reference. In the introduction to his translation, Li Funing takes special note of the sophisticated use of enjambments and the rhetorical mixture of long and short sentences in *Beowulf* (2005/6: 32-33), and his prose translation attends to this characteristic of the OE poem with remarkable dexterity. Grendel's approach to Heorot in lines 720-27 is rendered as follows:

這個失去了歡樂的怪物來到了大廳前面。當他用雙手輕推大廳用爐火煅造的箍帶加固起來的大門時，大門馬上讓路。罪惡的慾望驅使著他，他心裡充滿了怨恨。他用力把大廳的嘴撕開，打開了大廳的門。進入大廳後，這個凶惡的敵人就憤怒地踏上了發亮的地板。從他的雙目中射出一種難看的光亮，最和火焰相似。

(Li Funing 2005/6: 36)

[This joy-bereft monster came in front of the great hall. When he, with both hands, lightly pushed the great hall's door [that had been] fastened by fire-forged bands, the door immediately gave way. Evil desires drove him on; his heart was filled with rancor. He forcefully tore open the mouth of the great hall, opening the great hall's door. Upon entering the great hall, this vicious foe stepped wrathfully onto the shining floor. From both of his eyes emitted an ugly glow, most similar to a flame.]

[Cf. Donaldson 1966; 1979: 41: The creature deprived of joy came walking to the hall. Quickly the door gave way, fastened with fire-forged bands, when he touched it with his hands. Driven by evil desire, swollen with rage, he tore it open, the hall's mouth. After that the foe at once stepped onto the shining floor, advanced angrily. From his eyes came a light not fair, most like a flame.]

Throughout this passage Li Funing takes pains to retain the OE paratactic structures, its compounds, and striking embedding of sentence units of varying length and grammatical weight. Often the description of an action or the great hall takes precedence over that of the actor. The center of attention is not Grendel but his aggression, one that is sensed incoherently, repeatedly, like a nightmare difficult to wake up from. And all this while the door has to be opened (and fails to open, it seems) three times in three different ways until the intruder is finally shown. Even then the attention is quickly fixed on the flickering, ugly glint in the intruder's eyes. This overall effect of muffled, ambiguous horror differs substantially from that of Feng Xiang's energetic dramatic rendition. Their difference is unusual and unexpected in that although both translators are obliged to make significant syntactical changes and rearrange the line sequence, Li Funing's indirect translation remains closer to the original poem than Feng Xiang's direct translation.

Beowulf's fight with the fire-breathing dragon in lines 2569-80a provides another noteworthy example of Li Funing's tenacious translation.

```
       Ġewāt ðā byrnende        ġebogen scrīðan,
2570   tō ġescipe scyndan.      Scyld wēl ġebearg
       līfe ond līċe        læssan hwīle
       mærum þēodne         þonne his myne sōhte,
       ðær hē þȳ fyrste,        forman dōgọre
       wealdan mōste        swā him wyrd ne ġescrāf
2575   hrēð æt hilde.       Hond up ābræd
       Ġēata dryhten,       gryrefāhne slōh
       inċgelāfe,       þæt sīo ecg ġewāc
       brūn on bāne,        bāt unswīðor
       þonne his ðīodcyning     þearfe hæfde,
2580   bysigum ġebæded.
```

[Then came the burning one, coiled, slithering,
rushing to his fate. The shield protected well
the life and limb of the famous lord
for less time than he might have wished
if he, on that occasion for the first time in his life,
might prevail without fate assigning to him
glory in battle. Up [he] raised his hand
the Geatish prince, [and] stroke the horrible variegated one
with his heirloom sword in such a way that the edge failed,
bright against the bone, bit less strongly
than the folk-king had need of
hard-pressed by distress.]

隨後惡龍盤曲成火焰，在地面上滑行，急速走向它的命運。
堅實的盾牌保護著那位聲名彰著的君主的生命和身體，
但是這種情況比他預期的時間要短。在他一生當中，那還是第一次，也是第一天，
他沒有取勝，因為命運之神沒有把戰場上的榮譽分配給他。
業亞特人的君主舉起他的手，用鍛造成的利劍猛擊那發亮的怪物，但是

刀鋒沒有起作用，光閃閃地停留在龍骨上，沒有像危難中人民的君主所期望的那樣刺入龍身。

(Li Funing 2005/6: 52)

[Then the vicious dragon coiled in fiery flames, gliding on the ground, marching swiftly to its fate. The solid shield protected the renowned lord's life and body, but this condition [lasted] for a shorter time than he had anticipated. That was the first time in his life, also the first day when he was not victorious, for the deity of fate did not assign battle glory to him. The Geats' lord raised his hand, using a forged, keen sword to hack fiercely at that shiny monster, but the blade did not do the work, stayed gleaming on the dragon's bone, did not, as the folk-king in peril had expected, pierce into the dragon's body.]

[Cf. Donaldson 1966; 1979: 72-73: Then, coiling in flames, he came gliding on, hastening to his fate. The good shield protected the life and body of the famous prince, but for a shorter while than his wish was. There for the first time, the first day in his life, he might not prevail, since fate did not assign him such glory in battle. The lord of the Geats raised his hand, stuck the shining horror so with his forged blade that the edge failed, bright on the bone, bit less surely than its folk-king had need, hard-pressed in perils.]

In this passage Li Funing follows Donaldson's rendition quite closely. Especially significant and effective are the increasingly lengthened sentences that describe the dragon's movement, the failing of the hero's shield, and then that of his heirloom sword. The syntactical division of this passage into four sentences could alternatively use only three sentences when *ð*ǣ*r* of 2573a is read, not as an adverb "there," but as a conjunction "if" (cf. Klaeber 2008: 250-51). Either way, these large syntactical units are integral to the poetic effects of the passage. The battle represents a distressful occasion for Beowulf, bringing about a deeply regretful day. Juxtaposed with the dragon — the emblem of the adversary in heroic narratives — is the crumbling of everything vital to a heroic life. Now his shield and sword give in, soon later his fleeing retainers. Beowulf's own dwindling fighting ability is suggested by not only the overwhelming syntax of the verses but also the emphatic descriptions of the sword, bright, yet no longer biting, outmatched by the dragon's bone. Such is the effect of *brūn on bāne* of 2578a. Li Funing makes the darkly shining blade hold out just a bit longer and its lack of performance sting a bit deeper by replacing the locative preposition *on* with a verb phrase 停留在 *tingliu zai*, literally, 'stop and stay on'.

Feng Xiang's translation of the same passage of the fight with the dragon reads:

接著它張開萬片火鱗
2570   一撲而上，迫近了它自己的命運。
不幸，王公的鐵盾給予他生命和肢體的

掩護，稍遜他心中的期望。
第一次，也是末一次，
他必須以死相拼。命運
2575 沒有賜他凱旋而還的機會。
老王揮起祖傳的古劍，砍向
可怖的鱗甲。不料閃亮的利刃
沒有咬開骨鎖，危急關頭
寶劍辜負了噩運纏身的領袖。

[Then it opened ten thousand fiery scales
prancing forward, closing in on its own fate.
Unfortunately, the lord's iron shield gave his life and limb
less cover than his heart had expected.
For the first time, also the last time,
He had to wrestle with his life. Fate
Did not grant him the chance for a triumphant return.
The old king swung an ancient heirloom sword, slashing onto
The horrible bony scales. Unexpectedly, the shining keen blade
Did not bite open the bone locks; at that perilous moment,
The prized sword failed the leader besieged by evil fate.]

In comparison to Li Funing, Feng Xiang again allows much more extensive global and local changes of the original text. In particular, sentences are kept short throughout this passage, *brūn on bāne* of 2578a, gone, while explanatory metadiscourse such as "unfortunately" and "unexpectedly", added, making the failing of the weapons instant and final. Perhaps most astonishing of all is his reworking of lines 2569 and 2570a, recasting the fire-breathing dragon's coiling, gliding, and advancing movement into an all-out suicidal leap and the opening of "ten thousand fiery scales." If the rendition is audacious, the emphatic descriptions of the dragon's scales in these lines and line 2577 (可怖的鱗甲 *kebu de linjia*, 'horrible bony scales' for *gryrefāhne*) also use variations creatively. Added to these, it should be noted, is Feng Xiang's unusual reading of line 2568b *hē on searwum bād* just before the cited passage. The subject *hē* is taken to refer to, not Beowulf, but the dragon. The verse is therefore rendered to describe the creature 在鱗甲後窺測戰機 *zai linjia hou kuice zhanji*, 'peeking and scheming battle strategies behind his bony scales', i.e., his armor (*searwum*).

5. Conclusion

The different sets of translating strategies used by Li Funing and Feng Xiang have thus produced two very different renditions of *Beowulf*. From these two exemplary works several final observations can be drawn regarding the Chinese translations of *Beowulf* over a period of eighty years:

1. Most of these translations are indirect translations. Among them Li Funing's partial prose rendition stands out for a particular reason. While this translation shows sustained semantic, syntactical, and rhetorical negotiations with the original text via a modern English reference, it uses comparatively few Chinese traditional literary allusions, diction, or four-character idioms. This style of vernacular Chinese compares to that which the May Fourth modernists have envisioned for modern China. It is in this sense that Li Funing's rendition of *Beowulf* reads more "modern" than any other existing translations. Its lucid hard translation overcomes what Liang Shiqiu criticized as horrid foreignization practices in Lu Xun's translation, and what Lu Xun thought hard translation could do (but his own translation did not necessarily accomplish) is achieved by Li Funing's *baihua* vernacular translation of *Beowulf*.

2. As the only Old English-Chinese direct translation of *Beowulf*, Feng Xiang's rendition is at once controversial and thought-provoking: controversial because of its liberal syntactical rearrangements, omission, addition, and reworking of details of the Old English text; thought-provoking because of its original, combined use of Anglo-Saxon poetic tropes and equivalent classical and modern Chinese literary techniques such as parallelism, variation, and imagism, suggesting possibilities for future translation.

3. A historical review of the translations of *Beowulf* in modern vernacular Chinese cannot be concluded, however, without considering their ghosts, the alternate history of what could equally have taken place.
    a. There could have been, for instance, translations of *Beowulf* in classical Chinese, rendered as sensitively and innovatively as those classical renditions of Plato, Aristotle, Homer, Shakespeare, English and American Romantic writers, Voltaire, Ibsen, Rousseau, and Tolstoy published in the 1900s through 1920s by translators such as Lin Shu or members of the *Critical Review* Group who, at the height of the new literature movement, challenged the May Fourth radical view that classical Chinese had lost both literary vigor and political relevancy. When Zheng Zhenduo was translating *Beowulf* and searching for the Chinese foundational literature, Wu Fangji (1896-1932), a poet and one of the *Critical Review* multi-lingual scholars, had an ambitious plan to compose a three-part epic modeled on Dante's *Divine Comedy* in the traditional six-character verse form (Wu 1930: 166-67).
    b. There could also have been introductions and readings of *Beowulf* making informed use of the rich local literary and language resources

such as those in Cantonese and Taiwanese. In the early 1930s, during the same time when Liang Zhipan was editing *Hongdou* in Hong Kong, Su Weixiong (1908-68), a young scholar from Taiwan, was writing modern free-style poems intended to be recited in vernacular Taiwanese. His poems were published in *Formosa*, a subversive, oversea literary magazine for which he also served as editor-in-chief while studying in the English Department of the Tokyo University (Su 1933: 28-31). His nativism, however, and involvement in the new Taiwanese literature movement would prevent him from securing a teaching position after he returned to Taiwan under the Japanese colonial rule (1895-1945). In 1946 he was finally appointed to teach poetry in the English Department (later the Department of Foreign Languages and Literatures) of the National Taiwan University. His last publication *English Prosody* came out in 1967. To illustrate the metrical and rhetorical functions of alliteration in English poetry, he cited not only Old English *Beowulf* but also Taiwanese maxims as supplementary local vernacular examples (Su 1967: 172-80).

Existing translations of *Beowulf* have thus sharpened the home language issue in light of the historically complex make-up of the host culture and local audience. This diversity has complicated both the formation and the creative use of modern vernacular Chinese for translating substantial texts such as *Beowulf*. Suffused, however, with markings of historical language struggles between the past and present, home and foreign, dominant and subaltern, the Old English *Beowulf* also embodies a creative, intense and not infrequently violent literary and cultural translation. There is therefore an uncanny mirroring between the Anglo-Saxon production of *Beowulf* and its Chinese rendition at the core of their complex linguistic contention. Each engages a politically charged vernacular to seek out a diverse local audience during a historical period of intense identity crises, cultural wars, and battlefront conflicts. Viewed in this light, while perhaps not the most-frequented summit among the peaks of the Chinese translations of world literature, *Beowulf* represents nonetheless a worthy, if steep, mountain for the translators to climb.

Chinese translations of Beowulf 1926-2006: a chronological checklist

Xidi (Zheng Zhenduo) 西諦 (鄭振鐸). 1926. "Xite yu pi ao fu er fu" 西特與皮奧伏爾夫 ('Cid and Beowulf'). *Wenxue zhoubao* ('Literature weekly') no. 226 (23 May); reprint in: *Wenxue zhoubao* 文學週報 ('Literature weekly'), Vol. 3, Shanghai: Kaiming Shudian, 1928; Shanghai: Shanghai shudian, 1984, 463-65.

Xidi (Zheng Zhenduo) 西諦 (鄭振鐸). 1927. "Pi ao hu er fu" 皮奧胡爾夫 ('Beowulf'). *Wenxue zhoubao* ('Literature weekly') no. 265 (13 March); reprint in: *Wenxue zhoubao* ('Literature weekly'), Vol.4, Shanghai: Kaiming shudian, 1928; Shanghai: Shanghai shudian, 1984, 443-56.

([Liang]) Zhipan [梁之盤 1934. "Bei ao wu er fu" 貝奧烏爾夫('Beowulf'). *Hongdou man kan*紅豆漫刊 ('Red bean magazine') [Hong Kong], Shijie shishi zhuanhao — zhounian jinian kan世界史詩專號—週年紀念刊(Spec. anniversary issue on world epics) 2.3: n.p.

Chen Guohua陳國樺, trans. 1959. *Pei ou wuo fu*裴歐沃夫('Beowulf'). Beijing: Zhongguo qingnian chubanshe. Based on David Wright, *Beowulf: A Prose Translation*, Bungay, Suffolk: Richard Clay, 1957.

Yan Yuanshu顏元叔, trans. 1983. "Bei ao wu fu" 貝奧武夫 ('Beowulf'), in: *Yingguo wenxue: zhonggu shiqi* 英國文學: 中古時期 ('English Literature: the Middle Ages'). Taipei: Bookman, 1987. 177-214. Based on Charles W. Kennedy, *Beowulf, the Oldest English Epic* (1940). (Cf. Yan Yuanshu顏元叔 1974. "Gudai yingguo wenxue: shishi 'Bei ao wu fu'" 古代英國文學 史詩《貝奧武夫》('Old English literature: the epic "Beowulf"'). *Zhongwai wenxue* (*Chung-Wai Literary Monthly*) 3.6: 179-97.)

Liang Shiqiu梁實秋, trans. 1985. "Bei ao wu fu" 貝奧武夫 ('Beowulf'), in: *Yingguo wenxue xuan*英國文學選 ('Selections in English Literature'). Vol. 1. Taipei: Xiezhi gongye congshu, 3-136. Based on John Duncan Spaeth, "Beowulf," 1911; 1921, in: *British Poetry and Prose, Vol. 1: From Beowulf to Blake*, ed. Paul Robert Lieder, Robert Morss Lovett, and Robert Kilburn Root (1938).

Feng Xiang馮象, trans. 1992. *Bei ao wu fu*貝奧武甫 ('Beowulf'). Beijing: Sanlian. Based on F. Klaeber, ed., *Beowulf and the Fight at Finnsburg*, 3rd ed. (1950) and Charles L. Wrenn, ed., *Beowulf, and the Finnsburg Fragment*. 3rd ed., rev. by W. F. Bolton (1973).

Chen Caiyu陳才宇, trans. 1999. "Bei ao wu fu"貝奧武甫 ('Beowulf'). *Bei ao wu fu, Luolan zhi Ge, Xide zhi Ge, Igeer chuzhengji* 貝奧武甫, 羅蘭之歌, 熙德之歌, 伊戈爾出征記(*Beowulf, Song of Roland, Song of Cid, the Expedition of Igor*). Nanjing: Yilin chubanshe, 1-148. Based on John Porter, ed. and trans., *Beowulf, Text and Translation* (1991); also referencing E. T. Donaldson, trans., "Beowulf" (1996), in: *The Norton Anthology of English Literature*, 3rd ed. (1974).

Li Funing李賦寧, trans. 2005/2006. "Gu yingyu shishi 'Bei ao wu fu'" 古英語史詩《貝奧武甫》 ('The Old English epic "Beowulf"'), in: *Yingguo zhonggu shiqi wenxue shi*英國中古時期文學史 ('The history of the English literature of the middle ages'). Beijing: Waiyu jiaoxue yu yanjiu chubanshe, 28-61. Based on E. T. Donaldson, trans., "Beowulf" (1966), in: *The Norton Anthology of English Literature* [6th ed.] (1993); also referencing John Porter, ed. and trans., *Beowulf, Text and Translation* (1991).

References

Bjork, Robert E.
1997   "Nineteenth-Century Scandinavia and the birth of Anglo-Saxon studies", in: *Anglo-Saxonism and the construction of social identity*, ed. Allen J. Frantzen and John D. Niles. Gainesville, FL: University Press of Florida, 111-32.

Brooke, Stopford A.
1898   "Beowulf, the poem", in: *English literature from the beginning to the Norman conquest*. London: Macmillan, 68-83.

Donaldson, E. T. (trans.)
1966   "Beowulf", in: *The Norton anthology of English literature*, ed. M. H. Abrams et al. rev. ed.; 4th ed. New York: Norton, 1979, 29-83.

Fukuhara, Rintaro
1974   "Mr. William Empson in Japan", in: *William Empson: The man and his work*, ed. Roma Gill. London: Routledge & Kegan Paul, 21-33.

García, José María Rodríguez
2004   "Introduction: Literary into cultural translation", *Diacritics* 34: 3-30.

Guerber, Hélène Adeline
1896 "Beowulf", in: *Legends of the Middle Ages*. Project Gutenberg <http://www.gutenberg.org/etext/12455>.

Gunn, Edward
1991 *Rewriting Chinese, style and innovation in twentieth-century Chinese prose*. Stanford: Stanford University Press.
2006 *Rendering the regional, local language in contemporary Chinese media*. Honolulu: University of Hawaii Press.

Hall, J. R.
2001 "Anglo-Saxon studies in the nineteenth century: England, Denmark, America", in: *A companion to Anglo-Saxon literature*, ed. Phillip Pulsiano and Elaine M. Treharne. Oxford: Blackwell, 434-54.

Hearn, Lafcadio
1938 *A history of English literature*, ed. R. Tanabe and T. Ochiai. Tokyo: Hokuseido.

Hu Shih 胡適
1917 "Wenxue gailiang chuyi" 文學改良芻議 ('A preliminary discussion of literary reform'), in: *Zhongguo xin wenxue daxi* 中國新文學大系 ('Compendium to modern Chinese literature'). Vol. 1. Shanghai: Liangyou, 1935, 34-47.

Hung, Eva
2001 "Rewriting Chinese translation history." <http://www.renditions.org/rct/staff/bio/b.html>.

Imai, Sumiko
2008 "The stylistic features of *Beowulf* and Japanese translation", presented at the panel *Wordum Wrixlan: Anglo-Saxon Poetry in Modern Non-English Translation* during the 43rd International Congress on Medieval Studies, Kalamazoo, MI.

"Juan tou yu" 卷頭語 ('opening remarks')
1934 *Hongdou man kan* 紅豆漫刊 ('Red bean magazine') [Hong Kong], Shijie shishi zhuanhao — zhounian jinian kan 世界史詩專號—週年紀念刊 ('Spec. anniversary issue on world epics') 2.3: n.p.

Kennedy, Charles W. (trans.)
1940 *Beowulf, the oldest English epic, translated into alliterative verse with a critical introduction*. New York: Oxford University Press.

Klaeber, Frederick (ed.)
2008 *Klaeber's Beowulf and the Fight at Finnsburg*. 4th ed. by Robert D. Fulk, Robert E. Bjork & John D. Niles. Toronto: University of Toronto Press [1st ed. 1922; 3rd ed. 1950].

Lapidge, Michael
1993 "*Beowulf* and the psychology of terror", in: *Heroic poetry in the Anglo-Saxon period, studies in honor of Jess B. Bessinger, Jr.*, ed. Helen Damico and John Leyerle. Kalamazoo, MI: Western Michigan University, 373-402.

Li Yao-chung 李耀宗
2003 "Hanyi ouzhou zhonggu wenxue de huigu zhanwang" 漢譯歐洲中古文學的回顧展望 ('Chinese translations of European medieval literature: A retrospect and prospects'). *Guowai wenxue* (jikan) 國外文學 (季刊) (*Foreign Literature Quarterly*) 1: 23-33.

Liang Shiqiu 梁實秋
- 1927 "Wenxue piping bian" 文學批評辯 ('On literary criticism'), in: *Lu Xun yu Liang Shiqiu lunzhan wenxuan* ('Selected literary debates between Lu Xun and Liang Shiqiu'), 1-8.
- 1929 "Lun Lu Xun xiansheng de 'yingyi'" 論魯迅先生的硬譯 ('On Mr. Lu Xun's "hard translation"'), in: *Lu Xun yu Liang Shiqiu lunzhan wenxuan* ('Selected literary debates between Lu Xun and Liang Shiqiu'), 67-70.

Lu Xun 魯迅
- 1925a *Chule xiangya zhi ta* "Houji" 《出了象牙之塔》後記 ('Postscript to *Out of the ivory tower* [a translation of collected essays by Kuriyagawa Hakes]'), in: *LuXun quanji* ('Complete works of Lu Xun'), Vol. 10, 266-76.
- 1925b "Shanagshi" 傷逝 ('Regret for the past'), in: *Lu Xun quanji* ('Complete works of Lu Xun'), Vol. 2, 113-34.
- 1930 "'Yingyi' yu 'wenxue de jieji xing" 硬譯與文學的階級性 ('"Hard translation" and the class of literature'), in: *Lu Xun yu Liang Shiqiu lunzhan wenxuan* ('Selected literary debates between Lu Xun and Liang Shiqiu'), 77-98.
- 1933a "Wusheng de zhongguo" 無聲的中國 ('Silent China'), in: *Lu Xun quanji* ('Complete works of Lu Xun'), Vol. 4, 11-17.
- 1933b "Xiaopinwen de weiji" 小品文的危機 ('The crisis of familiar essays'), in: *Lu Xun quanji* ('Complete works of Lu Xun'), Vol. 4, 590-93.
- 2005 *Lu Xun quanji* 魯迅全集 ('Complete works of Lu Xun'). Beijing: Renmin wenxue chubanshe.

Lu Xun -- Liang Shiqiu
- 1982 *Lu Xun yu Liang Shiqiu lunzhan wenxuan* 魯迅與梁實秋論戰文選 ('Selected literary debates between Lu Xun and Liang Shiqiu'). Ed. Bi Hua. Hong Kong: Tiandi.

Mair, Victor H.
- 1995 "Anthologizing and anthropologizing, the place of nonelite and nonstandard culture in the Chinese literary tradition", in: *Translating Chinese literature*, ed. Eugene Eoyang and Lin Yao-fu. Bloomingdale and Indianapolis: Indiana University Press, 231-61.

Ono, Shigeru
- 2005 "A philological life", in: *Medieval English language scholarship: Autobiographies by representative scholars in our discipline*. Hildesheim; New York: Georg Olms Verlag, 129-43.

Osborn, Marijane
- 1997 "Translations, versions, illustrations", in: *A Beowulf handbook*, ed. Robert E. Bjork and John D. Niles. Lincoln, NB: University of Nebraska Press, 341-72.
- 2003 Annotated list of *Beowulf* translations. ACMRS online resources. Arizona Center for Medieval and Renaissance Studies, Arizona State University. <http://www.asu.edu/clas/acmrs/web_pages/online_resources/online_resources_annotated_beowulf_bib.html>.

Owen, Stephen
- 2007 "Genres in motion", in: *PMLA* 122.5: 1389-93.

Porter, John (ed. and trans.)
- 1991 *Beowulf, text and translation*. Pinner, Middlesex: Anglo-Saxon Books.

Saintsbury, George
1898 "Earliest Anglo-Saxon poetry", in: *A short history of English literature*. London: Macmillan, 1-8.

Sauer, Hans, et al.
2011 *205 years of Beowulf translations and adaptations (1805-2010): A bibliography*. Trier: WVT Wissenschaftlicher Verlag.

Schipper, William -- Tadao Kubouchi
1986 "Old English studies in Japan", *Old English Newsletter* 19: 24-31.

Spaeth, John Duncan (trans.)
1911; 1921 "Beowulf", in: *British poetry and prose, Vol. 1: From Beowulf to Blake*, rev. ed., ed. Paul Robert Lieder, Robert Morss Lovett, and Robert Kilburn Root. Boston: Houghton Mufflin, 1938, 7-34.

Shippey, T. A.
1998 "Introduction", in: *Beowulf, the critical heritage*, ed. T. A. Shippey and Andreas Haarder. London: Routledge, 1-74.

Stanley, Eric Gerald
2000 *The search for Anglo-Saxon paganism: Imagining the Anglo-Saxon past*. Cambridge; Rochester, NY: D.S. Brewer.

Su Weixiong蘇維雄
1933 "Chunye hen" 春夜恨 ('Regrets of a spring night'); "Yakou shiren" 啞口詩人 ('The voiceless poet'), *Formosa* 1: 28-31.
1967 *Yingshi Yunlu Xue* 英詩韻律學 ('English Prosody'). Taipei: The Commercial Press.

Sun Zhili孫致禮
1996 *1949-1968: Woguo yingmei wenxue fanyi gailun* 1949-1968: 我國英美文學翻譯概論 *(1949-1968: On translations of British and American literatures of the PRC)*. Nanjing: Yilin chubanshe.

Tinker, Chauncey Brewster
1903 *The translations of Beowulf, a critical bibliography*. Yale studies in English 16. New York: Holt. [Repr. 1974]

Venuti, Lawrence
1998 *The scandals of translation: Towards an ethics of difference*. New York: Routledge.

Wägner, Wilhelm
1883 "Beowulf", in: *Epics and romances of the Middle Ages*. Adapted by M. W. MacDowall and edited by W. S. W. Anson. Philadelphia: J. B. Lippincott; London, W. Swan Sonnenschein, 347-64.

Wang, C. H.
1975 "Towards defining a Chinese heroism", *Journal of the American Oriental Society* 95: 25-35.

Wang Jiankai王建開
2003 *Wusi yilai woguo yingmei wenxue zuopin yijie shi, 1919-1949* 五四以來我國英美文學作品譯介史, 1919-1949 *(The Translation of British and American Literary Works in China, 1919-1949)*. Shanghai: Waiyu jiaoyu chubanshe.

Wrenn, Charles L. (ed.)
1973 *Beowulf and the Finnsburg Fragment*. 3rd ed., rev. by W. F. Bolton. London: Macmillan; New York: St. Martin's.

Wright, David (trans.)
1957 *Beowulf: A prose translation*. Bungay, Suffolk: Richard Clay; New York: Penguin.

Wu Fangji 吳芳吉
    1930   "Wu Fanji lun shishi jihua shuba" 吳芳吉論史詩計畫書跋 ('Postscript to Wu Fangji's letter on epic and his writing plan for a Chinese epic'), in: *Wu Mi shihua* 吳宓詩話 ('Wu Mi's Remarks on Poetry'). Beijing: The Commercial Press, 2005, 166-68.

Zheng Zhenduo 鄭振鐸
    1927   "Yanjiu Zhongguo wenxue de xin tujing" 研究中國文學的新途徑 ('New course for the study of Chinese literature'). *Zheng Zhenduo quanji* 鄭振鐸全集 ('Complete works of Zheng Zhenduo'). Vol. 6. Beijing: Renmin wenxue chubanshe, 1988, 273-98.
    1932   *Chatuben Zhongguo wenxue shi* 插圖本中國文學史 ('Illustrated history of Chinese literature'). Beijing: Beijing chubanshe, 1999.
    1938   *Zhongguo suwenxue shi* 中國俗文學史 ('History of Chinese popular literature'). Beijing: Dongfang chubanshe, 1996.

Notes on contributors

MARY BLOCKLEY is a Professor in the English Department of the University of Texas at Austin. She is the author of *Aspects of Old English Poetic Syntax: Where Clauses Begin* (2001) Urbana: University of Illinois Press (Illinois Medieval Studies) and of articles on Old English meter and syntax, as well as English linguistics generally, including "Essential Linguistics for Students of the History of the English Language", pp. 18-23 in *Companion to the History of the English Language*, eds. Hal Momma and Michael Matto, Blackwell (2008) and "Speech Acts and Inscriptions: The Syntax of the Right Side of the Auzon/Franks Casket", pp. 171-178 in *More Than Words: English Lexicography and Lexicology Past and Present. Essays Presented to Hans Sauer on the Occasion of this 65th Birthday Part 1*, eds. Renate Bauer and Ulrike Krischke, Peter Lang, 2011. Current projects include papers on medieval vernacular syntax and morphology and the history of the paragraph in vernacular writing before 1800.

JULIA FERNÁNDEZ CUESTA is currently Associate Professor in English Language (History of English) at the University of Seville (Spain). Her main research interest lies in historical dialectology and, in particular, the evolution of Northern English. She has been the principal investigator of two European research projects on the development of northern English and has published widely on the topic. She is also responsible for the compilation of SCONE (The Seville Corpus of Northern English: <http://www.helsinki.fi/varieng/CoRD/corpora/SCONE/index.html>. In addition to studying the resilience of northern features in later varieties of Northern English, she is currently working on syncretism in the nominal morphology in the Lindisfarne gloss as part of a third research project on Northern English.

MARÌA F. GARCÍA-BERMEJO GINER is Associate Professor of English Historical Linguistics at the University of Salamanca, Spain. Her main research interests are English dialectology from the Early Modern English period to the early twentieth centry and the linguistic analysis of English literary dialects and English dialect literature. She is the project leader of the Salamanca Corpus, a digital archive of English dialect texts <http://salamancacorpus.usal.es/SC/index.html>. At the moment it includes 257 texts (over 6 million words) representative of English dialect literature, English literary dialects and glossaries published between 1500 and 1950. She has published extensively on historical English dialectology and the linguistic analysis of British English dialects.

TRINIDAD GUZMÁN-GONZÁLEZ is Associate Professor in the Department of Modern Philology at the University of León, where she teaches history of the

English language, and varieties of English. Her research focuses mainly on historical English phonology and morphology, with particular interest in the theoretical side. Some of her most recent publications about these issues include "Revisiting the revisited: Could we survive without the Great Vowel Shift?" (*Studia Anglica Posnaniensia* 39, 2003); "Out of the past: A walk with labels and concepts, raiders of the lost evidence and a vindication of the role of writing" (*IJES* 5, 2005) and "Assigned gender in 18th-century English prose: a corpus study" (*Creation and use of historical English corpora in Spain*, forthcoming). She also does lexicographical work, both in the elaboration and analysis of lexical databases in specialised registers (with the GRELIC team led by Isabel Verdaguer from Barcelona University) and Anglicisms in Spanish ("The impact of lexical Anglicisms in Spanish film magazines: a case study across time", *Historical Sociolinguistics and Sociohistorical Linguistics* 3, 2003). She has co-edited *SELIM*, the journal of the Spanish Society for Mediaeval English Language and Literature (2004-2011) and currently reviews for a number of publishers, both in Spain and abroad.

YUKO HIGASHIIZUMI received her PhD in English Linguistics from Dokkyo University, Saitama, Japan in 2004. She teaches Japanese as a foreign language at Tokyo Gakugei University and some other universities in Tokyo. She published *From a Subordinate Clause to an Independent Clause: A History of English because-clause and Japanese kara-clause* (Tokyo: Hituzi Syobo, 2006). Her research interests include historical pragmatics, grammaticalization, discourse analysis, and Japanese as a foreign language.

JOHN INSLEY was born in Preston in Lancashire in 1947. From 1967 to 1971, he was a student at Emmanuel College, Cambridge (Historical Tripos Part 1, Anglo-Saxon, Norse and Celtic Tripos as Part 2) and was awarded the degree of BA (Hons) in July 1971. Subsequently, he went on to do research at the University of Nottingham under Kenneth Cameron, the then Hon. Director of the English Place-Name Society, this research leading to his PhD thesis on Scandinavian personal names in Norfolk (1980), which was published by the Gustavus Adolphus Academy in Uppsala in 1994. He is the author of numerous articles on English onomastics and language history and has taught at the University of Erlangen-Nuremberg, the Free University in Berlin and the University of Heidelberg. He was awarded his *Habilitation* by the University of Heidelberg in 2002 and has been *außerplanmäßiger Professor* in Heidelberg since 2007.

KOUSUKE KAITA is a student of the doctoral programme of linguistics *Linguistisches Internationales Promotionsprogramm* (LIPP), Ludwig-Maximilians-Universität München, Germany, and at the graduate school of Humanities and Social Sciences, Chiba University, Japan. His publications include "The historical formation of English auxiliary *ought to* – with special reference to Late OE and

Early ME" (*Studies on Humanities and Social Sciences of Chiba University* 15, 108-116, 2007), "Distribution of OE *mid rihte* as an adverbial of propriety - with special reference to the textual variation" (*Historical Englishes in varieties of texts and contexts*, eds. Masachiyo Amano, Michiko Ogura, and Masayuki Ohkado. Frankfurt am Main: Peter Lang: 2008, 33-47) and "OE preterite-present verb *āgan* - its potential as an auxiliary" (*Cultural Heritage of Germanic Tribes*, ed. Michiko Ogura. Report on Research Project No.183. Graduate School of Humanities and Social Sciences, Chiba University, Japan: 49-74, 2010). He has just completed his doctoral dissertation entitled "Modal auxiliaries from Late Old to Early Middle English - with special reference to *āgan*, *sculan*, and *mōtan*", under the supervision of Prof. Dr. Hans Sauer.

NADĚŽDA KUDRNÁČOVÁ is Associate Professor at the Department of English and American Studies at the Faculty of Arts, Masaryk University, Brno, Czech Republic. Her research interests lie mainly within lexical semantics, cognitive semantics, syntax-semantics interface, construction grammar and psycholinguistics. She has published numerous articles in scholarly journals, collections of papers and conference proceedings. She is the author of the monograph *Directed Motion at the Syntax-Semantics Interface* (2008).

CHRISTOPHER LANGMUIR teaches history of English at the University of Seville (Spain). His main research interests are nineteenth-century philology and the *OED*. He has participated in the compilation of SCONE and is currently working on the multiple glosses in the Lindisfarne gospels.

ANNETTE MANTLIK completed her doctoral dissertation on "The historical development of shell nouns: A diachronic study of abstract noun constructions in English" at Munich University in 2012, where she was a researcher from 2007 to 2010. Mantlik studied philosophy at the Jesuit University of Philosophy in Munich (Bakkalaureat in 2001) and English and Roman Catholic Theology at Munich University (M. A. and Staatsexamen in 2007). Since July 2011, Mantlik has been research assistant to Prof. Beatrix Busse at the Chair of English linguistics at the University of Heidelberg. Her research interests include (historical) pragmatics, (historical) stylistics, construction grammar, (historical) syntax and lexicology. Currently, she is working on her *Habilitation* in historical English linguistics.

CARLA MORINI was Full Professor of Germanic philology at the University of Calabria, where she taught the history of the German language. She also taught at the Universities of Catania and Rome. She was also visiting professor and speaker at many universities and conferences in Italy and Europe (Florence, Naples, Palermo, Bari, Salerno, Venice, Parma, Verona, Manchester, Sevilla, Nizza, Utrecht, Bern, Belfast, etc). Her main interest is Anglo-Saxon language, literature and culture, especially the coat of mail in OE archaeological context, medical remedies, Apollonius of Tyrus, Ælfric of Eynsham's Life of St. Agatha, Life of St.

Lucy, Ælfric's Homilies, thunder and time prognostics, studies of OE words and their context. She is now retired and lives in Umbria, close to Perugia, on a manor named tenuta Poggio San Michele.

FUYO OSAWA is Professor at the Department of English of Hosei University in Tokyo. She received her MA and PhD in Linguistics from University College London. Her main academic interest is explaining syntactic changes, mainly English, within the framework of generative grammar. She has a special interest in the hypothesis that there might be a parallel between first language acquisition and diachronic change. Her work has appeared in the proceedings of various international conferences, periodicals, and books such as "Syntactic parallels between ontogeny and phylogeny", *Lingua* 113/1, 2003, 3-47; "The rise of IPs in the history of English", in *Historical Linguistics 2001* (eds. Blake and Burridge) 2003, 321-337; "The emergence of DP from a perspective of ontogeny and phylogeny", in *Nominal Determination* (eds. Stark, Leiss & Abraham) 2007, 311-337; "The emergence of DP in the history of English: the role of mysterious genitive", in *Historical Linguistics 2007* (eds. Dufresne et al.) 2009, 135-147.

HANS SAUER is Professor Emeritus at the University of Munich (LMU); currently he teaches as professor at the WSZMiJO (or Gallus) in Katowice, and as senior professor at the University of Würzburg. Previous posts and assignments include Eichstätt, Dresden, Innsbruck, Łódź, Palermo, Columbus/Ohio, Brno, Tokyo, Peking, Chongqing, Kuala Lumpur, and others. His research interests and publications include critical editions and studies of Medieval English texts, word-formation, glosses and glossaries, lexicography, plant names, *Beowulf* (especially translations and films), the history of linguistics and of English studies, varieties of English (e.g. advertising language; pidgins and creoles), interjections, twin formulae. He was a co-editor of *Anglia* and of the *Lexikon des Mittelalters*, and he still is a co-editor of *MET* (Middle English Texts) and of TUEPh (Texte und Untersuchungen zur Englischen Philologie); he has also co-edited a number of collective volumes.

CRISTINA SUÁREZ-GÓMEZ is Lecturer of English in the Department of Spanish, Modern and Classical Philology at the University of the Balearic Islands (Spain), and the Principal Investigator of the project "Morphosyntactic variation in New Englishes". In 2004 she received her PhD in English Historical Linguistics from the University of Santiago de Compostela. Her main areas of specialization are English historical syntax, historical pragmatics and dialectal variation in English, both in a synchronic and a diachronic perspective, and paying special attention to contact varieties. Her most relevant publications are about relativization in early English, dialectal variation in early English and grammatical variation in emergent varieties of English.

VERONIKA TRAIDL studied English linguistics and medieval literature, as well as modern English literature and Italian philology at the University of Munich (LMU) and completed her M.A. in 2012. She is currently writing her Ph.D. thesis on *Beowulf* films under the supervision of Prof. Dr. Hans Sauer. Her research interests include historical linguistics and medieval literature, but also the linguistic and cultural influence of Scandinavia on the English language and culture. She contributed to the "Electronic Ælfric Project" under the supervision of Dr. Aaron J. Kleist from Biola University in California and to *English Historical Linguistics 2008: Selected Papers from the Fifteenth International Conference on English Historical Linguistics (ICEHL 15), Munich, 24-30 August 2008, vol. II: Words, Texts, and Genres*, ed. Hans Sauer & Gaby Waxenberger, 2012.

STELLA WANG teaches writing at the University of Rochester in New York. She reads, writes, and publishes in English and Chinese, out of a choice that was profoundly influenced by her literary and academic training at the National Taiwan University, where she studied modernism and 20th-century British and American Literature. Without knowing a single word of Old English, she followed a hauntingly strange phrase first encountered in a translated text, "the greediest ghost" (i.e., fire) from *Beowulf* 1123a, which led her to pursue and eventually complete her doctoral degree in English at the University of Rochester, with concentrations in Old English Poetry and Anglo-Saxon Studies. In her professional work in the College Writing Program and her continuous writing and translation projects she finds coherence – a discovery that is as hard to come by in life as it is in writing, for which she remains awed and deeply thankful.

GABY WAXENBERGER was born in Muehldorf, Germany in 1956. After her studies (German and English) at Munich University, she completed her M.A. in 1984 (Middle English Lyrics of Ms. 2253 Harley) and her Ph.D. thesis (Categorization of Old English Nouns) in 1991. From 1986-2006 she was at the Catholic University of Eichstätt, Germany and worked for the chair of Historical Linguistics and English Medieval Literature. In the academic year of 1987-1988 she taught at the University of London (Westfield College). From 1995-2006 she also worked for the *Old English Runes Project* at the Catholic University of Eichstätt. Since April 2007 she has been teaching at the Department for English and American Studies at LMU Munich. In July 2010 she handed in her habilitation thesis on *Towards a Phonology of Old English Runic Inscriptions and an Analysis of Graphemes*. She is a part of the long-term project *RuneS* (*Runic Writing in the Germanic Languages*), funded by the Union of the German Academies of Sciences and based at the Academy of Sciences in Göttingen. This project includes the research centres at the universities of Kiel, Göttingen, Eichstätt-Ingolstadt, and Munich. Her major research interests lie in the field of runology and historical linguistics but she is also interested in Old English and early Middle English literature as well as in American and Australian English.

JERZY WEŁNA is Professor of English and Deputy Head of the Department of the English Language, Institute of English Studies, University of Warsaw, Poland. He is the author of several books and around 80 articles on English historical linguistics, especially phonology and morphology, among them *A Diachronic Grammar of English. Part One: Phonology* (1978), *Historical English Morphology* (1996), *A Brief Outline of the History of English* (2011; 3rd ed.) etc. He is the editor of the series *Warsaw Studies in English Historical Linguistics* and *Anglica. An International Journal of English Studies*.

Index

The index is, of course, selective. It lists important terms and concepts discussed in this volume, as well as words which are analyzed at some length. Authors of primary texts are also recorded, whereas authors of secondary literature are only mentioned if their work is discussed in some detail.

A

AB-language	xx, 69, 291
Abbreuiacion of Cronicles	73
abstract nouns	xiv, xvii, 133-135
adventus Saxonum	17-18, 41
agent	xiii-xv, xvii, xix, 163-182, 225, 227-228, 233, 235-239
Aldhelm	81
allophone	xiii, xv, 20-21, 24-28, 33-36, 38, 41-42, 45-46, 48-49, 65
Alpert, Herb	196
Ancrene Riwle	69-70, 74, 191
Ancrene Wisse	xx, 74, 217, 287, 290-291, 294
Anglo-Saxon Chronicle	xvi, 89, 122, 125
another	273
ansuz, rune	19-21, 28-29, 32, 36, 40, 45-46, 50-52, 60
antecedent	xix, 212, 214-215, 219-220
archaism	252-256, 292
Arderne	73
Athelstan	106-107, 109
Ælfric	90, 94-95, 122-123, 187
Ælfric's *Hexateuch*	94-95

B

baihua	303-304, 306, 322
Bale, John	247
barnes	xx, 254
Battle of Brunanburh	106-107, 109
Battle of Maldon	101, 105, 107, 109
Bayeux Tapestry	94-95, 110, 112
beadoleoma	312, 315
because	xiv, 186-187, 201-209
Benty Grange	96
Beowulf	xiii, xiv, xvi, xx, 81-82, 84-85, 88, 91, 102, 104-110, 122-124, 172, 175, 177, 180, 287, 289, 291-293, 295
Chinese translations	xiii-xiv, xx-xxi, 299-328
Birmingham	289
Blamire, Susanna	xx, 265-284
Boethius	71-72, 123-125
Book of Maccabees	95
Book of the Foundation	74
Boorde, Andrew	249
both	270-271, 279
breaking	18-19, 31, 33-35, 41-43, 270, 293
bright	271
broad	270
brother	273-274
Brut	69-70, 75, 166, 217, 291

brynja　82, 97-100
byrne　xvi, 82-86, 88-90, 92-93, 102-105, 108-109, 292
byrnhomas　82
Byron　11

C

Caistor-by-Norwich
　　Astragalus　22, 26, 30, 41-42, 45, 48, 50, 56
　　Brooch　26, 30, 36, 38-40, 49, 56
Caiyu, Chen　xx, 299, 314, 317
Camell, Thomas　xix, 245-246, 249-251, 255, 257-258
Campbell, Alistair　17-19, 29, 31-32, 34-35, 38, 44, 46, 294
canter　xvii, 164-165, 177-178, 180
Capgrave　71-73, 75
case system　237-238
causative　xvii, 163-170, 177-180
Caxton, William　69, 71-72, 75
causer　163, 167, 169, 171-172, 174, 178-179
causee　163, 165-166, 169, 170-174, 176, 178-179
Celts　82, 95, 138, 148-149, 288
Cely Letters　73-74
chain-mail coat　xiv, xvi, 81-120
Chappel, Geoffrey　250-251, 255
Chaucer, Geoffrey　xviii, xx, 71-72, 75, 185, 194, 254, 256, 267, 287, 291
Chessell Down
　　Pail　20, 23, 52, 56
　　Scabbard Mount　22, 42, 47-49, 52, 56
Chinese　xiii-xiv, xx-xxi, 299-328
Chinese translations, *see Beowulf*
Christ　87, 123-124, 126, 128
Chronicles of England　69

chronology, chronological　17-20, 25, 29, 32, 35, 38, 40-41, 48, 53, 68, 214-215, 288, 299, 323
Churchyard, Thomas　xix, 245-264
CLAN-construction　186
Clark, Ewan　266, 269-274, 277
clause-combining　201, 203-207
Cleopatra Glossary　93
close　272
Cloud of Unknowing　73
coat　85, 272
Cole, Elisha　255
collocation　123, 125, 128-129, 196, 270
colloquialism　250-256
come　273
Complaint of Our Lady　71-72
complement　xvii, 7, 128-129, 164, 185, 188, 191, 194, 215-216, 227, 229-230
compounding, *see* word-formation
conjunction　xiv, xviii, 66-67, 69, 185-199, 203-206, 288, 309, 320
connectives　xviii, 185-199
contraction　31, 256
conversion, *see* word-formation
Cooke, Sam　196
coordination　4, 201, 203, 207
Coriolanus　185
Cornish　249
coup　138, 140-141, 150-151
cow　273
Craigie, William　287
Cumberland, *see* dialect

D

dance　xiv, xvii, 163, 165, 173, 178, 180

demonstrative
- elements 211
- plural 274
- pronoun xviii, 188, 215

Deonise Hid Diuinite 73
Derufin 294
dialect
- Cumberland xx, 265-273, 275-279
- East Midland 65, 68, 70-75, 191
- Kentish xiv, xix, 75, 123, 213, 245-246, 249, 251-252, 256-258, 288, 290, 295
- Late West Saxon 81
- lexis 253, 259, 277-278
- Northern xiv, xix-xx, 68-69, 75, 190, 245, 249, 252-255, 258, 265-267, 270-276, 278-279, 291
- Northumbrian 81, 293
- Scoto-Cumbrian xx, 265-284
- Scots, Scottish, *see* Scots, Scottish
- Southern xiii-xiv, xix, 70-71, 74-75, 190-191, 203, 245-263
- Southern Middle English 191
- Southwestern xix, 74-75, 245, 247, 257-258
- West 191-192, 196
- West Mercian 291
- West Midland xx, 65, 68-70, 74-75, 191, 253, 290, 294
- Windhill 265

Dickens, Charles 195, 303
Dicts and Sayings 72
Donaldson, E.T. 318, 320
down 273

E

each 273
East Midland, *see* dialect
Edith 288
Ekwall, Eilert 289
Elene 83, 87, 105, 109-110, 124
Elucidarium 188
emergentism 3-4
English Mediaeval Lapidaries 71-72
enough xvi, 65-76
Entwade 294
éored 294
epistemic xviii, 202-206
Erchinoald 294
Erkenbrand 294
Ermyte, Richard 72-73, 75
etymology xvii, 85, 133-161, 267
evolution 4, 6, 7, 11, 66-68
- cultural evolution xv, 6-8

Exodus 102, 105-106, 108, 110, 122, 128

F

face 271
Fangji, Wu 322
father 274
Fight at Finnsburg 83, 289
find 157, 271
fine 158, 271
Fistula in Ano 73-74

fly xvii, 164-165, 169, 177-178, 180
Förster, Max 288, 290
found 273
for xiv, xviii, 185-199, 204
for ðam ðe 186-187, 193
forþon xiv, xviii
forþy xiv, xviii
frequency 66-67, 133, 185, 190-191, 204-205, 211, 214-215, 217, 219-220
Frodo Baggins 295
fronting 17-19, 27, 29-32, 38, 41, 272
functional category emergence 225
functional grammar 226-228
Funing, Li xx, 299, 301, 314, 318-322
fuþark xv, 17, 19-20, 50-52, 60
fuþorc xv-xvi, 17, 19-20, 27, 40, 60

G
gallop xvii, 164-166, 176-180
Gammer Gurton's Needle 257
Garfunkel, Art 196
gather 274
Gaytryge, Dan John 68
Genesis A & B xvi, 123, 126-127
Germanic origin 82, 136-137, 142-144, 146-147, 149-150
Gesta Romanorum 65, 69-70, 75
Gestalt 3
geweald agan/habban xiv, xvi, 121-131
Gibson, Craig 266
Gill, Alexander 246-247, 256-258
giwald hebbian xvii, 121, 126-127, 129
glossaries xvi, 92-93, 254-255

Gollum 293
Gordon, George 287
Gospels 121, 125-129
  Lindisfarne 128-129
  Rushworth 126
  West-Saxon 122, 126
Government and Binding theory 225, 228-229
Gower, John 71
Graham, Charles 266, 269, 272-273, 275-276
grammaticalization 201, 203, 207
Grendel 91, 302, 304-305, 315-318
Guohua, Chen xx, 299, 309-310

H
h-dropping xix, 9-10, 252
Haakon 100-101, 107
Hákonarmál 97
Hallkelsson, Tindr 100
Haribok 49
Harley Psalter 93-94
Harris, James 10-11
Hastings 289
Havelok xviii, 188-190, 192-193, 196
Hearn, Lafcadio 307
Heimskringla 97, 101
Heliand xvii, 121-123, 126-128
Helsinki Corpus of English Texts 211-214
Hengest 289-290
heriot 89-91, 109
Hermes 10-11
hernes 254, 256
hlenc, hlence xvi, 86, 108
Hobbit 287, 293
Hogg, Richard 52
hom, homa 85
Horace 267-269
Horsa 289
house 273
Howell, Thomas 249, 256

Hrafnsmál (Haraldskvæði) 99
hrægl 85
hring xvi, 85, 87-88, 92-93, 97, 102, 104, 108-109, 314
Hrothgar 91-92, 295, 302
hypotaxis 201, 204, 207

I
i-umlaut xv, 17-19, 24, 32-33, 35, 37-41, 44, 48
Ich xix, 247, 249, 258
Ichikawa, Sanki 307
idiom xvi, 121, 129
if 288, 320
impersonal constructions xiv, xix, 225-241
inanimate 166, 171-173, 178, 215, 219-221
infinitive xvi, 121-129, 134, 192, 194, 196, 276
Innsbruck Middle English prose corpus xvi, 65, 67, 70, 74
inscriptions xiii, xv-xvi, 17-64
intersubjectification 204

J
Jestbooks 247
Jiankai, Wang 306-307
Judith 82-83, 105, 107, 110
jump xvii, 164-165, 176, 178, 180

K
Katherine Group xx, 191, 287, 291
kenning 84-86, 97, 106, 108, 305, 308, 310, 312
Kentish, *see* dialect
kind 271
King Edward VI 250
King Harold 110
King Horn xviii, 65, 189-190, 192

Kuriyagawa, Fumio 307

L
labialisation 65
language change xiii, xv, 3, 5, 10, 13
language revolution 299
Lanterne of Liht 73-74
Late Modern English 170, 173, 175, 178, 180
Late West Saxon, *see* dialect
law 8, 136-137, 150, 157
    Danelaw 108-109
    Old English xvi, 89-92
Lawrence, John 307
Laȝamon 217, 291
leap xvii, 164-165, 175-176, 179
Lenker, Ursula vii, 185, 197, 204, 207
lexical-thematicity 225, 234, 237
lexicon 106, 133, 135, 138, 147-150, 167, 229, 310
Liber de Diversis Medicinis 65, 68
light 271
like 271
linguistic change, *see* language change
Lives of St. Augustine and St. Gilbert 72-73
loanwords xvii, 67, 70, 74, 82, 85, 136-141, 143-144, 146-150, 173, 293
Logonomia Anglica 246, 256
Lollard Sermons 73-74
London 40, 55-59, 65, 70-72, 75, 92-94, 190, 245, 247-248, 250-251, 253, 291
loose-knit networks, *see* networks
Lord of the Rings xiv, xx, 287, 293-295

Lorica 81-82, 92-96
Loveden Hill Urn 21, 32, 35, 42-45, 50, 57
Luick, Karl 17-18, 25, 29, 31-32, 34-35, 38, 41, 43, 65
Lydgate, John 168, 245, 256

M
MacDowall, W.M 302, 304
Macer Floridus de Viribus Herbarum 71
macro-linguistic 5, 8-9
malapropism 251-255
Mandeville 71-72, 75
manuscripts xv-xvi, 17, 20, 32, 67, 69-70, 74, 81, 92-95, 106, 109, 127, 191, 290-291
   illuminated 93-95
   south Midland group 291
march xvii, 163, 165, 173-174, 176, 178-180
Me thinks xiv, xix
medu 22, 45-47, 50-51, 53
meduseld 294
Meriton, George 249, 267, 270, 278-279
micro-linguistic 5, 9-10
middangeard 88, 312
Minimalist Program 229
Mirror of Saint Edmund 68-69, 75
monophthongization 24, 26, 29-30, 32, 41
more 270
morphology 4, 191, 226, 228, 238, 259, 277-278
   non-standard 278
More, Thomas 246-247
morning 272
Morte d'Arthur 65, 69-70, 75, 167
most 270
mother 274
much 273, 279

mystery 140-141, 151

N
naked 271
name 271
networks, network models
   loose-knit 8
   scholarly xv, 3, 10-12
   small-world 11-12
   social 3, 8, 10-12
nett 85, 102
Nichiwaki, Junzaburo 307
night 154, 271, 279
Northern, *see* also dialect
   English xx, 245, 249, 265, 271-272, 279
   Prose texts 68
Northernism 252-256, 289
Northumbrian, *see* dialect
notice 272
now 273

O
Oisc, Oiscingas 290, 295
Old English poetry 81-88, 108
Old Norse poetry 99-102, 108
Onions, Charles Talbut 287
Orosius 123, 125, 166, 186
out 273
Owl and Nightingale xviii, 188, 190, 191, 194, 196

P
pace xvii, 164-165, 177-180
pad 85
parataxis xvii, 195, 201-207, 305, 312, 315, 317-318
participle
   past 88, 229, 236, 256-257, 278
   present 194, 276
passive constructions xix, 164, 225-241

past participle, *see* participle
Paston Letters 72
Pater Noster 72-73
patient 163-164, 178-179, 188, 236-238
Payn, James 195
Pecock 74-75
perception 140, 151, 155
Peterborough Chronicle xviii, 187-188
phoneme xiii, xv-xvi, 17, 21, 24-29, 31-32, 35, 38-40, 42, 45-46, 49-53
    phoneme inventory 17, 49-53
phonemic split 17, 21, 24, 26, 28-29, 31-32, 34, 36, 40
phonological space 34
potestatem habere xvi, 121-122, 126, 128-129
pragmatic 164, 167, 170, 178, 202, 228
prance xvii, 164-165, 176, 178-180
pre-Old English xiii, xv, xxi, 17-64
prefixation, *see* word-formation
Present-Day English xvii-xviii, 133, 135, 148-150, 185, 188, 192, 195, 201-206, 211, 218, 231-239
present indicative 276
present participle, *see* participle
Prick of Conscience 291
programme 140, 151
pronouns
    personal 168-169, 190, 274-275
    relative xviii, 216-217
    wh- 215, 217-218
pronunciation 9, 66, 71, 75, 150-151, 256, 269-273
Prudentius 92-93
Psalterium Aureum 95

Psychomachia 92
punctuation 277
Puttenham, George 245

Q
–

R
Radagast 295
Ralph Roister Doister 247, 255
Ramsay, Allan 265, 267, 278
Ray, John 246, 255, 267
Redford, John 247
Redlingfield 289
Reeve's Tale xx, 291
Relational Grammar 225-228
relative clause xiv, xviii-xix, 194, 211-219
relativizers xix, 186, 216, 218, 220
    invariable xviii, 211-219
    pronominal 214, 216, 218
    wh- 211, 216
    zero 211, 218
Relph, Josiah xx, 265-284
retraction 19, 27, 31-32, 35
Revelations of Divine Love 73
Revelations of St. Brigitta 71-72
Riders of Rohan 294
right 133, 137, 271, 279
right-handed 271
Ritson, Isaac 269
roar 272
Rohan 295
rope 270
rounding 18, 27, 41, 70
run xiv, xvii, 163, 165-167, 169, 178, 180
runes, runic inscriptions xiii, xv, 17-64

S

Saint Olaf, king of Norway 100-101
Salomon and Saturn 82
same 271
Sardanapalus 10
Saruman 293-294
Scandinavian xvi, 47, 66-67, 74, 81, 95-97, 105-110, 137, 143-145, 147-148, 153, 157
scramasax 40, 57
scholarly networks, *see* networks
Scoto-Cumbrian, *see* dialect
Scots xx, 138, 219, 266, 269-270, 272, 274-275, 278-279
Scottish 67, 245, 254, 265-267, 270, 272, 278-279
scrud 85
searo-net 293
secondary agent constructions xiii-xv, xvii, 163-182
semantic
   bleaching 196
   range 185
   role 237-238
serc, serce xvi, 84-85, 88, 108
Sermon 68, 213
shall 274, 276, 279
shell nouns xiii-xv, xvii, 133-161
Shiqiu, Liang xx, 299, 309-313, 322
should 274, 279
Shu, Lin 303, 306, 322
sight 145, 154, 271
Skáldaspillir, Eynindr 97
Skallagrimsson, Egil 107
skanomodu coin 23, 26, 30, 37, 41, 48, 50, 58
Skelton, John 245, 247, 256
small-world networks, *see* networks
Smaug 293

Sméagol 293
social networks, *see* networks
sound change
   Pre-Old English xiii, xv, 17-64
Southern dialect, *see* dialect
Southernism 252, 256-258
Speculum Sacerdotale 71-72
Speculum Vitae 291
speech-act 202-206
Speght, Thomas 254
spelling xiii, xv-xvi, xx, 8, 32, 65-66, 69, 71-77, 147, 191, 251-252, 265-266, 269-274, 277-279, 288
   non-standard 277-278
Spong Hill Urn 21, 32, 35, 42, 50, 58
St Chad 291
standardization xiii, xv, 8-9, 11, 65, 75
story 140-141, 151-152
Strode, William 249
Sturluson, Snorri 97, 99-101, 107, 295
subordination 199-209
subjective meaning 205-207
subjectification 204
such 191, 273
suffixation, *see* word-formation
Swanhild 290
swim xvii, 163, 165, 169, 172-173, 178, 180
syntax xiv-xv, xix, xxi, 121, 127-129, 133-135, 164, 169-170, 179, 185, 191, 195, 211-212, 216-217, 219, 225-226, 228-229, 231, 234-239, 274, 306, 308, 312-313, 316-317, 320
syrce, syric 84-86

T

Tatian   122, 128-129
þat   xviii-xix, 211-223
þe   xiv, xviii-xix, 211-223
the   xviii-xix, 211-223
Thengel   294
Théoden   294
theory of games   4
these   274-275
though   65-77
those   274-275
Three Kings of Cologne   71, 75
through   65-76
time   271
Tolkien, J.R.R.   xiii-xiv, xx, 287-298
transitive   xvii, 163-182, 186, 226
transitive causative   163-182
translation, *see Beowulf*
Travels   72
trot   xvii, 164-165, 174-176, 178-180

U

Udall, Nicholas   247, 255-256
Undley Bracteate   20, 22, 26, 41, 45-46, 49-50, 58
Unter freyem Banner   110-111, 345
Utrecht Psalter   93

V

velar fricatives   xvi, 65-77
velarization   18, 42
Vices and Virtues   70, 192
Vikings   106-109
Vimose (Denmark) 110-111
vocalisation   65-68, 71-73, 75
voicing   xix, 191, 247, 249, 258

W

Wägner, Wilhelm   302, 304
Wakefield Master   245
walk   xiv, xvii, 163-165, 167-172, 178-180
waltz   xvii, 163, 165, 175-176, 178, 180
Walsingham   248, 289
Watchfield Purse Mount   22, 33, 35, 37-38, 48-49, 51, 59
wæd   85
wælstowes geweald agan xvi, 125
Weixiong, Su   323
Welbeck Hill Bracteate   23, 51, 59
Welsh   xx, 245, 250, 292
West Mercian, *see* dialect
Westfold   294
which   191
wills   xvi, 89-92
Windhill, *see* dialect
Wōden   295
Worcester   290
word-formation   136-137, 141-144, 146-147, 150
    compounding   xvi, 81, 84-88, 97-99, 102, 108, 141-144, 153-154, 156, 186, 289, 293-294, 308-314, 316, 318
    conversion   141-144, 152-153
    prefixation   141-145, 152, 154-158, 256
        counter-   144-145, 154
        dis-   144-145, 153-154, 158
        fore-   144-145, 154

        in-   144-145, 154, 156
        mis-   144, 154
        non-   144-145, 155
        out-   144-145, 155
        pre-   144-145, 155
        re-   144-145, 155-156, 158
        un-   141, 144-145, 154-155
        up-   144-145, 155
suffixation   48-49, 141-143, 145, 147, 151-152, 155-159, 250, 289-290, 293
        -ance 152, 155
        -ancy 156
        -al 156
        -ation 152, 156
        -ence 156
        -ency 156
        -er 156
        -hood 156
        -ing 156-158, 276
        -ism 157
        -ity 157
        -lec 157
        -le 157
        -ment 158
        -ness 141, 158-159
        -ure 159
World Wide Web   3, 11
Wright, Joseph   vii, 265-266, 269, 272, 275-277, 287, 290
writing   xiii, xv, 3-15, 196, 266-267, 269, 277-278, 303-304, 306-307, 310, 323
    runic   17-64
Wulfstan II   290
Wuse   49
Wyclif   74

X

Xiang, Feng xx, 301, 314-322

Xidi (Zheng Zhenduo)   xx, 301-305, 308, 322
Xun, Lu   303-304, 306, 309-310, 312-313, 322

Y

Yao-chung, Li   310
Year's Work in English Studies   xx, 287-288
Yuanshu, Yan   xx, 299, 309-312

Z

Zhipan (Liang Zhipan)   xx, 299, 301, 304-305, 307-308, 312, 323
Zhenduo, Zheng, *see* Xidi
Zhong, Fang   310

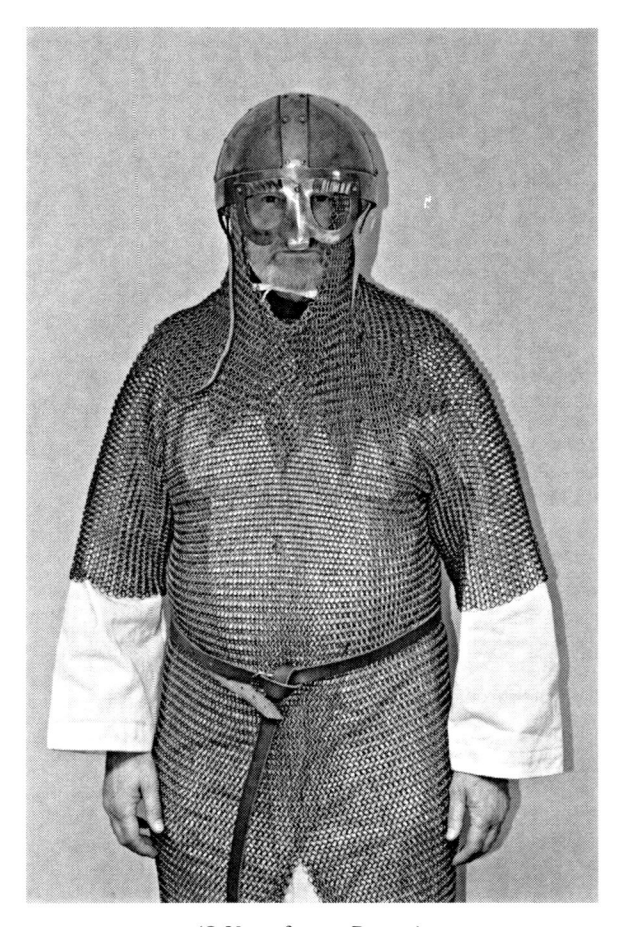

(© Unter freyem Banner)
Here the editors take their leave and say "Go little book."

Studies in English Medieval Language and Literature

Edited by Jacek Fisiak

Vol. 1 Dieter Kastovsky / Arthur Mettinger (eds.): Language Contact in the History of English. 2nd, revised edition. 2003.

Vol. 2 Studies in English Historical Linguistics and Philology. A Festschrift for Akio Oizumi. Edited by Jacek Fisiak. 2002.

Vol. 3 Liliana Sikorska: *In a Manner of Morall Playe*: Social Ideologies in English Moralities and Interludes (1350-1517). 2002.

Vol. 4 Peter J. Lucas / Angela M. Lucas (eds.): Middle English from Tongue to Text. Selected Papers from the Third International Conference on Middle English: Language and Text, held at Dublin, Ireland, 1-4 July 1999. 2002.

Vol. 5 Chaucer and the Challenges of Medievalism. Studies in Honor of H. A. Kelly. Edited by Donka Minkova and Theresa Tinkle. 2003.

Vol. 6 Hanna Rutkowska: Graphemics and Morphosyntax in the *Cely Letters* (1472-88). 2003.

Vol. 7 The *Ancrene Wisse*. A Four-Manuscript Parallel Text. Preface and Parts 1-4. Edited by Tadao Kubouchi and Keiko Ikegami with John Scahill, Shoko Ono, Harumi Tanabe, Yoshiko Ota, Ayako Kobayashi and Koichi Nakamura. 2003.

Vol. 8 Joanna Bugaj: Middle Scots Inflectional System in the South-west of Scotland. 2004.

Vol. 9 Rafal Boryslawski: The Old English Riddles and the Riddlic Elements of Old English Poetry. 2004.

Vol. 10 Nikolaus Ritt / Herbert Schendl (eds.): Rethinking Middle English. Linguistic and Literary Approaches. 2005.

Vol. 11 The *Ancrene Wisse*. A Four-Manuscript Parallel Text. Parts 5–8 with Wordlists. Edited by Tadao Kubouchi and Keiko Ikegami with John Scahill, Shoko Ono, Harumi Tanabe, Yoshiko Ota, Ayako Kobayashi, Koichi Nakamura. 2005.

Vol. 12 Text and Language in Medieval English Prose. A Festschrift for Tadao Kubouchi. Edited by Akio Oizumi, Jacek Fisiak and John Scahill. 2005.

Vol. 13 Michiko Ogura (ed.): Textual and Contextual Studies in Medieval English. Towards the Reunion of Linguistics and Philology. 2006.

Vol. 14 Keiko Hamaguchi: Non-European Women in Chaucer. A Postcolonial Study. 2006.

Vol. 15 Ursula Schaefer (ed.): The Beginnings of Standardization. Language and Culture in Fourteenth-Century England. 2006.

Vol. 16 Nikolaus Ritt / Herbert Schendl / Christiane Dalton-Puffer / Dieter Kastovsky (eds): Medieval English and its Heritage. Structure, Meaning and Mechanisms of Change. 2006.

Vol. 17 Matylda Włodarczyk: Pragmatic Aspects of Reported Speech. The Case of Early Modern English Courtroom Discourse. 2007.

Vol. 18 Hans Sauer / Renate Bauer (eds.): *Beowulf* and Beyond. 2007.

Vol. 19 Gabriella Mazzon (ed.): Studies in Middle English Forms and Meanings. 2007.

Vol. 20 Alexander Bergs / Janne Skaffari (eds.): The Language of the Peterborough Chronicle. 2007.

Vol. 21 Liliana Sikorska (ed.). With the assistance of Joanna Maciulewicz: Medievalisms. The Poetics of Literary Re-Reading. 2008.

Vol. 22 Masachiyo Amano / Michiko Ogura / Masayuki Ohkado (eds.): Historical Englishes in Varieties of Texts and Contexts. The Global COE Program, International Conference 2007. 2008.

Vol. 23 Ewa Ciszek: Word Derivation in Early Middle English. 2008.

Vol. 24 Andrzej M. Łęcki: Grammaticalisation Paths of *Have* in English. 2010.

Vol. 25 Osamu Imahayashi / Yoshiyuki Nakao / Michiko Ogura (eds.): Aspects of the History of English Language and Literature. Selected Papers Read at SHELL 2009, Hiroshima. 2010.

Vol. 26 Magdalena Bator: Obsolete Scandinavian Loanwords in English. 2010.

Vol. 27 Anna Cichosz: The Influence of Text Type on Word Order of Old Germanic Languages. A Corpus-Based Contrastive Study of Old English and Old High German. 2010.

Vol. 28 Jacek Fisiak / Magdalena Bator (eds.): Foreign Influences on Medieval English. 2011.

Vol. 29 Władysław Witalisz: The Trojan Mirror. Middle English Narratives of Troy as Books of Princely Advice. 2011.

Vol. 30 Luis Iglesias-Rábade: Semantic Erosion of Middle English Prepositions. 2011.

Vol. 31 Barbara Kowalik: Betwixt *engelaunde* and *englene londe*. Dialogic Poetics in Early English Religious Lyric. 2010.

Vol. 32 The Katherine Group. A Three-Manuscript Parallel Text. Seinte Katerine, Seinte Marherete, Seinte Iuliene, and Hali Meiðhad, with Wordlists. Edited by Shoko Ono and John Scahill with Keiko Ikegami, Tadao Kubouchi, Harumi Tanabe, Koichi Nakamura, Satoko Shimazaki and Koichi Kano. 2011.

Vol. 33 Jacob Thaisen / Hanna Rutkowska (eds.): Scribes, Printers, and the Accidentals of their Texts. 2011.

Vol. 34 Isabel Moskowich: Language Contact and Vocabulary Enrichment. Scandinavian Elements in Middle English. 2012.

Vol. 35 Joanna Esquibel / Anna Wojtyś (eds.): Explorations in the English Language: Middle Ages and Beyond. Festschrift for Professor Jerzy Wełna on the Occasion of his 70th Birthday. 2012.

Vol. 36 Yoshiyuki Nakao: The Structure of Chaucer´s Ambiguity. 2013.

Vol. 37 Begoña Crespo: Change in Life, Change in Language. A Semantic Approach to the History of English. 2013.

Vol. 38 Richard Dance / Laura Wright (eds.): The Use and Development of Middle English. Proceedings of the Sixth International Conference on Middle English, Cambridge 2008. 2012.

Vol. 39 Michiko Ogura: Words and Expressions of Emotion in Medieval English. 2013.

Vol. 40 Anna Czarnowus: Fantasies of the Other´s Body in Middle English Oriental Romance. 2013.

Vol. 41 Hans Sauer / Gaby Waxenberger (eds.): Recording English, Researching English, Transforming English. With the Assistance of Veronika Traidl. 2013.

www.peterlang.de